Warwick University Caribbean Studies

Financing Development in the Commonwealth Caribbean

Edited by
Delisle Worrell, Compton Bourne and Dinesh Dodhia

MACMILLAN
CARIBBEAN

First published 1991

Published by MACMILLAN EDUCATION LTD
London and Basingstoke
Associated companies and representatives in Accra,
Auckland, Delhi, Dublin, Gaborone, Hamburg, Harare,
Hong Kong, Kuala Lumpur, Lagos, Manzini, Melbourne,
Mexico City, Nairobi, New York, Singapore, Tokyo

Printed in Hong Kong

British Library Cataloguing in Publication Data
Caribbean Regional Programme of Monetary Studies
(21 1989 Barbados)
   Financing development in the Caribbean.
   I. Title   II. Worrell, Delisle   III. Bourne, Compton
   338.9729

ISBN 0-333-55204-0

Cover based on a painting by Aubrey Williams presented to the
Centre for Caribbean Studies, University of Warwick.

Series preface

The Centre for Caribbean Studies at the University of Warwick was founded in 1984 in order to stimulate interest and research in a region which is only now beginning to receive academic recognition in its own right. In addition to the publication of the papers from annual symposia which reflect the Centre's comparative and inter-disciplinary approach, other volumes in the series will be published in disciplines within the arts and social sciences.

This is the second volume in the series to focus on economics. Ramesh Ramsaran's *The Commonwealth Caribbean in the World Economy* (1989) was an overview whereas the present collection, deriving from a conference organised by the Commonwealth Secretariat, focuses on the problems of finance and investment. Events in Eastern Europe and the USSR, as well as the repercussions of 1992, free trade development in North America, and indebtedness, have all given an added urgency to the themes analysed and discussed here. Considerable unease is being felt throughout the Caribbean at the prospect of investment flowing eastwards and the threat of a contraction in aid funding.

In comparison with many other regions of the developing world, the Caribbean is well favoured but it may be questioned if the best use is being made of the advantages which it enjoys. This book addresses key areas of the economy where reform, and closer regulation and supervision of financial money markets is needed. Some of the chapters are highly technical but taken together this collection is a unique and comprehensive survey of all aspects of financial management, and is an important contribution to problems which have not been adequately covered in the economic literature of the region. Its findings and prescriptions should be pondered by all those with interests in and concern for the Caribbean.

Alistair Hennessy

Warwick University Caribbean Studies

Andrew Sanders
The Powerless People – The Amerindians of the Corentyne River

Kelvin Singh
The Bloodstained Tombs – The Muharram Massacre in Trinidad 1884

Editors: Jean Besson and Janet Momsen
Land and Development in the Caribbean

David Nicholls
From Dessalines to Duvalier – Race, Colour and National Independence

Editors: Malcom Cross and Gad Heuman
Labour in the Caribbean – From Emancipation to Independence

Harry Goulbourne
Teachers, Education and Politics in Jamaica, 1892–1972

Neil Price
Behind the Planter's Back – Lower Class Response to Marginality in Bequia Island, St Vincent

Douglas Hall
In Miserable Slavery – Thomas Thistlewood in Jamaica, 1750–86

Ramesh Ramsaran
The Commonwealth Caribbean in the World Economy

Editor: M. Gilkes
The Literate Imagination – Essays on the Novels of Wilson Harris

Miguel Barnet (Editor: Alistair Hennessy)
Runaway – The Autobiography of Estaban Montejo

Editor: Paul Sutton
Europe and the Caribbean

Patrick Bryan
The Jamaican People 1880–1902 – Race, Class and Social Control

Editors: Delisle Worrell, Compton Bourne and Dinesh Dodhia
Financing Development in the Commonwealth Caribbean

Contents

Foreword

The papers contained in this volume are a selection from those prepared for a Conference on Financing Development in the Caribbean held in Barbados in December 1989. The Conference was organised by the Commonwealth Secretariat jointly with the Regional Programme for Monetary Studies (RPMS) of the University of the West Indies, on the occasion of the latter's twenty-first anniversary meeting. It brought together senior finance executives from ministries and banking institutions of the region, as well as leading Caribbean academics, to reassess the issue of financing development in the region in the light of the difficult circumstances concerning external financial flows and domestic economic conditions facing most developing countries.

Since 1981, developing countries have experienced a large and sustained decline in the level of external private flows; unfortunately official flows have not expanded adequately while export credits have been negative or negligible. With large debt servicing burdens facing many developing countries, since 1983 a perverse situation has existed whereby there has been a net transfer of resources away from developing to developed countries. At the same time, severe adjustment pressures and the preservation of consumption levels have often resulted in sharp declines in domestic savings. The overall effect has been one of significant cutbacks in investment in highly indebted countries, with adverse implications for GDP growth rates.

Against the background of declining private external flows during the 1980s, the Commonwealth Secretariat made an early effort to reverse the situation. One of the main tasks of its long-standing programme on capital markets has been to keep governments abreast of developments in the capital markets and to describe new financing techniques through a regular confidential review *International Capital Markets*. The Secretariat has also conducted a number of studies and regional workshops on foreign investment policies and experiences over the past few years with a view to assist in improving policies. Its findings are analysed in the book *Developing With Foreign Investment* published by Croom Helm in 1987.

At their 1987 annual meeting, Commonwealth Finance Ministers expressed deep concern at the serious deterioration in private flows and called on the Secretariat to examine how Commonwealth capital-importing developing countries could be assisted in improving their access to foreign private capital. The resulting report, *Mobilising Capital for Development: The Role of Private Flows*, made a number of recommendations including a major proposal for the establishment of a Commonwealth Equity Fund (CEF), which Commonwealth Finance Ministers welcomed at their 1988 meeting. After two years of further work by the Secretariat and discussions with Commonwealth governments and interested capital market operators, the CEF – a private commercial fund without any official government financial support – has been established. It enables portfolio investors in international financial markets to invest in emerging stock markets of Commonwealth developing countries. The Hibiscus issue of the CEF of $56.6 million was launched in September 1990. The Secretariat is also beginning to work with Commonwealth governments, through seminars and studies, to broaden the possibilities of domestic and foreign investment, particularly through stock market development and assistance with privatisation.

Programmes aimed at encouraging domestic and foreign investment, including portfolio investment, form part of a wider recognition by Commonwealth governments of the long-term need to develop local financial markets as a means of encouraging both domestic savings (including their allocation to the most productive uses) as well as equity or other innovative forms of external flows. There is also increasing appreciation of the important role that official external flows can play in catalysing external private flows and in the development of local capital markets. The Conference on Financing Development in the Caribbean was held with these perspectives in mind.

I should like to express my appreciation to the RPMS for its collaboration in sponsoring the Conference and in preparing some of the papers for it; to the Central Bank of Barbados, the Caribbean Community Secretariat and the Caribbean Development Bank for their co-operation in carrying out this project; and to the World Bank and the Canadian International Development Agency for joining the Commonwealth Fund for Technical Co-operation in providing financial support. My special thanks go to Dr Delisle Worrell, Deputy Governor of the Central Bank of Barbados and Professor Compton Bourne of the University of the West Indies for agreeing to serve with Mr Dinesh Dodhia, Chief Economics Officer of the Economic Affairs Division of the Secretariat as general editors of this volume. The Secretariat's contribution was greatly assisted by the technical and organsational support provided by Mr Dinesh Dodhia and by Dr Bishakha Mukherjee and Ms Joyce Lestrade, Senior Economics Officers.

> B. Persaud
> Director and Head
> Economic Affairs Division
> Commonwealth Secretariat

Preface

This volume contains a selection of the presentations at the 21st Conference of the Caribbean Regional Programme of Monetary Studies, a conference that was sponsored jointly with the Commonwealth Secretariat in December 1989. That conference launched the Monetary Studies Programme on an extended analysis of financial performance in the Caribbean, expected to last several years. The Caribbean is caught up in the process of startling change which has characterised financial communities everywhere. New institutions have arisen in the past decade and new services have been instituted, presenting new challenges to the makers of monetary policy and to financial regulators. The Caribbean monetary authorities have been playing 'catch-up' just like monetary authorities elsewhere. The Caribbean has seen episodes of irrational interest rate behaviour, unexplainable monetary fluctuations, failures of financial institutions and tensions between the financial system and its regulators. In some countries, informal financial arrangements have thrived on the complexities and inefficiencies of the regulatory system.

The Conference took a first look at many of the issues pertaining to the role of finance in development, how that role has changed and the appropriate framework for accommodating to change. The present volume gives some selections from the rich menu of topics covered. The first chapters present an overview of the savings and investment process and the experiences of three countries – Barbados, Jamaica and Belize. The second section deals with non-bank financial institutions, and is followed by a discussion of the role of development financial institutions – the Caribbean Development Bank, the national development finance corporations and the development funds specifically targeted at small businesses. Two chapters look at aspects of the securities market with suggestions for developing the regional market in securities and addressing the need for venture capital financing. There are two chapters on aspects of financial regulation, discussing the experiences of Trinidad and Tobago and the Eastern Caribbean Central Bank and suggesting ways that the system might better deal with the current circumstances. The final section comprises chapters on external financial flows, debt and capital flight with suggestions on maximising the inflows of finance, addressing the external debt problem and reversing capital flight.

The volume continues the tradition established by the Caribbean Regional Programme of Monetary Studies of pursuing vigorous collaborative research among the central banks of the region, the University of the West Indies and the University of Guyana. This is the most recent of a long series of collections of studies and of monographs which have been produced by the Programme. Many have been published by the Institute of Social and Economic Research and have appeared in its journal *Social and Economic Studies*. A comprehensive bibliography of studies done under the Programme's aegis is available in June Stewart and Aldeen Payne, *A Bibliography of the Published and Unpublished Work of the Regional Programme of Monetary Studies* (Institute of Social and Economic Research, University of the West Indies, 1988).

The Monetary Studies Programme is grateful for the interest and support of the Commonwealth Secretariat for the enterprise which resulted in the current collection of studies. We are in debt to the organisers of the conference and in particular to Dr Bishnodat Persaud who vigorously promoted the idea. The conference was hosted by the Central Bank of Barbados and we owe a special debt of gratitude to Mr Rahman Mehter of the Central Bank for his efforts in co-ordinating the administrative arrangements. Pamela Arthur co-ordinated the process of editorial revision with the efficiency and dependability which are her trademark. We are also grateful to all the Commonwealth Secretariat staff who provided typing and other assistance in the preparation of the manuscript of this publication.

Delisle Worrell
Compton Bourne
Dinesh Dodhia
July 1990

The contributors

George Abbott is Senior Lecturer in Economics at the University of Glasgow, Scotland. His publications include *International Indebtedness and the Developing Countries* (Croom Helm, 1979).

Joseph Bailey is General Manager of the Jamaica Building Societies Association. He has published several papers and monographs on the Jamaican financial sector.

Karl Bennett is Professor of Economics at the University of Waterloo Canada. He has published extensively on Caribbean economic integration, the balance of payments, and economic growth.

Courtney Blackman is an independent consultant. He was Governor of the Central Bank of Barbados from 1972 to 1987. Dr Blackman has published numerous papers on aspects of Caribbean economic development.

Byron Blake is Director of Economics and Industry at the Commonwealth Caribbean Community Secretariat. Previously he worked at the Planning Institute of Jamaica. Mr Blake's publications are principally on the subject of economic integration.

Compton Bourne is Pro-Vice Chancellor, Deputy Principal, and Professor of Economics at the University of the West Indies. He has published extensively on finance and economic development and is the principal author of *Caribbean Development to the Year 2000* (Commonwealth Secretariat, 1988).

Martin Brownbridge is an economist in the Research Department at the Central Bank of Belize.

Paul Chen-Young is Founder and Executive Chairman of the Eagle group of financial enterprises in Jamaica. Earlier professional appointments include the World Bank, the Jamaican Development Bank, and the Workers' Bank of Jamaica.

Dinesh Dodhia is the Chief Economics Officer in the Director's office, Economic Affairs Division (EAD) of the Commonwealth Secretariat. He was formerly Chief of the Finance Section, EAD.

Stephen Emtage is Vice-President, Life of Barbados Ltd. He was Director of Finance and Planning in the Government of Barbados from 1967 to 1987.

Terrence Farrell is Senior Manager (Research and Information) at the Central Bank of Trinidad and Tobago. He is the author of a forthcoming book on monetary and financial policy in Trinidad and Tobago.

Claremont Kirton is Lecturer in Economics at the University of the West Indies (Mona Campus). He has published on commercial banking and economic planning.

Stanley Lalta is Research Fellow, Institute of Social and Economic Research, University of the West Indies (Mona Campus). He previously worked at the Caribbean Community Secretariat.

Eustace Liburd is Director of Research and Information at the East Caribbean Central Bank and has authored several journal articles on money and banking.

Clive Y. Thomas is Professor of Economics and Director of the Institute of Development Studies at the University of Guyana. His extensive publications on economic development include *The Poor and the Powerless* (Monthly Review Press, 1988).

Desmond Thomas is Lecturer in Economics at the University of the West Indies (Mona Campus). He has published on the Jamaican balance of payments.

Marion Williams is Advisor (Planning and Development) at the Central Bank of Barbados. She has written scholarly papers on regional financial co-operation and financial regulation.

Delisle Worrell is Deputy Governor of the Central Bank of Barbados. He has published extensively on Caribbean development. His recent publications include *Small Island Economies* (Praeger Publishers, 1986).

General notes

1 The term 'Commonwealth Caribbean' generally refers to the thirteen members of the Caribbean Community (CARICOM), as well as the British dependent territories of Anguilla, British Virgin Islands, Cayman Islands and the Turks and Caicos Islands. CARICOM members are as follows: The Bahamas, Barbados, Guyana, Jamaica, Trinidad and Tobago, Belize, Antigua and Barbuda, Dominica, Grenada, Montserrat, St Christopher-Nevis, St Lucia, and St Vincent and the Grenadines. The first five of these are often referred to as the More Developed Countries (MDCs) while the remaining eight are seen as the Less Developed Countries (LDCs). The last seven are members of the Organisation of East Caribbean States (OECS). Except for Montserrat, the other twelve members of CARICOM are independent countries and in some chapters Montserrat as well as other dependent territories are excluded when reference is made to the Commonwealth Caribbean, CARICOM, LDCs or the OECS.

2 Except where otherwise stated, all money figures used in chapters describing country experiences refer to national currencies. In all other chapters (except where otherwise stated) the term 'dollar' refers to the US currency.

3 In tables, the notation n.a. stands for data not available.

CHAPTER 1

Overview – The financial sector: Performance and challenges

Delisle Worrell

This volume of studies is concerned with the role that financial institutions have played in allocating financial resources, and the ways in which financial accumulation might be accelerated and its allocation improved so as to boost investment and accelerate growth. Greater efficiency in financial intermediation is desirable in itself, and is now made even more essential by the relative decline in finance available to the Caribbean from abroad. The issues raised in the studies in this volume include the diversity of financial services in the Caribbean, the availability of appropriate financial instruments and institutions, the influence of government finance on the allocation of private funds, the regulation of financial institutions, debt management and capital flight.

The supply of finance from industrial countries to the Caribbean (and to other developing countries) continues to decline as international banks adopt a more defensive stance, governments of OECD countries impose leaner budgets, and pressures mount to meet the enormous needs for finance of the countries of Eastern Europe. The Caribbean does have advantages which should help to avoid complete neglect: the countries have a strong democratic tradition, they are close to the US, English is spoken in the majority of countries and they have long standing cultural links with the US. Nonetheless, efforts must be intensified to find new sources of finance, to develop new instruments that will facilitate investment, and to secure greater efficiency in the use of external finance.

The papers are mainly concerned with ways to make more effective use of local saving, with less focus on the mobilisation of saving itself. Some of us argue that financial savings are more than sufficient, with excess of liquid funds in the banking systems of even those countries with the most dire economic performance. Moreover, there is an ample supply of foreign saving available for investment in projects which are internationally competitive. Neither of these sentiments is shared by all the authors of the volume. Another potential source of increased domestic saving in many countries is by governments, which will need to increase their savings on current account in order to stabilise their balance of external payments.

The supervisory authorities must encourage greater competition in the financial sector, in the interests of efficiency and innovation. To improve on their very poor record, development finance institutions should issue public shares, which would subject them to market discipline. They should have independent boards of directors, with private-sector involvement. Mergers of financial institutions across the region should be encouraged, to achieve economies of scale and scope, but safeguards must be established against regional monopolies. Strong fiscal incentives for equity financing are required, and a regional equity fund to provide venture capital, equity and loans is badly needed. Restrictions on capital flows and securities trading within the region should be relaxed, with more liberal exchange controls and the removal of restrictions on property ownership. These measures should be supported by provisions for improved labour mobility. A by-product of a more relaxed stance would be greater fiscal discipline imposed on individual countries.

However sympathetic the financial structure, investment will flower only if countries achieve external payments stability and sustain credible government policy. High real interest rates and constantly depreciating exchange rates are a disincentive to productive investment, and encourage speculation. Regulations and incentives should discourage leveraged buy-outs, foreign exchange deals and other practices which evidence a disjuncture between finance and production. Strong fiscal incentives should be provided for investment in the tradeable sector. Investment in education and human resource development should also be encouraged, as they yield very high dividends in the long run.

Financial regulation should be forward looking, and designed to correct weaknesses in the system before they reach the stage of inefficiency and failure. Regulations must be extended to cover the whole range of financial institutions – banks, near-banks, insurance companies, credit unions, pension funds, etc. Features of the regulatory framework should include:

- a licensing requirement that stipulates capitalisation, operating ratio requirements, qualification for management, limits of indemnity and reporting requirements;
- powers of on-site inspection and periodical inspection reports;
- powers of direct intervention by regulators;
- reporting standards for the external auditors of financial institutions;
- codes of conduct for relationships between management, auditors and regulators;
- adequate accounting standards and standards for reports to be made public, including the publication of sufficient operating data for an independent assessment of the financial institution's performance;
- winding-up provisions for failing institutions; and

- some form of deposit insurance.

The legal framework in all Caribbean countries will have to be updated, and the supervisory authorities expanded and upgraded.

Caribbean countries have varying expectations about levels of external indebtedness and possibilities of debt relief. Some countries are in dire need, others have manageable burdens. Regional muscle should be brought to bear on behalf of each country in need of relief, building on existing initiatives and modifying them to the Caribbean's needs.

There has been some capital flight from Guyana, Jamaica and Trinidad and Tobago, but the emigration of skilled personnel has been by far the greater loss. Some emigration is desirable, but the Caribbean needs to ensure that some emigrants are replaced by more highly-skilled immigrants. To provide that incentive the Caribbean must achieve balance of payments stability and a credible economic policy, and must remove burdensome foreign exchange, trade and other regulations.

Saving and investment

The first section of this book, on saving and investment, begins with C.Y. Thomas' analysis of the determinants of saving. The effects of income and interest rates were overwhelmed by changes in the economic, political and social environment in the Caribbean. Financial repression, crowding out of the private sector by the public sector and rapid inflation led to capital flight and diminished saving in most countries. The saving ratio rose in Barbados, but fell in Guyana, Jamaica and Trinidad and Tobago. In all four countries investment exceeded saving. Government savings were significant only in Trinidad and Tobago during the oil boom years; government savings were low in most cases, and negative for Guyana despite a strong tax effort in that country. Thomas notes the anaemic performance of stock exchanges in Jamaica, Trinidad and Tobago and Barbados. He recommends improvements in the regulatory framework, fiscal restraint, administrative improvements in securities exchanges and an amnesty on illegal capital outflows which are repatriated.

For Barbados, Emtage describes a period of sustained growth in output and economic diversification in the 1960s and 1970s, when investment, including foreign investment, domestic private saving and government saving, were all vigorous. In the 1980s the economy faltered, structural imbalances emerged and both investment and foreign investment declined. Government did not pre-empt funds at the expense of the private sector, however, and there was no bias against saving in the tax system. An increasing proportion of bank loans went to producers, and the proportion for consumers declined. Emtage suggests that a venture capital fund be set up, and that the Central Bank of Barbados expand its fund for medium-term financing of producers. He would like to see a wider range of stocks on offer on the Securities Exchange of Barbados.

Chen-Young records the diversification of the Jamaican financial system in the 1960s, with the establishment of a development bank, a securities exchange and several merchant banks. Jamaicans bought large blocks of shares in banks and insurance companies. In the 1970s the financial system was dominated by massive increases in public-sector borrowing, which precipitated and absorbed the increase in financial assets. The 1980s saw a curb in public-sector borrowing, and a new phase of diversification and innovation in the financial sector. Merchant banks and insurance companies were the fastest growing segments of the industry. Chen-Young believes that growth prospects in Jamaica would be enhanced if government expansion was geared specifically towards the producers of exports. Development banks should be wholesalers, with no direct interaction with customers, a model which has been adopted in Jamaica. Arrangements should be set up for a Caribbean regional securities exchange.

Brownbridge notes increased use of financial assets in Belize in the 1980s, in the face of economic difficulty. The surpluses of the Social Security Board made an important contribution to this process. The banking system was able to accommodate moderate increases in credit to government without reducing access to credit by the private sector. Brownbridge believes that the wide margins that commercial banks maintain between their interest rate offering on deposits and their interest charges on loans inhibited the expansion of credit.

Non-bank financial institutions

Bailey finds that non-bank financial institutions in Jamaica grew rapidly, both in the first half of the 1980s when there were tight financial regulations, and after 1986, when regulations were relaxed. In the earlier period it was trust company affiliates of commercial banks which grew fastest. The banks had excess funds and were subject to tight lending restrictions, while their trust affiliates were not. Insurance companies were also not subject to limits and they too expanded. After restrictions were eased merchant banks expanded most rapidly, offering new services such as leasing and the finance of insurance. High real interest rates encouraged the growth of financial institutions, but repressed most long-term lending and high-risk investment.

Desmond Thomas notes modest growth in building societies in Jamaica; they were at a disadvantage compared with commercial banks because of the low rate they were allowed by law to offer on deposits. The societies held an increasing proportion of liquid funds, earning interest at rates comparable to the returns they were allowed on mortgages, but the bulk of their revenue continues to be from mortgage interest.

Before Jamaica's independence credit unions expanded rapidly, according to Kirton, but the growth rate slowed in the 1960s. Most credit unions brought together workers in similar occupations, many in the civil service. Membership expanded in the 1970s but again contracted in the 1980s. Credit union savings increased in real terms and relative to deposits at commercial banks, but they remain at less than 10% of the total financial assets in Jamaica. The real interest rate on credit union deposits and members' shares has been negative for many years. Most credit union loans were for consumer purchases, but a significant minority were for small businesses.

Development finance institutions

Abbott believes that the Caribbean Development Bank (CDB) performed well as a bank, generating surpluses and maintaining a high credit rating, but it is poorly endowed with funds. The Bank has stimulated regional agricultural production, strengthened infrastructure in the smaller countries of CARICOM and complemented indigenous development within the region. It has established sound linkages with bilateral and multilateral funding agencies. Abbott recommends the accession of new members to bring additional capital resources and a shorter conduit for funds from the CDB to the private sector. The Bank should actively contribute to a regional strategy for managing external debt and should increase support for exports and regional trade. More funds should be allocated for revenue-earning projects, and relatively less for infrastructure, and the Bank should consider providing structural adjustment loans, though Abbott admits that this will involve sensitive policy issues.

Bourne argues that the lower interest cost of loans from development finance companies (DFCs) may be offset by the higher cost of doing business with them. He mentions 'protracted and expensive credit procedures'. Private finance institutions are offering increasing amounts of long-term credit, but to established customers. DFCs have enhanced the supply of credit from governments and from international agencies, but foreign agency stipulations have caused an excess of red tape and some anomalies, while government funds have too often been treated as grants by the recipients. DFC administrative costs have been high because of the high cost of administering small loans, weak management by enterprises and high default ratios. The Jamaican DFC has reduced lending costs by converting to a wholesale operation, but it is no longer able to apply social cost-benefit analysis in loan evaluation. Bourne concludes that sound macro-economic policy is the most important factor in the success of the DFC.

Lalta discusses national development foundations (NDFs), set up to provide loans, advice, training and technical assistance to very small businesses. NDFs are growing, and they have been effective in generating employment, particularly for women, and in ensuring a greater geographical dispersion of economic opportunity. Their deficits are large but declining, and they are mainly funded by external agencies. He envisages the NDF in the future providing credit references for clients applying to commercial banks, and acting as a strong small business lobby. The NDFs are moving in the direction of greater self-sufficiency (e.g. the Jamaica fund has set up an Endowment Fund to mobilise additional resources for its operations).

Equity and securities markets

Blackman's paper deals with the securities exchanges which replaced informal and episodic share trading in Jamaica (1969), Trinidad and Tobago (1981) and Barbados (1987). None has had much success in widening share ownership in their community. Blackman would like to see regional stock trading brought together in a single market to attain a 'critical mass'. He recommends the removal of exchange controls and legal barriers to property ownership within the region; freedom of movement of capital, entrepreneurship and skills; double taxation treaties among CARICOM members; exchange rate collaboration; and comparable treatment in all countries of CARICOM enterprises.

Williams discusses fiscal incentives and economic circumstances that might help to nurture venture capital.

Regulation

Farrell chronicles the evolution of financial regulation in Trinidad and Tobago. In the 1960s and 1970s the supervisors of financial institutions concentrated on compliance with reserve requirements, exchange controls and other central bank directives. They were forced by the growth of non-bank finance institutions (NFIs) and indigenous banks to widen their scope to include issues of solvency, probity and management competence. The legislative powers available to regulators proved insufficient, and some institutions failed, while the Central Bank undertook to rescue others, in order to maintain confidence in the financial system. Legislation was introduced to widen the powers of the central bank and a deposit insurance corporation was set up. The central bank has improved procedures for dealing with troubled institutions.

Liburd reports that banks in the Eastern Caribbean Central Bank (ECCB) region operate under individual banking acts of the eight countries which are members of ECCB, and the Bank has only residual authority. Members have agreed to implement a uniform banking act which will give the ECCB a central role in the granting of licenses and will stipulate uniform capital and reporting requirements.

External finance, debt and capital flight

Dodhia notes that the Caribbean experienced negative net resource transfers in the late 1980s, and official development assistance (ODA) has remained constant in nominal terms. The Caribbean is threatened by a shift away from aid to middle-income developing countries, and by the indiscriminate use of the per capita income criterion (notwithstanding a nod in the direction of factors such as social and economic infrastructure) as the basis for discriminating in the terms of financial assistance. To stimulate more export credit, Caribbean governments should step up expenditure on investment. Greater innovativeness on the part of export credit agencies and a stronger catalytic role to stimulate export credit from the World Bank and other development institutions was needed. A liberal regime for direct foreign investment is in place in the Caribbean but a more diversified appeal to foreign entrepreneurs might be fruitful, for example through licensing arrangements. Dodhia suggests the use of enterprise funds and credit insurance, and the setting up of equity funds to tap the savings of the Caribbean community abroad. Only a few Caribbean countries still have access to the foreign financial market: the Bahamas, Barbados and Trinidad and Tobago. Countries might also consider funding public projects with private foreign finance.

Blake documents the significant increase in Caribbean foreign debt in the 1980s, and the decline in net inflows over the decade. Loans were principally from official creditors and multinational financial agencies. There was a major debt rescheduling in Jamaica. Interest rates varied widely among countries and over time, but they were generally lower at the end of the decade than at the beginning. Guyana and Jamaica had burdensome debt service ratios and needed to secure debt reduction. Blake suggests a strategy for debt reduction and management involving contributions by all parties – debtor countries, bilateral creditors, multilateral financial institutions and private commercial creditors.

Bennett estimates significant net capital outflows from Guyana, Jamaica and Trinidad and Tobago, and substantial emigration from Guyana and Jamaica. He believes there is a large pool of saving in the Caribbean communities in North America and elsewhere which might be tapped by issuing shares of DFIs on the overseas market, establishing mutual funds in the overseas communities and issuing shares of building societies in those communities.

Part I

Savings and investment

CHAPTER 2

The mobilisation of savings in small states: The Commonwealth Caribbean

Clive Thomas

This chapter deals with issues centering on the mobilisation of private domestic voluntary savings in the Commonwealth Caribbean (CC). These are defined as voluntary reductions in consumption out of the disposable incomes of the resident household and private business sectors. Savings of public enterprises are excluded, although these are, strictly speaking, non-central government agencies. The reason is that governmental transfers and loans occupy such important positions in their operations as to make it impossible to study them adequately, without a detailed study of central government's revenue/expenditure/debt policies.

The major theoretical issues are reserved first, in order to lay the basis for some of the policy recommendations which emerge later. This is followed by a survey of recent data on savings trends and patterns in the region. Finally, policy issues drawn from the theoretical and survey analysis, along with others, are addressed.

Theory

In theoretical literature there are three broad approaches to the analysis of savings and growth. There is the 'prior-savings approach' of classical vintage, which stresses the importance of the prior accumulation of savings in generating growth. Savings is termed a prerequisite for investment, while investment outlets are deemed to be always in adequate amount, so that growth in output naturally follows the sequence of savings-investment-growth. The equilibrating variable is, of course, the rate of interest.

The Keynesian approach rejects this sequence and argues the primacy of investment. The encouragement of investment is the starting point, and this generates required savings either through the additional income it creates or the redistribution of income which can take place in favour of economic units more willing to save. The principal determining factor in saving is therefore the absolute level of current income. The marginal propensity to save is normally greater than zero and less than unity, but it is greater than the average propensity to save. As a result, as absolute income increases, so will the average propensity to save. It should be observed also, that at very low levels of income, dissaving can occur. This Keynesian formulation is based on a 'psychological law' of consumers' behaviour and early empirical studies employing cross-section techniques seemed to validate it.

The quantity theorists' approach identifies the determining factor in the saving process as government financing and monetary expansion.

Three major variants of these approaches have emerged, especially in relation to household saving. There is the Friedman 'permanent income' hypothesis in which saving is treated as a function of both permanent and transitory income (i.e. average expected future income and unexpected earnings). The transitory component of income is usually saved in its entirety. This, however, increases wealth and consequently expected future permanent consumption. 'Permanent' consumption is a constant proportion of 'permanent' income. This approach was invented to explain the time series data of Kuznets and Goldsmith which contradicted the Keynesian absolute income hypothesis, showing a proportional relation between income and consumption.

The second variant also developed as an explanation of these time series trend data. Dusenberry's 'relative income' hypothesis relates savings to current income, the previous peak in income, and the ratio of a person's consumption to that of the economic and social groups that person is in 'competition' with. It argues that people tend to maintain their consumption levels by dissaving or going into debt to maintain consumption levels. A substantial increase in income gives rise to increased savings levels. It follows that long-run and short-run savings behaviour are not identical.

Finally, the 'life-cycle' hypothesis treats household saving as a function of a lifetime planning horizon for consumption, with no net lifetime saving. Saving is done in the early years and used to maintain consumption in the later 'retirement' years when dissaving occurs. These approaches question the validity of the Keynesian view of the relationship of saving to income during a long period of 'steady state growth'. If there is zero growth in the population and income no net savings would occur in the society. Savings growth depends on a positive growth of population, per capita income or both. Findings of household budget surveys which show the average saving rate for higher-income groups to be higher than that for lower-income groups, are better accommodated in these theories.

This literature reveals no unambiguous delineation of the relationship of money and finance to real development; which is cause and which is consequence has not been clearly established. However, evidence now indicates unmistakeably that a well-developed monetary and financial system can aid (even if only marginally) the growth of economic activity, while a poorly organised and under-developed one can hinder it, and at times quite severely.

Econometric studies show that the ability and willingness to save out of GDP in developing countries is mainly a function of: the level of per capita income; the rate of growth of disposable income; and the distribution of income (especially its functional distribution between wages and profit). The main determinants of willingness to save are: the variety of financial institutions and savings instruments; the accessibility of these without inconvenience; the rate of interest in relation to risk and time preference of economic units, expectations as regards price changes; the demonstration effect of consumption and savings behaviour in other countries; and the general economical, social, and political environment in which economic activity takes place.

Following this type of analysis, Ramsaran (1988) sought to 'explain' bank deposit savings in Guyana, Barbados, Jamaica, and Trinidad and Tobago in terms of three variables, namely the rate of interest, the expected rate of inflation, and per capita income. They explained a high proportion of the variation in the level of bank deposits, although many results were indeterminate. In Guyana and Barbados inflation was positively related to changes in bank deposits, whereas in the other two territories they were negatively related. The interest rate variable had a positive sign in Jamaica and Guyana, but was negative in Barbados and Trinidad and Tobago. While per capita income was positively related to total bank deposits in all the territories, the associated standard errors were high.[1]

Similarly Najjar and Marcelle (1984) tested the relationship between the absolute level of measured income and savings, and the permanent income hypothesis that savings is a constant proportion of permanent income. Using ordinary least squares regression, sixteen relationships were tested for Trinidad and Tobago over the years 1963–83, but the results were not conclusive except that a close linear fit was found between national savings and national income whether using nominal, per capita or permanent income measures. When real variables are used the correlations are low.[2] Cross country comparisons and time series work show a savings function often simply depicted as:

$$S = -a_0 + b_0 Y \quad (1)$$

and savings per head of population:

$$S/P = -a_1 + b_1 (Y/P) \quad (2)$$

where S = savings, Y = income and P = population.

Savings is therefore a linear, but non-proportional function of income per head. The savings function S/GDP is given as:

$$b_1 - a_1 (GDP/P)^{-1}$$

(i.e. a hyperbolic function of GDP per head, in which the savings ratio rises with the level of per capita GDP but at a decreasing rate. As S/P approaches infinity S/GDP approaches the asymptote b).

The long-run association between domestic savings and growth is now well established. In its World Economic Survey (1988) the UN referred to a study which it conducted of savings in a sample of developing countries in the 1970s and 1980s and observed:

> The expected long-term relationship between domestic savings and growth held strongly for the sample countries during the 1980s; countries that grew fast also had a higher rate of savings. The average ratio of savings to GDP . . . remained practically unchanged, at the 1970s level of about 19 per cent . . . The association between the two variables was significant in both the 1970s and the 1980s.[3]

At the theoretical level it is important to shift the emphasis to take into account the role of savings in both short-run and long-run growth. The emergence of severe internal and external imbalances, (evident in many parts of the region) has independently emphasised the importance of domestic resources mobilisation in the restoration of macro-economic balance. This observation establishes the important, but often overlooked, significance of the relationship of macro-economic viability to long-run growth. Theoretically, therefore, regional approaches to planning for production balance which ignore financial balance (and hence savings) do so at the peril of both, since these are essentially dual aspects of one process. For this reason it is of particular note that the UN econometric exercise also showed that 'the long-term association between the savings ratio and the growth of GDP remained valid in the turmoil of the 1980s.'[4]

Over the years several economists have been critical of the single equation ordinary least squares regression model used in saving analysis. They stress correctly, the inherent simultaneity of such processes as savings and investment (Leff and Sato, 1975). They also point out the dangers of overemphasising aggregate magnitudes, ignoring the importance of regional, sectoral and other disaggregated elements. Some have also stressed the importance of a portfolio model approach which it is hoped would treat more adequately the effect of such variables as capital gains and losses on household saving behaviour, and the effects of the rate of interest on total saving, as distinct from its effect on the composition of that saving (Ortmeyer, 1985). The latter has emerged as an issue of some concern because current adjustment/stabilisation programmes have placed much emphasis on the virtues of a positive real rate of interest. Theoretically, an increase in the real rate of interest may deter consumption if linked to credit or restrictions on household purchases. It may also encourage individuals to save with the prospect of increased future consumption (a *substitution* effect). However, it could deter savings since the same level of asset accumulation generates a higher level of future spending (the *income* effect). The net effect can only be empirically established. The difficulty is that increased deposits in financial institutions may reflect a change in the composition of savings and not an increased propensity to save.

Recent econometric studies of savings behaviour reveal either explicitly or implicitly, the crucial role which the general economic, political and social environment plays in the savings process. This role is so important that it can, and frequently has, generated systemic disorders, leading to situations where none of the postulated relationships among the variables hold true. Consequently, there is wide agreement that in situations characterised by marked political instability, rapid inflation, financial repression, excessive public borrowing which crowds out private-sector access to resources and generates excess liquidity in the financial system, the willingness of economic units to save declines, capital flight and other forms of dissaving become significant, and both economic growth and macroeconomic viability are jeopardised.

Survey

There are two dimensions to a survey of savings trends and patterns; one is behavioural and the other institutional, including in the latter the variety and types of financial instruments available. Unfortunately, there is in the Caribbean a serious data limitation which has been recognised for several years now, but still cries out for remedy. Most of the aggregated savings data are obtained from the national accounts statistics. These do not measure savings directly, but obtain it as the residual difference of other directly measured aggregates; for example the difference between GNP and total consumption expenditure, or that between gross domestic investment and foreign savings defined as the balance of payments on current account adjusted by net factor payments abroad. From these accounts gross national saving plus external or foreign savings give the total supply of savings which is equal to gross capital formation. Savings is also measured net, in that consumption expenditure out of consumer credit is deducted from gross savings, and saving by one group used by another for consumption is not captured. Capital gains and losses induced by price changes are not treated adequately, nor is the treatment of consumer durables and certain elements of government expenditure.

In addition, estimates of net capital formation (one of the variables directly estimated) are affected by difficulties in the measurement of depreciation. As Ramsaran (1988) observes, the depreciation data in Trinidad and Tobago have ranged from 29–60% of capital formation during the years 1983–7, while in Jamaica these data ranged between 34–78% in the same period. Furthermore, inventory estimates are not reliable, while the national accounts data are *ex post* and therefore do not directly measure the saving *effort*.

Based on time-series and cross-country comparisons of investment, savings and growth, a number of rough indicators or targets can be found in the literature. Gross national savings are targeted at one-fifth of GDP or more for sustained growth, capital formation is targeted at above one-quarter of GDP, and the incremental capital-output ratio is targeted at 2–2.5. Foreign finance is expected to play a decreasing role in domestic capital expenditure, with both growth and domestic savings targeted to increase secularly. Some Caribbean countries exceed these targets by substantial margins while others fall short. Thus to take one example, a UN study (1987) gives Guyana an incremental capital-output ratio of 29.9% for the period 1970–81, which is far outside the target, while for the same period gross capital formation was equal to 28.2% of GDP, well within the target.

Tables 2.1 and 2.2 show data on real growth and the gross savings and investment ratios for Barbados, Guyana, Jamaica and Trinidad and Tobago for the period 1970–88, and for the OECS states for the period 1980–8. The

Table 2.1   *Growth, savings and investment (selected Caribbean countries)*

	Barbados			Guyana		
Period	Real growth	Gross savings ratio	Investment ratio	Real growth	Gross savings ratio	Investment ratio
1970	7.3	n.a.	n.a.	3.4	22	21
1971	4.0	n.a.	n.a.	2.8	22	18
1972	4.4	5	23	−2.0	19	18
1973	2.3	5	25	1.7	11	24
1974	13.5	8	22	7.0	28	21
1975	−1.9	9	19	10.4	33	30
1976	4.3	8	27	2.9	13	34
1977	3.7	5	20	−4.8	14	26
1978	6.1	15	23	−1.8	21	19
1979	7.7	14	24	−0.7	22	25
1980	4.7	19	25	1.9	19	27
1981	−3.2	13	28	4.5	11	31
1982	−5.0	16	23	−12.4	9	24
1983	−0.2	15	20	−9.3	3	22
1984	−3.4	17	16	2.1	16	27
1985	0.5	19	15	0.9	10	24
1986	4.7	16	16	0.2	16	25
1987	2.0	15	15	0.7	21	30
1988p	3.5	16	15	−3.0	14	26

Table 2.1   (Continued) Growth, savings and investments (selected Caribbean countries)

	Jamaica			Trinidad and Tobago		
Period	Real growth	Gross savings ratio	Investment ratio	Real growth	Gross savings ratio	Investment ratio
1970	11.9	25	31	3.6	10	21
1971	3.1	18	28	1.0	11	33
1972	9.2	19	26	5.8	6	30
1973	1.4	22	26	1.7	16	23
1974	−4.7	21	22	3.8	25	16
1975	−0.4	17	24	1.5	35	21
1976	−6.5	8	17	6.4	27	23
1977	−2.5	12	12	7.7	24	23
1978	0.5	12	13	7.6	24	27
1979	−1.5	13	18	7.3	22	27
1980	−5.8	9	15	6.8	30	28
1981	2.5	9	18	5.2	27	26
1982	1.1	8	20	1.7	13	27
1983	2.3	11	21	−7.3	6	27
1984	−0.9	10	21	−12.8	8	23
1985	−4.5	15	22	−2.9	6	17
1986	2.1	15	18	−6.4	0 4	23
1987p	4.9	16	19	−2.3	2	19
1988p	1.9	16	16	−4.0	13	15

Notes: Gross savings ratio is gross domestic savings as a percentage of GDP at current market prices.

Investment ratio is gross fixed investment as a percentage of GDP at current market prices.

p = provisional.

Real growth is annual per cent change in GDP at constant market prices.

Sources: Ramsaran (1988), for period 1970–6; World Bank (1988), for period 1977–89; Inter-American Development Bank Report, 1989 for 1988.

longer time series shows Barbados averaging nearly 5% growth between 1970 and 1980, and less than 1% since then. The saving ratio in Barbados, however, increased from 9% between 1970–9 to 17% between 1980–8. In the case of Guyana, Jamaica and Trinidad and Tobago, there were substantial declines in the savings ratios (approximately 50% in Guyana, 40% in

Table 2.2   OECS region: Savings, investment and growth

	1980	1981	1982	1983	1984	1985	1986	1987	1988
Antigua									
Real growth of GDP	8.7	4.7	1.5	7.4	7.1	7.8	8.4	8.8	7.6
Gross Domestic Savings[1]	8.4	11.8	10.5	18.1	15.4	17.8	13.9	16.1	n.a.
Gross Domestic Investment[1]	37.7	53.2	49.7	25.5	31.6	32.6	43.2	50.8	n.a.
Dominica									
Real growth of GDP	10.5	10.1	4.1	3.0	6.9	1.5	6.8	6.8	5.6
Gross Domestic Savings[1]	-22.9	-4.0	9.4	16.5	19.7	10.9	20.4	19.9	n.a.
Gross Domestic Investment[1]	55.5	37.3	33.6	32.3	44.9	32.7	25.1	28.1	n.a.
Grenada									
Real growth of GDP	-1.5	8.0	0.6	-2.9	2.0	3.7	5.6	6.0	4.3
Gross Domestic Savings[1]	n.a.	13.0	17.2	14.2	14.4	19.0	17.7	21.2	22.4
Gross Domestic Investment[1]	n.a.	47.0	62.8	52.2	39.4	39.4	40.2	40.1	45.0
Montserrat									
Real growth of GDP	9.4	5.7	2.7	-5.3	2.8	5.4	5.1	10.8	12.1
Gross Domestic Savings[1]	-13.4	-27.1	-25.1	-19.8	-11.5	-1.6	8.6	10.3	n.a.
Gross Domestic Investment[1]	46.7	52.7	45.2	33.5	21.9	30.5	39.2	44.2	n.a.
St Kitts-Nevis									
Real growth of GDP	3.9	5.1	6.3	-1.1	9.0	5.6	6.3	6.8	4.7
Gross Domestic Savings[1]	9.9	28.0	22.4	-0.4	19.4	26.0	17.4	16.8	13.9
Gross Domestic Investment[1]	48.4	38.3	40.0	36.6	29.4	37.2	32.8	33.6	n.a.

Table 2.2 (continued)   OECS region: Savings, investment and growth

	1980	1981	1982	1983	1984	1985	1986	1987	1988
St Lucia									
Real growth of GDP	-0.8	1.2	3.0	4.1	5.0	6.0	5.9	2.0	5.0
Gross Domestic Savings[1]	7.6	-2.3	14.4	23.3	16.2	30.0	41.1	38.2	n.a.
Gross Domestic Investment[1]	60.2	55.0	46.5	35.2	35.7	41.7	45.3	53.0	n.a.
St Vincent									
Real growth of GDP	2.7	7.4	8.5	5.8	5.3	4.6	7.2	5.7	8.4
Gross Domestic Savings[1]	-14.1	0.8	14.4	27.2	32.3	25.9	15.5	n.a.	n.a.
Gross Domestic Investment[1]	47.8	39.0	36.3	36.1	38.9	34.4	24.4	n.a.	n.a.

1 as a percentage of GDP.
Sources: Liburd and Bain (1988), World Bank (1988) and for Montserrat, UNECLAC (1987) and ECLA (estimates as cited in T. Harker, (1989).

Trinidad and Tobago, and 30% in Jamaica). All three of these countries averaged negative or close to negative growth in the 1980s.

The investment ratio exceeded the gross savings ratio in all four countries, indicating the role foreign finance played in domestic capital formation. For the period 1970–88 this financing averaged 40%, 31%, 29% and 32% for Barbados, Guyana, Jamaica and Trinidad and Tobago, respectively. In the case of Barbados, however, there was a substantial decline in the role of external financing between 1970–9 and 1980–7, from 62% to 16%, while in the other territories the reverse occurred over the same period: a near quadrupling of the ratio in Guyana, a near trebling in Trinidad and Tobago, and a near doubling of the ratio in Jamaica.

In all four territories the investment ratio exceeded the 'target' of one-quarter of GDP. National savings, however, only achieved the targeted ratio of one-fifth of GDP in Guyana and Trinidad and Tobago for the period 1970–9. Furthermore, only Barbados exhibited a reducing dependence on foreign savings.

The data on the OECS states (Table 2.2) cover a far shorter period and are therefore less useful indicators of trends. In general, however, investment ratios were substantially in excess of the targeted ratios derived from international comparisons, ranging between 36% and 47% of GDP. The gross domestic savings ratio behaved far more erratically, ranging from –18% of GDP (Montserrat where the investment ratio was 38%) to 17% of GDP.

The high level of foreign finance in capital formation in the region, as evidenced in the discrepancy between investment and domestic savings ratios, was complemented by the limited role public-sector savings played in the financing of capital formation (see Table 2.3). In Guyana there has been substantial public-sector dissaving, with a peak at 47% of GDP in 1985 and an average of 28% GDP for a period 1981–7. In Jamaica public-sector dissaving for the period 1977–85 averaged just over 4% of GDP, and in St Kitts it averaged 35% during 1981–5. Elsewhere, public-sector dissaving was not significant. Only in Trinidad and Tobago in the oil boom years (1977–81) were public-sector savings substantial, averaging over one-fifth of GDP, and accounting for most of the national saving.

Turning to the financialisation of savings, Crichton and de Silva (1988) show the total number of financial institutions in Trinidad and Tobago grew from 376 to 491 between 1973 and 1989. A number of new capital market institutions were established: a stock exchange, a unit trust, a deposit insurance corporation, a mortgage bank, and merchant banks. The institutional composition of financial institutions in Trinidad and Tobago showed important changes and the ratio of financial assets to GNP at current prices nearly doubled between 1973 and 1989 (i.e. rising from 0.54 to 1.01). Crichton and de Silva observed: 'for the most part, however, institutional

Table 2.3   Caribbean countries – Public sector savings, 1977–87*

	1977	1978	1979	1980	1981	1982	1983	1984	1985	1986	1987 [c]
Antigua	-3.6	-0.8	0.5	1.2	2.4	0.5	1.3	2.4	4.3	7.0	1.1
Bahamas	3.9	6.0	6.2	7.7	6.3	3.3	3.3	4.9	5.3	6.4	5.9
Barbados	3.0	6.7	5.8	4.5	2.9	4.0	5.6	3.9	2.8	1.9	0.1
Belize	1.4	6.3	4.1	4.6	-2.4	-0.3	-2.2	3.6	4.8	6.9	7.9
Dominica [a]	-4.4	-4.2	-28.3	-16.5	-3.8	-1.8	1.6	2.3	5.4	8.6	10.2
Grenada	5.5	2.5	0.6	-0.2	-0.6	2.0	5.3	2.1	4.5	2.2	n.a.
Guyana	-0.9	5.8	4.1	2.1	-18.0	-21.4	-37.0	-29.4	-46.8	-26.7	-19.9
Jamaica [b]	-6.2	-2.8	-4.2	-7.8	-4.0	-3.6	-8.6	-1.5	-1.0	4.0	5.5
St Kitts [ba]	11.2	5.0	4.7	4.3	-5.0	-3.4	-2.7	-1.0	-4.1	2.6	4.2
St Lucia	3.7	4.8	1.7	4.5	1.0	-0.3	0.1	4.2	6.3	8.9	11.0
St Vincent	0.2	-0.2	-1.4	0.2	1.1	0.8	-1.0	4.4	9.4	8.1	8.1
Trinidad	23.9	18.6	25.2	18.1	20.3	6.6	2.5	1.9	3.0	-1.4	n.a.

*   % of GDP.
a   Fiscal Year
b   Central Government.
c   Preliminary.
n.a.   Not available.

Source: World Bank (1988).

and structural change has been driven by deliberate policy action rather than by market signals. The Central Bank has played a major role in engineering structural change.'[5]

In Barbados, although the expansion of the financial sector was not as vigorous as in Trinidad and Tobago, the role of government policy was also key: 'In Barbados, the last decade was replete with official directives, restrictions and incentives in the interest of economic growth.'[6] The Government of Barbados established indigenous institutions (a stock exchange and a commercial bank) which have helped to alter the structure of financial intermediation in that country and to increase the ratio of financial assets to GDP from 1.03 in 1977 to 1.25 in 1987.

The OECS' financial system 'is still relatively under-developed in terms of the range of institutions and of financial assets available.'[7] Trading in equities and long-term securities is quite minimal; non-banks accounted for only 8% of financial intermediation. Government policy is central and is reflected in the creation of the Eastern Caribbean Central Bank, a number of development banks, and joint venture financial institutions. In Guyana, despite the emergence of substantial currency substitution and foreign currency black markets, financial assets as a percentage of real GDP rose from 79% in 1980 to 106% in 1986.

In all the territories commercial banks remain the key institutions in the financial system. For this reason, observations of their failure to allocate funds to the productive sector is of extreme importance. Thus Liburd and Bain estimate that commercial banks mobilise over two-thirds of the financial savings in the OECS states, yet only 9% of their assets represented claims on the productive sectors (agriculture, tourism and manufacturing).[8] A similar lament is made by Codrington and Coppin about Barbados, that: 'ten years of effort by the Central Bank has not led to increases in the share of total bank credit to the foreign exchange earning sectors – manufacturing, tourism and agriculture.'[9] Manhertz, writing a decade and a half earlier, had also observed this bias of the commercial banks' portfolio in Jamaica.[10]

The data in Table 2.4 show the distribution of financial assets by type of instrument for Trinidad and Tobago and the OECS region. The heavy concentration in loans and advances reflects the leading role of the commercial banking sector. The comparatively high level of foreign instruments in the OECS region reflects the more open financial system which exists there. If the Central Bank balance is taken together with holdings of government securities, the distribution is almost identical for the two sets of territories.

Although this chapter focuses on voluntary private domestic savings, a brief reference to the position of involuntary savings (taxation) is appropriate. Table 2.5 indicates a significant level of tax effort in the four MDCs of the CC, with the position of Guyana being particularly noteworthy, in the light of the prolonged depression being experienced in that country. In

Table 2.4   Distribution of assets of all financial institutions by type of instrument (Trinidad and Tobago and OECS region)

Item	Trinidad and Tobago (1988)	OECS Region (1986)
Cash in hand	1.6	7.1
Central Bank balance	4.6	8.0
Government Securities	7.5	4.7
Loans and advances	66.7	53.3
Foreign investments	12.8	20.3
Other[1]	6.8	6.6
Total	100.0	100.0

1   Includes commercial bills, mortgage loans and private securities.

Sources: Crichton and de Silva (1988), Liburd and Bain (1988), and Central Bank of Trinidad and Tobago.

general one would expect that given the pressures to maintain the government's current expenditure, government saving will be higher, the higher the level of the government's current revenue. Tax revenue is dependent not only on the income and expenditure subject to taxation, but on the rate of taxation, the efficiency of tax administration, as well as the level of co-operation of the citizenry at large in tax collection. The general ratios given in Table 2.5 mask these individual details and can therefore be misleading as true performance measures, although their significance should not be overlooked.

Table 2.6 shows tax effort in the OECS states, for indirect and direct taxation. The table also shows the marginal indirect and direct tax rates and the buoyancy of indirect and direct taxation for the OECS. Again the data show an impressive tax effort, averaging 27% for the years 1979–87. The average rates of both direct and indirect taxation were close to the marginal rates, while the elasticity of indirect taxation is 1.07% and that of direct taxation is 0.86%.

Arguably, the most important development in recent times in the process of financial intermediation in the region, has been the promotion of stock exchanges, as part of a wider encouragement of the growth of vibrant securities markets. The major objectives here have been to:

- broaden the range of assets available to potential savers;
- broaden the base of private capital ownership;
- encourage the growth of more financially sophisticated communities based on the regular information flows (published accounts, daily stock market reports, etc.);

Table 2.5 Tax revenue as a percentage of GDP,[1] 1970–88 (selected Caribbean countries)

	Barbados	Guyana	Jamaica	Trinidad and Tobago [2]
1970	n.a.	22	17	16
1971	n.a.	20	18	17
1972	23	22	18	18 (4)
1973	23	23	18	18 (5)
1974	20	31	17	30 (21)
1975	22	39	18	32 (24)
1976	22	30	18	33 (23)
1977	22	27	17	36 (23)
1978	25	24	20	32 (20)
1979	24	25	20	33 (21)
1980	23	25	19	40 (25)
1981	22	30	22	40 (26)
1982	23	31	25	34 (17)
1983	24	33	23	32 (13)
1984	24	34	23	33 (15)
1985	25	35	27	32 (14)
1986	24	41	28	27 (10)
1987p	24	30	28	28 (12)
1988p	23	37	27	27

p provisional.
1 at current market prices.
2 figures in brackets refer to revenues from the oil sector.

Source: Ramsaran (1987), and Inter-American Development Bank, Annual
Report, 1989.

- stimulate accounting and commercial law reform; and perhaps above all
- encourage the raising of investment funds through new issues, rather than from borrowing, in order to stimulate the growth of new ventures and to reduce the high debt ratios which characterise Caribbean enterprise.

Stock exchanges have either not grown rapidly enough or have exhibited marked instability. In December 1988, the oldest (1969) and the largest of the region's stock exchanges (Jamaica) with a capitalisation of J$3,279 million showed the value of traded stocks at J$137 million which was half that of the previous year, and less than half that of the peak year 1986 when this figure stood at J$377 million. After the first seven years (1978–84), the value of traded stocks had only reached J$26 million. The volume of transactions showed a similar trend to the value figures. In Trinidad and

Table 2.6   *Tax effort, marginal rate and buoyancy in the OECS, 1979–87*

Year	ITE	DTE	MITR	MDTR	BITE	BDTE
1979	.20	.10	n.a.	n.a.	n.a.	n.a.
1980	.18	.09	.09	.03	.48	.32
1981	.17	.08	.12	.05	.64	.54
1982	.17	.08	.17	.01	.89	.11
1983	.17	.09	.19	.14	1.02	1.51
1984	.18	.10	.31	.20	1.66	2.16
1985	.18	.10	.16	.20	.86	2.16
1986	.20	.10	.42	.07	2.25	.76
1987	.21	.10	.35	.05	1.87	.54
Average	.18	.09	.20	.08	1.07	.86

ITE   Indirect Tax Effort IDT/Y.
DTE   Direct Tax Effort DT/Y.
MITR   Marginal Indirect Tax Rate (change IDT/change in Income).
MDTR   Marginal Direct Tax Rate (change DT/change in Income).
BITE   Buoyancy of Indirect Tax – Elasticity – The percentage change in
       Indirect Tax relative to the percentage change in Income.
BDTE   Buoyancy of Direct Tax – Elasticity – The percentage change in
       Direct Tax relative to the percentage change in Income.

Source: Jones-Hendrickson (1988).

Tobago, a similar pattern is observed as the number of transactions quin-tupled between 1981 and 1982 and thereafter declined steadily to a level in 1987 which was only 25% above that of 1981. By 1987, the index of the unit value of shares traded had been reduced to one-third that of 1981, having risen to a peak in 1982 of over 40% above the 1981 level.

West Indian entrepreneurs exhibit a strong preference for debt as opposed to equity, in order to maintain family or other closed circle control of their enterprises. There have been internal weaknesses in the stock market as well, such as inadequate disclosure by firms.

Compared to other developing regions at a similar stage, the CC, and in particular the island territories, are generally recognised as having achieved a high level of financial intermediation. Despite this, informal finance, broadly defined, is a major source of small-scale saving and lending. Out-standing features of this form of finance include:

• the importance of personal relations to both lenders and borrowers, as well as in the formation of credit groups and associations. Many of these are part of local community support structures and the operators have a very good knowledge of the community and environment in which they operate;

- operators display flexibility, rapidity of response, and ease of transactions;
- the bureaucracy is minimal, and the regulations and administrative arrangements which they carry are well-suited to financially unsophisticated borrowers and savers; and
- the emphasis is to accept all savings no matter how small, and to emphasise availability rather than cost in lending. Loan rates are often very high, reflecting the absence of scale economies, the risks, and often the monopoly power which individual operators can command in circumstances when loans are resorted to out of distress. But in the communities this is often overlooked because of the emphasis on availability and flexibility.

Policy

The macro-economic environment

The typical ratio of commercial to non-commercial external debt in the region is 1:2, the reverse of the developing countries as a group. The well-publicised global trend of reduced private flows is now being paralleled with reduced multilateral and bilateral non-commercial inflows into the region, to the point that there is an excess of interest payment outflows over inflows. This situation dramatises the significant role mobilisation of domestic savings will have to play in the development of the region as all developing countries face a transition from relatively abundant and cheap international credit to expensive credit which is very difficult to access.

Rapid improvements in technology, as well as innovation in financial organisation, and the invention of new financial instruments, have also produced qualitative changes in the international financial environment, which pose unprecedented challenges to policymakers. A vast range of options now face those domestic residents who have access to international financial markets.

General economic policies must engender confidence if people are to be willing to save locally. Among the more important policies are: exchange rate stability; price stability; adequate access to foreign exchange; the absence of large government deficits and 'crowding out effect' of the private sector; the levels of financial repression; whether real rates of interest are positive or negative; and whether the tax structure generates incentives or disincentives to personal and corporate savings.

Data collection

A programme for the direct measurement of savings and the estimation of savings behaviour functions is also required. Frequent direct surveys of saving behaviour are required as independent cross-checks, along with the more widespread construction of flow-of-funds accounts. As Najjar and Marcelle observe: 'the disparities in the two sets of data [national accounts and flow-of-funds] highlight the urgent need for cross-checks amongst the major economic statistics'.[11] Data should be disaggregated to permit the determination of the right mix of incentives for the various groups in the society. This effort might be accompanied by promotional campaigns to encourage thrift. The neglect and/or abandonment of savings committees and commissions established in earlier periods is much to be regretted.

Targets and context

The empirical survey has indicated the erratic behaviour of regional performance in relation to targets derived from international comparisons and time series studies of a large number of countries. The particular problems of size, scale, high levels of migration, openness, proximity to the North American market, and the preponderant weight of foreign investment in the region make its economies very distinctive and atypical. Targets for the region should be based on its particular context and historical experiences, to be used as guides to internal progress and to form the basis for dialogue with external agencies which participate in the financing of regional development.

Public policy

In all successful market systems, the protection and nurturing of enterprises in their early phase of development, have been key features of public policy. In the Caribbean the areas where government initiative is called for include the further development of the regulatory framework of financial institutions, greater emphasis on securitisation and the development of stock market operations, informal finance, and the mobilisation of the savings of non-resident nationals. Governments must vigorously pursue measures to control and make more effective their own current expenditure while at the same time ensuring the steady growth of tax and non-tax revenues. The UN World Economic Survey (1988), already referred to, reported on a sample study of developing countries in which econometric data showed:[12]

• a close association between a high rate of growth of government savings and growth of GDP;

- that a large or growing deficit constrained growth;
- that prudent fiscal policies were associated with a higher rate of growth of output; and
- that an over-expansive fiscal policy in the face of supply constraints was harmful to growth.

The regulatory framework

Commercial banking should be opened to much greater competition from non-banks, by means of appropriate changes in the regulatory framework of financial intermediation. New or improved regulations are needed to govern:

- the activities of near-banks;
- the position of commercial banks as regards the holding of equity in other enterprises;
- the position of non-banks, especially insurance companies in the owner-ship of commercial banks;
- merger and take-over activities;
- capitalisation and debt ratios of enterprises;
- the prudential management of trust funds;
- the establishment of deposit insurance or safety-net facilities in the banking system; and
- stock market activities.

To economise on cost and maximise the effectiveness of available expertise a regional approach to the solution of these difficulties might well be considered. This would have the additional advantage of anticipating the need to harmonise these regulations to cater for increased regional co-operation.

The stock market

Reactivation of growth in the securities market requires a number of important policy measures, the more important of which are:

- a legal framework to complement self-regulation;
- the laws for public and private companies must be brought closer to-gether as regards disclosures, so that non-disclosure 'benefits' are not appropriated by private companies;
- the deliberate encouragement of increased competition in the stock mar-ket through an increase in the number of brokerage firms, including arms-length agencies of parastatals, joint enterprises and non-govern-mental associations;

- clear legal guidelines on broker liability, in the event clients are not given the quality of professional advice they pay for. To promote professionalisation, the relevant authorities should improve training of stock market operators and require clear, frequent, and up-to-date statements on the financial interests of broker firms;
- the removal of all administrative bottlenecks; and
- fiscal incentives geared to encourage companies to be listed on the exchange.

Non-resident national savings and capital flight

With the relatively large Caribbean diaspora residing in developed market economies, attention should be directed to mobilising savings of non-resident nationals, discouraging capital flight and encouraging capital repatriation. The major recommendations are that:

- consideration should be given to declaring an 'amnesty' on illegally-held overseas funds. This should be linked to legislative changes geared to place these funds under a regime of administration that is fair to all interests involved, while at the same time being realistic enough to accept that without incentives these savings will continue to be effectively outside the national economy. This proposal raises complex issues of law and ethics. In other situations the point has been made that such measures carry overtones of 'rewarding illegality'. It is for such reasons that careful consideration is being urged;
- providing exchange rate premiums for non-residents who send funds home for saving and investment. This proposal raises dangers of 'round-tripping' (that is a situation in which those who are entitled to these benefits seek to exploit the differences in exchange rates used for outward and inward transactions); and
- develop a dimension of the local securities market geared to the special requirements of non-residents, for example: the sale of offshore bonds, with special incentives for non-resident nationals and residents with overseas funds; allowing local financial institutions to accept funds as foreign currency deposits with certain convertibility and repatriation rights; and preferred access to the local security markets for non-resident nationals over other foreign investors.

Conclusion

A well-developed financial system with a range, depth and variety of financial assets and institutions is important to raising and sustaining the savings ratios in the region and creating the best conditions for the efficient allocation of these savings. Such a system is impossible without public confidence based on the free flow of information onto the market. At present, the fundamental disjunctures which exist in the market are those between the formal and informal sectors, between large and small savers and users of funds, and between public and private savings, and public and private domestic access to savings.

The remedies to these situations will require considerable public sector initiative, and perhaps a more prominent development role for the central banks.

Notes

1 Ramsaran (1988) p. 32.
2 Najjar and Marcelle (1984). The latter result leads them to question the appropriateness of the retail price index as the deflator of the series.
3 UN (1988) pp. 143–6. The coefficient of correlation between the savings ratio and growth of GDP for the 21 countries of the sample was 0.40 for the period 1971–80 and 0.54 for 1981–6. Both were statistically significant at the 5% level.
4 *Ibid.* pp. 143–6.
5 Crichton and de Silva (1988) p. 125.
6 Codrington and Coppin (1988) p. 1.
7 Liburd and Bain (1988) p. 2.
8 *Ibid.*
9 Codrington and Coppin (1988) p. 7.
10 Mannhertz (1971).
11 Najjar and Marcelle, (1984) p. 33.
12 UN (1988).

CHAPTER 3 | Savings and investment in Barbados

Steve Emtage

The focus of this chapter is the structure and development of the capital market in Barbados in the 1980s. The objective is to identify constraints on the efficient functioning of the market with regard both to the supply of and demand for loanable funds and to suggest any mechanisms which might address and overcome these constraints in order to improve allocative efficiency and raise the level of domestic investment. The approach will be pragmatic rather than theoretical, and as would be expected in a case study of a small open economy, domestic issues are considered against a regional and international background.

In conventional national income terminology, savings always equal investment deriving from the accounting identities $Y = C + S$ and $Y = C + I$, with savings being that part of income not spent on goods and services used for current consumption and investment that part of output devoted to projects providing goods not intended for immediate consumption. In an open economy, part of domestic investment may be financed by foreign savings or domestic savings may finance external investment. The relationship between domestic and foreign savings, and investment, is expressed in the savings-investment approach to the balance of payments. This approach to balance of payments equilibrium concentrates on the Keynesian relationship between savings and investment to explain the position of the current account of the balance of payments, for the differences between the exports of goods and services and the imports of goods and services is the counterpart of the difference between aggregate domestic savings and aggregate domestic investment.

While in ex-post fashion, the resource gap represented by the difference between exports and imports represents the part of domestic investment financed by foreign savings, it is still meaningful to speak of a savings and a foreign exchange gap where the rate of domestic savings or level of imports are less than that required to sustain a given target rate of growth of output. In such situations, the lack of realised savings and available foreign exchange constitutes a constraint on the attainment of the desired rate of growth.

The act of the individual refraining from current consumption is not synonymous with savings in the economists' sense. Through financial intermediation income not consumed by one household may be used for consumption purposes by another. Much of these financial savings will of necessity be used through the activities of financial intermediaries to satisfy the legitimate consumption needs of the country. Concrete evidence, however, supports the thesis that those countries which have devoted a high proportion of output to investment are also the countries which have the most impressive growth performances. This process involves not only replacing existing assets but more importantly adding to the stock of new income-generating assets and ensuring that assets replaced and installed are used efficiently.

The ratio of investment to GDP must be raised and sustained at a level consistent with the achievement of income and employment goals and an increasing proportion of that investment should be financed by domestic savings. The quantum and distribution of such savings are a matter of considerable significance. This is the subject matter of this chapter. Recent developments of the Barbados economy, particularly trends in gross fixed investment and its financing, are reviewed first. This is followed by a look at the functioning of the local capital markets. Finally, some suggestions for reform and improvement are considered.

Recent economic developments

In the two decades prior to the onset of the severe recession of the early 1980s, the Barbados economy experienced sustained real growth of between 3% and 5% per year. Against a largely favourable international economic background, the economy expanded and became more diversified.

The world economy in the 1960s was characterised by low inflation, monetary and exchange rate stability and continuous growth in trade in goods and services. The resulting rise in incomes in the developed countries, coupled with a marked reduction in the real cost of travel, led both to buoyant commodity prices and rapid growth of foreign travel expenditure. Barbados was well placed to take advantage of this favourable climate. With a well-developed social and economic infrastructure and political stability the economy responded to the external stimulus as well as to domestic policies aimed at promoting diversification and growth.

During the 1970s there were major shocks to the international economy with the escalation of oil prices and of inflation generally, and increased volatility in the capital and foreign exchange markets. These developments all had their adverse impact on Barbados but there were compensations – for example the rise of oil and commodity prices led to the rapid growth of intra-regional trade from which Barbados benefited greatly. So the 1970s, like the 1960s, were on the whole a period of economic expansion for the island.

The major structural change in these two decades was the relative decline in the importance of the agricultural sector and the increased contribution of manufacturing and services, particularly tourism, to total output. Within the agricultural sector real value-added in the sugar industry remained largely unchanged while there was a general increase of non-sugar agricultural output. The manufacturing sector initially responded to rising domestic incomes by exploiting opportunities for import substitution. Later, in the 1970s, with the advent of CARICOM and the impact of rising oil prices on the economy of Trinidad and Tobago, Barbados' manufacturers were able to gain a significant share of the regional market. Simultaneously there developed an enclave sector importing components principally from North America and re-exporting finished products under preferential tariff arrangements. In all this, Barbados was aided by the adoption of outward-looking policies which ensured that a competitive framework was maintained.

Mirroring these changes in economic structure were parallel changes in the structure of the labour force, with an increasing proportion of workers employed in the tertiary sector – commerce, tourism and public services. In some sectors (e.g. manufacturing), while the relative proportion employed did not change significantly, there were marked increases in productivity. Overall, despite increases in participation rates and in the labour force, unemployment fell progressively to about 10% in 1980. This growth in the employed labour force and increase in productivity was the result of strong growth in export demand accompanied by a high level of capital formation and maintenance of international competitiveness in the pricing of factors of production and finished goods.

In the period under review, capital formation remained high at between 20 – 30% of GDP. While foreign investment increased significantly, by the late 1970s domestic savings (which reached as high as 19% of GDP in 1980) were financing the greater part of this relatively high gross fixed investment. Indeed by 1980, Barbados' rate of domestic savings and investment compared favourably with the fastest growing developing countries. Steady economic growth and the diversification of the economy provided emerging opportunities for private-sector investment which accounted for some 80% of total capital formation. Apart from the growth of export demand, the fact that Barbados' costs of production remained competitive was a critical factor in ensuring the profitability of investment.

In the 1960s public-sector savings contributed significantly to public-sector capital expenditure, financing on average 40% of the total. External borrowing was limited and local borrowing and statutory funds financed the balance. During the 1970s, as current expenditure rose, surpluses on current account diminished, and increasing reliance was placed on foreign borrowing, mainly from multilateral financial institutions, to finance investment. With the establishment of the Central Bank in 1973 recourse was also had to the domestic banking system for credit. However, fiscal policy was able to adjust to exogenous shocks and contain the overall deficit to manageable proportions.

With strong export growth, adequate domestic savings and fiscal stability, the ratio of public external debt to GDP and the public-sector debt service ratio increased slowly, reaching only 14% and 2% respectively by 1980. The balance of payments came under pressure in the 1970s as a result of the escalation of oil prices but corrective policies succeeded in making the required adjustment without recourse to excessive foreign borrowing.

By comparison with the progressive growth and development of the economy in the 1960s and (despite the energy crisis) the 1970s, in the period since 1981 the economy has faltered and a number of severe structural imbalances have emerged. The international economic environment has not been favourable. The early part of the decade saw the industrialised countries plunged into the worst recession since the Second World War. Even though by the mid-1980s the recession had been overcome, certain features of the international economy continued to provide an unsettling framework for domestic economic policy. Volatility in exchange rates, decline in transfer of resources, falling commodity prices, increased protectionism and continuing high real interest rates have created serious problems for economies like Barbados, and these have been exacerbated by certain developments and inappropriate policy responses in the domestic economy.

Real output declined by nearly 7% in real terms between 1981 and 1982. Output in all the productive sectors declined as a result of the impact of the recession on external demand. Simultaneously with the fall in real output, the government was pursuing expansionary fiscal policies, with the public sector forced to borrow heavily from the banking system to finance its deficits. With inflation running at double digit levels and the balance of payments under pressure, the government decided to implement a stabilisation programme with the help of the IMF. As a result, the public-sector deficit was significantly reduced, price rises moderated and the deterioration in the balance of payments arrested. Positive growth has been recorded since 1985 although real output only surpassed its 1980 level in 1986.

Generally, growth has been strongest in the non-traded goods sectors – distribution, transport and storage, utilities, business and general services. Value-added in tourism only regained the 1980 level in 1988 and manufacturing has not yet found markets to replace those lost in CARICOM and the enclave sectors. While non-sugar agriculture has continued to show encouraging growth, the combined effects of reduced acreage and depressed prices have resulted in large losses in the sugar industry and the need to provide public subsidisation.

Accompanying the decline and stagnation in real output has been a significant drop in the ratio of investment to GDP. From an average of 24% of GDP in the period 1976–80, gross fixed capital formation slumped to an average of 16% of GDP in the period 1983–7. Assuming no change in the proportion of investment going to maintenance and creation of new fixed assets or in the incremental capital output ratio, this fall in the level of investment, if prolonged, would have a depressing effect on the long-term growth potential of the economy. While public-sector capital formation declined initially as government sought to correct fiscal imbalances by cutting capital expenditure, the major decline was in the level of private-sector capital formation from a high of 22% of GDP in 1981 to 11% in 1986.

This trend largely reflected a decline in the inflow of foreign savings, as domestic savings, although fluctuating, remained in the range of 14 – 16% of GDP in the period following 1981. External savings, which in the mid-1970s had financed as much as 70 – 75% of Gross Domestic Capital Formation (GDCF) in some years, steadily declined as a source of financing. In the period 1984–6, external savings actually became negative as reduced inflows of direct investment were accompanied by rising outflows to pay dividends as well as service large foreign loans contracted by the public utilities and others in the previous decade. The sharp fall in private investment was reflected in the external current account balance which became positive after 1984 as imports of capital goods fell significantly. In the absence of a high level of investment and of a satisfactory growth rate, this positive external balance emerged at the cost of the under-utilisation of the country's productive potential.

The trend of a declining ratio of GDCF to GDP and a reversal of private capital inflows is not, of course, unique to Barbados, but is the rule rather than the exception in Latin America and the Caribbean. For most heavily-indebted countries this largely reflects the crippling debt service payments and the virtual cessation of new commercial lendings. In the case of Barbados, while external debt service payments, particularly for privately contracted portfolio investment, have risen, the decline in GDCF represents, as well, a relatively sudden and significant fall in private foreign investment.

While there has been a noticeable decline in direct foreign investment in the developing countries in general, some countries have been able to continue to attract such investment. There are many factors which influence the flow of foreign investment – political stability, regulatory and tax frameworks, levels of social and economic infrastructure, etc. – but predominant among these is the scope for making a profit. Available data would seem to indicate that during the first half of the 1980s at least, Barbados' international competitiveness as a location for export activities declined. Wage increases ran ahead of both the rate of inflation and growth of real output in the traded goods sector. Coupled with a fixed exchange rate and tied to a currency which up to 1986 was escalating, the movement of wages relative to prices and production would have reduced Barbados' competitive position *vis-à-vis* that of its trading partners. More recently, as the rate of nominal wage increases has moderated and there has been renewed growth, the increase of unit labour costs has moderated. Barbados remains, however, in comparison with its CARICOM neighbours and other potential competitors, a high cost producer.

The combination of sluggish growth and declining investment has resulted in a significant rise in the rate of unemployment. While the number of jobs has expanded, the parallel growth of the labour force has matched the jobs created so that the unemployment rate has remained in the 16 – 18% range. Following the stabilisation programme introduced in 1982/83, there has been a steady deterioration in the public finances. While efforts have been made to increase revenue, efforts to control expenditure growth have been less successful. Capital expenditure and net lending have increased steadily while current expenditure, driven by wage increases and expansion of public-sector employment, has increased significantly in real terms since 1980. As a result, the overall public-sector deficit has risen to between 5 – 7% of GDP for the past three years. While in the earlier years a significant part of the deficit was financed from external sources, this consisted largely of project financing from multilateral and bilateral agencies. As the size of the deficits increased, however, the Government was forced to rely increasingly on domestic finance – the banking system and the surplus of the National Insurance Fund – and since 1985 mainly on commercial borrowing in the foreign capital markets.

An inevitable consequence of a slow growth economy combined with expansionary fiscal policies has been a weakening balance of payments situation. With weak export performance, rising debt service payments and the sustaining effect of increased disposable income (caused by a shift from direct to indirect taxation) on imports, the government has had to rely on its commercial borrowings to shore up the reserves. The changed maturity structure of the debt caused by a shift from institutional to market borrowing has also resulted in higher interest charges. Total debt service payments now amount to some 25% of the export of goods and services. With two-thirds of the Central Bank reserves sterilised in the CARICOM Multilateral Clearing Facility (whose operations have been suspended), the import cover of the country's foreign reserves remains uncomfortable.

The challenge facing the country is to restart export-led growth at a level which will induce the flow of savings and investment required to progressively reduce unemployment. Experience suggests that it is the increase in exports which is the causal factor not the increase in investment which only comes after. Assuming that the export demand exists, the question of ensuring that funds are available to create the necessary physical assets becomes the main concern.

Mobilisation and allocation of domestic savings

In analysing the process by which financial savings are transformed into domestic investment, it is useful to distinguish a number of related but fairly distinct mechanisms. The major mechanism is the accumulation of monetary assets by surplus sectors – households and institutions – and the allocation by various intermediaries of these funds to spending units which thereby create physical assets. Then there are self-financed investments effectuated by the corporate sector out of its own savings; and direct investment by households, corporations or the public sector in new or ongoing enterprises in the (mostly) private sector, through the Securities Exchange.

As in other countries at a similar stage of development, the level and growth of financial savings is determined mainly by the level and growth of nominal GDP, although there are other influential factors such as the distribution of income. Macro-economic policy can affect the rate at which such financial savings are transformed into physical assets by influencing the share of real credit allocated to public and private consumption. The main mechanisms are the size of the public-sector deficit and the impact of changes in fiscal policy on the distribution of incomes and the incentive to accumulate monetary assets or to consume income.

The size of the public-sector deficit and how it is financed is important because of its potential impact on the level of private-sector investment. Whether the public-sector deficit is caused by public-sector consumption or investment, the possibility exists that credit allocated to its financing may hold down or depress private investment – the so-called 'crowding out' effect. It is argued that, by repressing private investment, crowding out reduces the rate at which the stock of productive capital grows and thereby tends to reduce the rate at which productivity, per capita income, and total output grows (Stein, 1983). Additionally, the persistence of deficits of the order of 5 – 7% of GDP, in the absence of an adequate savings rate, can lead to progressively higher and unsustainable debt/GDP ratios.

The current foreign exchange crisis in developing countries obscures the potentially adverse impact on the growth of income and employment of large and persistent reliance on domestic debt to finance the deficit. Because servicing domestic debt does not involve any direct transfer of foreign currency, it is considered as merely shuffling paper between domestic units, which though affecting income distribution, has no significant consequences for the real economy. This is a short-sighted and misguided view. Bourne, in noting that government domestic debt finance makes great demands on private financial surpluses in many of the region's economies, states that this raises several important issues and that 'there is some basis for concluding that there is considerable scope for improving the favourable influence of government expenditure on national economic development' (Bourne, 1987).

Initial reaction to analyses of available data does not lend weight to the view that there has been any crowding out of private-sector investment in the period under review. While there has been a significant expansion of domestic credit to the public sector in absolute terms, the share of such credit going to this sector has shown no substantial increase. Net domestic credit from the banking system to government expanded in the mid-1970s with the initial ability of the Central Bank to accommodate the government's overdraft requirements, but after rising to about 25 – 30% of the total in the period 1976–8, it has since fallen and fluctuated between 22% and 24% for the past 4 –5 years. Similarly, the share of the total assets of the consolidated financial sector held by the government, after rising from 9% to 18% between 1970 and 1975 has remained constant around 20% since. In a similar vein, in the past few years, particularly in the period since 1985, excess liquidity in the banking system has been quite marked, with banks holding as much as 27% in excess of their required holdings of stipulated government securities, at a time when the average treasury bill rate was less than half the prime bank rate.

It can therefore be safely stated that 'crowding out' of the private sector has not been a contributory factor to the dramatic fall in the ratio of GDCF to Gross Output in the period since 1983. With excess liquidity in the banking system, the cause would have to be found either in institutional deficiencies in transforming financial assets into physical assets or in a lack of effective demand for bankable projects.

This current situation does, however, mask a potential long-run problem for the economy. Should the coalescence of the right external environment with the appropriate mix of domestic policies lead to a return to strong export-led growth and demand for domestic credit, the size of the domestic debt and the level of debt service payments could present a problem and act as a brake on increased investment. Between 1980 and 1986, the domestic debt/GDP ratio rose by 50% to 30%, while interest and amortisation payments rose from 14% to 20% of current revenue. Unless the public-sector deficit can be reduced to more manageable levels of around 2 – 3% of GDP, there is the possibility that the need to borrow just to maintain the level of debt service payments would act as a constraint on future growth.

The propensity of the household and corporate sectors to accumulate monetary assets – which are what Bourne describes as the 'conduit' for investment (Bourne, 1988) – can be significantly influenced by the incentives and disincentives built into the tax system. At one extreme, it is said that the Japanese policy of offering tax-free savings accounts at the windows of 22,000 post office branches (the Marayu) was a powerful factor in raising and sustaining the household savings rate to 17% of GDP. At the other extreme, it is argued that the taxation of interest on savings and the write-off allowed on hire-purchase and other consumption expenses in the US has contributed to the fact that the household savings rate there has fallen as low as 4% of GDP (Bernstein, 1988).

Incentives undoubtedly influence the form in which real or financial assets are accumulated. Relief on the payment of mortgage interest and for repairs and maintenance have encouraged house ownership, although there have been frequent changes in the quantum of relief in response to the financing needs of the government. Savings through insurance is also encouraged through tax relief on premiums, although the experiences of Canada (where there has never been relief) and the UK (where relief was withdrawn) suggest that people will buy insurance with or without incentives. Other incentives can have perverse effects – for example, deposits in credit unions are offered special relief but, ironically, a major part of these deposits finance consumption expenditure.

In order to promote the growth of share ownership and encourage equity financing, successive governments in Barbados have introduced concessions aimed at reducing the transaction costs of holding shares and in effect subsidising share purchase. Thus, what was in fact, but not in name, a capital gains tax on the appreciated value of shares was abolished, and new share purchase and the issuance of bonus shares made tax exempt. These incentives have made share purchase an attractive alternative to other forms of asset accumulation but institutional and other factors have restricted the availability of shares for purchase. The inconsistency of public policy is once more shown by the fact that at the same time as share ownership was being encouraged, the tax relief previously given on dividends through the dividend credit was progressively being reduced.

The government has also sought to use tax incentives in a selective manner to finance its own operations or to fund the lending activities of its own financial institutions. Thus, interest on National Savings bonds and on certain debentures are tax free up to different limits. Since, in recent years, these funds were used to finance non-capital expenditure, the ultimate effect is to increase public consumption and build up future claims on government revenue. Interest on certain other types of development bonds raised to finance long-term lending or house construction is also partially tax exempt as is interest on savings deposits at the publicly-owned National Bank.

The ultimate effect of these incentives on the volume of financial savings is not easy to quantify. There is no doubt that changes in existing, or introduction of new, incentives affect the allocation of savings between various instruments and intermediaries. Similarly, changes in interest rate differentials have demonstrably altered the distribution of savings between demand, savings and time deposits. Of more significance would appear to be changes in macro-economic policy affecting the level of disposable income. For example, between 1978 and 1984, total deposits of the financial sector grew at roughly the same rate as nominal GDP. In 1985 and 1986, however, total deposits grew at a faster rate, moving from 58% of GDP to 66%. This increase in the rate of growth of total deposits coincided with the intensification of the shift in the tax burden from direct to indirect taxation, which increased disposable incomes significantly.

The conclusion to be drawn from this belief analysis is that there is no anti-savings bias in the Barbados tax system. Although policy has been inconsistent in some cases, there is a fairly wide range of incentives and instruments available to the investing public. However, while these incentives may influence the form in which assets are held, the major underlying influence on the level of financial savings remains the rate of growth of nominal GDP and the overall balance between direct and indirect taxation through its influence on disposable incomes.

The financial system

The financial system in Barbados comprises the consolidated banking system and the non-bank financial intermediaries. The consolidated banking system is defined to include the Central Bank and seven commercial banks (five branches of foreign-owned banks and one privately and one publicly-owned domestic bank). The non-bank financial intermediaries include the trust companies (subsidiaries of the commercial banks), two publicly-owned entities – the Barbados Development Bank and the Barbados Mortgage Finance Company – and three finance companies. Other non-bank financial institutions include a number of general purpose and life insurance companies, credit unions and consumer societies and nine offshore banks. Completing the structure of the financial system is the Securities Exchange which began operations in 1987.

Commercial banks

The commercial banks dominate the financial system, capturing about 80% of private-sector financial savings. The other significant recipients of financial savings are the trust companies which in the period 1984–6 controlled about 10% of the total deposits of the consolidated financial sector. The remaining is shared between the finance companies, credit unions and the offshore banks. The dominance of the commercial banks, however, has been reduced as a result of the diversification of the financial system and the emergence of several new intermediaries. Thus in comparison with the current situation, in the period 1974–6 commercial banks captured some 85% of private sector financial savings.

Total deposits in commercial banks rose at roughly the same rate as nominal GDP between 1974 and 1984 and at a faster rate in the period 1985–7, reflecting the increase in disposable income resulting from the marked shift from direct to indirect taxation. The same trend is reflected in the movement of deposits held by various classes of depositors. Up to 1984, households contributed about 60% to the total, with business firms and financial institutions contributing between 15 – 17% each. Since 1985 there has been a significant increase in the share of deposits contributed by households, with the figure reaching as high as 65%. Apart from the effects of the change in tax policy, there has been a slowdown in the build up of deposits by financial institutions as the government has utilised a greater part of the surplus of the National Insurance Fund to finance its burgeoning deficit and the insurance companies allocated more of their funds to satisfy the strong demand for residential and commercial mortgages. With the increase in disposable income and the narrowing of interest rate differentials, an increasing proportion of deposits are being held in the form of savings as opposed to time deposits.

With the slowdown of economic growth since 1980 and the rapid build up of deposits, considerable excess liquidity has emerged in the banking system. This is revealed in several ways. For instance, the ratio of loans to advances which was 86% in the period 1974–6 had declined to 76% in the period 1984–6. Again, cash reserves held by commercial banks remained in the 1980s above the required level and (as noted earlier) the banks have been holding over the past four years 25 – 30% more of stipulated government securities than required by the Central Bank.

During the past ten years, available evidence points to a significant shift in the distribution of loans and advances by the economic sector. As discussed earlier, the critical factor in analysing the role of financial intermediaries is the extent to which financial savings get transformed into physical assets. Because there is no published data which would permit such a detailed analysis to be undertaken, a rough approximation of the extent of such transformation would be the proportion of credit allocated to what could be described as the productive sectors and to the sector which contributes most to private consumption. The former consist of tourism, manufacturing, agriculture, public utilities and construction and the latter the personal and distribution sectors.

In the ten-year period, the proportion of total loans/advances going to the productive sectors rose from 42.1% to 53%, while that going to the personal and distribution sectors declined from 42.5% to 36% (see Table 3.1). The same trend is illustrated by the fact that consumer credit outstanding declined from 12.4% to 10% of total credit between 1974/76 and 1984/86. As the commercial banks have shifted their focus towards the productive sectors, some of the newer financial intermediaries – finance companies and credit unions – have moved to fill the gap.

As the commercial banks have expanded their lending to the productive sectors, there has been a corresponding change in the maturity structure of their loans, as the following data indicates. There has been a significant shift in the proportion of loans/advances to the private sector lent for periods in excess of five years from 14% of the total in 1974/76 to about one-third ten years later (see Table 3.2). Within the productive sectors, loans to the tourism and manufacturing sectors and for the development of public utilities are increasingly longer term (see Table 3.3). (The reduction in the term of lending to the agricultural and construction sectors probably reflects the fact that other financial intermediaries – the Agricultural Division of the Barbados National Bank and the finance companies – have emerged as alternative sources of finance).

Non-bank financial intermediaries

The trust houses of the commercial banks have emerged in the past decade as important intermediaries in the financial system. Between 1980 and 1985 their deposit base increased by over 200%, from 4.3% of total deposits of the financial sector to 10% between 1974/76 and 1984/86. Trust houses engage almost exclusively in long-term lending. Accordingly, they only seek longer term deposits, and to attract such deposits have to pay a higher average borrowing rate.

Trust houses specialise in mortgage lending. Indeed, they were set up by the commercial banks for this specific purpose presumably to ensure a better matching of assets and liabilities; currently only some 4% of commercial bank credit to the private sector is in the form of mortgages. Some two-thirds of the trust houses' lending is for residential mortgages. Because the residential mortgage rate is controlled by the Central Bank (currently at 9%), commercial mortgages which carry higher rates of interest are of considerable importance in determining overall profitability.

The trust houses are one of a trilogy of institutions which cater for the mortgage market, the other two being the insurance companies and the publicly-owned Barbados Mortgage Finance Company (BMFC). A quarter of the total credit to the private sector goes into mortgages. The trust houses account for 40% of the total, the insurance companies for about 30%, the

Table 3.1   Barbados commercial banks: Loans/Advances by sectors (% of total)

	1974/76	1984/86
Productive sectors		
Tourism	11.6	12.4
Manufacturing	9.3	14.2
Agriculture	4.0	4.0
Public utilities	6.0	8.2
Construction	11.2	14.2
Total	42.1	53.0
Personal and distribution sectors		
Personal	25.0	22.0
Distribution	17.5	14.0
Total	42.5	36.0

Source: Central Bank, *Annual Statistical Digest 1987*

Table 3.2   Maturity structure of commercial bank loans (% of total)

Years	Overdraft	Under 3 years	3–5 years	Over 5 years
1974/76	46	27	13	14
1984/86	41	18	10	31

Source: Central Bank, *Annual Statistical Digest 1987*

Table 3.3   Maturity structure of credit to productive sectors (% over 5 years)

	1974/76	1984/86
Tourism	3.4	26.0
Manufacturing	32.0	49.0
Agriculture	26.0	16.0
Public utilities	0.0	74.0
Construction	21.0	16.0

Source: Central Bank, *Annual Statistical Digest 1987*

BMFC 20% and the commercial banks 10%. The BMFC provides finance mostly to lower and lower-middle income groups and is funded by long-term loans mainly from the National Insurance Fund.

The insurance companies, which together provide about 10% of total credit to the private sector, have become increasingly important in the process of financial intermediation. There are no up-to-date consolidated data on the insurance industry but total annual premium income generated by the life and general companies is probably in the region of $150 million. The life companies are increasingly moving to meet the demand for investment products by marketing a variety of fixed and variable rate policies. Because of their need for a high degree of liquidity, general companies hold 70% of their assets in the form of short-term deposits and government paper, while the life companies with longer term liabilities hold about 60% of their assets in the form of mortgages and real estate. In total, the insurance industry holds only 5% of their consolidated assets in shares, reflecting the shortage of marketable shares rather than any reluctance to hold equity.

The other non-banking financial institutions of some significance are the finance companies and the credit unions. At the end of 1986, the three finance companies then operating had combined assets of $40 million and only 2% of the total deposits of the financial sector. These institutions lend for the lease or purchase of private motor vehicles, taxis and other commercial vehicles and construction and office equipment. About 20% of these loans/leases could be classified as for consumption purposes, the major proportion therefore being for lease/purchase of vehicles and equipment – which the commercial banks, for various reasons, have not found attractive and which is not being adequately filled by any other institution.

The main problem with these companies has been that all are under-capitalised and some have been badly managed but have not been subject to Central Bank control and regulation as have the commercial banks and the trust houses. Because there have been no minimum capital requirements and restrictions, on the size of loans in relation to paid-up capital etc., imprudent lending policies (lack of adequate security) led in 1987 to the collapse of one company with the consequent loss of depositors' funds. Legislation to bring the finance companies within the ambit of the Central Bank's control is pending.

The financial institutions which have shown the most rapid growth have been the credit unions. Although they remain small in relation to the banks and insurance companies, they have increased in number from 23 in 1980 to 40 in 1986 with total membership moving from 5,500 to 20,000 and total assets from $5.5 million to $42.2 million in the same period. The credit unions mostly lend for home improvement, real estate and purchase of motor vehicles and other consumer goods. Indeed, their rapid growth is probably not unrelated to the fact that, as they are not subject to Central

Bank regulations, they have permitted their members to circumvent the hire purchase and credit restrictions formerly imposed by the Bank, particularly in the purchase of major consumer durables.

The remaining non-bank financial institution of significance is the Barbados Development Bank (BDB). Although it is not a financial intermediary in the sense of raising deposits to make loans, it is important as the major conduit for chanelling long-term funding from international institutions like the World Bank, the Inter-American Development Bank, the European Investment Bank and the Caribbean Development Bank to productive sectors of the economy. It is a major source of foreign exchange for development purposes and of long-term finance. While it charges market rates of interest for most of its loans, it can offer loans with maturity up to 15 years.

Although its loans comprise less than 10% of the loans of the financial sector, the BDB is a significant lender for capital projects of the tourism and manufacturing sectors. Its loans to the tourism sector are equivalent to 50% of commercial bank credit and for the manufacturing sector about 25%. It often co-finances projects with the commercial banks, (the BDB providing long-term funds and the commercial banks, working capital). As a development bank, the BDB has been able to finance worthwhile projects which do not meet formal commercial bank criteria and has also been able to reschedule debt when its clients have faced recessionary conditions. It has also been innovative and has opened special windows for groups such as small manufacturers and operators in the service industries, who would have difficulty in accessing commercial credit.

However, as a consequence of this approach and of the inevitable political pressure to accommodate special interests and not to enforce repayment conditions systematically, the Bank has built up a large non-performing portfolio. Failure to make adequate provision for bad debts in a timely fashion has forced large write-offs of these debts, which has eroded the equity base of the institution. Because the Bank operates under a government guarantee, normal tests of insolvency do not apply. But as long as the Bank continues to fail to make an accepted rate of return on its investments, it is using scarce resources inefficiently and imposing a cost on the rest of the economy.

Self-financing

While access to financial savings through the medium of intermediaries is vital for new and untried enterprises, well-established firms with a proven track record have the alternative of financing fixed investment by internally generated cash or issuing shares. In the latter case, the decision on the method of finance will depend on a number of factors including the financial strength of the company, the relative cost of borrowing as against equity, the dividend pay-out policy, etc.

Although no comprehensive data are available on the sources of financing of fixed assets for the corporate sector as a whole, Arthur Young International produce an annual summary of the published financial statements of selected Barbadian companies. The companies are grouped into three categories: general trading, manufacturing and processing, and public utilities. The sample is not representative of a cross-section of the corporate sector because it does not include firms whose principal business is tourism or agriculture, or any of the newer manufacturing operations. However, the sample includes all the companies listed on the Securities Exchange and together these firms accounted for roughly one-half of the corporation tax paid and one-third of expenditure on fixed assets by the private sector in the period 1984–6. So while conclusions drawn from analysis of the data cannot be generalised for the corporate sector as a whole, the report is of relevance because the companies surveyed are major contributors to employment, income, investment and tax revenue in the economy.

The available data indicate that the gearing ratios of the companies in the sample remained relatively stable in the period 1984–7. As Table 3.4 shows, most of the companies are low-geared with only four of them (out of 19) having more than 50% of their total financing contributed by loan capital. In many cases, this low gearing ratio is not the result of a policy of financing investment by issuing shares, but from the ability of many of these companies to finance their expansion internally.

Table 3.4   Barbados companies: Sources from which expenditure on fixed assets and investments were financed, 1984–7 (% of total)

	External financing	Internal financing
General trading companies		
1984	27	73
1985	31	64
1986	15	85
1987	29	71
Manufacturing and processing		
1984	49	51
1985	18	82
1986	10	90
1987	29	71

Source: Arthur Young International.

The public utilities' pattern of financing fixed investment is different from the other companies in the sample because not only is their need for capital much larger but their tariffs and dividend pay-out are also controlled by the regulatory agency. These companies are more reliant on external borrowing and share-capital. In fact, in the period under review, the only shares issued by the other companies were bonus shares to the employees, so that the overwhelming proportion of such external financing which is undertaken is in the form of borrowing rather than share issues.

The reasons for the preference for borrowing are not hard to find. Dividend yields are currently in the region of 8% to 12% making share ownership the most attractive outlet for financial savings over the past several years. As the survey observes 'with the present low rates of interest prevailing in Barbados, providing a company can afford to borrow, it is true to say that debt financing is cheaper than equity financing'. The differential is even more marked when account is taken of the fact that interest payments (unlike dividends) are tax deductible.

In this situation, the decision to finance investment out of retained earnings or borrowings rather than by selling new shares appears as quite a logical reaction to a given market situation. There may, however, be other factors at work. In the first place, many of the older established companies accept deposits from customers. This was a practice which developed over many years when the banking system was less competitive and the companies (particularly in the distribution sector) were able to attract deposits by offering higher interest rates. The practice has persisted, and these deposit-taking institutions remain outside the framework of the regulation of the Central Bank. The deposits are, of course, unsecured and in fact one company which had substantial deposits went into liquidation with consequent losses to many small and large depositors. The point is, however, that the ability of some companies to attract deposits probably reduces their need to borrow long-term or issue new shares.[1]

The second factor is that many companies consider their shares to be undervalued and therefore the prospect of diluting ownership by presenting a windfall to new shareholders may act as a disincentive to equity financing. The authors of the Survey note that 'Price/Earnings ratios are in most cases still very low, suggesting that there is considerable room for improvements in share prices' with 50% of the companies showing P/E ratios below 5. It is possible, therefore, as the market values of shares rise to more nearly reflect the earnings records and the rate of dividends paid, the attractiveness of raising capital by issuing shares may increase.

A third reason for relying on self-financing or bank financing as opposed to equity financing is the reluctance to dilute ownership and control, especially of predominantly family-owned businesses. The importance of this factor is impossible to quantify but no doubt is significant in many cases. Although many older trading and manufacturing companies are listed on the stock exchange and so are accustomed to public disclosure and accountability, control remains vested in a minority of the shareholders who also dominate the Board of Directors and executive management. They may not wish to have their control eroded by expansion of shareholding.

The Securities Exchange

Prior to the establishment of the Securities Exchange in June 1987, there was no organised framework for the purchase and transfer of shares. Shares were either sold in settlement of outstanding liabilities or traded informally by trust companies or solicitors who brought together buyers and sellers. High transaction costs and illiquidity of share ownership were significant deterrents to the wider acceptance of shares among the investing public.

The establishment of the exchange created a mechanism for the orderly purchase and transfer of securities under a regime which reduced transaction costs and assured owners of such securities that their financial assets could be quickly converted to cash. A major objective of establishing the stock exchange was to facilitate equity financing of business expansion and to encourage the wider participation of the public in the ownership of private enterprise. While there has been sustained activity on the exchange in the transfer of existing shares with share prices advancing, there was only one new issue through the exchange since the inception of trading. At the end of 1987, 13 companies with 189 million shares and market capitalisation of $243 million were listed for trading. In the six months to the end of 1987, 1.5 million shares with an aggregate value of $3.6 million were traded. In the period December 1987 to June 1988 some 1.48 million shares with a market value of $4.2 million were traded.

Trading in shares constituted only a small part of the stock of shares currently held, as would be expected. The shortage of new issues constrains expansion. Since the exchange began operating, an issue of 1 million shares (in a public utility) totalling $5 million was put on the market and oversubscribed by a factor of three but this was not issued through the exchange. The effectiveness of the stock exchange is constrained by the fact that equity financing is the least attractive alternative method of financing investment for established companies. However, the success enjoyed to date in providing share transfers indicates that the public is willing to place their financial savings in good quality equities.

Changing international and domestic environment

Before considering what improvements or modifications may be introduced into the financial system in Barbados, it is helpful first to look at what implications the changing international environment and changing structure of the economy may have for the future level and pattern of savings and investment. The major factors likely to impact on the domestic economy appear to be:

- the marked reduction in net foreign capital inflows which will result from the combination of higher debt service payments and reduced inflows of loans from multilateral agencies and commercial banks;
- the integration of international capital markets and persistence of a regime of largely floating exchange rates;
- reduced opportunities for emigration which has in the past provided an important outlet for surplus labour and remittances for the support of dependant relatives;
- the long-term decline of the prospects for the export of primary commodities, the result of negative income elasticity of demand, development of substitutes and more efficient use of industrial inputs;
- increased protectionism in the markets of the developed countries. At the same time, the major industrial countries are forming trade groupings with each other which pose potential threats to those LDCs which have preferential agreements with one or other of these groups. Thus the Integrated European Market of 1992 and the US/Canada Free Trade Agreement could impact adversely on Lomé, CBI, CARIBCAN, etc; and
- the rapid rate of technological change in the developed countries and the need for flexible policy responses from the domestic economy. Broad and Cavanagh, in an article in the Fall 1988 edition of *Foreign Policy*, point to a series of corporate developments which have stunted demand globally, leaving increasing numbers of people at the margins of market activity; 'Prominent among these are . . . corporate substitution for Third World raw materials, and labour-saving technological innovations in the developed world'. Lower labour costs are no longer likely to be a critical factor in determining locational advantage, and the quality of the human resource will hold the key to success in the twenty-first century.

The relatively sheltered environment of the past few decades – for example, special arrangements for sugar, access to concessional finance, outlets for nationals to emigrate to greener pastures – can no longer be counted on in the future. The major problem facing the economy will be the creation of enough jobs to reduce the present level of almost 20% of unemployment of the labour force.

Future developments hold out opportunities and also pose challenges (e.g. in the expected strong growth of trade in all kinds of services). What is required is far-seeing and informed national economic management which can anticipate and plan for change, and an adaptable and well-educated work-force capable of coping with rapid technological development.

Against this background, the domestic economy will undergo further structural changes. The most important emerging trends appear to be:

- increased share of the service sector in total output and employment. This will involve the continued growth of recreational and leisure activities as the tourism industry maintains its position as the leading sector, and the further development of the island as an offshore financial centre and the premier regional location for multilateral, bilateral and commercial organisations operating in the Eastern Caribbean. In addition, prospects are good for the promotion of the island as a venue for establishing health and educational facilities catering for residents and non-residents alike;
- changes in the structure of the manufacturing sector from labour-intensive to knowledge-intensive activities. While this sector will continue to cater for the domestic and regional market and possesses the potential to fill particular needs in preferential markets, it cannot perform the role of the leading sector. In the article referred to above ('No New NICs') Broad and Cavanagh, after surveying the growth of protectionism and the slow down in the rate of growth in world trade, conclude that it is questionable whether export-oriented industrialisation can be the optimal route to growth in the future; and
- continued decline in the relative contribution of agriculture to GDP and employment. Sugar exports will be a valuable source of foreign exchange, however, so long as market access is guaranteed. The production of non-sugar crops and exploitation of the marine resources can make a significant contribution to foreign exchange savings.

These changes, which are already reshaping the Barbadian economy, can be expected to intensify. Change can also be expected in the size and role of government and in the composition and structure of the business sector. In order to contain the size of the public sector deficit to sustainable proportions without raising taxation to levels which will have a disincentive effect on individual effort, the government will be forced to address the expenditure side of the budget. This will involve both privatisation of existing public assets and services as well as requiring individuals to assume greater responsibility for providing for their health, education, pension and other needs. Already, private profit-centered hospitals offering non-critical services funded through private health insurance are being established.

Other emerging changes in the private sector have implications for the functioning of the capital market. There has been a marked increase in the number of small businesses. For example, in the retail sector, the one-stop general purpose shop has virtually disappeared as the market has become more sophisticated, and small specialist shops have taken their place. Similarly, in the tourist sector many small operators provide services in water sports, catering and entertainment. Many more people are also self-employed – for example, in the professions, in repairs and maintenance, etc. These changes produce new needs which the institutions and regulators must move to meet.

Future development of the capital market

For a country of only a quarter of a million people and GDP of $2.6 billion, Barbados has a relatively well-developed and diversified capital market. There is a range of functioning financial institutions catering to the diverse needs of the borrowing public. In the past decade, the needs of the productive sectors for short- and medium-term finance have been increasingly addressed and with the establishment of the stock exchange, the institutional structure for transferring financial savings into physical assets is now virtually complete. Where deficiencies have been identified, mechanisms to address these have been put in place. With one exception which will be discussed shortly, there are no obvious institutional gaps in the capital market in Barbados.

However, there is room for improvement in the operations of the existing institutions, both privately and publicly owned. In particular, although there are six commercial banks operating in Barbados, the market is more oligopolistic than competitive in nature, as is evidenced by the uniformly high cost of services provided, which is reflected in the quite large differential between the average borrowing and lending rates. In this regard, the publicly-owned bank has had no visible impact in stimulating competition, which was supposed to be one of its main objectives.

At present, two important needs appear not to be adequately met – the need for risk capital and for more long-term financing. The capital market, as presently structured, does not provide an adequate proportion of resources for high-risk operations. To address this problem the Central Bank has been promoting the idea of the establishment of a Venture Capital Corporation (VCC). As proposed, the VCC would provide equity, long-term loans and support services to small- and medium-sized businesses, especially in the manufacturing sector. The corporation would not only share the risk of investment with the shareholders of the company in which it invests but would provide advice of a technical, managerial and marketing nature as well. To have maximum impact, the VCC would have to be properly staffed to spot project proposals with good chances of success. Potential for growth and expansion and modernisation would be the main criteria for selection.

The VCC should be funded principally by the private sector financial institutions. Although initial support by way of tax concessions and capital subscription from the government would be necessary, there is a good possibility that an efficiently run corporation could attract external funding from institutions like the International Finance Corporation, the World Bank and the Inter-American Development Bank.

While the establishment of a Venture Capital Corporation would directly assist those enterprises which are unable to raise risk capital directly, in the long run, the stock exchange must expand the range of its operations to make a major contribution to raising new capital for business expansion. The priority must be to get more public companies listed. Beyond this, the present exchange control rules which make it rather cumbersome for non-residents to trade need revising. As one of the strongest regional economies at the present time, Barbados stands to gain from liberalisation of capital movements. Opening up the buying and selling of shares more to regional and international investors might well provide the basis for an expansion of trading activity, an increase in share values and an increase in equity financing for business expansion. The compartmentalisation of regional capital and labour markets through the application of national foreign exchange and work permit regulations have made it difficult for regionally-owned businesses, which operate in many territories, to do so with maximum efficiency.

Although the data confirm that commercial banks over the past ten years have progressively increased both the proportion of credit allocated to the productive sectors and the proportion lent over five years, as Delisle Worrell states, 'the maturity structure of finance for investment remains most unsatisfactory' (Worrell, 1986). The experience of the Barbados Development Bank referred to earlier indicates that the commercial banks' reluctance to get involved in many of the projects on offer is not just ultra-conservative business practice, since many have proven to be failures. However, there is both the scope and the need for the banks, as the major recipients of financial savings, to become more involved in long-term lending. The conventional argument that as they borrow short they can only lend short is unconvincing, since their deposits are stable and expanding.

A suitable vehicle to encourage the banks to devote more resources to the long end of the market could be an expanded Industrial Credit Fund. This revolving fund, set up with World Bank and Central Bank money, has been quite successful in involving the commercial banks in getting more familiar with and accustomed to appraising projects for long-term financing. The amounts disbursed have been modest but the learning experience for the staff must have been valuable. The original World Bank loan has been drawn down and when the Fund is replenished, the opportunity should be taken to enlarge its size by inviting the banks to commit more of their resources in joint financing arrangements. In addition to normal long-term lending, the Fund should specifically target export-oriented activities. A technical assistance component should be added to enable special training to be offered to the staff to permit them more readily to evaluate projects on the basis of economic and financial criteria and not on the adequacy of security alone. In this way, the banks themselves would be better equipped to assist prospective investors in formulating project proposals that advance especially the small-business sector.

Facilities for long-term lending could also be improved if a market in corporate bonds could be built up for trading on the stock exchange. If the Central Bank (as it should) does tighten up on the practice of deposit-taking by firms, it is likely that it will gradually be phased out. As an alternative, these firms and others could find that raising long-term capital by the issuance of convertible stock or fixed-rate bonds a cheaper form of finance than commercial bank borrowing. It might be necessary initially to get such issues underwritten, and for an appropriate fee, insurance companies or the commercial banks could be encouraged to undertake the underwriting once some degree of liquidity is assured through trading on the exchange.

One benefit of increasing the variety of instruments tradeable on the stock exchange would be to improve the prospects for the operation of an institution which up to now has only had moderate success in Barbados – the Mutual Fund. These funds are supposed to offer the investor the advantages of diversification and professional management, but in Barbados, because of the paucity of traded paper, the one fund operating has not been able to offer competitive yields, although it has attracted some interest as purchases of its shares qualify for tax concessions. However, the fund offers real possibilities for bringing into the market many small savers who now are probably excluded. To the extent that corporate bonds, government bonds and equities are traded on the exchange, the Mutual Fund should become a much more viable institution.

At the macro level, there are many factors inhibiting the development of the export sector, which is important for stimulating future economic growth and raising levels of fixed investment. The Barbados Export Promotion Corporation, the government agency charged with promoting exports, has identified poor quality, deficient design, uncompetitive pricing, slipshod packaging, inadequate market research and lack of capacity as major inhibiting factors in constraining the growth of exports. There is, therefore, a pressing need for product development, market development, and research and development on the basis of which informed investment decisions can be made. In addition, in areas such as furniture-making and garment manufacture many firms need new equipment and modernised workplaces. There is also a lack of resources for refinancing. Sometimes an undercapitalised business experiences temporary financial difficulties – perhaps caused by failure to update technology or loss of market share – and needs refinancing, while steps are taken to deal with the problems. At present, such a business would likely go under because existing financial institutions by and large are not geared to refinancing them.

There is a need to allocate more resources to cater for these various needs. In some cases (e.g. product and market development) there is no reason why funds should not be forthcoming from the commercial banks once such expenditure is seen as an essential component of a viable proposal. With regard to refinancing and research and development it might be necessary, through loan guarantees or establishing separate funding, for the government to take the lead in ensuring the availability of funds.

An economy which becomes progressively reliant on knowledge-intensive services and industries for employment will require a labour force with a wide array of skills – professional, technical, managerial and supervisory. Accordingly, the creation of a more organised structure for channelling funds into investment in human capital will become a priority. As responsibility for financing tertiary-level training of all kinds becomes increasingly the responsibility of the individual, facilities for medium- to long-term lending will have to be put in place. At present, funds are either made available through the Student Revolving Loan Fund which has a maximum income criterion, or through commercial bank borrowing, usually for very short periods (but sometimes through mortgages for longer periods). While problems of repayment are common to most educational loan schemes, a properly structured system of loans through the commercial banks (with appropriate guarantees) with the main security being mandatory deductions from future income (as is the case in some Nordic countries) should be feasible.

Finally, attention should be paid to reversing the quite dramatic decline in private foreign investment which has occurred since the early 1980s. While this is partly reflective of a global trend, as well as the relative loss of competitiveness of the economy, the role of private foreign investment in the past, in bringing new technology and markets and raising the level of skills, calls for a special effort to identify and encourage the formation of joint ventures to exploit in particular the opportunities opened by access to markets of the EC, the USA and Canada under preferential arrangements. This would require more intensive promotion, improved training facilities, and a serious attempt to improve the efficiency with which the bureaucracy processes the granting of various permissions and licenses. In addition, it could require a more liberal approach to the access of foreign investors to short- and medium-term loans for working capital purposes.

Notes

Values are in Barbados dollars (BDS$1.00 = US$0.50)

1 Central Bank statistics reveal that these non-bank deposit-taking institutions had $70 million on deposit at 30 June 1988.

CHAPTER 4 | The Jamaican financial sector

Paul Chen-Young

Overview of the Jamaican economy

The Jamaican economic experience of the last three decades shows the impact of three distinct phases of economic policy, reflecting different ideological positions of various administrations in independent Jamaica, and coinciding with major international trends.

Firstly, in the 1960s, there was a worldwide surge towards industriali-sation in the developing countries, with strong private overseas investment. Secondly, in the 1970s, the oil crisis created a shock effect and produced nationalistic moods in the developing world in pursuit of a new interna-tional economic order. In the 1980s, with the advent of President Reagan and Prime Minister Thatcher, there was a strong ideological shift to market economies. The magnitude of the debt crisis became the focus of interna-tional attention and a major determining factor in many national economic policies.

Jamaica attained independence in 1962, during what some now regard as the halcyon days of economic development. The government of the period pursued a liberal economic policy, the thrust being towards industri-alisation, and the development of the mining and tourism sectors. Pragmatic economic policies prevailed, and the country went through a period of steady growth and economic expansion. Between 1962 and 1970, growth in GDP averaged 5.8% per annum. Manufacturing increased its percentage share of GDP from 7.1% to 13.4%. The increase in mining was from 15.2% in 1967 to 17.7% in 1970. In the tourism sector the number of hotel beds increased from 7,553 in 1964 to 13,758 in 1970, a growth of 82%.

The strategy embarked upon by the government to spur the manufac-turing sector was a combination of fiscal incentives and a major factory expansion programme. Major incentives were granted through the Indus-trial Incentives Act, the Export Industry Encouragement Law, and the Pioneer Industry Encouragement Law. These laws offered a combination of income tax and duty-free concessions. They were supported by protection-ist measures, with a wide range of quantitative restrictions. In the tourism sector, the Hotel Incentives Act also provided fiscal concessions. In addition, the government undertook its own major hotel building programme.

In the mining sector, bauxite output grew by just over 100% from 5.84 million metric tons in 1960 to 11.82 million metric tons in 1970, while alumina exports grew by approximately 153% from 0.68 million metric tons in 1960 to 1.72 million metric tons in 1970. The major international companies operating in Jamaica then were the Kaiser Bauxite Company, Alcan, Alcoa and Reynolds. With the increase in exports and capital inflows, the country's net international reserves rose from US$92.7 million to US$141.0 million over the same period.

In the decade of the 1970s, which marked the second phase, a new government was elected (1972) and soon afterwards had to face a dramatic change in the world economy with the advent of the oil crisis in 1973. The government responded by introducing a bauxite levy which was regarded by the companies as a breach of contract and quasi-nationalisation. This action, coupled with a declaration of democratic socialism as the official development strategy, led to a series of actions and responses which resulted in a loss of business confidence by local and foreign investors.

The controversial levy brought in US$1,206.4 million from 1974 to 1980. Part of the proceeds was used to finance costly social programmes as well as the Jamaica National Investment Corporation, a public-sector investment bank set up to undertake major projects. This institution was eventually transformed into the National Investment Bank of Jamaica in the 1980s. The investments of both entities have been notably unsuccessful.

There was a general reversal of most of the indicators during the period 1973 to 1980. GDP declined at an average annual rate of 2.6%; agriculture fell 0.8%, manufacturing 4.5% and construction 11.3%. The fiscal deficit moved from 3.6% of GDP in 1973/74 to 17% by 1980/81; net international reserves declined from US$204 million in 1973 to negative US$432.3 million by 1980; unemployment stood at 27.9% in 1980, as compared with 21.4% in 1973.

Towards the end of the 1970s the government discontinued an adjustment programme with the IMF, the prime contention being the unwillingness of the government to accept austerity and structural adjustment programmes. During this impasse Jamaica experienced severe shortages, a flight of capital and people, and severe economic dislocation. Net private foreign capital outflows in 1980 were US$119.5 million as against an inflow in 1970 of US$162.3 million.

In the third phase, the government elected in 1980 reversed the socialist policies of the previous government and immediately re-opened negotiations with the IMF and other overseas lenders. Emphasising private enterprise, and encouraging foreign investment, the government negotiated a structural adjustment programme which included fiscal, monetary, tariff and administrative reforms. It also initiated an export-oriented industrial policy aimed at creating a dynamic export manufacturing sector.

These new policy initiatives, which were endorsed by international agencies and the major donor countries, created a more positive investment climate, facilitated by substantial inflows of aid.

Between 1981 and 1984, total capital inflows stood at US$1.397 billion. In specific areas of reform, success was also achieved:

- the share of government expenditure as a percentage of GDP fell from 45% in fiscal 1981/82 to 31% in fiscal 1984/85;
- the current account deficit fell from 20.8% of GDP in 1981/82 to 3.8% in 1986/87;
- the central government deficit fell from 17% of GDP in 1981/82 to 2.1% in 1986/87; and
- the share of investment grew from 20.8% of GDP in 1981/82 to 23.1% in 1986/87.

The structural adjustment programme which is still being adhered to by the government elected in 1989, has succeeded in creating a positive investment climate. But it has caused a severe cut-back in social services. It has also led to a sharp increase in the external debt from US$1.866 billion in 1980 to US$4.004 billion in 1988.

The financial sector

Jamaica's financial infrastructure was already well-developed in the 1960s and there have been many innovations since then. There is now a central bank, a development bank, a stock exchange, 12 commercial banks, 15 trust companies, 27 merchant banks, 17 life insurance companies, 4 general insurance companies, 15 building societies, 125 credit unions, and a unit trust.

The 1960s

The monetary policies pursued by the Bank of Jamaica (BOJ) were generally conservative, with minimum financing of government debt. A major objective of the policy in this period was to establish the credibility of the BOJ as a central bank, and to develop an independent monetary policy. In 1966, the automatic link with the pound sterling was removed, and the power to declare an independent par value for the Jamaican pound was established. Foreign assets, which in 1967 totalled US$63.4 million, rose to US$112 million by 1970.

The Jamaica Development Bank (JDB), an outgrowth of the Development Finance Corporation (DFC), commenced operations in 1969, its primary objective being to channel domestic and external financial resources into the major developmental areas: agriculture, tourism, manufacturing and housing. The balance sheet of DFC was stripped so that only satisfactory assets could be carried over to the Jamaica Development Bank. It discontinued lending for housing, but continued to finance manufacturing, tourism and agriculture. It was funded both by the government and commercial banks, as well as by international lending agencies. In 1970, lending was allocated as follows: agriculture 14%; manufacturing 62%; and tourism 24%. The company's net worth was J$31.7 million.

The stock exchange was established in 1969 under the auspices of the Bank of Jamaica which provided office space and a subsidy for its operations. No securities exchange commission exists, but the exchange is governed by a Council comprised of four brokers, the Central Bank Governor, and the Financial Secretary. It operates under a set of regulations dealing with matters such as takeovers, block transactions, reporting requirements of companies listed, brokers fees, etc. (In June 1989 there were 45 companies operating on the stock exchange with a total capitalisation of $1.66 billion.)

The 1960s witnessed the Jamaicanisation of the banking and insurance sectors, largely by policy pronouncements of the government and not by legislation. There were 10 commercial banks at the end of 1970, of which only Citibank, Barclays, Canadian Imperial Bank of Commerce and Bank of Montreal remained as branch operations. Bank of Nova Scotia and Royal Bank of Canada were localised although majority control was still held overseas. The first local bank to be established was the Jamaica Citizens Bank, which was supported by public offering. Commercial bank activities were in the conventional areas of trade financing and working capital financing. Assets of the commercial banks moved from $168 million to $430.3 million in 1970.

Merchant banks were started as subsidiaries of overseas banks, namely Citibank, Chase Manhattan, Bank of America and Crown Continental. They were intended to provide services such as project financing, underwriting and advice for corporate restructuring, mobilising funds locally and overseas. Partly because of the absence of adequate business opportunities, they diversified into real estate financing. All except the subsidiary of Citibank have since closed operations in Jamaica.

Credit unions and building societies generally cater for small savers, and are quite vibrant, having the largest membership of any financial institution in Jamaica. Building societies have been operating for over 100 years and cater for long-term savers with lending activity geared towards housing. Their assets have increased from $10.965 million in 1964 to

$72.473 million in 1972. Assets for the credit unions increased from $4.2 million in 1964 to $8.4 million in 1970.

Insurance companies experienced a significant degree of localisation in the 1960s. Many overseas companies either sold their portfolio or invited local equity participation. For example, Life of Jamaica, which is now Jamaica's largest life insurance company, started operations in the 1960s using as its base, the acquisition of the North American Life Assurance portfolio.

The 1970s

Growth in the financial institutions continued in the 1970s, but this period marked a turning point in the operations of some of the key financial institutions.

There was little or no change in the operations of credit unions and building societies, which continued to operate along traditional lines, and maintained growth. Assets of the building societies moved to $311.06 million by 1980. (In 1988, their assets stood at $1.86 billion). Assets of the credit unions moved to $7.2 million in 1976 and to $14.8 million by 1980. (In 1988, assets totalled $47.8 million).

The commercial banking sector also continued to operate along traditional lines, but among the commercial banks, the Bank of Montreal terminated its operations while Barclays was purchased by the government, making that institution the first wholly Jamaican-owned commercial bank (National Commercial Bank). Later, the Government Savings and Loan Bank was transformed into the Workers Bank, another wholly-owned commercial bank. Eventually the overseas interests in the Jamaica Citizens Bank were purchased by a local group. The commercial banking sector was significantly transformed, with local interests being the significant players. Along with this control and minority participation in the case of Bank of Nova Scotia and Royal Bank of Canada, there was a noticeable change in the top management with Jamaicans assuming senior positions.

Assets of the commercial banking sector grew from $430.3 million in 1970 to $2.1 billion in 1980. During this period, there was a marked shift in credit allocation, with credit to the government increasing from $41.6 million in 1970, to $343.1 million in 1980. As a percentage of lending, the figures were 12.8% in 1970 and 24% in 1980, the increase no doubt being used to finance the public-sector deficit which increased to a high of approximately 17% of GDP by 1980/81.

As in the case of commercial banks, the central bank was to play its part in financing the public-sector deficit, with adverse impact on its balance sheet. In 1970, the BOJ's credit to the government (net) was $21.9

million, with credit being 16.92% of its assets. In 1976 this increased to $373.5 million representing 79.8% of its assets; by 1980, the respective figures were $1.3 billion and 56.5%.

It could be argued that the runaway deficit of the public sector was facilitated by BOJ's policies during the 1975/76 period. Instead of acting independently, the BOJ acceded to the borrowing requirements of the government and removed the statutory ceiling on treasury bills, as a result of which, net credit to the government jumped from $161 million in 1974/75 to $374 million in 1975/76, an increase of 132%. Since then the BOJ has never restored its independence, and no statutory ceiling for its holding of treasury bills has been set; the only limitation stipulates that holdings of treasury bills must not exceed a stated proportion of revenue estimates. The BOJ also ventured into investments which proved unwise, as a shareholder in the Jamaica Development Bank (J$8.0 million in 1980), by granting unsecured loans (J$10.0 million) to the Development Bank without government guarantee, and by guaranteeing direct lending from an overseas government entity to a private sector fish processing complex.

The 1970s also saw the demise of the Jamaica Development Bank. What started out as a properly capitalised, well-funded and properly managed entity, ended up as a bankrupt institution in 1978 with a negative net worth of $18.9 million, having lost all credibility with international financial institutions. Its failure stemmed primarily from:

- lax management bowing to political pressure in the granting of loans;
- excursions into unprofitable direct investments in its own subsidiaries as well as in operating entities; and
- attempts to do too much without the proper management infrastructure.

The JDB attempted to tackle two of the areas of grave concern in Third World countries, that is, venture capital financing and the small business sector. It created a subsidiary called Development Venture Capital Finance Company to offer venture capital financing and also was responsible for small business lending through the Small Industry Finance Company Limited (SIFCO). It failed in both cases. The Venture Capital Company failed because it was not properly funded and did not have the management to move such projects. It ended up making few venture capital investments and relied instead on interest income to cover expenses. SIFCO ran into problems due to poorly prepared projects, insufficient equity and weak management by its clients, common to this difficult area of financing.

In February 1972, the Jamaica Mortgage Bank began operations. A wholly-owned government organisation, it was established to operate primarily in the secondary mortgage market; however, it also lent in the primary market, where important gaps existed. Its primary lending focused on financing schemes, and its operations were channelled through the Caribbean Housing Finance Corporation, a company jointly owned by the Commonwealth Development Corporation and the Jamaica Mortgage Bank. Its secondary mortgage operations were intended to bring liquidity in the financing of the housing sector. It dealt primarily with the building societies, which would sell mortgages in times of tight liquidity, and repurchase in times of high liquidity. Although this programme was partially successful, the building societies did not find themselves in tight liquidity for any extended period, and were not prepared to sell much of their loan portfolio. Few transactions took place.

The Jamaica Mortgage Bank was to suffer a fate similar to that of the JDB. Firstly, it borrowed overseas funds without passing on the exchange risk, and had its net worth wiped out from devaluation losses. Secondly, it financed housing projects on which there was a poor collection record. Its net worth moved from $3.6 million in 1976, to a negative worth in 1980.

The 1980s

The government elected in 1980 determined that the private sector should not be starved of credit because of public-sector demands. Overall net credit to the government was increased from $1.6 billion in 1980 to $3 billion in 1988, but, in percentage terms, the government's share of total credit fell from 67.6% to 34% over that period. The liquid assets ratio and credit controls were phased out and a programme for the reduction and eventual elimination of the reserve requirement was put in place.

A foreign exchange auction system was introduced and the exchange rate stabilised between 1986 and 1988, an accomplishment few thought could be achieved. The efficiency of this mechanism allowed for a smooth phasing out of import restrictions. By 1988, net foreign assets of the Bank of Jamaica stood at negative J$5,523.5 million, as against J$130.7 million in 1971.

The rediscount facility introduced in the 1970s was continued, along with the pre- and post-shipment financing facilities. However, because of the shift to more private-sector credit by the commercial banks, utilisation of the post- and pre-shipment facilities was minimal.

A new strategy on development financing was introduced in the 1980s, with the creation of the National Development Bank and the Agricultural Credit Bank. Given the experience of the old Development Finance Corporation and the JDB, the new institution's purpose was to mobilise external resources for development lending, using commercial banks and near-banks as the conduit.

The National Development Bank (NDB), was to fund projects in tourism and manufacturing and the Agricultural Credit Bank (ACB) was to fund projects in the agricultural sector. These institutions allow an agreed margin to the approved financial institutions (AFIs) who take on the risk. In the case of the ACB, approved financial institutions were expanded to include the People's Co-operative Banks. Despite strong initial opposition from the banking sector and from certain groups in the private sector, the model has proved a success. As at 1987, the balance sheet for the NDB showed assets of $213.3 million and a net worth of $78.8 million while that of the ACB showed assets of $254.3 million and a net worth of $77.1 million.

Assets of the commercial banks, which stood at $2.1 billion in 1980, increased to $5.7 billion by the end of 1988. Credit allocation to the government, which in 1980 was $358 million or 12.7% of total lending, rose to $1,729.3 million in 1988, representing 22% of total lending.

While in the 1970s there was a marked decline in merchant bank activities, 1982 marked the emergence of a vibrant merchant banking sector with the establishment of Eagle Merchant Bank. This company was capitalised at $1 million, and embarked on an aggressive marketing programme. As a merchant bank it could not take current accounts nor engage in foreign exchange activities, but it competed with the commercial banking sector by paying attractive rates on certificates of deposit and by creating new financial instruments. Eagle Merchant Bank has created the most comprehensive range of related services in what is called the Eagle Financial Network. The entities involved include a unit trust, an insurance brokerage, a life insurance company, a mortgage guarantee insurance company, a stock brokerage, a financial consultancy and a commercial bank.

In 1983 there were six merchant banks with assets of $109.7 million. By 1988, the number of merchant banks had increased to 27, with assets of $1,957 million. This increase included the creation of new merchant banks as well as conversions of trust companies into merchant banks. The dramatic growth in merchant banks has had a profound effect on the entire banking and financial sector through increased competition and innovation.

Merchant banks provide lease financing for new equipment and commercial vehicles, and for refinancing of existing equipment. Enterprises can improve cash flow from the new or used sale of assets by leasing them back. Because lease payments were treated as expense items for income tax purposes, there were also significant tax benefits. Merchant banks lend at medium term (3–5 years) primarily to the productive sector. They also provide advice on corporate restructuring, underwrite new share issues, arrange loan syndications and provide some equity financing.

The success of the merchant banks depends on their ability to win public confidence in attracting deposits, in identifying good lending and investment opportunities, and most importantly in making decisions with minimum delay. Apart from equity, funding is from deposits, limited to 20 times paid-up capital and reserves. In the case of commercial banks, the ratio is 25 times. With the advent of the National Development Bank and the Agricultural Credit Bank, access to these institutions enhanced the lending capabilities of the merchant banks.

Life insurance companies have played an extremely important role in the mobilisation of long-term savings and through the investments they have made. Today, life insurance companies are the second largest mobilisers of savings after commercial banks. When localisation started in the 1970s, assets of life insurance companies stood at $168.4 million. By 1986, the assets increased to $1.9 billion.

The investment policy of life insurance companies over the last two decades has moved from a conservative approach to a dynamic policy oriented towards directly productive activities. In the 1970s the bulk of the life insurance companies' investments were in government paper, stocks, deposits and real estate. Life insurance companies were primarily responsible for the modern office buildings constructed in the 1980s, which now form the New Kingston complex.

The Structural Adjustment Programme of the 1980s created a new awareness among the investing public that future growth potential rested on investments which offered export growth potential, as well as domestic investments.

Life insurance companies have participated in syndicated loan financing for both equity and loans for new projects (for example in tourism), and have taken a more aggressive attitude in acquiring existing productive entities with export potential. Life insurance companies now manage most of the pension funds in Jamaica, with their own resources representing the largest pool of investible funds.

Lessons and implications from Jamaica's experience

If monetary policy is not exercised independently of fiscal policy, overall credit creation and its allocation simply react to fiscal developments – sometimes merely to finance deficits. The build up in the public-sector deficit to some 18% of GDP in the 1970s was financed mainly by credit from the central bank and the commercial banking sector with net government credit rising to 48.97% of total credit in 1979. When the Bank of Jamaica buckled to pressures from the government in 1975/76, it was unable to check the flow of bank credit to finance the government's increasing deficit. Since then, the BOJ has virtually lost its independence as a monetary authority.

The issue of the level of bank credit in relation to the government's deficit raises the question: to what extent can governments, especially in developing countries, use the Keynesian pump-priming to foster economic development? Public expenditure – whether from domestic or externally generated funds – creates a high import demand because the import propensity of these economies is so high. Additionally, even if domestic investment is in line with domestic saving, import demand rises with the growth in investment. If investment is deficit financed, this creates inflationary pressure, eventually leading to devaluation. Unless expenditure is channelled into export-oriented production activities, the eventual impact is further dependency on external borrowings and an eventual depletion of foreign exchange reserves.

It would appear prudent for economic policymakers in countries such as Jamaica to have a judicious combination of a Keynesian-type expenditure model, geared to productive export activities, and monetary policy which will create a stable financial environment. In the nearby Eastern Caribbean currency area, where money supply and credit creation are rigidly linked to the change in external reserves, the countries involved have managed to hold inflation rates down and to maintain the value of their currencies. It is sound economic policy for developing countries to set desired levels of international reserves and use such targets to determine the level of credit creation. This is the centrepiece of the IMF programme, where targeted levels of external reserves have to be achieved.

Government-owned development banks run the risk of becoming entities subject to strong government influence in channelling resources into specific enterprises. While they start off with the best intentions, excellent boards, and even sound management, they are expected to do too much, too quickly, and to assist too many projects, some of which are politically favoured. As these development banks bend to public and political pressure, they tend to lose their independence and to suffer a deterioration in their balance sheet. The model currently in use, whereby the development bank acts as a mobiliser of funds, especially from overseas entities, and recycles them through AFIs (i.e. commercial banks and 'near banks') which take the commercial risk for an agreed spread (currently 3 points) has proved reasonably successful. But, for this model to succeed, there has to be a close working relationship between the development bank and the AFIs at the management level, to minimise the lead time from the preparation of the project to the approval by both the AFI and the development bank. Despite the apparent bureaucracy, the system has worked reasonably well without too many delays.

In streamlining the process under this model, the next logical step would be for the development banks to issue credit lines to the AFIs, thus allowing for only one decision-making entity, but with certain reporting obligations. This has started on a modest scale for small-enterprise lending. Only recently this model type lending was put in place with the establishment of a US$15 million credit line from the International Finance Corporation to two commercial banks and a merchant bank in Jamaica.

The question of risk-sharing between the development bank and the AFI, under this model, has proved contentious. It is becoming clear that, in the area of agricultural lending, there is a strong case for risk-sharing. The contribution of the ACB in the present model is unlikely to be significant unless a risk-sharing formula with the AFIs is put in place.

The Export-Import Bank, 50% of whose shares are owned by the Bank of Jamaica, plays a similar role to the NDB. However, it differs in negotiating credit lines from private as well as public sources primarily to finance trade credit. In some instances, such as with the US EXIM Bank, credit lines are channelled through the commercial banks which take the credit risk. In other cases, the Export-Import Bank finances the customers directly. It has been argued that the NDB and the Export-Import Bank should be merged. But both have developed at different times and, in the case of the Export-Import Bank, its experiences have been varied (it was upgraded from the Jamaica Export Credit Insurance Corporation which was mainly involved in trade financing). While theoretically a merger of both organisations would seem sound, experience to date suggests that separation makes sense. When institutions are working effectively, despite the possible economies of scale to be derived from amalgamation, it is best not to disturb them.

Credit controls have been applied only to the banking system and have proved ineffectual for a number of reasons. Not all lending institutions are subject to these controls. For example, life insurance companies and building societies are exempt. In the former case, they have been providing lease financing, which itself raises a legal issue on how to impose credit ceilings on the purchase and lease back of assets. With regard to mortgage lending, again there is discrimination with credit limits being imposed on trust companies while there are none for life insurance companies and building societies. There is also the problem of sector classifications where limits are imposed on the distributive and personal sectors but none on productive sectors. What happens, for example, when a large distributor provides new material financing to a small manufacturer of furniture or holds inventory which would normally be held by the producing entity? Is this credit to production or distribution? Fortunately, Jamaica has lifted credit controls except in the case of 'personal' credit.

The lesson to be learnt is that there is far more to be gained from relying on proper macro-economic policies in the control of credit creation than on administrative controls. Currently, monetary policy is managed by certificates of deposit which serve as a type of open market operation, although the latter is primarily of a demand management type, to 'sop up' liquidity. Nevertheless, the use of certificates of deposit as part of an open market operation policy is a useful instrument in increasing or decreasing liquidity.

Localisation of the financial sector has been successful because it was achieved pragmatically and on a negotiated basis, without any acrimony with overseas parent companies. When Citibank and American Life Insurance Company objected to localisation because of their then world-wide policy, they were allowed to continue to operate. Citibank continued to be treated like all other banks without discrimination. But, in the case of the life insurance industry, foreign companies were obliged to pay a special tax on premium income.

The success achieved in localisation is reflected in many areas. Firstly, nearly all entities have grown financially stronger. Secondly, boards and management are dominated by local personnel who, by maintaining high standards of service, have allowed these institutions to be more responsive to the needs of society. Thirdly, the image of banking and insurance has moved away from a staid approach to one of greater innovation and dynamism. Finally, because decision-making has been localised, the response time to financing requests has been shortened.

The advent of merchant banking in the 1980s has impacted positively on the banking system. These 'near-bank' institutions have intensified competition for deposits, credit offerings, project financing, loan syndication and other types of financial services. Innovation and improved services have benefited the consumer. For example, instead of relying on working capital financing as their main type of activity, commercial banks either directly or through their own merchant banks are more aggressively involved in lease, term and project financing. Accordingly, conservative commercial banking has virtually disappeared in Jamaica and there is now innovation and dynamism in the sector.

The keen interest displayed by the banking and insurance sectors in project financing, through loan syndication and co-financing, marks a major turning point in the financial sector. Institutions recognise that they must be more intimately involved in the development effort through both equity and loan financing. It is also acknowledged that co-financing of large ventures is the way to spread the risks while investing in income-producing capacity. This is most noticeable in the tourism sector, in recognition of the vital importance of the export development drive. Banks and insurance companies have the large capital base and the resources to undertake projects with large capital outlays which would not get off the ground without participation.

The Jamaican experience successfully challenges the view that deposit and loan maturities must be matched. It is necessary only that confidence exists in the banking system and that the resources applied for direct investments are matched by adequate levels of reserves, including rediscounting arrangements with the central bank, to meet unusual withdrawals by the public.

The final point to be made is in reference to the proposal for a Caribbean stock exchange. This is a logical extension of the free movement of goods within CARICOM. Implicit in the proposal is the further development of the capital market within CARICOM and the free movement of capital within the region, both of which were envisaged with the CARICOM treaty as necessary to the deepening of CARICOM.

The possibilities for a CARICOM stock exchange far outweigh the dangers. The greatest obstacle to implementation is the Alien Land Holding Act in Trinidad and Tobago (where a stock exchange exists), and in other East Caribbean countries. Once these Acts are amended to treat all CARICOM nationals on the same basis, trading in CARICOM stocks can become a reality through: the harmonisation of stock exchange regulations in Trinidad and Tobago and Barbados; the simultaneous listing of shares on the three exchanges, with computer linked facilities, including settlement arrangements; the appointment of a Joint Securities Exchange Commission, to monitor activities and upgrade rules as necessary; settlement through the banking system, arranged under the CARICOM Clearing Facility; and co-ordinated efforts for the exchange and dissemination of financial information on listed companies, on a CARICOM basis, coupled with special promotional and educational programmes.

The successful divestment of the National Investment Bank of Jamaica (NIBJ), the Caribbean Cement Company and Telecommunications of Jamaica Limited (Telecom), suggests that the Jamaican public is now aware of and interested in shares listed on the stock exchange. The broadening of opportunities within CARICOM, especially to include countries without a stock exchange, would be a very positive development for the integration movement. Liberalisation of immigration laws within the region would be a logical extension to liberalising the capital market.

Conclusion

The history of Jamaica's financial institutions over the last three decades reflects the economic strategies pursued. The 1960s – an essentially *laissez-faire* period – saw the laying of the foundation for a range of financial institutions. The socialist adventure of the 1970s saw the eclipse of some of these institutions and marked the turning point in the independence of some national institutions, such as the central bank, the steep decline of the stock exchange, and a decline in the investment climate.

In the 1980s, the re-orientation of economic policy to the private sector created the atmosphere for the development of a vibrant financial sector. Merchant banking in its new form and the willingness of financial institutions to be more actively involved in development financing, have created support for investment activities of all types. The strong infrastructural base of financial institutions laid in the first decade provides a good foundation for economic development.

The Jamaican system has demonstrated an inherent dynamism which flowered in a climate of less state-dominated economic policy. Financial institutions which are forced to accommodate political pressure lose their autonomy and find their finances in disarray. In recent times, financial institutions have demonstrated a capacity to respond to new challenges, particularly in the area of co-financing of large projects, and in their willingness to undertake equity and loan financing.

CHAPTER 5

The growth of financial savings in Belize and its contribution to economic growth

Martin Brownbridge

This chapter examines the growth and utilisation of domestically generated financial savings in Belize during the 1980s. The emphasis of the chapter is on private-sector financial savings which have been mobilised through domestic financial intermediaries and are potentially available to finance domestic investment. The financial instruments available to savers in Belize are examined first; these consist mainly of commercial bank deposits and member shares in credit unions, although a very limited range of primary securities are also available. Then, developments in the Belizean economy during the 1980s are outlined; the country experienced a serious recession in the early part of the decade largely due to a sharp deterioration in the terms of trade, and had to undertake a balance of payments stabilisation programme in the mid-1980s, but over the last two years the economy has displayed vigorous growth. This is followed by an examination of the growth of the main domestic financial assets available in Belize; interest-bearing bank deposits and shares in the credit unions have both displayed strong growth during the 1980s and the possible reasons for this growth are discussed. The utilisation of these savings to finance domestic economic activity is also examined. The chapter ends with some tentative conclusions regarding the role played by financial savings in facilitating economic growth in Belize.

Financial instruments available to savers in Belize

In common with many other developing countries Belize has a poorly-developed financial system in the sense that the range of assets and liabilities available to potential savers and borrowers is very limited. The financial system is dominated by the commercial banks, whose operations are confined largely to retail rather than investment banking. The commercial banks attract the bulk of the private sector's financial savings and are by far the most important intermediaries for channelling domestic savings into domestic investment. Virtually the only alternative outlet for the public's savings is provided by credit unions and a government savings bank. A very limited range of primary securities and equities is available but they are not yet held in any significant volume by the non-bank public. The Central Bank holds deposits of the central government and some public-sector enterprises.[1]

The four commercial banks in Belize offer savers non-interest bearing demand deposits and interest bearing savings and time deposits. Demand deposits are held largely by businesses and salaried workers and are probably held mainly for transactions rather than for savings purposes. Savings deposits are a relatively convenient form of saving for lower- and middle-income members of the public. These deposits are liquid and the minimum deposit requirement before interest is paid is relatively low. The current nominal interest rate payable on savings deposits is between 5% and 6% per annum. In recent years they have offered a positive if small real rate of return.

The banks offer time deposits of up to one-year maturity which currently pay between 7% and 9.5% per annum in interest. Most time deposits, however, are of maturities of up to three months. A minimum deposit of BZ$5,000 is required by two of the banks while a minimum of BZ$25,000 is required by the other two. This must effectively exclude a large part of the population from purchasing these assets. Time deposits are mainly held by the wealthier sections of the public, by cash surplus businesses, and increasingly recently by some of the public enterprises and statutory bodies.

The Central Bank has, since its establishment in 1982, stipulated the minimum interest rates paid on commercial bank savings and time deposits (as well as a minimum lending rate). Minimum rates have been adjusted on average every one to two years mainly in response to the need to influence aggregate demand in the economy. Attention has also been given to ensuring that domestic deposit rates of interest remain competitive with those in the US because US financial assets are a potential substitute for domestic bank deposits. There is a large number of Belizeans living and working in the US and their remittances, which are estimated to have amounted to around BZ$30 million annually in recent years, provide an important source of foreign exchange.

The credit unions, of which there are 17 known to be active in Belize, attract savings largely because they can also offer credit facilities to savers who would normally have difficulty in obtaining commercial bank loans. Savers have the opportunity of either buying shares in a credit union (which entitles them to become a member) or in making a deposit, although virtually all savings in the credit unions are in the form of shares rather than deposits.[2] Shares yield a dividend of around 5–6% and are relatively illiquid but can be used as collateral for loans from the credit unions. Credit unions in effect recycle money between their members to facilitate spending on house building, education, small businesses and purchases of consumer durables, etc. Any surplus funds are invested in the commercial banks.

The Government Savings Bank offers a 5% interest rate on deposits. The deposits of this institution are apparently held mainly by the elderly and have experienced very little growth in recent years. Savers in theory can also purchase treasury bills. These are auctioned regularly by the Central Bank. They are normally of 90 days maturity and currently offer an annual nominal yield of just about 7.5%. In addition, longer-dated government debentures are also available. The non-bank public, however, has shown virtually no interest in buying treasury bills or debentures and these securities have instead been held by the Central Bank, the Social Security Board and the commercial banks; the latter in order to meet statutory liquidity requirements and to absorb excess liquidity. Little attempt has been made to widen the market for treasury bills partly because the government's borrowing requirement has been reduced considerably in recent years. The public was offered the opportunity to purchase equity in Belize Telecommunications Ltd. (BTL) when this company was partially privatised in 1988, but the bulk of these shares were actually bought by the commercial banks, the Society Security Board and a foreign investor (British Telecom). BTL preference shares were bought by the Central Bank. In addition, the public can hold financial savings in the form of life insurance policies. No aggregate data on the assets and liabilities of these companies are available but most of their funds are probably invested abroad through the parent companies. Life insurance policies might therefore more usefully be regarded as savings held mainly in the form of foreign assets. Any funds invested locally are likely to be held as commercial bank deposits.

At the end of 1988 the non-bank Belizean private sector held almost BZ$200 million of commercial bank deposits, just over BZ$25 million of (recorded) member shares in credit unions, BZ$4 million of deposits in the Government Savings Bank and BZ$2.4 million of BTL shares. Total non-bank private-sector domestic financial assets (excluding cash) therefore amounted to about BZ$230 million at the end of 1988, of which approximately 85% were in the form of commercial bank deposits and about 11% in the form of credit union shares.

The tax system in Belize provides the public with an incentive to hold financial assets by exempting interest earnings and credit union dividend payments from income tax. There is also no capital gains tax.

Economic developments in Belize during the 1980s

The world economic recession and the fall in commodity prices during the first part of the 1980s had a severe impact on the Belizean economy. Real output increased only marginally between 1980 and 1983, while real incomes fell substantially as a result of steep falls in the value of sugar and other exports. Export earnings declined by 20% between 1980 and 1983. Most sectors of the economy, with the exception of public administration and the utilities, experienced very little real growth in this period and private-sector investment fell sharply. Meanwhile consumer prices, reflecting the still high rates of inflation in the industrial countries, rose by over 30% during the first four years of the decade.

The economy made a brief recovery in 1984 but a balance of payments crisis and growing public-sector deficits led to the implementation of a stabilisation programme supported by the IMF in the second half of that year and in early 1985. The stabilisation programme involved fiscal reforms and monetary restraint and was designed to improve the finances of the public sector, contain the growth of aggregate demand and restore the balance of payments to a more viable position. The fiscal reforms included raising indirect taxes and utilities charges while the policy of monetary restraint consisted of an increase in the reserve and liquid asset ratios of the commercial banks and an increase in minimum deposit and lending rates of interest. Private-sector borrowing from the domestic banking system fell in 1985 and remained depressed in the following year. Meanwhile the growth of private-sector bank deposits accelerated substantially.

The balance of payments began to improve in 1985 due to substantial official capital inflows combined with the impact of the policy-induced demand restraint on imports. Although the consumer price inflation of the early 1980s had abated significantly by 1985, incomes in real terms were stagnant with export earnings suffering another sharp decline due to the continuing difficulties of the sugar industry. In addition private investment suffered another fall.

Economic growth remained modest in 1986 but by the end of the year a second successive annual balance of payments surplus and an improvement in public-sector finances allowed monetary policy to be eased in an effort to stimulate private-sector investment. Meanwhile the growth of the citrus, banana, garment and tourist industries was beginning to reduce the country's dependence on sugar for foreign exchange earnings.

The reduction of the macro-economic imbalances in 1985/86 was followed by a major acceleration of economic growth in the following two years, with output in real terms estimated to have expanded by 13.3% in 1987 and a further 7.9% in 1988. The growth, which was accompanied by a rapid increase in private-sector borrowing, was strongest in the construction industry and in some services. A major impetus to the economy was provided by a substantial expansion in both private- and public-sector investment. The former, financed from both local and foreign sources, increased by over 150% between 1986 and 1988 and encompassed sectors such as export agriculture, tourism, light manufacturing and residential construction. Export earnings, boosted by a rise in the unit values of sugar and citrus concentrate and the volume of banana and garment exports, increased by 17% in 1987 and 10% in 1988.

Trends in financial savings during the 1980s

The stock of domestic financial assets in Belize has expanded during the 1980s both in real terms and as a proportion of the nominal value of the economy. Growth has encompassed both bank deposits and shares held in the credit unions while the sources of growth have been in both the private and the public sectors.

A well-known measure of 'financial deepening' in an economy with very limited non-monetary financial assets is the broad money GDP (or GNP) ratio – the inverse of the income velocity of broad money. The M2/ nominal GDP ratio in Belize has risen from 36.5% in 1980 to 59.4% in 1988.[3] The growth in M2 – in real terms it expanded by 87% between 1980 and 1988 – is largely a reflection of the growth in bank deposits and in particular interest bearing deposits by the private sector and to a lesser extent by the Belize Social Security Board.

Commercial bank deposits

Commercial bank deposits increased in real terms by 95% between 1980 and 1988 (see Table 5.1).[4] The strongest growth was displayed by time deposits, with the share of time deposits in total bank deposits rising from 39% to 55% during this period.

Table 5.1   Belize: Commercial bank deposits by type, 1980–8 (Level outstanding at year end [BZ$ million])

Year	Demand	Savings	Time	Other	Total	Growth %	Real growth %
1981	25.3	31.2	36.8	0.7	94.0	12.8	−1.7
1982	23.1	27.8	53.8	0.5	105.2	11.9	0.0
1983	20.6	26.6	66.9	1.3	115.4	9.7	5.5
1984	22.4	30.9	85.1	1.9	140.3	21.6	18.5
1985	28.6	32.3	81.1	1.6	143.6	2.4	−3.3
1986	27.3	31.8	90.6	1.5	151.2	5.3	6.0
1987	30.8	37.8	105.1	1.7	175.4	16.0	13.2
1988	39.5	45.9	126.3	1.9	213.6	21.8	19.4
1989	46.8	62.6	137.0	2.0	248.4	16.3	12.6

Sources: Central Bank, CSO, World Bank.

Demand deposits have been the slowest growing component of private-sector bank deposits, expanding by 37% in real terms between 1980 and 1988. Virtually all of the growth in real terms has taken place over the last two years. Business deposits have been the most rapidly growing component of private-sector demand deposits. Demand deposits, along with cash, are likely to be held by the private sector primarily to facilitate financial transactions. Changes in the level of these deposits, combined with currency in circulation have quite closely reflected changes in the value of nominal GDP during the 1980s. The ratio of these assets to GDP

Table 5.2 Belize: Private-sector monetary assets as a share of GDP, 1980–8

Year	GDP	Currency (c)	Demand deposits (dd)	c+dd	c+dd/GDP %
	($m)	($m)	($m)	($m)	
1980	308.1	17.5	22.9	40.4	13.1
1981	309.4	19.0	21.5	40.5	13.1
1982	291.6	20.6	18.5	39.1	13.4
1983	302.4	21.4	20.5	41.9	13.9
1984	339.0	22.8	27.4	50.2	14.8
1985	335.2	22.6	25.0	47.6	14.2
1986	354.3	25.9	27.8	53.7	15.2
1987	425.3	29.6	35.9	65.5	15.4
1988	480.4	34.1	41.9	76.0	15.8

Year	GDP	Savings deposits (sd)	Time deposits (td)	sd+td	sd+td/GDP %
	($m)	($m)	($m)	($m)	
1980	308.1	31.1	35.7	66.8	21.7
1981	309.4	27.6	50.6	78.2	25.3
1982	291.6	26.4	58.5	84.9	29.1
1983	302.4	30.4	71.9	102.3	33.8
1984	339.0	31.4	65.2	96.6	28.5
1985	335.2	31.3	75.4	106.7	31.8
1986	354.3	36.1	85.2	121.3	34.2
1987	425.3	43.4	101.9	145.3	34.2
1988	480.4	59.6	97.9	157.5	32.8

Source: Central Bank, CSO.

(the inverse of the velocity of circulation) has remained relatively stable at between 13.1% in 1980 and 15.8% in 1988 (see Table 5.2). The behaviour of these assets is consistent with a conventional quantity theory of money demand with a small trend fall in velocity.

Time and savings deposits held by the private sector registered substantial growth in real terms between 1980 and 1988; the former by 102% and the latter by 41%. As a share of GDP, private-sector time and savings deposits combined have risen from 21.7% in 1980 to 32.8%, and this has been the most important element of the financial deepening of the Belizean economy during the 1980s. These deposits are held primarily as savings instruments, and given the limited availability of alternative interest bearing assets in the economy, they are by far the most important outlet for the financial savings of the private sector in Belize.[5]

The growth of private-sector interest bearing deposits has occurred in two distinct phases; between 1980 and 1983 and between 1984 and 1988. In the first phase the Belizean economy experienced serious difficulties, with domestic purchasing power falling by about 18% between 1980 and 1983 and annual consumer price inflation averaging over 10% in 1980 and 1981, conditions conducive to the accumulation of financial assets.

The growth in interest bearing deposits during this period was concentrated entirely in time deposits. Private-sector savings deposits actually declined by 2% in nominal terms and by 18% in real terms and this suggests

Table 5.3   Belize: Commercial bank weighted average interest rates, 1980–8 (per cent)

Year	Weighted average deposit rate	Weighted average savings deposit rate	Weighted average time deposit rate	Weighted average lending rate	Consumer price inflation
1980	6.7	7.0	10.6	15.6	14.8
1981	9.3	7.5	14.5	19.1	11.9
1982	10.4	7.7	14.9	18.6	3.9
1983	8.3	5.8	11.5	15.3	2.6
1984	6.6	4.8	9.2	13.8	5.9
1985	8.8	7.8	11.6	14.7	−0.6
1986	9.0	7.7	11.8	14.7	2.5
1987	7.3	6.3	9.8	14.2	2.0
1988	6.3	5.7	8.6	13.6	3.3

Source: Central Bank, CSO, World Bank.

that low-income households were unable to add to their stock of financial savings in the face of sharply falling real incomes.

Time deposits increased by 69% in real terms and by 101% in nominal terms between 1980 and 1983, a marked acceleration in nominal rate of growth, compared with that of the late 1970s.[6] This sharp growth was probably influenced by the high rates of interest paid on these deposits. Weighted average nominal time deposit rates increased from 10.6% in 1980 to 14.9% in 1982 (see Table 5.3). The rise in nominal interest rates combined with the fall in inflation increased ex-post real interest rates to 11% in 1982 and almost 9% in the following year, although ex-ante real rates may have been much lower due to the persistence of inflationary expectations.

The high rates of interest available on time deposits may have attracted funds from the business sector which would otherwise have been used for internally financed capital investment. Private fixed capital investment is estimated to have fallen from \$52 million in 1981 to \$32 million in 1983 (see Table 5.4). With the economic recession and falling living standards limiting domestic market opportunities and with depressed world commodity prices, the expected rate of return, discounted for risk, of many prospective capital investments in Belize may not have matched that available from time deposits.

Private-sector time deposits declined in 1984 although there was a small rise in savings deposits. Part of the fall in time deposits may have been attributable to capital outflows as a result of a reduction in the interest rates paid on these deposits, and a decline in Belizean time deposit rates relative to those in the US.[7]

Table 5.4   Belize: Gross fixed capital formation 1980–8 (BZ\$ millions)

Year	GFCF	Public sector GFCF	Private sector GFCF	GFCF/GDP %
1980	88.7	n.a.	n.a.	28.8
1981	95.8	43.7	52.1	31.0
1982	81.0	45.7	35.3	27.8
1983	71.3	39.2	32.1	23.6
1984	85.0	36.1	48.9	25.1
1985	71.6	36.7	34.9	21.4
1986	80.0	41.1	38.9	22.6
1987	119.2	46.2	73.0	28.0
1988	158.6	56.6	102.0	33.0

Sources: Central Bank, CSO and IMF.

The country continued to experience balance of payments problems in 1984 and in response implemented a stabilisation programme. As part of the programme the Central Bank raised minimum deposit rates by 3 percentage points in January 1985 in order to stimulate financial savings. The actual weighted average nominal rate paid on time deposits increased as a result from 9.2% in 1984 to 11.6% in 1985 and 11.8% in the following year, while that paid on savings deposits rose from 4.8% in 1984 to 7.8% and 7.7% in 1985 and 1986, respectively. During this period consumer price inflation is estimated to have declined from 5.9% in 1984 to 2.5% in 1986.

The growth in private-sector interest bearing deposits resumed in 1985. Over the four years to the end of 1988 these deposits expanded by 63% in nominal terms and 52% in real terms. Both time and savings deposits registered large increases during this period – the former by 40% and the latter by 77% in real terms – suggesting that the growth of financial savings was encompassing a wider section of the public than had been the case earlier in the decade.

Public-sector deposits in the commercial banks have also experienced substantial growth during the 1980s, expanding tenfold from a small base (see Table 5.5), to 19% of total commercial bank deposits by the end of 1988. The Belize Society Security Board (BSSB), founded in 1981, held 60% of public-sector deposits in the commercial banks at the end of 1988. These deposits are a form of indirect financial or contractual savings for its 30,000 individual contributors.[8] Some utilities and other statutory bodies have also accumulated deposits in the commercial banks following an improvement in their operating finances in recent years.

Table 5.5 Belize: Public and private sector commercial bank deposits 1980–8 (Level outstanding at year end [BZ$ millions])

Year	Public sector	Growth %	Real growth %	Private sector	Growth %	Real growth %
1980	3.6	–22.8	–32.8	89.7	14.9	0.0
1981	5.0	38.9	24.1	99.7	11.1	–0.7
1982	10.6	112.0	104.0	103.5	3.8	–0.1
1983	15.6	47.2	43.5	122.8	18.6	15.7
1984	18.1	16.0	9.6	124.0	1.0	–4.6
1985	18.2	0.6	1.2	131.7	6.2	6.9
1986	24.6	35.2	31.9	149.1	13.2	10.5
1987	30.7	24.8	22.3	181.1	21.5	19.1
1988	46.9	52.8	47.9	199.4	10.1	6.6

Sources: Central Bank, CSO, IMF.

Commercial bank lending

The expansion of their deposit liabilities during the 1980s has allowed the commercial banks to increase lending to both the public and private sectors. Private-sector borrowing expanded by 69% in real terms between 1980 and 1988 with most of the increase concentrated in the final two years of this period. The sectoral composition of commercial bank loans and advances is shown in Table 5.6. During the 1980s the share of agricultural loans in total commercial bank lending has fallen from 26% in 1980 to under 14% while the share of lending for construction and some of the service industries has increased.

Lending to the private sector expanded at a modest rate in real terms over the 1980/84 period, growing by an average of 6% per year. As mentioned above, private-sector investment was badly affected by the impact of the recession on exports and domestic demand and by very high interest rates. Credit to the agricultural sector, and in particular to the sugar, rice and banana industries, fell very sharply.[9] Nevertheless the growth of lending to the private sector accounted for the bulk of the increase in the commercial banks' deposit liabilities in this period.

Over the following two years private-sector borrowing from the commercial banks declined by 10%, undoubtedly due in part to the effects of the increase in minimum interest rates and the liquid assets ratio in early 1985. However, by 1987 the banks had accumulated a large volume of excess liquid assets and this, combined with the lowering of minimum interest rates at the end of the previous year, put some modest downward pressure on lending rates. With the economy starting to display more vigorous growth assisted by higher export earnings, private-sector borrowing increased rapidly in the second half of 1987 and the expansion continued in the following year. Loans to the private sector rose in real terms by 20% and 31% in 1987 and 1988 respectively, stimulated by a large increase in demand for loans for residential construction. Lending to most other private sectors of the economy, including agriculture, also increased during this period.

The growth in credit to the private sector has facilitated a major expansion in gross fixed capital formation (GFCF). Private-sector GFCF expanded by 88% in 1987 and a further 3% in 1988 (see Table 5.4).[10] Private-sector GFCF has also been financed by a substantial inflow of foreign investment. Private direct foreign investment is estimated to have amounted to BZ$16 million in 1987 and BZ$28 million in 1988 (i.e. 22% and 28% of total private sector GFCF in 1987 and 1988, respectively) and has been concentrated in export agriculture, light manufacturing such as garment assembly and the tourism industry. Public investment has relied heavily on foreign sources of finance.

Table 5.6   Belize: Commercial bank lending by sector, 1980–8 (Loans outstanding at end of year [BZ$ millions])

Sector	1980	1981	1982	1983	1984	1985	1986	1987	1988
Government services	2.5	4.2	14.4	15.1	16.5	16.7	12.3	8.2	4.3
Public utilities	0.2	0.8	0.6	2.2	3.9	1.1	0.8	6.3	5.8
Agriculture	24.1	24.1	22.7	17.2	16.7	14.3	12.8	21.5	28.8
Commercial fishing	0.7	0.4	0.5	0.9	0.8	0.7	1.5	1.6	2.6
Forestry	3.1	2.7	2.8	1.0	1.5	0.4	0.3	1.8	0.6
Manufacturing	12.5	11.9	15.0	18.6	19.9	21.1	16.7	14.2	17.5
Tourism	0.7	1.0	1.4	1.1	1.2	1.5	1.6	4.1	5.9
Building and construction	9.2	11.9	12.6	13.1	15.4	15.4	19.0	23.4	33.9
Real estate	0.9	1.2	1.4	3.1	4.7	3.1	3.6	4.2	7.7
Financial institutions	0.2	0.4	0.3	1.4	0.0	0.7	1.1	2.2	2.0
Distribution	25.2	36.3	44.4	42.7	45.9	45.9	44.0	51.0	61.5
Professional services	1.1	0.9	0.8	0.9	0.9	1.4	1.1	1.7	2.1
Transport	1.6	1.8	2.0	3.5	2.7	1.9	2.3	4.2	7.5
Entertainment	0.4	0.4	0.9	0.7	0.8	0.7	0.6	0.8	1.0
Mining and exploration	0.0	0.0	1.9	5.0	6.0	5.8	5.0	4.7	5.8
Personal loans	9.6	10.9	10.7	14.9	16.1	10.8	12.4	15.2	24.9
Sundries								-1.2	-1.7
Total	91.9	108.9	132.3	141.4	153.0	141.4	135.0	163.9	210.2

Source: Central Bank.

There is, however, a widespread perception in the country that the commercial banks remain too conservative in their lending strategies and that the credit needs of small businesses in particular are not being adequately met by the banks.

Commercial bank lending to the public sector, both directly and through purchases of government securities, began expanding rapidly in 1982. The relatively slow growth of private-sector borrowing prior to 1982 had led to a large increase in commercial bank liquidity and this was channelled into financing the deficits of the central government and some of the public utilities. The private sector, via the commercial banks, had in effect taken on a large part of the burden of financing the public sector's domestic debt from the Central Bank, and this played an important role in helping to stabilise the economy in the mid-1980s.[11]

During 1987, following the reduction of minimum deposit and lending rates of interest in December 1986, the excess liquidity with the commercial banks ranged between 11.0% and 18.7% of deposits. The high levels of liquidity continued in the first part of 1988 and prompted banks to discourage time deposits and instead channel additional deposits into the less costly savings deposits. This highlights the difficulty faced by the banks in expanding credit to the private sector even during a period when the economy was growing rapidly and they had ample liquidity.

Evidently the banks are confronted with a narrow credit base, with a limited number of large private enterprises to which they can lend. Some of the larger tourism projects have been financed from foreign loans and loans to the manufacturing sector have increased very little. The major growth areas of bank lending have been residential construction and personal loans.

Currently the banks enjoy a spread of about 7.8 percentage points between their weighted average deposit and lending rates of interest. This spread has increased from 6.1 points in December 1986. The banks have preferred to maintain a rising trend in their interest rate spread rather than lowering interest rates to stimulate loan demand and reduce their excess liquidity. They obtain a yield of 7.5% from excess liquid assets invested in treasury bills and obtain even higher yields currently on their holdings of short-term foreign assets. These yields are consistently higher than the average cost of deposits and reduce the pressure on the banks to raise their levels of lending. The continuation of high levels of excess liquidity represent a potential loss of momentum for growth.

Savings in the credit unions

The rate of growth of member shares in the credit unions during the 1980s has been similar to that of private-sector deposits in the commercial banks.

Member shares increased by 67% in real terms between 1980 and 1988, with the rate of growth having accelerated significantly over the last two years (see Table 5.7). The pattern of growth of these savings during this period suggests that changes in incomes (and especially urban incomes) have probably had most influence over this expansion.

Table 5.7   Belize: Credit unions: assets and liabilities 1980–8 (BZ$ millions)

	1980	1981	1982	1983	1984	1985	1986	1987	1988
Assets									
Loans	13.3	14.2	15.4	16.6	18.9	20.5	22.2	26.0	31.6
Bank deposits	0.9	1.3	1.6	1.9	1.9	2.1	2.5	2.9	2.8
Other assets	0.5	0.3	0.4	0.5	1.0	0.9	0.7	1.0	1.3
Total assets	14.7	15.8	17.4	19.0	21.8	23.4	25.4	29.9	35.7
Liabilities									
Members' shares	11.2	11.6	12.7	13.9	15.3	16.5	17.9	21.8	25.3
Reserve funds	2.2	2.9	3.2	3.5	3.7	4.1	4.6	2.5	2.8
Other liabilities	1.3	1.3	1.5	1.6	2.7	2.7	2.9	5.7	7.6

Data for 1980–85 are estimates.
Sources: Central Bank, Holy Redeemer Credit Union, Registrar of Co-
operatives and Credit Unions.

Credit union loans have expanded at a slightly faster pace than member shares, increasing by 75% in real terms between 1980 and 1988. As with the commercial banks, lending for residential construction, improvement and repair has become an increasingly important part of the credit unions' loan portfolios during the 1980s. These loans accounted for between 40% and 50% of total credit union lending in 1988, with lending for business investment accounting for another 20%.[12] The bulk of lending by the credit unions is therefore used to finance various forms of domestic investment rather than simply consumer spending.

Conclusions

The stock of financial assets in Belize has expanded in real terms during the 1980s leading to a considerable 'financial deepening of the economy'. This has occurred despite the very difficult economic circumstances facing the country for much of the decade and the very limited range of financial instruments available to savers. The growth of savings by the private sector has been concentrated in commercial bank time and savings deposits and to a lesser extent in the shares of credit unions. Bank deposits have also been enhanced by the surpluses of the Social Security Board.

It seems likely that one reason for the growth of private-sector bank deposits, and particularly time deposits, has been the relatively high interest rates prevailing for most of the 1980s. The Central Bank, since 1982, has attempted to maintain incentives for savers by stipulating the minimum nominal rates of interest to be paid on commercial bank time and savings deposits. This, together with falling rates of consumer price inflation, has ensured that positive real interest rates have been available on these deposits for most of the subsequent period.

The expansion of the stock of financial savings in Belize has made two important contributions to the economy in the 1980s. First, it helped to stabilise the economy in the mid-1980s as private-sector savings were used to finance the public-sector deficit. Second, the build up of the liquidity in the commercial banks was channelled into rapid expansion of credit to the private sector in 1987 and 1988. This credit was used to finance a range of domestic economic activities including a major expansion of fixed capital investment, and in particular residential construction. In addition, credit union lending, much of it also used to finance residential construction, increased greatly during 1987 and 1988.

Real output expanded vigorously in 1987 and 1988 after several years of very slow growth. The expansion of commercial bank and credit union lending to the private sector over the two years undoubtedly facilitated the growth in output although there were a number of additional factors which also made an important contribution. These included the inflow of direct foreign investment, the recovery of certain commodity prices, the repair and expansion of the country's public infrastructure and the reduction of macro-economic imbalances. Nevertheless, much of the investment which took place in several important growth industries such as construction, trade, and parts of the tourist and agricultural sectors relied of necessity upon local sources of finance.

The growth of financial savings in the coming years is likely to continue if rising incomes, the modest rates of inflation and the preferential treatment of tax deposits continue to prevail. Economic policies in the USA and the UK give high priority to the control of inflation and as imports from these countries account for the bulk of imports into Belize the chances of restricting domestic inflation rates to modest levels are bright. The contribution which further steady growth of financial savings can make to the achievement of high growth rates of the Belizean economy in the years ahead is likely to depend crucially on the success achieved in channelling these savings into the productive sectors, both large and small.

Private-sector credit demand needs to be stimulated by a reduction in lending rates of interest by the banks and a narrowing of their interest rate spreads. At the same time, banks must work out imaginative credit schemes whereby their lending is increased without any undue rise in the risks incurred. In particular, small enterprises in the tourism and services sector need to be financed in order to create opportunities for increased employment and incomes. Small farm development should also be undertaken especially in the banana and citrus industries which have been expanding in recent years. Lower interest rates would also stimulate credit demand for housing construction, an industry with a large employment potential. The banks also need to review their norms for minimum collateral so that greater emphasis is placed on the viability of projects financed and less on the amount of collateral that the entrepreneur is prepared to provide. It will be difficult to channel the flow of financial savings into productive investment unless the small enterprises are also brought into the ambit of bank lending in greater measure.

Notes

1 A more detailed analysis of the financial system in Belize is given in Luben (1983) and Central Bank of Belize (1988).
2 The value of deposits in the largest credit union amounted to less than 0.1% of the value of members' shares in 1989.
3 M2 consists of currency with the public plus all commercial bank deposits held by the non-bank private sector, plus all deposits in the Central and commercial banks of the non-central government public sector. GDP is calculated at factor cost.
4 Nominal asset values have been deflated by the Consumer Price Index.
5 Although the stock of private-sector financial savings as a share of GDP has been increasing, the IMF estimates that the private savings ratio measured as a flow of funds (i.e. the share of income saved in any given year) has fallen from 21.5% in 1981 to 9.8% in 1987. The increase in the stock of time and savings deposits during the 1980s is equivalent to about 3% of GDP per year on average.
6 Private-sector time deposits increased by 61% in nominal terms between 1977 and 1980. Calculating the increase in real terms is not possible because of the absence of a CPI for this period. Private-sector time and savings deposits combined increased by 40% in nominal terms between 1977 and 1980 as compared with 53% between 1980 and 1983.
7 Central Bank of Belize, 1985, pp. 18–19. Minimum deposit and lending rates were lowered at the beginning of 1983 by between 2 and 3 percentage points and minimum lending rates were reduced by a further 2 percentage points in January 1984. These reductions were in response to declining international interest rates. However, the differential between deposit interest rates in Belize and those in the US, which had widened in favour of Belize in 1981, 1982 and 1983, narrowed significantly in 1984.
8 The Belize Social Security Board also holds deposits in the Central Bank, treasury bills, government securities and equity in Belize Telecommunications

Ltd. The rapid growth in its financial assets is partly a reflection of the age structure of its contributors, (i.e. there are at present far more people paying contributions than making claims).

9　The fall in commercial bank credit to the sugar and rice farmers was partly offset by an increase in credit from the Development Finance Corporation, a public-sector development bank which utilises mainly foreign sources of finance.

10　These figures are in nominal terms. Calculating the increase in real terms is difficult because of the absence of a price index for private-sector investment expenditures. It is also not possible to give a breakdown of GFCF by sector.

11　Since 1985 public-sector net credit from the domestic banking system (the commercial banks and the Central Bank) has fallen as a result of the improved financial position of the central government and the public utilities combined with the build-up of deposits by the Social Security Board. The public sector became a net lender to the domestic banking system in 1988 following the sale of nearly half of the government's equity in BTL.

12　Estimate based on a breakdown of loan approvals made by the Holy Redeemer Credit Union, the largest credit union in Belize in 1988. The HRCU accounted for approximately 75% of recorded credit union lending in 1988.

Part II

Non-bank financial institutions

CHAPTER 6

The role of non-bank financial institutions in the Jamaican economy, 1979–88

Joseph Bailey

The assets (and liabilities) of bank and non-bank financial institutions in Jamaica grew at a substantial rate in real terms over the ten-year period 1979–89. However, there was only marginal increase in aggregate real income (Gross Domestic Product) over the same period. The increase in real resources mobilised by financial institutions, and the evident growth in the level of financial intermediation was not associated with a corresponding increase in aggregate real incomes during the period. This chapter will analyse the developments which might contribute to an explanation of this paradoxical situation, with emphasis on the role of the non-bank financial institutions.

Generating development

The mobilisation of savings and the development of the financial structure are issues central to the process of development. Development depends on increasing the savings rate and on the capacity to transform savings into financing for investment and development. An increasing proportion of savings should be held in financial instruments which can be transformed from units or sectors with surplus resources to those entities which need the resources for investment and expansion. Non-bank financial institutions contribute to the development process because they add to the variety of instruments which are available to an increasingly diverse group of saving entities. They are also able to utilise the resources mobilised for capital investment in specific areas, such as the financing of investment in housing and residential construction.

As financial transformation grows, and the role of financial institutions expands in the developmental process, the ratio of financial assets to income (GDP) is expected to increase (Goldsmith, 1969). A necessary condition for the transformation of savings into finance for investment and growth is that the rate of return on investment should be high enough to justify the use of such resources. Real loan rates should not be so high as to reduce or inhibit the opportunities for the profitable use of such capital.

Over the 1979–89 period, exchange rate devaluation and problems associated with the shortage of foreign exchange were dominant issues in the economic problems confronting the government of Jamaica. There is much controversy concerning the precise impact of exchange rate devaluation on growth and development. Nevertheless, a certain view-point appears to be gaining general acceptance that devaluation may have a net deflationary impact on aggregate real income and output in the economy (Taylor, 1989). This may occur through the redistribution of income from low to high-income earners as a consequence of devaluation and a high marginal propensity to save of such income earners. This scenario might, in part, explain the high volume of resources mobilised by financial institutions during the period against the background of marginal change in aggregate real incomes, and the fall in the value of the Jamaican dollar to less than a third of its previous US dollar value.

Interest rate policy associated with maintaining the stability of the exchange rate would also help to reinforce this pattern of development. Under the conditions which existed during the period, stability of the exchange rate became the main policy objective, and domestic interest rates were used to maintain this stability.

The relationship of interest rates to the rate of return on investment has not been fully assessed, but it is very likely that in many instances this policy caused loan rates to rise well above the rate of return on investment. Hence, while resource mobilisation remained high, the demand for finance might have been weakened, lending to less than optimal levels of real investment.

A vibrant underground economy is believed to have developed during the period. Although there are no available estimates of the size of this underground economy, the evidence of the substantial increase in real resources within the financial system, set against the background of marginal growth in reported aggregate real incomes, both support the hypothesis of its existence and help to explain the disparity in the rates of growth of output and financial assets.

Finally, the overall macro-economic policies of the government, if strongly interventionist in character, can have an adverse effect on the extent to which resources can be transformed into investment and growth.

In tracing the development of non-bank financial activity during the period, two sub-periods can be distinguished. The first relates to the years 1979–84, and the second to the developments in the 1985–8 period.

The 1979–84 period

This period was characterised by much turbulence in exchange rate and monetary policy developments as the government attempted to deal with the deteriorating foreign exchange situation. Government policy was strongly interventionist in character, despite the removal of control on some prices and the removal of subsidies on others. There was substantial public-sector borrowing from the banking system with consequent increases in the money supply. The growth in public-sector demand for resources was associated with quantitative controls on credit to the private sector and other regulations affecting commercial banking transactions. These included an increase in the liquid assets ratio of the banks to 44% by 1984, and an increase in the cash reserves ratio to 10% in the same year. The increase in domestic demand was reflected in pressures on the exchange rate and price increases, particularly in 1984, when retail price inflation was 34.9% (see Table 6.1). There was a substantial depreciation of the exchange rate over the period with the US dollar appreciating by about 172.4% against the Jamaican dollar. There was a cumulative decline in real GDP of 2.4% over the six year period.

Despite the high demand for resources by the public sector, the ratio of non-bank assets to GDP increased from 25.2% in 1979 to a peak of 32.8% in 1983, as Table 6.2 portrays. There was a more rapid increase in the ratio for the banking system which more than doubled during the period, rising from 71.9% of GDP in 1979 to 147.1% in 1984.

Growth in real assets of non-bank institutions averaged 18.2% during the period, and the trust companies experienced the most rapid growth rate, averaging 30.5% yearly. These institutions benefited from their close rela-

Table 6.1   Jamaica: Real sector variables and the real interest rate, 1979–88

Year	% Change in GDP deflator	Real GDP ($ M)	Real GDP growth (%)	Real treasury bill rate
1979	16.6	1940.0	−1.8	n.a.
1980	17.9	1838.8	−5.7	7.5
1981	8.4	1875.5	2.5	1.4
1982	9.2	1898.7	1.2	0.0
1983	16.5	1942.2	2.3	−3.8
1984	34.9	1925.0	−0.9	−13.8
1985	25.0	1837.2	−4.7	−3.0
1986	17.1	1870.1	1.9	−1.0
1987	12.2	1967.5	5.2	6.6
1988	13.7	1977.6	0.5	3.8

Sources: National Income and Product, 1988 Statistical Institute of Jamaica; *Statistical Digest,* (various issues), Bank of Jamaica.

Table 6.2 Jamaica: Assets of the financial system, 1979–88 ($ Millions)

	1979	1980	1981	1982	1983	1984	1985	1986	1987	1988
Banking System[1]	3,090.8	4,319.8	5,059.1	5,907.8	9,840.1	13,759.8	17,803.2	20,371.2	22,079.0	27,000.9
Central Bank	1,447.0	2,219.4	2,424.9	2,757.4	5,520.4	8,333.8	11,180.8	12,131.0	12,478.6	14,188.5
Comm. Banks	1,643.8	2,100.4	2,634.2	3,150.4	4,319.7	5,426.0	6,622.4	8,240.2	9,600.4	12,812.4
Non-bank Fin. Inst.[2]	1,083.9	1,245.1	1,465.4	1,798.0	2,293.3	2,869.0	3,637.3	4,266.6	5,369.9	7,204.2
Life Ins. Co[a]	375.8	452.0	523.4	590.1	737.8	868.1	1,108.1	1,231.4	1,451.2	1,584.2
Bldg. Soc.	254.9	331.1	387.6	500.3	580.1	675.2	802.2	1,049.3	1,353.7	1,864.4
Merchant Banks	123.6	84.2	92.7	109.8	125.2	221.1	348.0	636.4	1,200.6	1,956.7
Trust Cos.	130.1	132.5	162.6	251.0	373.6	544.3	735.8	682.5	592.7	871.3
Fin. Houses	52.0	56.6	61.3	59.4	120.4	139.2	163.8	123.1	147.5	178.7
Credit Unions	114.6	146.7	185.1	224.4	269.8	312.6	347.0	379.1	432.2	492.7
Others[b]	32.9	42.0	52.7	63.0	86.4	108.5	132.4	164.8	192.0	256.2
(1)/GDP (%)	71.9	90.5	95.3	100.7	140.7	147.1	159.6	153.0	140.5	150.3
(2)/GDP (%)	25.2	26.1	27.6	30.6	32.8	30.7	32.6	31.3	34.2	40.1

(a) Data for three largest life insurance companies – Mutual Life, Life of Jamaica and Island Life.

(b) Estimates are based on the assumption that these stocks represent about 25% of commercial bank assets.

Sources: Statistical Digest, Bank of Jamaica; Annual Reports, Building Societies Association.

tionship to the commercial banks, and were able to bid competitively for deposits at a time when there was less competition from merchant banks and finance companies. Credit unions and building societies grew at average annual growth rates of 19.4% and 18.6% respectively. These institutions provide the facility of 'tied' savings which are linked to the provision of mortgage loans for residential construction, and to loans for consumption.

The assets of finance companies grew on average by 22.3% in the period, and were particularly high in 1983 when these institutions took an active role in the operation of the parallel market for foreign exchange and in the establishment of a special retained account for import financing. The assets of the life insurance companies[1] grew at an average of 15.1% being particularly low in 1984 when the rate of growth amounted to 1.6%. The average rate of growth of the merchant banks was the lowest among non-bank institutions, averaging 12.8% for the period. These institutions experienced substantial decline in 1980, and this has been associated with a reduction of external financing during the year. Their assets grew substantially in 1984, but for the period as a whole the overall rate of growth was moderate as the institutions had not yet assumed the highly competitive stance which has been evident since 1985.

Other miscellaneous forms of non-bank financial intermediation, such as the transactions of attorneys-at-law, informal credit revolving schemes (the 'partner') and miscellaneous money lending entities which fall outside the scope of central banking control, are assumed to have grown at least on a par with the growth of assets of the commercial banks. The flow of such resources have been tentatively estimated at about 2.0% of the assets of the commercial banks. These funds are estimated to have increased, on average, by about 28.4% yearly over the period.

The 1985–8 period

In spite of the restrictive monetary and credit conditions and high interest rate regime which prevailed for most of 1985, there was clear indication by the end of the year of attempts to restructure the financial system and to reduce the interventionist policies of the government. Global ceilings on commercial bank credit were removed and revisions to the banking legislation were initiated.

In 1986, liberalisation of the monetary system continued with reduction in the liquid assets ratio of the commercial banks from 48.0% to 38.0%. This removed the pool of funds available to the government at preferential rates of interest, which was a major source of distortion in the interest rate structure. The external transactions showed a sharp reduction in the current account deficit to US$108.1 million during the year, while the reduction in the fiscal deficit to 4.9% of GDP reflected a broadening of the income tax base with the imposition of new taxes on a wide range of commodities. There was also relative stabilisation of the exchange rate and, consequently, inflation fell to 10.4% from 23.3% in the preceding year.

1987 saw a continuation of the financial sector reform programme and a liberalisation of exchange control as part of an overall structural adjustment. Inflation fell to 8.4%, the fiscal deficit was reduced to 1.0% of GDP and real growth rose to 5.0% for the calendar year. This programme of economic liberalisation continued in 1988 with the reduction of the savings deposit rate from 15.0% to 13.0%. This was a signal for reducing nominal interest rates as a means of influencing investment activity. There was also a relaxation of exchange control regulations, particularly with respect to foreign travel and remittances.

But the economic programme was severely interrupted by a natural disaster (Hurricane Gilbert) in September of that year. Resulting from the reinsurance inflows consequent on the damage caused by the hurricane, the monetary system became very liquid with a build-up of substantial deposit balances in the banking system. However, inflation, which was running at a relatively moderate rate before the hurricane, still amounted to only 8.8% compared with 8.4% in the preceding year. The public-sector deficit rose following increased expenditure by government as part of its post-hurricane reconstruction efforts, but it was still relatively low compared with the levels which had been achieved in the pre-1985 period.

For the five-year period aggregate real growth amounted to 2.9% compared with –2.4% for the preceding period 1979–84. Within the framework of the more liberalised macro-economic environment there was an acceleration in the level of financial intermediation by the non-bank institutions. The ratio of non-bank financial assets to GDP rose from 32.6% in 1985 to a peak of 40.1% in 1988. These changes reflected strong real growth in the financial assets of these institutions, averaging 31.5% for the period, compared with an average of 18.2% during the 1979–84 period.

By far the most spectacular growth occurred in respect of the merchant banks, whose assets grew at a yearly average of 80.7%. These institutions developed a large and diversified asset portfolio, including lease financing, insurance premium financing and credit for investment in tourism, manufacturing, construction and other areas associated with growth in the economy. The assets of the building societies showed the next highest average rate of growth with 34.6% for the period, which compared favourably with an average of 18.6% in 1979–84. Life insurance companies were next in importance with an average growth rate of 22.1%, followed by the trust companies with 20.1%, credit unions with 16.9% and finance companies with 12.9% (a decline from 22.3% during 1979–84); this can be attributed to the reorganisation and transformation of some of these entities into the business of merchant banks, which correspondingly accounted for part of the rapid growth rate in the assets of these institutions during the period. The growth rate of the group of miscellaneous financial intermediaries including attorneys-at-law, was estimated at 29.4% for the period, and follows the trend established by the commercial banks. These estimates must be treated with some caution, however, because of the weak basis of estimation.

The increase in the rate of financial intermediation by non-bank institutions during the period can clearly be related to the programme of financial liberalisation and the reduced interventionist stance of the government. This was reflected chiefly in the reduction of the public-sector deficit and the existence of positive real rates of interest which was achieved not by raising nominal rates but by the reduction in the rate of inflation.

Flow of funds

The flow of funds into the non-bank financial intermediaries rose from $161.2 million in 1980 to $1,834.3 million in 1988, an increase of over ten times (see Table 6.3). The distribution of resources moved in the direction of short-term deposits and shares held in building societies and credit unions. These short-term balances accounted for 48.6% of the sources of funds in non-bank institutions in 1980 compared with 74.3% in 1988. The

Table 6.3   Jamaica: Sources of funds of non-bank financial institutions, 1980–8 ($ Millions)

Year	Capital and reserve	Deposits and shares	Life insurance fund	Loans	Other	Total
1980	44.2	78.3	53.6	13.6	–28.5	161.2
1981	3.1	164.3	52.7	5.1	–4.9	220.3
1982	11.9	224.7	53.4	23.6	19.0	332.6
1983	19.6	323.5	88.6	9.3	54.3	495.3
1984	41.8	300.0	108.4	99.1	26.4	575.7
1985	34.0	454.7	149.1	–23.8	154.3	768.3
1986	125.3	406.3	166.4	13.6	–82.3	629.3
1987	71.2	836.5	121.8	–26.8	100.6	1,103.3
1988	63.2	1,362.7	140.1	148.5	119.8	1,834.3

Sources: Annual Reports of merchant banks, trust companies and finance companies, Annual Reports of three largest life insurance companies, *Fact Book* 1988, Building Societies Association, Annual Report of Jamaica Credit Union League.

shift to deposits appeared to be associated with changes in the real rate of interest which became positive in real terms in 1981, 1987 and 1988. Corresponding to this change was the relative decline in the proportion of resources accounted for by the life insurance funds which fell from 33.2% of the total in 1980 to 7.6% in 1988. If life insurance funds are associated with long-term savings then the shift in favour of deposits reflects a possible preference for short-term over long-term savings during the period. This development can be related to the volatility in the financial and money markets which existed, and was a direct consequence of the sustained depreciation of the exchange rate which occurred during the period.

A large proportion of short-term deposit balances, particularly those held in the building societies, possess the character of long-term funds, since they are 'tied' to the provision of housing credit. Hence the apparent shift in favour of short-term funds may not be as great as is indicated in the tables. Resources obtained from capital and reserves remained small, and no discernible pattern of change was observable over the period. To a certain extent, the same was true in respect of loans and other sources of funds.

With regard to the uses of funds (see Table 6.4), the proportion of resources allocated to mortgage financing (both residential and non-residential) in the 1980–4 period varied between 28.1% and 41.2%, and was the largest single use of funds except in 1981, when there was an almost equal distribution between corporate securities, personal loans, liquid balances and mortgage loans. However, in the high real interest rate regime between 1985 and 1988, the use of funds for mortgage financing fell off sharply. This decline in mortgage loans can be attributed partly to weak demand in response to high positive loan rates. Correspondingly, the large build up of liquid balances reflected institutional preferences for high-yield, low-risk instruments in the environment of a fairly volatile money and capital market. Substantial resources were also put into other loans, particularly in 1985, 1987 and 1988. This was a reflection of strong demand for the new credit facilities, such as lease financing which was provided mainly by the merchant banks.

A relatively high volume of funds was also put into government securities between 1985 and 1988. These funds comprised largely treasury bills and certificates of deposit issued by the Bank of Jamaica. These securities provided relatively high yields, and satisfied the same institutional preference as was reflected in the demand for liquid balances. The provision of personal loans remained an important use of non-bank funds, but the proportion declined in the later years compared with the situation between 1980 and 1984. Overall, the pattern of use of funds appeared to have shifted in favour of short-term as against long-term assets, matching the change in the source of funds.

Table 6.4   Jamaica: Use of funds by non-bank financial institutions, 1980–8 ($ Millions)

Year	Fixed assets	Real estate	Government securities	Corporate securities	Residential mortgages	Non-residential mortgages	Personal loans	Liquid balances	Other loans	Other	Total
1980	4.9	0.8	3.2	33.4	105.7	−47.2	51.1	33.9	−7.7	−26.9	161.2
1981	12.0	0.5	−21.2	60.8	59.8	2.3	55.7	65.6	20.2	−35.4	220.3
1982	16.2	2.5	11.9	33.5	121.1	16.0	51.9	22.7	45.0	11.8	332.6
1983	22.0	40.5	3.0	0.5	152.7	35.2	78.5	100.4	42.9	19.6	495.3
1984	47.2	37.3	−7.0	45.0	170.8	19.2	66.3	124.4	26.5	46.0	575.7
1985	101.8	26.0	113.9	92.7	64.2	−3.5	59.8	135.3	249.5	−71.4	768.3
1986	113.8	23.8	75.9	100.3	41.3	9.9	67.6	294.5	−80.7	−17.1	629.3
1987	24.3	48.3	70.3	−3.8	78.6	46.0	60.5	240.5	400.0	138.6	1,103.3
1988	28.4	26.3	202.8	72.0	174.3	207.2	121.6	479.3	473.3	49.1	1,834.3

Sources: Annual Reports of merchant banks, trust companies and finance companies, Annual Reports of three largest life insurance companies, *Fact Book* 1988, Building Societies Association, Annual Reports of Jamaica Credit Union League.

Conclusion

An increase in the level of financial intermediation is a necessary, though not sufficient, condition for growth and development. Integral to the overall process of development is the extent to which macro-economic policies implemented by the government provide a satisfactory environment for the financial intermediation process.

In the 1979–84 period a relatively high rate of resource mobilisation by non-bank institutions was associated with cumulative negative real growth in the island's economy. On the other hand, between 1985–8, within an environment of financial liberalisation, strict fiscal management and low inflation, financial intermediation attained a relatively high level, but in this case was associated with real growth expansion in the economy. The implication is that the financial sector reform programme initiated by the government in 1985 (with World Bank assistance), is a vital element in the growth and development of the Jamaican economy.

Note

1 The data relate only to the three largest companies which are believed to account for about 70% of aggregate life insurance business in Jamaica.

CHAPTER 7 | The role of building societies in financing development in Jamaica, 1964–88

Desmond Thomas

Building societies represent an important response to the historic problems of land-hunger and inadequate housing conditions affecting low-income groups in Jamaica. Since first being established in Jamaica in the 1860s, they have grown to take a conspicuous position in the financial landscape. They represent a distinguishing feature of the Jamaican financial market by comparison with those of the other English-speaking Caribbean countries where building societies have made hardly any impression. They are an integral part of community life, especially in rural areas where, until the relatively recent expansion of commercial banks, they have been the dominant financial institution. They have the distinction of a strong indigenous base in Jamaica although at inception they were heavily influenced by expatriate religious leaders. Within the last two or three decades, building societies have undergone a process of consolidation, characterised by merger activity, which has given them a more conspicuous role in capital markets. In 1989, two new building societies were formed, marking a growing trend of interest in these institutions as profitable investment opportunities. This trend is noteworthy given the traditional perception of building societies as non-profit organisations.

This chapter will outline the performance of building societies in the mobilisation of savings and their effectiveness as a vehicle for providing resources for housing. They have had growing competition in recent decades from old institutions such as commercial banks and new institutions such as merchant banks and trust companies which are competing for savings and the National Housing Trust (NHT) which has a specific role in relation to housing.

Building societies are compared with commercial banks and credit unions. Commercial banks are chosen because they are the largest, most influential financial institutions and credit unions have similarities with building societies in terms of the people they are supposed to serve. The analysis deals with the period 1964–88 for which data are available; in some instances, data are only available up to 1986.

Building societies in Jamaica: A brief history

It is possible to identify three overlapping phases in the history of the building societies movement in Jamaica. The first phase may be termed the establishment phase when the original building societies were launched and consolidated their influence throughout Jamaica. The first building societies were set up in Jamaica in the middle of the nineteenth century and new ones were started up until the 1950s. By the 1920s, building societies were a well-established institution in Jamaica. The second phase was a period of further consolidation lasting from the 1950s until the 1980s, characterised by many mergers and growing modernisation. Mergers created the large building societies that exist today, giving individual firms a more conspicuous role in the Jamaican capital market. This was also a period of growing competition in the capital market characterised by the expansion of financial institutions. The third, current phase has witnessed a new surge of interest and the creation of new building societies.

The first building societies in Jamaica appeared about three decades after emancipation. The early post-emancipation period was characterised by growing tensions between the sugar planters and colonial administration, on the one hand, and the emerging peasantry, on the other (*see* Woolcock, 1987). The former slaves who had been expected to continue working on the sugar plantations chose to leave the plantations and establish themselves in independent production. At the same time, the sugar industry experienced a marked decline in production with exports falling from £1.3 million in 1832 to £½ million in 1870. The sharpening tensions between the economically besieged planters and the emerging peasantry erupted in the Morant Bay Rebellion of 1865.

One of the critical problems of this period was the peasants' access to land for housing and growing crops. An attempt was made by the Baptist Church, led by William Knibb, to settle the former slaves in villages across the island and although considerable progress was made with the establishment of up to 200 villages by 1842, the problem of land availability persisted.

Building societies were established to facilitate ownership of land and the movement was spearheaded by the churches. The Kingston Benefit Building Society, which was founded in 1864, was the first building society in Jamaica. The leading figure in its establishment was the Reverend W.S. Gardner, who was a Congregational Minister at the time. The Kingston Benefit Building Society failed in 1907.

Over the next century, building societies proliferated. By 1959, 21 building societies had been created, as listed in Table 7.1. Members of the clergy, including the Anglicans, Baptists and Congregationalists played a conspicuous role. Many societies have survived although most have merged

Table 7.1   Building societies founded in Jamaica

Date of establishment	Name of building society
1864	Kingston Benefit*
1874	Westmoreland Benefit
1875	St James Benefit
	St Ann Benefit
1878	Jamaica Permanent
	Victoria Mutual
1893	Hanover Benefit
	Browns Town
1897	St Thomas Mutual
1915	St Mary's Benefit
1925	Middlesex**
1931	Clarendon
1932	Jamaica Central*
1939	The Metropolitan*
	St Catherine's Mutual*
1942	Progressive Mutual
	Surrey Mutual
1952	Farmer's General Mutual*
	Jamaica National*
1955	Manchester Mutual
1959	Allied

* These building societies went out of existence.
** Originally Western St Mary's Building Society. Renamed in 1945.

Sources: Woolcock (1987), Building Societies Association of Jamaica.

with others. In addition to the Kingston Benefit, five societies went out of existence, namely, Jamaica Central, Metropolitan, St Catherine Mutual, Farmers and General Mutual and the first Jamaican National (not to be confused with the present Jamaica National).

Building societies were established to assist members, especially the low-income groups, in obtaining freeholds and developing their properties by pooling their savings. Provision was also made for a limited amount of borrowing. Some societies, such as the Western St Mary Benefit, went beyond the acquisition of dwellings and displayed a specific concern with helping peasants to finance farming activities. Societies were widely dispersed across the island, operating in urban and rural areas.

The 1970s witnessed a spate of mergers among building societies reducing their number to five, namely, Hanover Benefit, Jamaica National, Jamaica Savings and Loans, Victoria Mutual and Allied. Table 7.2 presents a chronology of these mergers. The building societies continue to offer services island-wide through a network of branches. Improved efficiency has been advanced as the justification for the mergers, as the enlarged societies updated their facilities.

Table 7.2 Jamaica building societies: List of mergers

Date merged	Merging societies	Name of new society
January 1967	Westmoreland Benefit Manchester Mutual	Westmoreland Building Society
December 1970	St Ann's Benefit Browns Town Benefit St James Benefit Westmoreland Building	Jamaica National Building Society
September 1972	Progressive Mutual Jamaica Permanent	Jamaica Permanent Building Society
June 1975	Trelawny Benefit Northern United	United Benefit Building Society
December 1975	Middlesex Surrey Mutual	Jamaica Savings and Loan Building Society
September 1976	Jamaica National Jamaica Permanent	Jamaica National Building Society
October 1978	Victoria Mutual Clarendon Benefit	Victoria Mutual Building Society
September 1983	Jamaica National St Mary's Benefit	Jamaica National Building Society
April 1986	Victoria Mutual United Benefit	Victoria Mutual Building Society

Sources: Building Societies Association of Jamaica, *Fact Book* (1986); Woolcock (1978).

After a lapse of 30 years, new building societies are starting to be formed. Two new building societies were formed in 1989, both as subsidiaries of financial groups. These new efforts are proprietorships linked to groups which are in the business of maximising profits. The element of mutuality which motivated building societies at their inception is giving way to conventional business motives. However, the attractiveness of building societies as investment opportunities is matched by their failure with respect to the goal of providing housing for low-income people.

Regulation

The operations of building societies in Jamaica are governed by the Building Societies Act of 1897. Under the Act, a building society may carry out mortgage lending on a security of freehold and may foreclose such mortgages. However, the proceeds of foreclosures have to be disposed of and converted into money as soon as practicable in keeping with the general restriction against ownership of property by building societies. The only land and buildings which a society may own are those necessary for conducting its business. The building society may also lend on security of up to 80% of shares which have no prior lien on them. The Act also stipulates the ceiling for penalties for infractions such as accumulating arrears and makes mortgages not greater than $16,000 exempt from duty. The total borrowing by building societies, including deposits by the public, is limited to 75% of mortgages outstanding. The Act allows the regular rules governing building societies to be waived in making loans for the development of a housing scheme, slum clearance scheme and other kinds of schemes aimed at benefiting low-income groups, provided that the approval of the Minister of Housing is obtained for the scheme.

Apart from the Act, there is a considerable level of self-regulation of the industry through the Building Societies Association of Jamaica. The Building Societies Association of Jamaica was established in 1959 to 'formulate and promote the adoption and observance of regulations of their business in Jamaica' and to assist in the 'securing and maintaining of public confidence in the Movement' (Woolcock, 1987, p. 26). It includes all the building societies except the Allied Building Society. Its decisions with respect to minimum reserve and liquidity ratios are binding upon its members and, in addition, it makes recommendations on other aspects of operations. Its members are required to hold 7% of total assets in liquid form and to hold reserves of not less than 3.5% of total assets.

Building societies are not subject to the control of the Central Bank in setting their interest rates but the rates actually set tend to be influenced by what is happening in the banking sector. Up until 1985, the lending rate was set by the Minister of Finance but since then, this has been an area of self-regulation. Building societies usually mobilise funds at lower rates of interest than commercial banks and so are invariably able to carry out mortgage lending to the household sector at lower rates than those obtained in the banking sector. For example, in February 1990, the interest rate offered by building societies on shares is about 12% and the lending rate for household mortgages is 19%, 10 – 15% below those charged by commercial banks.

The fact that building societies are not strictly subject to the Bank Act gives them some advantages in the financial markets. For example, they do not withhold income tax on interest earnings while commercial banks are required to do so, and this helps them to attract funds. In addition, building societies do not have to adhere to credit ceilings which have been imposed on the banking sector although they are expected to exercise some self-regulation in this regard.

The growth of building societies in independent Jamaica

Two aspects of the general economic conditions prevailing in Jamaica since the early 1970s bear special relevance for the growth and performance of building societies in Jamaica in the last two decades. Firstly, this period has been one of economic stagnation, marked by deteriorating average income and living standards, high inflation and a balance of payments deficit. Secondly, the responses to the balance of payments problem have involved rising rates of interest. Economic stagnation and high inflation have conspired to make the problem of access to adequate housing more acute as low and middle-income groups have watched the prices of homes climb out of their reach. Ironically, the real sector deterioration has been accompanied by a boom in the financial sector as a whole in which building societies have shared. Monetary developments, including the tendency for high market interest rates to prevail, have played a significant role in the pattern of growth experienced by building societies.

Building societies achieved vigorous growth between 1964 and 1988 in nominal terms but this growth appears to be more modest in real terms. Total assets and liabilities which stood at $22.8 million in 1964 reached $1,860.5 million in 1988 representing an average rate of annual increase of 20.1% (see Table 7.3). This was a slightly faster rate of growth than that experienced by commercial banks which displayed an average annual rate of increase of assets and liabilities of 19.8%. It was, however, slightly lower than that experienced by credit unions, the assets and liabilities of which grew annually at 22.7% from 1964 to 1986. If the period 1964–88 is broken up into three sections of eight years each, one sees that the growth rate of the building societies has been steadily increasing over the period. Building societies registered average annual rates of growth of 17.5%, 18.0% and 25.1% in the periods 1964–72, 1972–80 and 1980–88, respectively. This is partly a reflection of rising inflation.

Over the period 1964–86, price levels increased by some 1,642%. When this inflation rate is taken into account it may be observed that the real rate of growth of assets and liabilities was 4.5% per annum. By comparison, the average annual rate of growth of real GDP over the same period was 1.2%.

Mobilisation of savings

The main sources of savings for building societies are share accounts and deposit accounts held by the public. In addition, building societies are permitted a limited amount of borrowing under the Act. Share account

Table 7.3   Jamaica: Total assets and liabilities of building societies, commercial banks and credit unions as at 31 December, 1964–88

Year	Building societies	Commercial banks	BS/CB	Credit unions	CU/BS
	(J$000)	(J$000)	(%)	(J$000)	(%)
1964	22,800	n.a.	n.a.	4,626	20.3
1965	25,614	199,594	12.8	5,356	20.9
1966	28,322	216,490	13.1	6,321	22.3
1967	32,550	240,902	13.5	6,665	20.5
1968	39,190	305,874	12.8	8,920	22.8
1969	47,713	388,606	12.3	8,889	18.6
1970	54,551	452,682	12.1	10,063	18.4
1971	67,947	543,081	12.5	11,356	16.7
1972	82,782	665,587	12.4	13,421	16.2
1973	97,858	770,264	12.7	19,743	20.2
1974	114,425	910,903	12.6	25,560	22.3
1975	137,908	1,010,875	13.6	36,078	26.2
1976	156,886	1,066,100	14.7	48,811	31.1
1977	189,829	1,183,899	16.0	65,636	34.6
1978	222,446	1,538,621	14.5	94,495	42.5
1979	253,624	1,643,774	15.4	127,285	50.2
1980	311,058	2,100,353	14.8	168,161	54.1
1981	387,536	2,634,167	14.7	214,961	55.5
1982	500,280	3,150,399	15.9	258,733	51.7
1983	579,999	4,320,389	13.4	307,415	53.0
1984	675,199	5,426,014	12.4	353,125	52.3
1985	802,237	6,622,963	12.1	387,024	48.2
1986	1,047,282	8,241,008	12.7	417,374	39.8
1987	1,353,708	9,600,366	14.1	n.a.	n.a.
1988	1,860,494	12,812,423	14.5	n.a.	n.a.

BS = building societies; CB = commercial banks; CU = credit unions.

Source: STATIN, *Monetary Statistics*; BOJ, *Statistical Digest*, June 1989.

holders are members of the society. Membership gives one priority in obtaining mortgage loans and members are entitled to a part of the dividends declared by the building society, though their returns fluctuate with the fortunes of the society. Deposit accounts earn interest only and their interest earnings are guaranteed.

The supply of funds through shares and deposits to building societies has grown at an average annual rate of 19.1% in nominal terms and 4.6% in real terms over the period 1964–86 (see Table 7.4). By way of comparison, deposits in commercial banks rose from $138.9 million in 1965 to $6,203.5 million in 1986, at an average annual growth rate of 19.8%. Shares plus deposits in credit unions grew at an annual rate of 21.5% from 1964 to 1986 reaching $379.1 million. Credit union deposits grew at the fastest rate over the entire period but building societies have registered a higher annual average rate of growth than credit unions in the 1980s.

The good performance of building societies in mobilising funds is remarkable in the context of rising market rates of interest in recent years. Interest rates offered by building societies are lower than those offered by other institutions such as commercial banks and margins have been increasing in favour of these other institutions (see Table 7.5). In these circumstances, it is reasonable to expect that building societies would encounter great difficulty in attracting funds. The steady growth of the funds mobilised may be attributed to a number of factors:

• the access to mortgage financing which goes with the holding of share accounts is an appealing feature in the context of the chronic shortage of housing. (In addition, share accounts entitle their holders to share loans);
• unlike commercial banks, building societies do not withhold taxes;
• a considerable amount of advertising and promotional activity has been undertaken by building societies; and
• building societies have displayed important qualitative features such as the personal nature of services.

Building societies are able to mobilise resources cheaply relative to other institutions in the financial sector. The composition of the funds mobilised has shifted in favour of shares. Share accounts have grown unremittingly in absolute terms since 1964. Their proportion of total liabilities has increased from 48.1% in 1964 to 88.6% in 1986 while the proportion of deposits has declined from 43.3% to 4.7% (see Table 7.4). This shift has been promoted by the building societies because of the flexibility it allows in dealing with fluctuations in their earnings. From the point of view of savers, there is some incentive to choose share accounts in so far as they entitle holders to priority in qualifying for mortgages. In addition, tax withholding is applied with respect to deposits but not share accounts.

The strong growth of building societies is reflected in increases in the number of deposit and share accounts within the last two decades. From 99,698 accounts in 1969, the numbers increased to 542,106 in 1987. This represents an average annual rate of growth of 9.8%. This growth in the number of accounts has, however, been slowing down over the period indicated above. Over the sub-periods 1969–74, 1974–81 and 1981–7 the average annual growth rates were 12.2%, 10.1% and 7.7%, respectively. Moreover, the growth in the number of accounts has not kept up with the

Table 7.4   *Jamaica: Mobilisation of savings by building societies, 1964–86*

Year	Shares (J$000)	Ratio of shares to liabilities (%)	Deposits (J$000)	Ratio of deposits to liabilities (%)	Shares and deposits (J$000)	Reserves (J$000)	Reserve/ assets ratio (%)
1964	10,956	48.1	9,902	43.3	20,856	1,560	6.8
1965	12,600	49.2	10,788	42.1	23,388	1,756	6.9
1966	14,518	51.3	11,204	39.6	25,722	2,042	7.2
1967	17,328	53.2	12,462	38.3	29,790	2,332	7.2
1968	20,456	52.2	15,684	40.0	36,140	2,652	6.8
1969	24,943	52.3	19,253	40.4	44,196	3,087	6.5
1970	29,729	54.5	20,745	38.0	50,474	3,455	6.3
1971	37,286	54.9	26,241	38.6	63,527	3,944	5.8
1972	47,016	56.8	30,611	37.0	77,627	4,684	5.7
1973	56,104	57.3	35,623	36.4	91,727	5,372	5.5
1974	64,938	56.8	42,271	36.9	107,209	6,131	5.4
1975	77,919	56.5	51,540	37.4	129,459	7,070	5.1
1976	90,404	57.6	55,940	35.7	146,344	8,241	5.3
1977	113,824	60.0	61,871	32.6	175,695	8,557	4.5
1978	148,745	66.9	61,717	27.7	210,462	10,776	4.8
1979	176,985	69.8	64,109	25.3	241,094	11,650	4.6
1980	218,586	70.3	76,129	24.5	294,715	15,079	4.8
1981	284,695	73.5	81,790	21.1	366,485	18,640	4.8
1982	374,607	74.9	98,774	19.7	473,381	21,130	4.2
1983	456,286	78.7	89,070	15.4	545,356	32,212	5.6
1984	542,410	80.3	84,464	12.5	626,874	47,175	7.0
1985	682,036	85.0	57,898	7.2	739,934	54,659	6.8
1986	929,833	88.6	49,704	4.7	979,537	63,784	6.1

Source: STATIN, *Monetary Statistics;* BOJ, *Statistical Digest,* June 1989.

Table 7.5 Jamaica: Comparative lending rates: Commercial banks and building societies, 1977–87 (per cent)

Year	Commercial banks	Building societies
1977	11.7	7.1
1978	10.5	7.0
1979	8.9	n.a.
1980	10.3	7.2
1981	11.6	7.7
1982	9.6	8.4
1983	13.1	8.3
1984	14.4	11.0
1985	21.3	11.8
1986	19.0	12.3
1987	17.5	11.2

Interest rates quoted are *averages* taking into account, in the case of building societies, mortgage lending as well as lending at rates closer to market rates of interest.

Source: IMF, *IFS 1981*; Building Societies Associations of Jamaica, *Fact Book*, several issues.

rate of increase of the total value of accounts. Consequently, the average value of accounts has risen steadily from $387 in 1969 to $2,319 in 1987. At this rate, average accounts have failed to keep up with the pace of inflation.

Assets

A convenient breakdown of the total assets of building societies is in terms of mortgages, liquid funds and other loans and assets (see Table 7.6). Liquid funds consist of government securities, other similar 'investments' and cash in hand. Included in the category of other loans and assets are commercial loans, and resources devoted to building or otherwise acquiring physical facilities to carry out their operations.

The most salient development on the asset side in recent years has been a marked shift in composition from mortgages to liquid funds. Liquid funds have been the fastest growing part of total assets with an annual average growth rate of 26.4% from 1964 to 1986. Meanwhile, mortgages grew by 16.7% annually (i.e. at a lower than average rate for assets as a whole). In 1964, liquid funds were 13% of mortgages outstanding but by 1986 this

Table 7.6   Jamaica: Distribution of building societies' assets, 1964–86 (J$000)

Year	Mortgages	Liquid funds	Other loans and assets
1964	19,466	2,464	800
1965	22,422	2,236	896
1966	24,824	2,518	950
1967	28,476	2,920	1,126
1968	33,150	4,034	1,988
1969	39,892	3,711	3,110
1970	47,310	4,335	2,906
1971	54,758	10,822	2,367
1972	64,632	14,543	3,607
1973	74,620	18,165	5,073
1974	87,062	21,215	6,148
1975	105,889	25,665	6,354
1976	122,929	25,085	8,872
1977	133,811	47,288	8,730
1978	163,246	49,301	9,899
1979	187,372	58,020	8,232
1980	223,859	76,666	10,533
1981	269,623	105,741	12,172
1982	355,824	123,982	20,474
1983	442,498	121,009	16,492
1984	525,410	127,299	22,490
1985	546,570	214,547	41,120
1986	580,897	428,409	37,976

Source: STATIN, *Monetary Statistics.*

ratio had reached 74%. The rapid growth of liquid funds has been most dramatic in the 1980s, a period characterised by high interest rates. The relative growth of liquid funds is a discomfiting development in light of the primary mission of building societies to facilitate access to housing.

The shift to liquid funds has been accompanied by a sharp rise in the proportion of building society income generated by liquid funds, although mortgage income remains the largest source of income. From close to 90% in the 1960s, the share of mortgage interest in the total earnings of building societies declined to 62% in 1986. Liquid funds yielded typically over 20% of total income in the 1980s and reached 32% in 1986, up from around 5% in the 1960s (see Table 7.7).

The shift towards liquid funds is partly explained by lagging demand for mortgages. Sharply rising inflation combined with falling average

Table 7.7 Jamaica: Building societies: Income and expenditure, 1964–86 ($m.)

Year	Total income and expenditure	Mortgage interest	Interest on other investments	Int/bon. on shares, deposits	Oper./ admin. expenses	Sur- plus
1964	1.6	1.4	0.1	0.8	0.5	0.3
1965	1.8	1.6	0.1	1.0	0.6	0.3
1966	2.1	1.8	0.1	1.1	0.7	0.3
1967	2.4	2.1	0.1	1.3	0.7	0.4
1968	2.8	2.4	0.2	1.6	0.7	0.4
1969	3.6	2.9	0.3	2.0	1.0	0.5
1970	4.0	3.3	0.3	2.2	1.2	0.5
1971	5.3	4.3	0.5	3.1	1.7	0.5
1972	7.0	5.3	1.0	4.1	2.1	0.8
1973	8.5	6.2	1.3	4.9	2.8	0.8
1974	10.9	7.7	1.9	6.4	3.7	0.8
1975	14.3	10.8	1.4	8.2	4.7	1.4
1976	16.7	13.3	2.0	9.6	5.6	1.5
1977	19.2	15.1	3.1	12.0	6.5	0.8
1978	22.1	15.9	4.9	12.8	7.9	1.3
1979	25.7	18.6	5.9	14.9	9.2	1.6
1980	33.8	25.0	7.2	19.2	12.1	2.4
1981	43.1	30.6	9.5	25.4	15.2	2.5
1982	57.0	39.1	12.6	35.3	18.7	3.0
1983	69.0	51.4	15.3	42.5	23.5	3.1
1984	90.7	69.4	20.0	55.9	31.4	3.4
1985	123.9	93.5	28.7	80.8	39.3	4.5
1986	161.0	100.1	51.3	106.1	47.9	7.0

Int./bon. = Interest and bonus on share and deposit accounts.
Oper./admin. = operating and administrative expenses.

Source: STATIN, *Monetary Statistics*, several issues.

real incomes made housing unaffordable for the majority of the low- and middle-income population. In addition, there are indications that administrative hurdles have been used to slow the pace of construction activity, given the high foreign exchange costs of building. Consequently, the growth in the demand for mortgages has fallen behind the growth in funds mobilised. The impact of inflation is dramatically reflected in the sharp increase in the average value of mortgages over the years from $3,593 in 1964 to $80,998 in 1986 and the number of mortgages is less in 1986 than it was in 1964 (see Table 7.8).

Rising market interest rates have increased the attractiveness of liquid funds. The growth rate of liquid funds has accelerated during the 1980s coinciding with very high market rates of interest which reached a peak of 21% in 1985 (see Table 7.5). Liquid funds have turned out to be a highly profitable, relatively riskless way of holding assets.

Mortgages are secured for different types of housing, including dwelling houses, agricultural enterprises, commercial and semi-commercial buildings, undeveloped lots and land development. The composition of total mortgages is dominated by those for existing houses which are changing hands, the proportion in this category varying between 88% and 98% in value (see Table 7.8). This gives rise to the criticism that the operations of building societies are linked to speculative activity rather than the creation of more housing. Mortgages for agricultural enterprises have typically been 1% to 2% of total mortgages since 1964.

Other loans and assets matched the growth rate of total assets with a nominal growth rate of 19.2% from 1964 to 1986 (see Table 7.6). This growth rate reflects a steady pace of modernisation of the facilities and operations of building societies.

The reserves of building societies have grown rapidly, keeping pace with liabilities. The BSAJ regulation that reserves observe a minimum ratio to assets of 3.5% has been upheld by the movement as a whole (see Table 7.4). The source of reserves is 'accumulated surpluses or earnings retained to protect depositors against losses that may arise on the asset side'. Therefore, although building societies are basically non-profit organisations, the need to maintain reserves is the principal motivation for surpluses.

Conclusions

The period since independence in Jamaica has been one of vigorous growth for building societies, but there have been significant changes in the character of the movement. In the first place, the perception of the building society as a business in the conventional sense has gradually replaced its traditional role as a non-profit institution, devoted specifically to improving the access to low-income groups to adequate housing through the pooling of their savings. Reflections of this profitability are the expansion of the building societies movement over the last three decades and, more specifically, the upsurge in interest displayed by the establishment of two new societies in 1989. The new building societies are proprietorships rather than mutual societies and are attached to financial groups where the traditional rationale is profit-making.

The basis for the profitability of building societies is the fact that they continue to be able to mobilise funds cheaply and are in a position to take

Table 7.8   Jamaica: Analysis of the value of loans, 1964–86

Year	Total mortgages ($000)	Housing ($000)	Agricultural enterprises ($000)	Commercial or semi-commercial ($000)	Land development ($000)	No. of mortgages (no.)	Average mortgage (l$)
1964	5,454	4,748	68	554	84	1,518	3,593.0
1965	6,198	5,572	84	484	58	1,529	4,054.6
1966	5,944	5,518	64	298	64	1,456	4,082.4
1967	7,270	6,786	70	358	56	1,648	4,411.4
1968	9,180	8,574	32	494	80	1,721	5,334.1
1969	12,600	11,385	29	1,057	129	2,122	5,937.8
1970	13,167	11,760	141	1,059	207	1,759	7,485.5
1971	12,449	11,188	144	1,007	110	1,486	8,377.5
1972	20,407	18,719	146	1,259	283	1,984	10,285.8
1973	23,358	21,984	206	872	296	1,819	12,841.1
1974	26,202	24,695	111	1,028	368	1,738	15,075.9
1975	37,367	35,672	752	542	401	2,633	14,191.8
1976	29,313	28,622	–	383	308	1,747	16,779.1
1977	24,878	24,204	36	268	370	1,522	16,345.6
1978	43,773	41,242	37	430	2,064	2,248	19,472.0
1979	46,657	44,798	–	1,311	548	2,152	21,680.8
1980	58,302	56,452	958	573	319	5,240	11,126.3
1981	74,360	66,466	1,501	2,423	3,970	2,295	32,400.9
1982	119,735	107,593	3,584	4,732	3,826	3,041	39,373.6
1983	122,103	114,598	1,507	2,684	3,314	2,364	51,651.0
1984	118,271	109,842	1,260	3,610	3,559	1,890	62,577.2
1985	84,756	80,860	1,716	796	1,378	1,259	67,320.1
1986	81,160	78,648	–	1,138	1,374	1,002	80,998.0

Source: STATIN, *Monetary Statistics.*

advantage of the high interest rates prevailing in financial markets. On the one hand, building societies are able to use the appeal of qualitative aspects of their services to attract funds in spite of the competition of higher interest rates being offered by other financial institutions. On the other hand, building societies have been able to earn high interest in financial markets, thus boosting their profits, and this has been linked to a marked shift in their assets portfolio towards holdings of liquid funds. Consequently, the actual performance of building societies in Jamaica is in violation of their traditional image as an organisation struggling to fulfil their mission with smaller margins than other financial institutions.

The high interest rates experienced are linked to the general policy direction of stabilisation efforts since the 1970s. Moreover, the shift towards liquid funds in the operations of building societies is a manifestation of the phenomenon of high financial intermediation accompanied by stagnant real growth which is a striking feature of the Jamaican economy since the 1970s.

While the viability of building societies grows, difficulties in facilitating access to housing for low-income people become more noticeable. High inflation in the prices of houses, high interest rates and deteriorating real per capita income have pushed decent housing out of the reach of the poor. One initiative aimed at helping low-income groups has been a scheme called the mortgage certificate programme in which the funds of building societies (and other financial institutions) may be combined with funds from the National Housing Trust in order to reduce the interest rate on mortgages. A satisfactory solution to the problem of low-income housing continues to elude policymakers and the construction industry.

Notes

1   I am grateful for the assistance and co-operation of a number of persons who provided information, namely, Mr J. Bailey, General Manager of The Building Societies Association of Jamaica (BSAJ), Mrs A. McKenzie, Director of Economic Accounting Division, Statistical Institute of Jamaica, Mrs J. Maxam, BSAJ and Mr A. Stone, National Housing Trust. I also knowledge the valuable comments of participants at the 21st Annual Conference of the Regional Programme of Monetary Studies.
2   The measure of inflation used here is the GDP deflator. See IMF, *International Financial Statistics 1988.*

CHAPTER 8 | Credit unions in Jamaica: Performance, problems and prospects

Claremont Kirton

The main objectives of the credit union movement include the encouragement of increased levels of household savings, provision of short-term 'provident' loans at low cost, granting of loans to small-scale, productive enterprises, and provision of financial counselling geared mainly, though not exclusively, towards improvement in household financial management. Such objectives are important in developing countries, especially in the context of the need for increased domestic savings mobilisation, and the allocation of funds to those economic units like small-scale firms whose loan financing requirements are not adequately satisfied by the traditional lending institutions.

Credit unions are simple financial institutions using few inputs and producing even fewer outputs. Most credit union operations in the Caribbean are based on the CUNA International (the international association of credit unions) model where members deposit their savings in a pool which is then made available for lending to fellow members at strictly regulated interest rates. Whenever there exists a residual of loan revenue over operating costs, members receive dividends or interest rate rebates.

It is generally assumed that in comparison with the larger bank and non-bank financial intermediaries, credit unions provide better accessibility to the working people, allow for more popular participation of members in decision-making, are more adaptable to local needs, and may also make available lending and deposit facilities neglected by other financial institutions. Credit unions play an important role in domestic savings mobilisation by facilitating untapped categories of savings, while providing for credit allocation to neglected areas of the economy.

Funds mobilised by credit unions are generally made available to depositors and, especially in rural areas, this may facilitate the allocation of funds in rural communities from which they have been mobilised. In many developing countries, rural credit requirements greatly exceed available supply from the commercial banking sector and the larger non-bank financial intermediaries. Credit unions may meet this supply shortfall. In almost all credit unions, members' ability to access funds via loans is dependent on prior saving, and a commitment to continue saving in the credit union.

Credit unions: A general overview

Croteau's work initiated detailed academic research on credit unions and provided valuable information on their economic behaviour in the United States (Croteau, 1963). Subsequently, a number of institutions and scholars have examined credit union behaviour in developing countries (COLAC, 1978; Kang, 1981; Dublin, 1983; Stemper, 1987). The published work on credit unions in Jamaica is limited to a study conducted by the National Savings Committee in 1972.

Generally, credit unions operate outside the regulatory framework which governs the operations of commercial banks and the more traditional non-bank financial intermediaries. They are sometimes not identified as being part of the formal financial system, leading some analysts to place them in the category of 'semi-formal' or even 'informal' financial institutions. The majority of credit unions operate under government regulations, usually those concerning co-operatives, which specifically delineate their roles and functions. Governments in some countries provide financial and technical support to credit unions in an attempt to reduce the dominance of certain informal financial agents, such as money-lenders.

In Jamaica, credit union operations are regulated by the Co-operative Societies Law (Chapter 75). Credit unions operate under the control of the Registrar of Co-operatives who must ensure that they comply with the statutory regulations governing their operations. In addition, the Registrar of Co-operatives is empowered to investigate the operations of credit unions and, where necessary, dissolve and liquidate those credit unions whose operations are assessed to be unsatisfactory.

At the end of 1987 there were nearly 40,000 credit unions affiliated to the World Council of Credit Unions (WOCCU) operating throughout the world. Just under two-fifths were located in the USA (38%), while about one-third (31%) operate on the African continent, with 446 (or 1% of total) operating in the Caribbean. Of the 65.7 million recorded credit union members internationally, some 50.1 million (76% of total) were from the USA; the available data show that there were just over 650,000 members in the Caribbean. Savings deposits in credit unions throughout the world were US$173.7 billion in 1987, with 86% mobilised in US credit unions. World credit union loans outstanding amounted to US$119.9 billion (1987), while assets were about US$190 billion. Caribbean credit unions are reported in 1987 as having total deposits of just over US$300 million, loans outstanding of US$158.6 million, and total assets of US$331.4 million.

Credit unions in Jamaica, 1941–62

Credit union operations in Jamaica began in 1941 with the establishment of the Clerks Co-op Credit Union. Located in Kingston, this credit union started with 98 members and total deposits of J$520. In 1943, the six existing credit unions formed themselves into a League which was then registered with the relevant government authority. Both the number and membership of credit unions increased significantly over the period up to 1950. By 1950, there were 39 credit unions with 3614 members with savings averaging J$21 per member (see Table 8.1). Recognising the increasing importance of co-operatives generally and more specifically the credit union movement, the government implemented legislation (Co-operatives Societies Law, Chapter 75) in 1950 which stipulated guidelines for the operation and regulation of credit unions. During the same year, the Jamaica Credit Union League was affiliated with CUNA International, thus facilitating its access to a range of services, including deposit and loan insurance. Jamaica was the first country member of CUNA International outside North America.

Between 1950 and 1955, the number of credit unions almost doubled, membership reached 10,000, and total nominal savings deposits were almost J$400,000. This period of Jamaica's economic history was characterised by impressive economic growth rates; the average annual real product growth rate was 10.1%, with the construction sector being dominant; real per capita income grew at an annual average of about 7%, while real net domestic savings also increased. The growth in real credit union savings averaged over 40% per annum during the period 1950–5. Credit union annual average real savings growth rates for the period exceeded the annual average nominal growth rates of both gross national product and national income. No data is currently available on any other credit union liabilities, assets, or their geographic dispersion for the 1950–5 period.

The period 1955–60 in Jamaica saw a slowing down of macro-economic growth to an annual average real growth rate of just over 7%, due mainly to reduced activity in the construction sector. Average annual growth rates of credit union numbers and membership declined in the period 1955–60, relative to the preceding five years; the average annual growth rate of credit unions was down to 20% from 25%, while the comparable figures for membership trends were 15% and 8%, respectively. However, in real terms, credit union annual average savings growth rates exceeded those of the preceding period, being around 50% per annum.

By 1962, the credit union industry in Jamaica had 26,448 members in 113 credit unions, an average of 234 members per credit union, with nearly J$3 million in savings deposits. At that time, credit union savings as a

Table 8.1   Jamaica: Credit unions' early growth (selected indicators, 1941–62)

Year	Number of credit unions	Number of members	Total savings	Average savings per member	Total loans	Total assets
			(J$000)	*(J$)*	*(J$000)*	*(J$000)*
1941	1	98	0.5	5	n.a.	n.a.
1942	4	196	1.2	6	n.a.	n.a.
1943	6	843	5.4	6	n.a.	n.a.
1944	18	1,450	14.7	10	n.a.	n.a.
1945	25	1,820	21.1	12	n.a.	n.a.
1946	31	2,209	41.3	19	n.a.	n.a.
1947	30	2,298	42.9	19	n.a.	n.a.
1948	35	2,350	58.2	25	n.a.	n.a.
1949	34	2,887	54.7	19	n.a.	n.a.
1950	39	3,614	75.5	21	n.a.	n.a.
1951	45	4,523	104.7	23	n.a.	n.a.
1952	52	5,200	142.6	27	n.a.	n.a.
1953	63	6,500	203.4	31	n.a.	n.a.
1954	67	8,700	300.0	34	n.a.	n.a.
1955	73	10,000	390.0	39	n.a.	n.a.
1956	81	13,336	592.1	44	n.a.	n.a.
1957	89	14,789	837.7	57	n.a.	n.a.
1958	92	18,279	1,143.6	63	1,331.8	1,331.8[1]
1959	99	21,000	1,500.0	71	1,445.6	1,562.7[1]
1960	101	22,245	1,879.3	84	1,880.8	1,943.7[1]
1961	110	25,000	2,265.1	91	2,195.2	2,467.0[1]
1962	113	26,448	2,864.2	108	2,651.6	2,996.0

[1] Approximated as the greater of (Loans + other assets) or (Shares/ deposits + reserves).

Sources: Jamaica Co-operative Credit Union League (JCCUL), *Annual Report 1987*; Department of Statistics, *Monetary Statistics*, various issues.

percentage of total personal savings in Jamaica was 11%, rising slightly from about 9% in 1958. The composition of total credit union assets for the first five years for which data are available (1958–62) indicates the major quantitative significance of loans, which account for an annual average of 93% of total assets. The loans/savings ratios of the credit union movement averaged 100.1% for the period, reflecting what may be interpreted as both a commitment to, and confidence in, member borrowers.

Credit unions after political independence, 1962–72

During the first decade following political independence, economic growth in Jamaica was significantly slower than in the previous decade. The national level of real savings mobilisation was correspondingly diminished and the number of credit unions remained relatively stable (see Table 8.2). The average annual growth rate in the number of credit union members was nearly 7%. In 1962, there were 113 credit unions with 26,448 members, with average credit union membership of 234. By 1972 membership had grown to over 50,000 in 125 credit unions, with an average membership of 406. During the 1969–72 period, the Credit Union League upgraded its promotional activities. This may be one of the reasons which explain the pattern of membership growth during those years.

Kingston and St Andrew (predominantly urban areas) accounted for an average of two-thirds of credit union membership in Jamaica. In the parishes of Western Jamaica (Hanover, St Elizabeth, Trelawny, and St James), the credit union movement was virtually non-existent during the period even though fairly high levels of economic activity in mining, tourism, and agriculture existed in those parishes.

Credit unions are usually organised only within groups having what is termed a 'common bond'. Historically, in many countries, the most pre-

Table 8.2 Jamaica: Credit unions (selected indicators, 1963–72)

Year	Number of credit unions	Number of members	Average members per credit union	Total savings	Average savings per member	Credit union total loans outstanding
				(J$m)	(J$)	(J$m)
1963	125	28,000	224	3.5	126	3.2
1964	127	31,000	244	4.2	135	3.9
1965	126	32,000	254	4.6	144	4.4
1966	130	35,000	270	5.5	158	5.2
1967	131	36,000	275	6.3	174	5.9
1968	132	37,865	287	6.9	181	7.1
1969	132	39,185	297	7.8	198	7.9
1970	128	41,256	322	8.4	205	8.3
1971	127	45,583	359	9.6	210	9.2
1972	125	50,723	406	12.7	251	13.1

Sources: Computed from data in JCCUL, *Annual Report 1987*;
Department of Statistics, *Monetary Statistics*, various issues.

valent form of this bond is employment, followed by trade unions, churches, and co-operative societies. Community-type credit unions have tended to be the least prevalent. In Jamaica between 1963 and 1972, the number of credit unions whose common bond related to employment (occupational-type) moved from nearly half to about 60%. Significantly, the second most important type of credit union during the period was the community-based one, accounting for an average of 25%.

In terms of both membership and savings mobilised, the occupational credit unions dominated, with 54% of total membership and 65% of total savings mobilised in 1963, and about 60% of total membership and three-quarters of total savings by 1972. Although the number of community-based credit unions declined slightly during the period, both their share of total membership and their percentage of total savings remained stable. Associational-type credit unions were relatively unimportant in terms of numbers, membership, and savings deposits.

Government sector and sugar industry worker-based credit unions were dominant between 1962 and 1972. These two occupational-type credit unions accounted for at least one-fifth of the total number of credit unions, averaging over one-third of total membership, and mobilising nearly half of total credit union savings.

No time series data exists on the distribution of credit unions by asset size during the specific review period. However, the data for 1971 show that of the 127 credit unions, 98 (or 77% of the total) had asset sizes of under J$100,000. Only five credit unions (1971) had asset sizes of over J$500,000, three of which operated in the government sector. The small asset size of the majority of credit unions indicates their macro-economic impact was minimal.

Total nominal credit union savings increased from J$3.5 million (1963) to J$12.7 million in 1972 (see Table 8.2). The nominal value of average savings per member in credit unions almost doubled over the period moving from J$126 to J$251. The annual growth rate of savings deposits averaged 16% for the period, while savings deposits remained the dominant source of total credit union liabilities, averaging nearly 90%.

When savings mobilised by the credit unions are compared with those by commercial banks during the review period, the most significant years for credit union savings were 1964 to 1967 when their savings levels peaked at just over 5% of those mobilised by commercial banks, demonstrating that credit unions did not provide effective competition to commercial banks. As a percentage of Gross Domestic Product (GDP), credit union savings were miniscule, accounting for less than 1% annually during the 1963–72 period.

Between 1963 and 1972, nominal interest rates on credit union deposits exceeded those offered by commercial banks on savings deposits (see

Table 8.3); real interest rates on credit union savings were positive, except for two years – 1966 and 1971. However, during this period, as already indicated, credit union savings declined as a percentage of total commercial bank savings. This suggests interest rate insensitivity by Jamaican savers during the period.

The value of loans granted by credit unions during the 1963–72 period almost quadrupled (see Table 8.2). The average annual loan growth rate of 15.6% was slightly less than that of savings. Loans continued to be the dominant credit union asset, with loan/asset ratios averaging over 80%. For 1968, 1969 and 1972, credit unions were net lenders of funds (or dis-savers) as evidenced by loans/savings ratios of over 100%. More detailed information indicates that, in 1966, only those credit unions associated with public utilities were net lenders; by 1971, however, five categories had reached that position (church, government, education, manufacturing and public utilities). In 1966, none of the parishes had credit unions which were net lenders of funds; by 1971, credit unions in Kingston/St Andrew, Clarendon and Manchester, had loans/savings ratios exceeding 100%.

Credit union lending for the review period averaged under 3% of commercial bank loans. Unfortunately, there is no detailed information on sectoral loan allocations to facilitate further analysis. However, the credit union contribution to consumer instalment lending is considerable. Credit unions were beginning, by the late 1960s, to emerge as important suppliers of instalment credit. Credit union real loan rates were positive throughout the period and exceeded prime lending rates of commercial banks (see Table 8.3); this may be one of the possible explanations for low credit union loan demand.

Development of the credit union movement since 1972

Since 1974 successive governments have attempted to restructure the economy, largely in response to external factors. Financial institutions operating locally have been the target of various aspects of monetary, exchange rate and other macro-economic policies.

The number of credit unions operating in Jamaica has contracted since 1972. However, the average membership has increased nearly seven times. Significantly, membership growth rates declined during the 1980s, in the context of positive growth trends of the country's main macro-economic indicators. The most recent data (see Table 8.4) indicate that the credit union movement experienced a net loss in membership during 1986. Although there are more urban than rural credit unions, membership of rural credit unions has grown to nearly half the total number over the period since 1972.

Table 8.3 Jamaica: Comparative deposit and loan interest rates, 1963–87

Year	Commercial banks[1] Savings rate	Commercial banks[1] Average weighted deposit rate	Credit union savings rates[2] Nominal	Credit union savings rates[2] Real[β]	Credit union loan rates[2] Nominal	Credit union loan rates[2] Real[β]	Commercial bank loan rates Prime lending rates Nominal	Commercial bank loan rates Prime lending rates Real[β]	Commercial bank loan rates Average weighted loan rates Nominal	Commercial bank loan rates Average weighted loan rates Real[β]
1963	3.0	n.a.	6	n.a.	12.0	n.a.	6.4	n.a.	n.a.	n.a.
1964	3.0	n.a.	6	6.4	12.0	12.4	7.0	7.4	n.a.	n.a.
1965	3.0	n.a.	6	5.6	12.0	11.6	7.0	6.6	n.a.	n.a.
1966	3.5	n.a.	6	-3.6	12.0	2.4	7.5	-2.1	n.a.	n.a.
1967	4.0	n.a.	6	2.2	12.0	8.2	8.0	4.2	n.a.	n.a.
1968	3.0	n.a.	6	3.1	12.0	9.1	7.0	4.1	n.a.	n.a.
1969	3.5	n.a.	6	2.3	12.0	8.3	8.0	4.3	n.a.	n.a.
1970	3.5	n.a.	6	0.1	12.0	6.1	8.0	2.1	n.a.	n.a.
1971	3.0	n.a.	6	-0.3	12.0	5.7	7.0	0.7	n.a.	n.a.
1972	3.5	n.a.	6	3.3	12.0	9.3	8.0	5.3	n.a.	n.a.
1973	4.0	n.a.	6	-13.1	12.0	-7.1	9.0	-10.1	n.a.	n.a.
1974	6.0	n.a.	6	-24.2	12.0	-18.2	11.0	-19.2	n.a.	n.a.
1975	6.0	n.a.	6	-14.8	12.0	-8.8	10.0	-10.8	n.a.	n.a.
1976	7.0	10.2	6	-5.1	12.0	0.9	11.0	-0.1	n.a.	n.a.
1977	7.0	6.8	6	-6.2	12.0	-0.2	11.0	-1.2	13.65	1.4
1978	7.0	6.1	6	-20.0	12.0	-14.0	11.0	-15.0	13.60	-12.4

Table 8.3 (continued) Jamaica: Comparative deposit and loan interest rates, 1963–87

| Year | Commercial banks¹ | | Credit union savings rates² | | Credit union loan rates² | | Commercial bank loan rates | | | |
| | Savings rate | Average weighted deposit rate | Nominal | Real³ | Nominal | Real³ | Prime lending rates | | Average weighted loan rates | |
							Nominal	Real³	Nominal	Real³
1979	7.0	8.0	6	-10.7	12.0	-4.7	11.0	-5.7	13.96	2.7
1980	9.0	9.0	6	-11.9	12.0	5.9	13.0	-4.9	16.68	1.2
1981	9.0	11.4	6	-2.4	12.0	3.6	13.0	4.6	16.25	7.8
1982	9.0	11.4	6	-3.2	12.0	2.8	13.0	3.8	16.43	7.2
1983	9.0	12.3	6	-10.5	12.0	-4.5	13.0	-3.5	17.02	0.5
1984	13.0	17.2	6	-29.0	12.0	-23.0	18.0	-17.0	20.10	-14.9
1985	20.0	19.6	6	-19.0	12.0	-13.0	23.0	-2.0	29.20	4.2
1986	15.0	14.8	6	-11.1	12.0	-5.1	23.0	5.9	25.60	8.5
1987	15.5	15.5	6	-6.3	12.0	-0.3	23.0	10.7	25.19	12.9

1 Rates prevailing at end of December of relevant year.
2 Rates are set at a maximum of 6% by law for savings and 12% for loans.
3 Real values are calculated using the GDP deflator.

Source: Computed from Bank of Jamaica, Statistical Digest; Department of Statistics, Monetary Statistics.

A 1987 survey of credit union members in Jamaica has provided some interesting results (Jamaica Credit Union League, 1987). First, nearly one-half of credit union membership (48%) was in the 26–35 year age group; approximately one-quarter of the employed work force falls into this age category. Only about 15% of membership is between 16 and 25 years old, while this age group accounts for nearly one-quarter (23%) of the employed work force; the credit union movement in Jamaica is not attracting the younger potential saver. Second, the sex distribution of credit union membership follows fairly closely the sex distribution (male 60%, female 40%) of employment in the formal economy. Third, the dominant occupational groups which comprise the membership of credit unions in Jamaica are clerical workers (23%), artisan/craft workers (20%), and service workers (20%). The professional/administrative and self-employed categories are less significant. The data indicate that the majority of credit union membership falls into the lower income category.

When we examine credit union categories during the 1970s, the evidence suggests a declining role for those operating in the sugar industry, and those involving workers in the government sector. Credit unions in the industrial/agricultural, teaching, and community categories showed increases in the percentages of total savings mobilised. Community-based credit unions moved from about one-fifth of total membership and almost 10% of total savings in 1972 to 45% of total membership and over one-quarter of total credit union savings mobilised in 1978. This particular growth trend may have reflected the increased emphasis placed by the government on community development during the 1970s.

Measured in nominal terms, savings mobilised by credit unions increased from J$16.8 million in 1973 to J$432.3 million by the end of 1987 (see Table 8.5), with an increase in average nominal savings per member from J$279 (1973) to J$1,373 (1987). Savings deposits remained the most important component of total credit union liabilities, accounting for an average of over 80% during the period, and rising slightly during the 1980s. Rural based credit unions increased their share of the total to one third, and had a higher average annual growth rate of savings mobilised (32%) when compared with those operating in urban centres (26%).

In real terms, credit union savings deposit growth was much slower, moving from J$21.9 million in 1973 to J$54.1 million in 1987, peaking in 1983 at about J$75 million. When compared with real savings of commercial banks during the period, real credit union savings accounted for an average of 9.6%. This ratio was, however, much higher than the comparable one for the 1962–72 period. As a percentage of real GDP, real credit union savings remained insignificant, averaging only 2.5% over the 1973–87 period; this average, however, was greater than that of the earlier decade.

In Table 8.3, certain aspects of credit union deposit rates are examined.

Table 8.4 Jamaica: Growth of credit unions (numbers/membership), 1973–87

Year	Number of credit unions	Number of credit union members	Average membership per credit union	Number of credit unions[1] – regional breakdown (%)		Number of members regional break-down (%)	
				URBAN	RURAL	URBAN	RURAL
1973	113	60,027	531	65.5	34.5	n.a.	n.a.
1974	112	68,179	609	65.2	34.8	63.9	36.1
1975	113	81,067	717	65.5	34.5	58.5	41.5
1976	103	92,062	894	71.8	28.2	60.7	39.3
1977	103	111,388	1081	71.8	28.2	57.8	42.2
1978	98	142,262	1452	72.4	27.5	55.1	44.9
1979	96	171,100	1782	72.9	27.1	52.9	47.1
1980	96	197,647	2059	72.9	27.1	52.5	47.5
1981	96	221,619	2309	72.9	27.1	52.7	47.3
1982	96	252,109	2626	72.9	27.1	52.4	47.6
1983	97	274,128	2826	73.2	26.8	52.2	47.8
1984	96	292,871	3051	74.0	26.0	52.4	47.6
1985	95	299,642	3154	74.7	25.3	51.9	48.1
1986	91	298,527	3281	74.7	25.3	50.2	49.8
1987	89	314,840	3538	74.2	25.8	50.5	49.5

1 'URBAN' refers to Kingston and St Andrew (i.e. the 'Corporate Area'); 'RURAL' refers to the remaining twelve parishes.

Source: Jamaica Co-operative Credit Union League.

Table 8.5　Jamaica: Credit unions savings deposits – growth and composition, 1973–87

Year	Total savings deposits	Average savings per member[1]	Savings deposits regional breakdown (%)		Total savings/ total liabilities (%)
			URBAN	RURAL	
	(J$m)	(J$)			
1973	16.3	279	78.0	22.0	81.5
1974	22.3	327	75.2	24.8	84.0
1975	31.5	389	72.5	27.5	86.0
1976	42.0	456	71.3	28.7	84.2
1977	57.1	513	68.7	31.3	86.6
1978	84.8	596	65.0	35.0	86.0
1979	114.7	670	64.0	36.0	86.8
1980	146.8	743	63.6	36.4	86.8
1981	185.1	835	64.9	35.1	86.1
1982	224.4	890	66.7	33.3	86.7
1983	269.8	984	67.2	32.8	87.8
1984	312.7	1068	67.5	32.5	88.5
1985	347.1	1158	67.9	32.1	89.5
1986	379.1	1270	66.7	33.3	90.8
1987	432.3	1373	66.7	33.3	n.a.

1　Figures are rounded to the nearest dollar.

Source:　Computed data in Jamaica Co-operative Credit Union League (data reported to the Bank of Jamaica); Department of Statistics, Monetary Statistics, various issues.

These deposit interest rates have been set by law at 6% per annum. In addition to being more attractive than comparable commercial bank savings rates in nominal terms up to the end of 1973, credit union real rates of interest on savings deposits were positive between 1964 and 1972, except for 1966 and 1971. Since 1972, however, real credit union deposit rates have been negative.

If credit union savers are free of money illusion, it is reasonable to assume that negative real interest rates affected credit union savings growth. This is further reinforced by the credit union Member Survey results which indicate that 'low returns on savings' was an important factor influencing persons away from membership of local credit unions. It is also likely that certain transaction costs may have impacted negatively on incentives for depositors. Although service charges are assumed to be relatively low, and transportation costs based on journeys to and from credit union offices are expected to be minimal as a result of nearness of credit union offices to workplace or home, one possible disincentive is the generally slow service provided by credit unions with respect to savings withdrawals. Additionally, the limitations placed on large withdrawals which require in some instances up to six months' notice, and the constraint that members who have outstanding loans are not allowed to withdraw funds, may act as disincentives to deposit growth.

In the period under review, credit union loans remained the dominant component of their asset portfolio. Their loan/asset ratios averaged over 80% between 1973 and 1987 (see Table 8.6). During the 1970s, the Jamaican economy was characterised by major economic dislocation, negative economic growth and economic contraction. To the extent that credit unions were able to maintain their high loans/savings ratios, they demonstrated a level of resilience in periods of economic crisis.

Credit union loans outstanding in nominal terms increased from J$16.8 million in 1973 to over J$400 million in 1987. In real terms, credit union loans peaked in 1973 at J$73 million and have declined since. The geographical distribution of credit union loans follows closely the pattern of savings mobilised; the data indicates that, as a percentage of total, both credit union savings and loans in rural communities were increasing. During the 1970s and up until 1980, the growth rates of credit union savings and loans in rural areas significantly outstripped those of the urban areas. These trends suggest that credit unions' loan finance played a crucial role in rural Jamaica in facilitating a minimum level of economic survival during the economic crisis of the 1970s.

The total loans/savings ratios during the period continued to be very high, averaging over 95%, reflecting a high level of commitment to borrowers. Additionally, as a percentage of total loans to the private sector, credit union loans have been increasing since 1973, and have been much higher

Table 8.6   Jamaica: Credit union loans outstanding – growth and composition, 1973–87

Year	Credit unions' total loans outstanding	Credit union loans – regional composition (%)		Total loans/ total assets	Total loans/ total savings
		URBAN	RURAL		
	(J$m)			*(%)*	*(%)*
1973	16.8	80.2	19.8	82.7	100.0
1974	22.4	76.2	23.8	85.8	100.0
1975	31.5	73.7	26.3	86.3	99.9
1976	42.1	71.9	28.1	86.5	100.3
1977	55.8	69.5	30.5	85.2	97.8
1978	83.2	66.6	33.4	86.6	98.1
1979	112.6	65.3	34.7	84.2	98.2
1980	144.2	64.7	35.3	85.1	98.2
1981	184.1	65.6	34.4	85.6	99.4
1982	219.5	67.7	32.3	84.8	97.8
1983	265.2	67.7	32.3	86.3	98.3
1984	299.9	68.6	31.4	84.9	95.9
1985	328.6	68.7	31.3	84.9	94.7
1986	353.9	67.0	33.0	84.8	93.3
1987	404.6	67.2	32.8	n.a.	93.6

Source: Computed from data in Jamaica Co-operative Credit Union League; Department of Statistics, *Monetary Statistics, 1977;* Statistical Institute of Jamaica, *Monetary Statistics, 1986.*

than was the case in the previous decade.

Credit union loans are usually made for 'provident and productive purposes'. Loans are usually appraised by a loan committee comprising management personnel from the credit union. Loans are limited to credit union members 'in good standing' (i.e. those who have no outstanding arrears on previous loans); potential borrowers may be required to provide guarantors or 'co-makers' if certain loan preconditions are not satisfied.

As for the sectoral distribution of loans, for the most recent period for which detailed information is available (1982–87), housing/construction-related loans accounted for an average of 43% of total, the personal category averaged 37%, while the share of business-related loans averaged 15% (see Table 8.7). In the housing category, nearly half of the loans were for consumption (rent, purchases of household goods, and other loans for household purposes) rather than investment activity. All of the sub-categories in the personal category refer to consumption loans, mainly instalment credit. If one assumes that all credit union lending goes to provide instalment credit, then these institutions have been the dominant source of such lending in Jamaica since 1977, rising to 96% of total in 1984.

'Business-related' loans by credit unions rose from 13% to 21% of total loans during the review period. Since loans are restricted to credit union members who are mostly in the lower income category, it is reasonable to assume that these borrowers are involved in micro-enterprise activities which have been the source of considerable employment creation and income generation in Jamaica, especially since 1980.

In nominal terms borrowing costs have not changed since 1963, and up until 1979 were higher than commercial bank prime loan rates. Over the last decade, however, both commercial bank prime and average-weighted nominal loan rates have been much higher than credit union loan rates. This, however, has not been reflected in any marked increases in credit union lending. Real credit union loans have actually declined since 1983. Since 1983, in real terms, credit union loan rates have been negative.

Prospects for the Jamaican credit union industry

In 1985, the dominant views of both management and the broad membership of credit unions concerning the future prospects of the credit union movement in Jamaica were generally pessimistic (Magill, 1985). Firstly, credit union growth rates were projected to show declining trends and the sector was expected to 'shrink in size and importance'. Secondly, it was anticipated that commercial banks and other traditional financial institutions would provide significant competition for potential credit union sav-

Table 8.7   Jamaica: Credit union loans by categories[1], 1982–87 (Percentages of total loan portfolio)

Categories of loans	1982	1983	1984	1985	1986	1987
Housing/construction related	*44.28*	*47.24*	*44.39*	*42.65*	*37.71*	*42.78*
Purchase of land/building	8.34	9.79	10.37	9.73	6.12	12.66
Home improvement	13.83	15.67	15.03	10.79	12.82	8.41
Rent/mortgage and utility	4.49	3.05	1.01	4.32	0.95	1.54
Household furniture/appliances	14.01	14.56	13.25	14.95	15.84	12.99
Household request	3.61	4.17	4.73	2.86	1.98	7.18
Personal	*36.68*	*34.39*	*36.58*	*40.17*	*43.00*	*33.23*
Vacation and travel	3.71	3.44	2.31	2.76	3.22	2.93
M/Vehicle purchase/repair	21.77	18.41	17.58	16.67	16.92	16.44
Medical expenses	3.41	3.42	3.28	3.68	3.21	3.10
Education	4.87	6.19	7.15	6.35	6.69	5.86
Legal expenses	0.62	0.67	0.69	0.71	0.92	0.71
Wedding and funeral	1.71	1.74	2.06	2.21	2.01	2.01
Insurance premiums	0.06	0.11	0.35	0.28	0.14	0.17
Personal requisites	0.53	0.41	3.16	7.51	9.89	2.01
Business-related	*13.32*	*13.80*	*12.71*	*13.45*	*15.25*	*20.90*
Agriculture	3.28	3.79	4.18	3.09	3.13	4.40
Business (general)	10.04	10.01	8.53	10.36	12.12	16.50
Miscellaneous	*5.72*	*4.57*	*6.32*	*3.73*	*4.04*	*3.09*
TOTAL	100	100	100	100	100	100

1   Pertains to categories of (new) loans *granted.*

Source: Adapted from data reported to the Bank of Jamaica.

ings deposits, leading to a reduced credit union share of the domestic financial market. Thirdly, it was predicted that there would be increasing levels of credit union loan delinquencies, more account closures and fewer members. Fourthly, with decreased savings, credit union loan capacity was projected to decline. Fifthly, based on the generally negative expectations, credit union operations were expected to become less viable, leading to staff reduction and reduced services.

These projections were generally accurate. From the available data, some of which we have already discussed, trends in credit union numbers and membership declined after 1985, although membership levels increased marginally in 1987. Credit unions' real savings and loans also declined. Unpublished information indicates that credit union loan delinquencies have increased since 1985; expenses have been growing faster than income, and the estimated average expenses/income ratio for credit unions had reached 77% in 1986 showing an increasing trend from 63% in 1980.

Although the general prognosis for credit union growth in Jamaica still appears to be pessimistic, there exists considerable developmental potential with respect to the behaviour and operations of these institutions. The first aspect of this potential can be discussed in the context of the pattern of ownership of credit unions. These institutions are basically member-owned; members' savings provide almost all of the funds available to credit unions. In Jamaica, the largest segment of credit union membership comprises working people; they also participate in the overall management and operations. Most importantly, they share in the profits of the credit unions, which may be interest income on savings deposits and shares or interest rebates to borrower members. Credit unions may also provide financial and management services to segments of the population which may not otherwise have obtained such expertise. However, at present, credit union management structures in Jamaica are generally weak and skills must be upgraded.

Secondly, credit unions have historically encouraged the savings habit. Increasing domestic savings mobilisation is an integral part of any development process, and is particularly important for those developing countries with limited access to foreign funding. Although not spectacular in terms of savings mobilisation domestically, trends in real credit union savings in Jamaica suggest that some potential exists. Many urban and rural households have a readily available alternative to non-financial forms of savings via the deposit services provided by credit unions. The existence of such services may also be assisting in the monetisation process, especially in rural areas. Credit unions in Jamaica should examine the services which they now provide with a view towards becoming 'full service' institutions, offering a much wider range of financial instruments and commercial bank-type services. A review of deposit interest rate structures is also necessary.

The third issue relates to loan portfolio behaviour. Credit union lending policies are geared towards members' needs. Credit union loan applications are processed by a loan committee, usually elected by the membership from among its ranks. The committee is expected to be more sensitive to loan requirements than traditional financial institutions might be. In the Jamaican context, credit unions need to review carefully their sectoral allocation of loans. It is true that credit unions may be allocating funds to those sectors of the society neglected by the major financial institutions. However, the credit unions in Jamaica ought to be required to place more emphasis on productive loans and reduce their existing specialisation on instalment credit. It may be necessary to upgrade the loan appraisal arrangements and employ professional staff who are able to provide financial counselling to potential borrowers, so as to limit the trend towards increasing loan delinquency.

Finally, credit unions in Jamaica have reported mainly low net incomes or losses over the last few years in spite of low costs involved in credit union savings mobilisation, and the expected low administrative and operating costs. It seems that administrative practices are weak and operating procedures relatively backward. Credit unions must upgrade their administrative organisation and streamline their overall operations.

Part III

Development finance institutions

CHAPTER 9 | The Caribbean Development Bank

George Abbott

During the twenty years of its existence, the Caribbean Development Bank (CDB) has exercised a decisive influence on developments within the Caribbean, both as a source of development finance and as the primary driving force behind the move towards regional co-operation and integration. All the signs are that it will continue to play a major role in the development of the region. It is equally clear that the Bank will face new and serious challenges as it attempts to respond to the needs of its members. Among other things, this will require it to expand the range and scope of its activities and operations, perhaps even cut back some of its existing programmes, and to seek new sources of funding. This chapter reviews CDB's principal operations and activities since its inception, and evaluates its contribution to the process of regional co-operation and integration. It also identifies a number of problems which are likely to confront the CDB during the 1990s and assesses its capacity to cope with them.

Functions of the CDB

The CDB is essentially a dual-purpose institution: firstly, a bank and, secondly, a regional development agency. Its functions include:

- helping members to co-ordinate their development programmes so as to achieve more effective utilisation of resources, making them more complementary and promoting the orderly expansion of trade, particularly among the members;
- mobilising additional financial resources for the development of the region;
- financing projects and programmes of a regional developmental nature;
- providing appropriate technical assistance to its regional members;
- promoting public and private investment within the region;
- promoting regional and locally-controlled financial institutions and a regional market for credit and savings; and

- stimulating and encouraging the development of capital markets within the region.[1]

This list shows not only the extent to which the CDB is involved in the affairs of the region, but also the essential dichotomy which it faces. As a bank, it has to operate according to strict financial and banking criteria and conventions. These require it, for example, to back sound projects which earn a satisfactory rate of return; to establish and maintain an appropriate international credit-rating, and to operate competitively in international financial and money markets.

On the other hand, as a development agency, it is required 'to contribute to the harmonious economic growth and development of the member countries in the Caribbean and to promote economic co-operation and integration among them, having special and urgent regard to the needs of the less developed members of the region'.[2]

It has therefore to provide enough resources on appropriate terms to meet the developmental needs of its regional members. Further, the stipulation that it must pay particular attention to the needs of its less developed members means that it has to provide soft loans and other subsidised forms of credit.

Membership

The Bank's Charter allows for regional as well as non-regional members. Initially, there were 16 regional and two non-regional members. In 1988, membership stood at 24, of which 20 were regional and four non-regional. The former includes Anguilla, Antigua and Barbuda, Bahamas, Barbados, Belize, British Virgin Islands, Cayman Islands, Dominica, Grenada, Guyana, Jamaica, Montserrat, St Kitts and Nevis, St Lucia, St Vincent and the Grenadines, Trinidad and Tobago, and the Turks and Caicos Islands. Other regional members are Colombia, Mexico and Venezuela. The original non-regional members were Canada and the United Kingdom. France became a non-regional member in 1984 and Italy in 1988. Negotiations are in progress for Germany to become a non-regional member. The regional members can draw on CDB's resources. The non-regional members cannot.

The Bank also makes a functional distinction between its more developed (MDC) and less developed (LDC) Caribbean members. The MDCs include the Bahamas, Barbados, Guyana, Jamaica and Trinidad and Tobago; and the LDCs Anguilla, Antigua and Barbuda, Belize, British Virgin Islands, Cayman Islands, Dominica, Grenada, Montserrat, St Kitts and Nevis, St Lucia, St Vincent and the Grenadines, and the Turks and Caicos Islands. CDB has concentrated its operations and activities on the latter group of countries.

Capital structure, contributions and voting rights

The CDB started operations in 1970 with an authorised capital of 10,000 shares, each with a face value of US$5,000. This gave it a capital base of US$50 million, half of which was in paid-up capital and the rest callable. In 1988, the CDB was capitalised at US$410 million, of which US$95 million was paid-up capital and US$315 million callable. Effectively, therefore, the proportion of paid-up capital has fallen from 50% to 23% of total capitalisation.

The Bank's Charter stipulates that not less than 60% of its total authorised share capital should be held by its regional members and not more than 40% by its non-regional members. This was used as the basis for the initial subscription of its regional and non-regional members. Subsequent increases in its authorised share capital have altered the initial division in favour of regional members. In 1988, the CDB's authorised capital stood at 62,302 shares, of which its regional members held 64.4%.

The increase in the share of regional members has been due mainly to the admission of Colombia, Mexico and Venezuela, each of which holds 3.34% of the total shares. There have also been major changes in individual members' subscriptions. When the Bank started in 1970, for example, Jamaica held the largest number of shares (22.4%) of any member (regional as well as non-regional). It now holds 17.74%, the same proportion as Trinidad and Tobago, which started with an initial subscription of 15.4%. On the other hand, the proportionate share held by each of the other Caribbean members is now less than when it joined, except for Barbados, whose share has gone up from 2.8% to 3.34%. Canada and the United Kingdom, each of which started with 20%, are now down to 11.14% each. France and Italy, the other non-regional members, each hold 6.68%. There will have to be another allocation of quotas when Germany becomes a member.

The regional members also have a built-in majority in terms of voting rights. Article 32 of the Agreement allows each member 150 votes plus one additional vote for each share of capital stock held. In 1970, they held 60% of the capital stock and 64.9% of the voting rights. By 1988, their share of the Bank's capital was 64.4% and they held 65.1% of the total voting rights. Both the ownership and control of the CDB rest effectively, therefore, with its regional members.

However, in terms of contributions to the Bank's resources, they are minority holders. In 1988, the CDB's total resources came to US$733.2 million including capital subscriptions, loans, grants and trust funds, but excluding net income of some US$41 million from the Bank's ordinary capital resources. The Commonwealth Caribbean members accounted for 13.0%, and the other three regional (i.e. Latin American) members 11.9%.

In other words, the regional members contribute less than one-quarter of the CDB's resources. Non-regional members (Canada, the United Kingdom, France and Italy) contributed 36.4% between them. The rest (38.7%) came from non-members, of which 17.4% was contributed by the United States, making it the largest single contributor. A further 15.3% came from multilateral financial institutions, and the rest, 6.0% represented contributions from Sweden, Nigeria, The Federal Republic of Germany and the Netherlands.

The disparity is even greater in respect of the CDB's soft resources which totalled US$510.3 million in 1988. The contribution of its Commonwealth Caribbean members, the principal beneficiaries, amounted to 5.7%. The other regional members contributed 11.6% making a total of 17.3% contributed by its regional members. Non-regional members contributed a further 42.1%. The other 40.6% was contributed by non-members, of which the United States alone contributed 23.6%, making it again, by far the largest single contributor to the Bank's resources. The share of multilateral institutions dropped to 8.9%, while that of Sweden, Nigeria, Germany and the Netherlands went up to 8.1%.

Although ownership and control rest with the regional members, the CDB depends very largely on outside sources for its funding, particularly the United States. The extent and pace at which it extends its operations depend therefore, on the co-operation and contribution of non-members. So far, no major problems have arisen, but clearly the situation is untenable in the long run, given that (a) soft resources and special funds finance the largest share of the CDB's operations, and (b) the CDB's ability to borrow for ordinary operations is limited by the callable capital of Canada, France, Italy, Trinidad and Tobago, the United Kingdom and Venezuela. Of these, only Trinidad and Tobago can draw on the Bank's funds.

Ordinary and special operations

The CDB's financial resources consist of (a) Ordinary Capital Resources (OCR), and (b) Special Funds Resources (SFR). The former includes its authorised capital stock; funds borrowed by the Bank; funds received in repayment of loans; income received from loans; special resources; and other funds which are not part of special funds. The latter also consists of special funds contributed initially, or subsequently earmarked for inclusion in any special funds. It also includes repayment on earlier special loans or guarantees and income derived from the operation of such special funds.

The Bank's Charter specifically requires that 'The ordinary capital resources of the Bank shall at all times and in all respects be held, used, committed, invested or otherwise disposed of, entirely separate from special funds resources. Each special fund, its resources and accounts shall be kept entirely separate from other special funds, their resources and accounts'.[3]

OCR cannot, therefore, be used to finance special funds operations, and vice versa. More than that though, individual special funds, of which there are several, can only be used for the purpose for which they are intended. Similarly, liabilities incurred under any fund are limited to the operation and available resources of that particular fund. While these requirements do undoubtedly conform to the principles of sound financial and accounting practice, they create inflexibility and reduce the scope for internal economies, particularly in the case of special funds for development projects and programmes.

The most important of the special funds is the Special Development Fund (SDF), which is used to make or guarantee loans of a high developmental priority, calling for longer maturities, longer grace periods and lower interest rates than those set for ordinary operations. In 1988, the average rate of interest on SDF loans was 3% per annum. Grace periods average 8.8 years and maturity 26.8 years. Table 9.1 shows the average terms of lending on SDF loans for the three borrowing groups and the proportionate share of total loans approved in 1988.

In all, 17 projects totalling $44.7 million were approved in 1988. Of these, 13 went to Group III borrowers, the so-called LDCs. Jamaica was the only Group II borrower. It received three loans, one of which, amounting to $15 million, was for rehabilitation of hurricane damage. This had the effect of virtually doubling in a single year the amount of loans approved. Total disbursements however, amounted to $17.1 million, the same level as in 1987.

Very definite limits are set on the CDB's authority to lend, invest or borrow. The total amount of loans, equity investment and guarantees which

Table 9.1   Caribbean Development Bank: Terms of lending on SDF Loans in 1988

	Maximum maturity[a] (years)	Maximum grace period (years)	Interest rate (per cent)	Share of total (per cent)
Group I	20	5	5	1.9
Group II	30	7	4	40.8
Group III	40	10	2	57.3

a including grace period.

Source: CDB Annual Reports 1987 and 1988, Barbados.

it is allowed to have outstanding in respect of its ordinary operations at any one time is limited to the amount of its unimpaired subscribed capital, reserves and surplus and other funds included in its ordinary capital resources, exclusive of the special reserve set aside for meeting the Bank's liabilities. The total amount of funds which can be invested in equity capital is limited to 10% of the aggregate amount of the unimpaired paid-up capital stock of the Bank actually paid up at any one time together with the resources and surplus included in its ordinary capital resources, excluding the special reserve. Equity investment is also limited to 10% of the equity capital of the entity of enterprise concerned. In its special operations, total loans outstanding in respect of each special fund cannot, at any one time, exceed the total amount of the unimpaired capital of the fund.

Table 9.2 shows total resources and the different funds operated by the CDB between 1983 and 1988. Ordinary Capital Resources constitute its hard funds, and go mainly to the MDCs, with small amounts to the LDCs for private enterprise and public-sector activities which are commercially viable or financially self-liquidating. The terms of repayment attached to these loans are harder than SDF loans. The rate of interest, for example, is 9.5% per annum. In 1988, OCR loans outstanding amounted to $132.8 million.

Special funds are the Bank's soft window. They provide cheap loans for projects of a high developmental priority which are not usually self-liquidating. They constitute the chief means of supporting small enterprises indirectly through loans to national development finance corporations and infrastructure projects which support such enterprises. A basic rationale for their use is the need for development assistance to ease fiscal pressures and the external debt service burdens of very small and open economies where size and resources make development costly and limited in scope.

Most of the CDB's soft loan operations have been concentrated in the LDCs. Initially, this was done by the MDCs foregoing their entitlement to draw on the resources of the Special Development Fund (SDF), the largest of CDB's special funds. Later, it was decided that in the allocation of soft funds between LDC and MDC members, where aid donors do not stipulate the shares, the former should get no less than 70% of the total, taking one year with another. It was also decided that the LDCs could borrow up to 90% of the project cost while the MDCs would be restricted to 80%. By deliberately favouring the smaller, poorer members, it is hoped to counterbalance the natural tendency towards polarisation, and for the benefits of integration to accrue to the more developed members. In 1988, total loans outstanding on Special Funds Resources were almost US$264 million.

The Venezuelan Trust Fund was established with a contribution of 53,750,000 Venezuelan bolivars and US$12.5 million from the government of Venezuela. The purpose of this Fund is to contribute to the financing of

Table 9.2   Caribbean Development Bank: Total resources, 1983–8 ($US'000)

	1983	1984	1985	1986	1987	1988
1 Ordinary Capital						
Resources	164,166	171,988	190,010	192,703	197,343	210,469
a) Paid-up capital	65,708	74,302	80,237	80,237	80,237	94,813
b) Ordinary reserves, special reserves, current net income	25,407	23,639[d]	29,141	30,144	34,280	41,044
c) Borrowings	73,051	74,047	80,632	82,322	82,826	74,612
2 Venezuelan Trust Fund	16,133	15,814	14,822	13,129	11,994	11,073
3 Special Funds Resources[a]	299,581	361,134	375,277	392,147	423,967	511,679
a) Special Development Fund	<u>137,749</u>	<u>178,154</u>	<u>197,417</u>	<u>219,470</u>	<u>244,779</u>	<u>334,505</u>
i) Contributions	78,983[b]	133,176	150,082	168,660	187,795	279,187
ii) Borrowings	33,257	31,362	33,518	35,996	38,521	35,466
iii) Accumulated net income	25,509	13,616	13,817	14,814	18,463	17,585
iv) Other[c]	–	–	–	–	–	1,602
b) Other special funds	<u>161,832</u>	<u>182,980</u>	<u>177,860</u>	<u>172,677</u>	<u>179,188</u>	<u>177,174</u>
i) Contributions	19,580	33,252	35,004	27,983	24,027	24,093
– Canada	10,813	10,386	10,012	10,092	10,501	11,116
– United States[c]	4,619	15,486	13,171	7,832	5,172	4,786
– Other[c]	4,148	7,381	11,821	10,059	8,354	8,191
ii) Borrowings	<u>137,821</u>	<u>145,905</u>	<u>140,228</u>	<u>140,014</u>	<u>148,443</u>	<u>144,067</u>
– Nigeria	5,000	4,800	4,600	4,400	4,200	4,000
– Trinidad and Tobago	4,167	4,167	2,778	2,646	2,558	2,088
– United States	97,762	97,593	97,413	95,230	95,039	93,930
– IDB	11,592	8,179	13,209	13,059	12,278	11,686
– IDA	14,414	13,882	14,787	15,710	23,447	22,537
– EC	4,881	17,284	7,441	8,969	10,921	9,826
iii) Accumulated net income and current net income	<u>4,431</u>	<u>3,823</u>[d]	<u>2,628</u>	<u>4,680</u>	<u>6,718</u>	<u>9,014</u>
TOTAL (1, 2 and 3)	479,880	548,936	580,109	597,979	633,304	733,221

a Excluding the Venezuelan Trust Fund.

b Includes an amount of $14.6 million held on behalf of Canada as accumulated net income.

c Non-reimbursable technical assistance.

d Restated as a result of prior year adjustments.

Source: CDB Annual Reports (various years).

projects and programmes which may have a significant effect on the development of regional members, especially the LDCs, through better utilisation of their natural resources and the promotion of industry, agriculture and agro-industry, and the financing of exports and investment programmes for the development of tourism. The Venezuelan Investment Fund has the right to the return of all sums received in repayment of loans and to the net income earned. In 1988, the value of the Fund stood at $11 million.

Operations and activities

The principles governing lending operations are very explicit. The CDB is required, for example, to concentrate on financing projects which form part of a development programme whether at the national, sub-regional or regional level. It is also required to provide loans or guarantees to national development banks and other financial institutions, such as development finance corporations, where the scale of operations is too small to warrant direct supervision by the Bank. In making loans, it has to pay particular attention to the ability of the borrower to obtain finance elsewhere as well as to meet its service obligations. Any risk which it undertakes must be suitably and adequately compensated. Procurement of goods and services financed by its loans must normally be undertaken within the region, and help to develop and strengthen undertakings, entities and skills of individuals within the region. Further, the CDB must ensure a reasonable distribution of the benefits of its operations as well as maintain reasonable diversification in its investment in equity capital.

In appraising projects, the CDB must have regard to their technical, commercial, financial, economic, cost-benefit, legal, organisational and managerial, environmental and social points of view; their effect on the general development activity of the country concerned; their contribution to the removal of economic bottlenecks; the capacity of the borrowing country to service additional external debts; the introduction of appropriate technologies to raise the contribution to domestic output and productivity; and the expansion of employment opportunities. In effect, it follows the same procedures and criteria used by the World Bank and other multilateral financial and development institutions.

There is a deliberate bias in the CDB's financial operations towards its LDC members. Between 1970 and 1988, the cumulative total of net approvals of loans, including contingent loans and equity, amounted to $665 million. Of this, 55% was allocated to LDC members and 45% to MDCs. Net approvals from special funds over the same period ran to $428.4 million, of which 73.7% went to LDCs and 26.3% to MDCs. In 1988, cumulative grant financing amounted to $75.2 million, with more than 90% going to the LDCs.

On a cumulative basis, disbursements, including grants, at the end of 1988 amounted to $545.3 million, or 76.4% of total net approvals, which is better than average for most multilateral financial institutions. About 69% of all disbursements for project financing has been funded by soft resources with the larger share going to the LDCs. To date, 58% of all disbursements and 72% of all concessional special funds resources have gone to projects in these countries. In summary, up to the end of 1988, the CDB provided a total of $714 million as loans, equity and grants of which 91.4% were loans and 8.3% grants. Equity accounted for less than one half of one per cent. With a total of approximately $2 million over 20 years in three LDCs, it is clearly the Cinderella of the Bank's operations. Agriculture, manufacturing and tourism took 90%. Table 9.3 gives the percentage distribution of loans, contingent loans, equity and grants approved by sector for each member country between 1970 and 1988.

CDB's banking role and operations

The CDB has powers to borrow funds in its members' territories or elsewhere, buy or sell securities, underwrite and/or guarantee securities in which it has invested, or otherwise has an interest, invest or deposit funds in any member country and assist regional members in matters relating to the foreign placement of official loans.

As the figures in Table 9.2 show, borrowings under its OCR in 1988 were well down on previous years; US$74.4 million, or 10% of total resources is conservative by international banking standards. Net income from ordinary operations in 1988 was US$6.5 million, more than double the figure for 1987. A significant part of this gain (US$1.9 million) was realised as a result of the devaluation of one member's currency. If this is excluded, net income would have increased by 50%. However, investment income, having declined from US$3.6 million in 1986 to US$2.7 million in 1987, a drop of 30%, remained stable, while the average yield on investment, including capital gains realised, was 8.5% compared with 10.4% in 1986.

Borrowing for SFR operations exceeded US$144 million in 1988, US$44 million less than in the previous year. This does not include borrowings for the Special Development Fund which also declined in 1988. The United States is by far the largest supplier of cheap, subsidised credit to the CDB. Significantly, Trinidad and Tobago is the only Caribbean member to make a loan to the CDB, in the days when oil prices were booming. But times have changed. Trinidad and Tobago's economy is not as buoyant nor its prospects as bright as they were ten years ago. One must therefore regard this as a one-off operation, particularly as none of the other Caribbean members have followed its lead. The value of this loan in 1988

Table 9.3   Caribbean Development Bank: Percentage distribution of loans, contingent loans, equity and grants approved (net) by sector for each country, 1970–88

Country	Directly productive sector					Economic infrastructure and other								Multi-sector	Percentage of total
	Agriculture, forestry and fishing	Manufacturing	Tourism	Mining	Total	Power and energy	Water	Transportation and communication	Housing	Education (including student loans)	Health	Sanitation	Total		
Anguilla	4	26	10	–	40	31	4	5	8	4	–	–	52	8	1
Antigua and Barbuda	20	34	9	–	63	1	–	2	12	6	–	–	22	15	2
Bahamas	5	14	8	–	27	–	26	31	–	–	–	16	73	–	4
Barbados	6	25	6	–	37	–	1	38	3	14	4	2	62	1	7
Belize	22	16	2	–	40	11	–	34	7	3	–	–	55	5	8
British Virgin Islands	22	28	3	–	53	39	–	1	–	6	–	–	46	1	2
Cayman Islands	3	4	3	–	10	10	–	52	2	1	–	25	90	–	4
Dominica	16	11	–	–	27	11	2	29	8	9	–	–	59	14	8
Grenada	13	13	–	–	26	–	5	43	10	9	–	–	67	7	6
Guyana	28	44	–	–	72	9	–	12	3	4	–	–	28	–	6
Jamaica	15	29	6	–	50	–	5	9	13	2	1	–	30	20	19
Montserrat	17	19	–	–	36	20	–	5	–	19	–	–	44	20	1
St Kitts and Nevis	9	23	4	–	36	–	–	28	10	15	–	–	53	11	4
St Lucia	8	24	9	–	41	2	13	21	6	10	–	1	53	6	8
St Vincent and the Grenadines	10	26	–	8	44	12	3	23	4	8	–	–	50	6	8
Trinidad and Tobago	91	6	–	–	97	–	–	–	–	–	–	–	–	3	2
Turks and Caicos Islands	2	15	27	–	44	–	–	44	4	6	–	–	54	2	1

Table 9.3 (continued)   Caribbean Development Bank: Percentage distribution of loans, contingent loans, equity and grants approved (net) by sector for each country, 1970–88

Country	Directly productive sector					Economic infrastructure and other								Multi-sector	Percentage of total
	Agriculture, forestry and fishing	Manufacturing	Tourism	Mining	Total	Power and energy	Water	Transportation and communication	Housing	Education (including student loans)	Health	Sanitation	Total		
Regional:															
LDC Focus	3	2	1	–	6	2	–	77	–	–	–	–	79	15	6
MDC Focus	–	–	–	–	–	–	–	100	1	–	–	–	100	–	1
LDC/MDC Focus	3	4	10	–	17	4	1	3	1	17	–	–	26	57	2
Total	14	21	4	0	39	5	4	27	6	6	1	2	51	10	100

Source: Caribbean Development Bank Annual Report 1988, Barbados, Appendix 1 – F, p. 84.

was put at US$2 million, less than half of one per cent of the CDB's total resources. The CDB's ability to raise loans within the region is thus very much open to question.

This is in direct contrast to its efforts at mobilising resources outside the region. From an initial capital base of US$50 million, the CDB has expanded the combined resources of its OCR and SFR to over US$733 million, virtually all from non-Commonwealth Caribbean countries. Its efforts to mobilise domestic resources and develop capital markets within the region have been confined to making two public bond issues of US$15 million in Trinidad and Tobago. These early successes have not been repeated. The CDB has, however, channelled substantial resources to local financial centres and development finance corporations for on-lending. At least one-third of all its lending was absorbed in this way.

At one level, this is indicative of the CDB's success in strengthening and promoting the financial infrastructure and institutions of its Commonwealth Caribbean members. At another level though, it goes to the heart of a major dilemma. The proliferation of national development banks, finance corporations and related financial institutions imposes a serious strain on the CDB's technical and professional services. Secondly, most of the smaller member states do not have enough qualified and trained staff to service these institutions. Consequently, there has been a lot of slippage in terms of performance and repayment. The Caribbean Investment Corporation, for example, had to be wound up, and several LDCs are in arrears on repayment of outstanding loans.

For a long time, the CDB has been concerned over the multiplicity of special funds, most of which are pre-packaged for specified projects. A reduction in the number (though not the resources) of these funds, and, more particularly, some liberalisation and rationalisation of their operational requirements would clearly reduce operating costs and improve efficiency. It has also repeatedly expressed concern over the proliferation of statutory corporations acting as executing agencies for projects financed by the Bank. The inefficiency and operating standards of many of these financial intermediaries, particularly in the LDCs, not only adversely affect its international credit-rating (as a Bank) but also make it more difficult for CDB to raise replenishment funds and so fulfill its developmental role to the full.

The CDB has performed reasonably well as a Bank. It is in surplus and it has a high credit-rating. As Table 9.4 shows, it also compares favourably with the World Bank and other regional development banks in terms of profitability (income before interest as a proportion of total assets) and its liquidity ratio (liquid assets as a proportion of undisbursed loans). The table also shows how poorly endowed the CDB is as compared with the other multilateral financial institutions. It urgently needs to increase its capital base and its capacity to raise additional resources.

Table 9.4   Performance indicators of the regional banks and the World Bank 1986

		Inter-American Development Bank	African Development Bank	Asian Development Bank	Caribbean Development Bank	World Bank
1	Establishment (Year)	1960	1964	1966	1970	1945
2	Membership (Number)					
	initial[a]	20	25	31	18	n.a.
	Present total	44	75	47	23	135[b]
	Regional countries	27	50	32	20	–
	Developed countries	18	17	18	3	26[b]
3	Voting power (%)					
	Initial					
	Developing	58.18	100.00	35.34	64.90	n.a.
	Developed	41.82	nil	64.66	35.10	n.a.
	Present total					
	Developing	54.01	67.93	45.088	67.37	37.55[b]
	Developed	45.99	32.07	54.912	32.63	62.45[b]
4	Authorised capital (US$m.)					
	Initial amount	813	250	1,100	50	–
	Present amount	34,073[c]	6,605	19,663	347	77,526[b]
	Subscribed by					
	Developing	9,538	4,583	7,973	225.6	24,149
	Developed	24,535	2,022	11,503	121.4	55,273
	Paid-in total	2,600	1,625	2,354	80.2	6,850
	Callable total	31,474	4,877	17,122	266.7	72,571
	Callable, developed	14,509	n.a.	10,118	93.7	n.a.
5	Statutory funds (US$m.)[d]					
	Cumulative total	8,397	4,291	7,745	435.0	40,723
	Recent replenishment	703	2,700	3,600	118.5[g]	12,400
6	Other funds (US$m.)					
	Cumulative total	1,188	305	82	–	–
7	Gross borrowings (US$m.)					
	Cumulative total	12,155	2,156	7,561	148.4	65,846
	1986	1,911	202	813	–	10,500
8	Loan approvals ($m.)					
	Cumulative total	35,438	8,445	19,491	678.4	n.a.
	Average (84–85)	3,222	1,225	2,048	47.2	15,426
	All statutory funds					
	cumulative total	10,666	3,603	6,175	–	n.a.
	Average (84–86)	273	746	651	–	3,248
9	Loan disbursements (US$m.)					
	Cumulative total	24,027	3,139	6,092	491.3	n.a.
	Average (84–86)	2,328	497	645	42.6	11,219
	All statutory funds					
	total	–	1,297	2,384	–	n.a.
	Average (84–86)	568	212	367	–	2,743
10	Assets (US$m.)	17,847	3,470	11,354	179.1	108,224
11	Profitability (%)[e]	7.5	6.0	7.7	6.8	6.3
12	Liquidity (%)[f]	40.7	44.5	71.0	62.5	68.8
13	Administrative expenses (US$m.)	165	92	86	7.2	746

a Initially the IDB had one developed member; AfDB had none; ADB had 15.
b IBRD only.
c Including inter-regional capital.
d Fund for Special Operations (FSO) in the IDB; African Development Fund (AfDF) in the AfDB; and Asian Development Fund (ADF) in the ADB. World Bank figures are for IDA, the Special Fund and the African Facility.
e Profitability is income before interest as a proportion of total assets.
f Liquidity-ratio is liquid assets (cash and investments) as a proportion of undisbursed loans.
g Pledged for the period 1988 to 1991.
n.a. not applicable.
    not readily available.

Sources: Compiled from annual reports of the respective institutions.

Regional co-operation and integration

Since its inception, the CDB has worked tirelessly to promote regional co-operation and integration. It has helped members to co-ordinate their development programmes so as to achieve better utilisation of their resources, make their economies more complementary and to promote the orderly expansion of their international trade, particularly intra-regional trade. It has accordingly promoted projects which have a direct integration aspect principally in agriculture, transportation, industry and energy.

In the field of agriculture, the CDB has promoted and financed regional agricultural projects, including fisheries and livestock, as part of the Regional Food Plan, adopted by CARICOM in December 1975. More recently, it helped in the development and adoption of the New Marketing Arrangements for Primary Agricultural Products and Livestock which aims to increase the region's net foreign exchange earnings through a reduction of its food import bill and an increase in the value of agricultural exports marketed both within the region and to other Third World countries. It also played a major role in devising the Agricultural Sector Programme (1987–91) for the co-ordination and integration of agricultural policies and programmes within the region.

The CDB's policy in the industrial sector has been to support and promote projects which will not only make industrial development throughout the region more complementary, but also lead to more orderly market-sharing and the development of internationally competitive enterprises. To this end, it works closely with CARICOM in devising guidelines and instruments for implementing the Common Market trade and development policy (e.g. Customs Tariff, Rules of Origin and the Fiscal Incentive Regime). It also helped to mount the first Caribbean Manufacturers' Exhibition in Barbados in 1985. On a cumulative basis, 9% of CDB's funds have been allocated to regional projects, with the main emphasis placed on the LDCs.

Additionally, it provides funding for numerous other regional programmes, workshops and projects.[4] The rewards have not, however, been commensurate with its efforts. Performance in the productive sector, the main focus of its attention, has been at best, patchy. Agriculture, in particular, remains a major headache. Also, several programmes have either stalled or had to be wound up because of financing and implementation problems. The major expansion of intra-regional trade, one of the main planks of its regional co-operation and development policy, has not materialised. Indeed, the reverse has happened. Most of the region's growth in trade is with non-regional members. Further, imports have increased while exports show very little growth, adding to the members' balance of payments problems.

On the positive side, the CDB's policy of special treatment for the LDCs has definitely paid off. Their economies are stronger, essential infrastructure has been put in place, and their growth rates exceed those of the MDCs. Inflation is also much lower in the LDCs. The danger of polarisation and uneven distribution of benefits inherent in regional co-operation and integration has been largely avoided. However, while CDB funds have played a crucial role in developing and strengthening the economies of the LDCs, they may eventually prove counter-productive to the process of regional integration. Lacking a history of economic co-operation and a strong basis for integration, the LDCs have always preferred to go it alone, and the CDB's funds have strengthened the economies of individual members to stand on their own. A considerable number of Bank-financed projects are duplicated throughout the LDCs, and there has been little progress in the harmonisation of their economic and financial policies, structures and systems.[5]

The CDB has developed important links with bilateral as well as multilateral donors and agencies. Among other things, it provides an effective channel for disbursing and monitoring donors' aid programmes, most of whom prefer to centralise operations and deal with the CDB, rather than operate a series of small aid programmes in individual countries. The expertise and contact acquired have proved invaluable for improving the administration and effectiveness of aid to the region. Additionally, it has developed valuable contacts and working relations with various international institutions and governments which contribute to its SDF and other special funds.

It has also made a major contribution to regional aid policy and co-ordination. It participates in the work of the Caribbean Group for Co-operation in Economic Development (CGCED) which serves as a mechanism for the co-ordination and strengthening of external assistance to the Caribbean and for the continuing review of national and regional activities related to economic development of the region. Further, the CDB was very active in the promotion of the Caribbean Development Facility (CDF) as a mechanism for channelling foreign resources to help finance essential imports and to offer supplementary financing mainly for local costs in the execution of development programmes and projects.[6]

The future

The CDB has coped well with the problems of the past. It has gained the respect and confidence of the international financial community. This is a major achievement. Quite clearly though, it is being asked to do too many things with the limited resources at its disposal, and there is the danger of spreading its resources and energies too thinly over too wide a field. With twenty years of operational experience to draw on, now would seem an appropriate time to undertake a major and comprehensive review of its activities and operations. Among other things, this would identify its strengths and weaknesses, assess its achievements, and help to develop new strategies and policy responses to the problems of the 1990s.

One of the first problems to be addressed is undoubtedly the adequacy of resources. The CDB just does not have enough resources to finance all its operations. In 1988, for example, OCR loans fell to 20% of total gross loan approvals (10% lower than the previous year) mainly as a result of the shortages of loanable funds. The admission of Italy and Germany when formalities are completed, will provide a fresh injection of capital. But this will only be enough to finance its operations until 1991, after which, the problem will resurface. A substantial increase in capital is urgently needed to ensure that it does not start the 1990s with a serious liquidity crisis on its hands. The CDB is itself aware of this possibility, and has already initiated negotiations for a general increase in capital. It has also decided to have a regular (four-yearly) review of capital adequacy.

The admission of these two non-regional members will obviously facilitate borrowing in international capital markets. More needs to be done though, within the region itself, to increase the CDB's lending and borrowing capacity as well as to develop and exploit regional capital markets. The Bank could, for example, issue local currency bonds in member countries, or encourage member governments to do so, either at home or within the region. There is a considerable amount of liquidity within the region which can easily be mobilised, if the appropriate financial instruments existed. The CDB must take measures to develop this market.

New members bring new resources. However, given the requirement that ownership and control must rest with the regional members, the admission of non-regional members is limited to the status of minority shareholders. Further, the statutory limits placed on the number of shares which they can hold and their voting rights mean that new non-regional members can only be accommodated within very narrowly defined limits, or by a reallocation of existing non-regional members' quotas. This is what happened in the case of France and Italy, when Britain's and Canada's quotas were reduced to make room for them. A similar rearrangement will be necessary in order to accommodate Germany.

On the other hand, there are not many Caribbean countries left to join the CDB. In any case, their membership will not significantly increase its resources. There are also not many other regional (i.e. Latin American) countries anxious to join the CDB. Nor are there likely to be, for a variety of reasons. Regional membership seems, in effect, to have reached its limit. The CDB is thus faced with a dilemma which is very much of its own making. An increase in the membership of its regional (i.e. majority) shareholders is unlikely to strengthen its capital base sufficiently, or to provide enough additional resources to finance expansion of its OCR operations. At the same time, its Charter restricts the extent to which non-regional members (i.e. countries with the necessary resources) can subscribe to the Bank's capital. It is a case where those who have the resources cannot increase their share of the CDB's capital, while those who do not have the resources, can do so.

The division of subscriptions and voting rights clearly lies at the heart of this dilemma. It may have made sense to reserve majority rights to regional members at the outset. But times have changed. So, too, have the nature and functions of international capital. The CDB has established itself as a reputable and efficient multilateral financial institution. It no longer needs to prove itself. There is also no longer any need to get hung up on outdated dogma. Regional ownership and control are no longer an essential prerequisite for the CDB. They are, in fact, an unnecessary and expensive restriction in its operations and ought to be relaxed. A more appropriate division of subscriptions and voting rights should therefore be devised, which would reflect the realities and requirements of the 1990s, and at the same time preserve the essential characteristics of the CDB.

As the data in Table 9.4 show, the other regional banks have already gone some way towards reducing the disparity in terms of capital subscriptions and voting rights between (i) regional and non-regional members, and (ii) developed and developing countries. The African Development Bank, for example, started out with all the voting rights reserved for African members. The proportion has now fallen to roughly two-thirds mainly to accommodate the admission of developed countries. More significantly, its authorised capital jumped from $250 million to $6.6 billion as a result. Similarly, the Inter-American Development Bank had one developed country member when it was established in 1960. The number now stands at 18 (out of a total membership of 44). Of the Bank's share capital, 72% is held by these developed country members, who collectively hold 46% of the voting rights.

Two things emerge from this brief comparison. Firstly, any major injection of new capital will have to be accompanied by a revision of the distribution of voting rights in favour of those providing the funds. In the case of the CDB, this obviously requires the admission of additional non-regional members and a readjustment of the present statutory division of voting rights between regional and non-regional members. Secondly, the original preoccupation with ownership and control has largely been super-seded and rendered irrelevant by the need to attract additional external resources and the rapid globalisation of international capital markets. The other regional development banks have successfully responded to these developments without compromising the regional characteristics of their existence and operations. There is no reason to suggest that the experience of the CDB will be different.

The review body which is currently studying the need for a general increase in capital will have to address this dilemma. Among the questions which need to be thoroughly examined are (i) what constraints, if any, does the statutory requirement of regional ownership and control impose on the efficiency and conduct of the CDB's banking and financial operations, and how can these be removed? (ii) what does the concept of Caribbean charac-teristics of the CDB mean in the context of the globalisation of international capital markets? (iii) how, and in what respects, would the nature and characteristics of the CDB be affected, if the present division of subscrip-tion and voting rights were varied? and (iv) how would an increase in the proportion of the CDB's callable capital, which presently stands at 76%, affect its operations? The corresponding figure for the Inter-American Development Bank and the World Bank exceeds 90%. How can the CDB's capital base be restructured to bring it into line with that of these institu-tions, and what effect will this have on the regional members' ability to provide the necessary guarantees?

The CDB urgently needs to decide what its role and relationship with the private sector should be, and the extent to which it should get involved in activities traditionally reserved for that sector. Its private-sector portfolio has not been fully developed and remains out of focus with the rest of its operations. Less than 4% of all its loans have gone to the private sector, and even then a substantial proportion of them has gone bad. According to the 1988 Annual Report, 'Provision for loan losses increased by 73% to $1.9 million, mainly because of difficulties in the Bank's private-sector loans portfolio. At the end of 1988, cumulative provisions for loan losses amount to $10.4 million, or 7.8% of loans outstanding, compared with 7.3% at the end of 1987'.[7] The private sector, for its part, complains that there are many layers of administration, each with its own conditionality leading, in turn, to a bewildering array of cross-conditionality; also, that there are too many delays in procurement, validation and other administrative procedures which increase costs and engender uncertainty.

The Bank has responded to these criticisms by improving its operating policies and procedures, restructuring its financial packages, and generally trying to win the confidence of the private sector. It provides up to two-thirds of the foreign exchange of project cost, subject to acceptable loan/equity ratios. However, much remains to be done, particularly in the field of equity financing, where the Bank's policies are unnecessarily cautious and conservative. The limits imposed on the level of participation in equity financing are now a serious constraint on its operations, and need to be relaxed.

Such a move would, in fact, be consistent with the present trend adopted by the World Bank and other regional development banks in respect of co-financing, parallel financing, joint ventures and other forms of participation with the private sector. The Bank must make this one of its main priorities for the 1990s. The Report of the Task Force appointed to survey the needs of the private sector should provide valuable guidance on the extent of the CDB's involvement and support for the private sector.

The debt crisis has not affected the CDB as such, mainly because it only lends to Caribbean members, and the amounts involved are not significant by world standards. In 1988, total loans outstanding amounted to $404 million. In terms of its current operations, total disbursements in 1988 ran to $58.2 million, almost $5 million up on the previous year. However, when repayments ($34.6 million) are taken into account, net transfers ($23.6 million) increased by only $1.7 million, hardly enough to keep pace with the region's demand for additional resources.

More important than aggregates though, is the fact that (i) hard loans are rapidly driving service payments up, and (ii) the amount of loans on 'non-accrual status' (i.e. the arrears) shot up sharply in 1988.[8] Arrears on OCR loans in 1988, for example, stood at $28 million, an increase of $5 million on 1987. This reduced the CDB's income by almost $4 million. In addition, arrears on the CDB's soft loan operations in 1988 exceeded $31 million, resulting in a further loss of almost $1 million. In essence, therefore, the makings of a major debt problem already exist, and all the signs are that it will get worse with the 1990s.

Furthermore, the CDB is not the only official creditor with debts outstanding in the region. Substantial amounts are also owed to various bilateral and multilateral creditors. In addition, the proportion of commercial debts is steadily increasing. The debt problem will therefore deteriorate rapidly for all the well-known reasons. So far, the Bank's response to the problem of arrears and mounting indebtedness has been to seek to declare itself a preferred creditor; a position adopted by the World Bank and other multilateral financial institutions. This is hardly an effective or sympathetic way to deal with the problem. A lot more thought and analysis is required for a viable long-term regional debt management strategy, in which the CDB plays a central role. This is undoubtedly the most significant contribution the Bank can make to resolving the debt problem of its members.

Additionally, there is the problem of export promotion, trade liberalisation and the need for additional financing facilities for intra-regional trade purposes. The pressure for action on these fronts will intensify as the Common External Tariff (CET) in the OECS gets fully operational and intra-regional trade revives. While most members have some form of government-sponsored export credit and insurance guarantee agency, these are still in their infancy, and vary vastly in terms of resources, operational coverage and experience. Also, they operate through the commercial banking system and are expensive. Having decided not to set up a Caribbean Export Bank, the CDB will have to explore and develop ways of accessing existing sources of export credit and of encouraging regional institutions to increase the supply of pre- and post-shipment credits on appropriate terms.

The CDB will also have to explore ways of reactivating the Caribbean Multilateral Clearing Facility (CMCF) which was wound up in 1983. The major problem to be resolved concerns the outstanding debts of Guyana which owes $98 million, virtually the total amount of credits available to the Facility. Can these be written off, or consolidated, and if so, how will this affect the credit-rating and operations of the new facility? Other outstanding issues concern such questions as, what commodities should be included; should it cover existing patterns of intra-regional trade, or encourage new ones; what proportion of foreign exchange coverage should it provide; and how can additional external resources be mobilised to supplement its operations? Notwithstanding the problems ahead, the CDB must find ways of re-establishing the CMCF (or some variant of it).

The CDB is required to maximise its net income, increase reserves, maintain a low loan/loss ratio and to satisfy all the other criteria of sound financial intermediation. At the same time, it is required to act as a development agency as well as to promote regional co-operation and integration. Although the CDB has tried valiantly to straddle these three fences, it really is faced with an impossible task, given the resources at its disposal, the multiplicity of its special funds and the compartmentalisation of its operations.

Nowhere is this more evident than in the LDCs. On the one hand, these members do not have enough bankable projects to utilise productively the Bank's hard funds (i.e. for the CDB to operate effectively as a Bank). On the other hand, they are the principal beneficiaries of its soft loan operations (its development agency role). The provision of subsidised loans and cheap credit is obviously intended to bring them to a stage where they can graduate to using the CDB's hard funds productively. This has not happened. The CDB's dual role is perceived essentially as being geographically rather than functionally separate – hard funds and bankable projects for the MDCs, and soft fund operations for the LDCs.

The CDB has to resolve this anomaly particularly as (i) its regional MDCs are now experiencing serious economic and financial problems and will increasingly look to it to provide additional development financing; and (ii) like other multilateral financial institutions, it will inevitably experience replenishment problems of its soft loan facilities. The LDCs have in fact done very well. With 13% of the region's population, they received 55% of total net loans and 90% of all grants. They hold 6.5% of the CDB's shares and contribute even less to its total resources. The concentration of the CDB's operations in the LDCs has helped them to outperform the MDCs. Perhaps now is the time to redress the imbalance in the pattern and distribution of its operations.

There is also need for the CDB to re-examine its sectoral priorities. The early emphasis on agriculture and tourism as the leading sectors seems to have given way to manufacturing and transport and communications without any appreciable improvement in overall economic performance of the beneficiary countries. The division between the directly productive sectors and economic and social infrastructure projects is, in fact, heavily skewed in favour of the latter. Given its limited resources and the economic and social characteristics of its members, it is legitimate to ask whether the present pattern of expenditure is appropriate for the region. Because regional members are small, export-oriented, middle-income countries, the regional policy imperative must surely be to increase revenue-earning capacity on a path of self-sustained growth. The CDB needs to re-orient its programmes to this end.

Finally, there is the question whether the CDB should get into structural adjustment. In the 1980s Jamaica was the only Caribbean regional member which had a structural adjustment programme with the World Bank. Guyana would, no doubt, have had one (or more) as well, if it had managed to sort out its problems with the IMF, the other key actor in the adjustment process. Before Jamaica embarked on an adjustment programme, its GDP fell by 20% between 1973 and 1980, and its public-sector deficit ranged between 14% and 18% of GDP. Without an adjustment programme, Guyana's economic performance continued to deteriorate. In 1987, its public-sector deficit amounted to 22.4% of GDP, and its per capita income is now the lowest of the CDB's members. It is, therefore, the obvious, perhaps the only, candidate for an adjustment programme.

However, to provide support for structural adjustment is very expensive. Only the World Bank and the IMF have the resources to mount and maintain these programmes. Also, there is no alternative for countries whose economies are facing protracted balance of payments and other structural problems other than to adjust. Experience from elsewhere suggests that although structural adjustment works, it takes time and ties up a lot of resources. Also, it requires sacrifices and hard policy decisions from the adjusting country.[9]

In summary, the 1990s will present the CDB with a series of major challenges. Several of these have been identified in this chapter, in particular, the shortage of funds. The CDB must increase its capitalisation. It must also mobilise additional resources in the region as well as internationally. The Caribbean is, in fact, well served by a variety of financial and commercial institutions, and there is no shortage of liquidity within the region. The CDB needs to develop new instruments and forms of financial co-operation with the private and commercial sector and the financial institutions for tapping into this market. This will require it to decide what its role and relationship with the banking and commercial sectors will be during the 1990s. Not much thought seems to have been given to this matter. The challenges which have been identified will require, *inter alia*, the CDB to expand its operations, not on all fronts at the same time, since it does not have the resources for that, but on a selective basis. There are too many separate special funds. Some of these can be consolidated and supplemented so as to allow greater *virement* of funds and flexibility of operations. They will also require the CDB to amend its Charter in several important respects. But this is not a bad thing. The essence of any viable institution is its ability to adapt to changing circumstances.

Notes

1 For a more detailed account, see, *CDB – Its Purpose, Role and Functions – Twenty Questions and Answers*; and *CDB, The First Ten Years 1970–1980*, Letchworth Press Ltd., Barbados, 1980.
2 Article 1, *Agreement Establishing the Caribbean Development Bank*, 1970. Barbados.
3 Article 12, *op. cit.*
4 For a detailed discussion of these programmes, see *Annual Reports*, Caribbean Development Bank, Barbados.
5 See George Abbott, *Fiscal Harmonisation in the Eastern Caribbean*, Commonwealth Secretariat, London, 1988. (Mimeo).
6 For a fuller account of CDB's contribution to regional integration, see *CDB – Its Purpose, Role and Functions, op. cit.* pp. 20–21.
7 *Annual Report 1988*, Caribbean Development Bank, Barbados, p. 70.

8 The Bank places in non-accrual status all loans on which payment of interest, other charges or principal is overdue by more than twelve months.
9 See *Adjustment Lending – An Evaluation of Ten Years of Experience*, Country Economics Department, Policy Research Series, The World Bank, Washington DC, December 1988.

CHAPTER 10

The role of Development Finance Corporations in the Commonwealth Caribbean

Compton Bourne

Development Finance Corporation (DFC) is the label generically applied to institutions established for the specific purpose of providing finance for economic development. DFCs have also been described as development banks, specialised credit agencies, and 'credit boards'. Although their primary function is finance, DFCs in many instances have been assigned other functions, including investment promotion services and technical assistance in the production operations of their clients.

Development finance corporations have a firm place in the financial sector of Commonwealth Caribbean economies. Every country has at least one DFC. This type of financial institution has been in existence for a considerable length of time in a few economies, notably Jamaica where the first DFC was established in 1951,[1] but in most cases its origin does not extend beyond the early 1970s. With few exceptions in the Caribbean, DFCs are public enterprises – with statutorily-defined goals, objectives and functions; with senior management appointed by the political directorate, and with overall operations subject to ministerial control; and with much of their loanable resources provided by government or guaranteed by government.

The present decade has witnessed quite substantial changes in the financial sector of the Commonwealth Caribbean. New financial institutions, new financial instruments, and new financial services have been introduced with important implications for the structure, organisation and functioning of the financial sector.[2] In relation to DFCs, several privately-owned DFCs have been established.[3] Furthermore, the organisation of the government-owned DFCs has undergone substantial change in some countries, notably Jamaica and Trinidad and Tobago.[4] These developments of recent vintage invite reconsideration of the role and operations of DFCs in the Commonwealth Caribbean.

Rationale for DFCs

The *raison d'être* for development finance companies is to be found in the discordance between the financial requirements of rapid and sustained economic development and the credit allocation practices of private financial institutions. One cannot fully comprehend the appeal of development finance companies in developing countries without an appreciation of the concept of development finance.

One dimension of development finance is the provision of financial capital to remove or at least relax the savings constraint on physical capital accumulation. Another important dimension is the quality of financial services. The specific qualitative attributes are the term-to-maturity of financial obligations and the extent of risk-bearing by financial institutions. These derive from the long-term investment capital requirements of new ventures and production innovations and the greater-than-normal perceived riskiness of such activities. Financial flows to development enterprises or projects would tend to be less liquid and more risky than flows to already established enterprises and projects. A third dimension to the concept of development finance is the use of 'social cost-benefit' criteria instead of 'financial rate of return' criteria in credit allocation decisions. Social cost-benefit criteria take explicit account of externalities associated with the project as well as established internal performance standards not necessarily measured or measurable in market prices or not necessarily generating project income. Financial rate of return criteria disregard externalities and calculate only those outcomes that impose project costs or yield project income. In many cases, the two sets of criteria lead to conflicting financing decisions.

The fourth aspect of development finance is the widespread policy of subsidised interest rates. Several arguments are frequently advanced in support of interest rate subsidies. One is that low interest rates are a necessary incentive to investment and to adoption of new technologies. Another argument is that new projects are unlikely to generate sufficiently high financial rates of return to be feasible at market rates of interest. It is also claimed that low interest rates are required to compensate for disincentives and distortions elsewhere in the economic system.

These arguments are questionable on several counts. Credit supply constraints rather than price incentive effects on credit demand might be dominant, so that the critical policy consideration should not be the use of interest rates to induce loan demand but the establishment of an institutional and economic framework supportive of an expanded loan capacity and loan supply. Furthermore, adding interest rate distortions to existing distortions in production and trade is not self-evidently second-best policy and might in fact increase allocative inefficiency and encourage adoption of inappropriate capital-intensive production technologies.

In reality, the situation has been evolving in the direction of greater participation in development finance by the major private credit institutions. The term structure of commercial bank lending is now considerably longer than it used to be. For example, the Eastern Caribbean Central Bank reports that long-term loans comprised 74% of commercial bank loans in the OECS economies in December 1987, compared with 51% in 1982. As another example, the percentage of Barbadian commercial bank term loans with maturity greater than five years increased from 26% in 1975 to 45% in 1987. The growth of non-bank financial intermediaries, especially merchant banks and finance companies has also resulted in an expanded supply of venture capital, unsecured lending, and capital equipment leasing services, all of which generally enhance the quality of finance.

However, the pace and nature of the spread of financial services are not entirely satisfactory. Financial resource flows favour well-established enterprises *vis-à-vis* new entrepreneurs. Key economic sectors appear to be relatively neglected. Credit allocation decisions are guided by financial rate of return criteria and do not reflect social benefit-cost considerations. Furthermore, there is an underlying fragility to much of the unsecured lending resulting from the lack of transparency in lender-client relationships and the close corporate inter-relationship between some financial institutions and their credit customers.[5]

DFCs are an institutional device for ensuring greater convergence between the supply side of domestic finance and the demand for development finance. DFCs are required to specialise in long-term lending, to adopt social benefit-cost criteria in credit allocation decisions, and to charge concessionary rates of interest. Frequently, also, DFCs are required to undertake other supportive activity of a developmental nature not usually conducted by other financial institutions. These include provision of technical assistance, investment promotion, and equity financing. There is also typically some credit targeting of particular categories of potential loan beneficiaries. The rest of this chapter provides a detailed discussion on these aspects of the role of DFCs.

Goal setting or goal ascription

Development finance corporations are ascribed a set of statutorily-defined objectives which they should seek to attain by manipulation of the credit resources and other resources at their command. In theory, these objectives define the preference functions of DFCs. The objectives have been variously defined in terms of economic development, employment creation, generation of national income, import-substitution, export earnings, and wealth creation at national, sectoral or sub-sectoral levels. In essence, the preference functions ascribed to development finance corporations are social preference functions. Theophilus (1986) maintains that there are contradictory public and political expectations of DFCs. They are expected to yield commercial returns on their operations as well as to function as instruments of social and welfare policies.

DFCs and borrowing costs

The cost of credit obtained by borrowers in formal financial markets is comprised of explicit interest rate charges, implicit interest charges, and transaction costs. Transaction costs include transportation and related expenses incurred in sourcing and servicing the loan, the opportunity cost of waiting time, and expenses (such as legal fees, costs of forms, application fees) associated with the processing of the loan application. Official attention is mainly focused on explicit interest rates, even though it is readily appreciated that implicit interest charges (e.g. through compensating balances requirements) must be incorporated in accurate estimates of true interest costs.

Development finance corporations impose explicit interest charges considerably below those prevailing at commercial banks and other financial intermediaries. In most Commonwealth Caribbean countries, DFCs' loan rates are less than 8% per annum while commercial bank loan rates range from 10% to 15%, and the latter institutions seem no less prone to implicit interest charges than the DFCs. Through their concessionary or 'below-market' loan rates of interest, DFCs may lower average loan rates within the formal financial sector provided the loan market is segmented and there is no credit arbitrage between the two segments. The extent to which DFCs' interest rate practices increase the interest rate elasticity of the credit supply function of the entire market would vary directly with the share of the DFCs credit portfolio in the total supply. Because DFCs are a small part of the total formal financial sector, this role is rather limited in a quantitative sense.

Concessionary rates of interest may be rationalised in qualitative terms. One possibility is that in the absence of interest rate subsidies the net operating revenues of new entrepreneurial activities would be insufficiently attractive either because of initial marketing difficulties or because their unit operating costs are high during the learning phase. Figure 10.1 illustrates the positive impact of credit subsidies on loan demand and investment. The marginal revenue curve MR represents the loan demand-interest rate relationship defined by the borrower's net operating revenues. MC is the DFC's loan offer function. The socially desired level of loans, L*, will only be demanded at interest rate R* which is less than the market rate R.

However, it is worth noting that interest rate subsidies are not the only means of fostering socially optimal loan demand. Direct fiscal transfers, tax allowances, and higher commodity prices are options. Any of these increase marginal revenue (say from MR to MR_1), permitting higher affordable rates of interest.

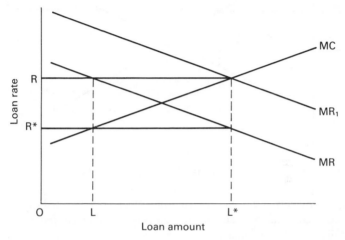

Fig 10.1   Interest rate subsidies and net operating revenues effects on loan demand.

The second justification for concessionary interest rates is along the following lines. DFCs have unusually high unit lending costs in their early years of operation when their staff might be inexperienced, systems are new or untried, and loan volume is small. However, both risk costs and administrative costs would be expected to decline because of learning by doing and economies of scale (Anderson and Khambata, 1985). These unusually high lending costs should not be passed on in their entirety to credit customers. The subsidy policy is thus defended in terms of moral restraint in the exercise of market power. Moreover, it can be expected to diminish as lending costs approach their normal level. Figure 10.2 depicts the early phase marginal cost curve as MC and the 'mature' phase marginal cost curve as MC_1. When MC prevails, the equilibrium loan rate is R and loan amount is L whereas when MC_1 prevails the loan rate is R_1 (less than R) and the loan amount is L_1 (greater than L). The maxim is to price on the basis of MC_1.

It is possible that interest rate concessions are negated considerably by transaction costs incurred by DFC customers. Little attention has been paid to transaction costs as a component of total borrowing costs in appraisals of Caribbean DFCs despite widespread complaints among credit applicants about protracted and expensive credit appraisal procedures and long

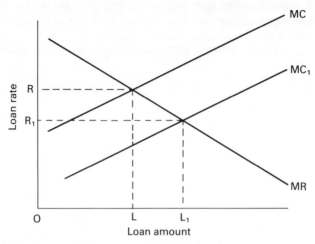

Fig 10.2   Loan pricing at run marginal lending costs.

disbursement lags. Evidence drawn from other countries indicated that transaction costs can outweigh interest costs in development financing and might dissuade credit demand.[6]

DFCs as agents of technical change

Almost invariably, DFCs provide technical assistance services to their credit customers. There is thus a combination of financial assistance and technical assistance. The latter set of activities may be an expression of the explicit technical change-promoting role of DFCs. Not only do they provide credit, they may also seek to introduce improved production practices, upgrade capital equipment, and increase managerial knowledge and skills among their credit clientele. The provision of credit is itself a vehicle for technological improvement given the bias in investment expenditures towards capital goods and the embodiment of technology in those goods.

However, some scepticism may be entertained about the role of DFCs as agents of technical change. First of all, technical assistance activities in practice are more in the nature of credit supervision intended to reduce the incidence of credit diversion and to enhance loan repayment performance. Secondly, DFCs are so thinly staffed with the requisite production, marketing, and enterprise management expertise that their technical services must be deficient in both scope and quality. A considerable expansion in technical resources would be required to make the technological progress role meaningful. It is not self-evident, however, that technical assistance is necessarily the business of DFCs and that DFCs can have a comparative

advantage in this sphere. It might be more efficient to transfer these functions to specialist agencies.

Funding and the availability of credit

The major contribution DFCs are expected to make is in the supply of
credit. DFCs are intended to increase the availability of credit to development enterprises in general or to particular sectors, industries, or types of
eligible enterprises classified by production, income, or net worth. The
extent to which they do so depends upon the strength of their own finances,
their credit allocation policies and practices, and the loan repayment performance of their credit customers. Each of these warrants discussion.

To begin, one may note that the loan portfolios of most DFCs have
grown significantly during the present decade. Table 10.1 presents some
details on disbursements for a sample of DFCs. In some instances there has
been a decline since 1985. Despite their recent expansion, the DFCs have
not made a major quantitative impact on the total provision of loanable
funds in their respective economies. Table 10.2 shows that DFC loans are
no more than 12% of the loan balances of commercial banks alone, not to
mention the entire commercial loan system.

The loan volume of DFCs is mainly a consequence of their funding
policies. Their main sources of funds are the local government, regional and
extra-regional multilateral financial institutions, and foreign governmental
agencies. Table 10.3 presents some approximate data on the liability structure of a few DFCs in recent years. Share capital and accrued reserves
typically comprise between 10% and 20% of total liabilities. Government
loans and grants include receipts from the central government and from
government-owned commercial banks, and national insurance funds. In
several instances they comprise between 20% and 46% of total financial
liabilities. The Caribbean Development Bank is a major funding agency for
DFCs in the OECS member countries, the Virgin Islands and Belize, but not
in Jamaica, Barbados, Guyana, Trinidad and Tobago, or The Bahamas. The
main extra-regional multilateral funding agencies are the Inter-American
Development Bank, the World Bank, and the European Investment Bank,
while the main foreign governments contributing to DFCs are the USA and
Canada. The multilateral financial institutions feature more importantly in
Jamaica, Barbados, Dominica, and Trinidad and Tobago. Foreign governments comprise a particularly large source of funds in Jamaica and Guyana.
It should not be imagined that the patterns are static. The DFCs experience
periods of low capitalisation. The multilateral financial institutions had no
role in Trinidad and Tobago until 1984, and have contributed no new flows
to Guyana in recent years.

It is clear that DFCs have built up experience in intermediating between international financial institutions and foreign governmental agencies and the local borrowing community. This role is highly important in situations where economic development is constrained both by a savings gap (i.e. insufficiency of national savings relative to warranted investment) and by a foreign exchange gap (i.e. insufficiency of foreign exchange resources relative to those warranted by investment and production plans).

Table 10.1   Disbursements by DFCs: (selected Caribbean Countries), 1980–88 $m (local currency)

DFC	1980	1981	1982	1983	1984	1985	1986	1987	1988
Jamaica ACB[1]			1.0	4.3	5.3	66.9	93.4	127.2	n.a.
Barbados Dev. Bank	5.0	11.0	20.6	15.7	14.9	19.0	21.6	23.7	30.5
Dominica AIDB	0.9	2.0	2.6	3.6	4.2	5.1	6.4	n.a.	n.a.
GAIBANK	n.a.	23.3	24.6	29.4	40.5	28.8	n.a.	n.a.	n.a.
T&T ADB	48.3	41.3	61.3	26.4	24.8	24.7	19.7	19.8	19.9
T&T DFC	49.1	66.8	80.4	87.4	56.7	50.8	69.7	39.1	50.6
Virgin Island Dev. Bank	0.15	0.34	0.37	0.58	1.09	1.31	1.01	n.a.	n.a.
St Lucia Dev. Bank		0.52	1.66	3.84	4.03	5.4	n.a.	5.8	7.1
Dev. Bank of St Kitts-Nevis	n.a.	n.a.	n.a.	1.31	1.96	3.03	3.57	4.5	

[1]The Jamaica ACB started operations in 1982 and St Lucia Development Bank in 1981.
Source: Annual reports of the individual financial institutions.

Table 10.2   DFC loans outstanding as per cent of commercial bank loans outstanding (selected Caribbean countries).

DFC	Year	%
Jamaica ACB	1967	5.8
Barbados Development Bank	1988	9.4
Dominica AIDB	1986	12.2
GAIBANK	1985	0.5
T&T ADB	1983	3.1
T&T DFC	1987	3.1
Bahamas Development Bank	1988	1.8
St Lucia Dev. Bank	1988	8.3
Dev. Bank of St Kitts-Nevis	1987	7.8

Source: Annual reports of the DFCs and Quarterly Statistical Digest (Bulletin) of the central banks of the respective countries.

Table 10.3 Percentage structure of liabilities of selected DFCs (selected Caribbean countries).

DFC	Year	Capital	Local government Grant/loan	CDB	Multilateral financial institutions	Foreign governments	Other	Total[1]
Jamaica ACB Ltd.	1986	14.9	23.9	3.0	17.4	37.1	3.7	100.0
Barbados Dev. Bank	1987	3.3	18.7	1.6	34.3	–	42.1	100.0
Dominica AIDB	1986	7.9	7.9	55.6	26.8	–	1.8	100.0
GAIBANK	1985	10.6	–	–	–	89.4	–	100.0
T&T DFC	1988	23.5	21.4	–	32.9	–	22.2	100.0
Bahamas Dev. Bank	1988	42.0	46.4	8.6	–	–	3.4	100.0
Virgin Islands Dev. Bank	1986	15.0	33.2	50.4	–	–	1.4	100.0
St Lucia Dev. Bank	1988	20.9	27.2	34.5	7.0	–	10.3	100.0

[1]Totals may not necessarily add due to rounding.
Source: Annual reports of the individual financial institutions.

However, the exercise of this function is not without its problems. Bourne and Graham (1980) have highlighted the inordinate and restrictive influence of funding agencies on credit portfolio choice, the maturity structure of the credit portfolio, and interest rate practices. In brief, funding agencies exclude segments of the potential credit market on the basis of type of production activity and income or wealth status; prohibit the financing of working capital or refinancing of debt with their credit tranches; and stipulate both the interest rate spread and on-lending loan rate of interest. These limit the ability of the DFCs to engage in portfolio diversification by enterprise type or activity or by loan maturities, and limit the scope for cost-recovery. Furthermore, there are considerable exchange rate costs associated with foreign currency funding in those Caribbean economies characterised by persistent and large exchange rate depreciations. In cases where the costs are borne by the credit customer, loan delinquency may escalate to crippling proportions, as the Jamaican experience of the late 1970s demonstrates (Bourne and Graham (1980)). In some cases, the foreign exchange rate risks are legally borne by the local government but, as Theophilus (1986) notes ruefully, in practice the DFCs 'carry the can'. In such instances, the damaging effect on the DFCs' balance sheet is more immediate and certain.

Difficulties related to portfolio restrictions and interest rate policies also ensue from local government funding. A pervasive problem closely linked to the dependence of DFCs on government finances (as well as on foreign agencies' capital guaranteed by the local government) is the widespread perception among credit clienteles that DFCs are agencies for providing financial grants *de facto* as distinct from credit which intrinsically carries repayment obligations. The perception that DFCs are grant institutions rather than credit institutions is reinforced by several features of their operating milieu: their own weak loan enforcement systems; the extreme tardiness and prohibitively expensive nature of the Caribbean judicial machinery; community approbation of property repossession and sale; and political interference with DFC management.

There is an element of temporal fragility in the specialisation of DFC funding. Bourne and Graham (1980) have commented on the discontinuity of funding and the short, episodic life cycles which seem to characterise rural development banks. The underlying reasons are the fragility of public finances in primary commodity exporting economies, loss of confidence among funding agencies, the shifting balance of forces in political competition for public-sector financial resources, and the corrosive effect of loan defaults.

Commonwealth Caribbean DFCs have had little experience with domestic resource mobilisation from private institutions and individuals. This is so despite the fact that the statutes of most DFCs envisage and permit domestic issue of financial liabilities. Only the Barbados Development Bank and the Virgin Islands Development Bank have made sustained efforts at bond financing or deposit financing. DFCs may be able to stabilise their funding and even increase the volume of their financial resources by deposit mobilisation, issues of bonds and shares, and by collaboration with other financial institutions on various methods of indirect financial intermediation.

Deposit mobilisation offers not only the prospect of enhanced funding, but also the possibility of sizeable economies of scale. One important source of cost complementarity is the financial information assembled on depositors who are also credit customers, thereby enabling better and less costly appraisal of creditworthiness. Commonwealth Caribbean DFCs have been largely resistant to the expansion of their functions to include deposit services. A frequent objection is that these services would be too costly for the DFCs and would be uncompetitive with the commercial banks and other established depository institutions. Another objection is that it would compromise their developmental mission. With respect to the matter of competitiveness, it should be noted that new entrants to the deposit market have in fact succeeded in attracting deposits, mainly on the basis of interest rate competition with the commercial banks. True enough, the corollary is higher loan charges, but if the binding constraint on potential development projects is the availability of funds (as maintained by say, neo-liberalists), then the case for deposit mobilisation remains strong. Evidence from the wider Caribbean also suggests that Commonwealth Caribbean DFCs might be unduly pessimistic about their prospects in the deposit market. Despite low per capita incomes among their clientele, rural development banks in the Dominican Republic succeeded in attracting a large number of savings accounts and sizeable deposit balances (Gonsalez-Vega *et al.*, 1988; Poyo, 1988).

The growth of demand for corporate equity, particularly that of financial institutions, presents additional opportunities for financial innovation by DFCs directed towards improving their capitalisation and increasing their lending resources. Development finance corporations may issue bonds. This has been done successfully by the Barbados Development Bank. A great deal depends upon the financial history of the DFC and upon the overall stability of the financial system. DFCs that do not have a reputation for financial soundness and profitability are likely to experience difficulties in persuading potential investors to hold their debentures. Similar problems would confront stock issue. However, whereas confidence in DFCs' bonds may be strengthened by government guarantees, such a possibility is absent for stock issues.

Another seemingly difficult problem arises in relation to stock issue, namely the retention of the predominant model of government ownership.

Stock acquisition by private enterprises and individuals would constitute a departure from this model. However, it is perhaps time for reconsideration in the light of two factors. Firstly, the public ownership model is not universal, and already within the Caribbean privately-owned DFCs are beginning to appear. Secondly, some degree of divestment of state ownership has started in several countries on quite pragmatic economic grounds. Public ownership may not be necessary to ensure that DFCs pursue their development mandate.

The final set of domestic resources mobilisation opportunities involve intermediation between the DFC and other financial institutions. This indirect intermediation takes the form of DFCs incurring financial liabilities to the other domestic financial institutions. One possibility is DFC indebtedness to commercial banks. Commercial banks, as already noted, are the major mobilisers of domestic financial savings, but display an aversion to long-term, risky loans to development enterprises. DFC on-lending of funds provided by commercial banks can bring about an improvement in the social efficiency of financial intermediation without compromising the solvency and profitability of commercial banks. Commercial banks are concerned with the liquidity of their asset portfolios. Liquidity targets are principally met by statutory reserves and short-term money market instruments. However, a second line of defence is the short-term nature of commercial loans. An important consideration, therefore, is the extent to which loans to DFCs will have the requisite liquidity. One mechanism for achieving this is to include them in the set of commercial bank assets eligible for rediscounting by the Central Bank. This involves no deviation from the Central Bank's role as lender of last resort, but instead takes advantage of that role by extending it beyond the traditional short-term government securities and commercial paper.

Another mechanism relies upon the existence of statutory reserve requirements imposed upon commercial banks. Some proportion of those reserves may be earmarked for on-lending by the Central Bank to DFCs. In this scheme, the commercial banks have claims on the Central Bank (not on the DFCs), and the Central Bank has claims on the DFC. There is therefore no danger of capital loss to the commercial banks as a barrier to their participation in the scheme. Indeed, since the reserves are statutory, they have no option but to participate. There may be a practical difficulty presented by a tendency for Ministries of Finance to treat government recurrent budgetary requirements as a priority claim on statutory non-cash reserves. The scheme also requires the Central Bank to take a more activist developmental role.

A small proportion of commercial bank assets can make a big difference to the on-lending resources of DFCs. For instance, 1% of commercial bank assets would add another $9.4 million to the Bahamas Development

Bank's loan portfolio, $100 million to the Trinidad and Tobago's ADB and DFC, $3.4 million to the St Kitts-Nevis Development Bank, $31.8 million to GAIBANK, and $15 million to the Barbados Development Bank.

Similar mechanisms can be applied in the case of other institutions falling under the regulatory preview of Central Banks. Institutions such as trust companies and merchants banks are also large mobilisers of long-term deposits. For instance, in Barbados in 1986, deposits in trust companies were a fifth of those mobilised by commercial banks.

It is also useful to consider their application to institutions outside of the Central Bank's regulatory framework. The main ones are the life insurance companies, pension funds, and national insurance funds which are vehicles for contractual savings. In the case of national insurance funds, some lending to DFCs already occurs in some countries. The Dominica Security Fund has provided loans to the Dominica AIDB; the Bahamas National Insurance Board to the Bahamas Development Bank; and the Barbados NIB to the Barbados Development Bank. However, there is a need to import a greater degree of reliability or stability to these loan arrangements. Market persuasion or inducement may be usefully reinforced by use of statutory reserve requirements. Since the specialist long-term lenders of contractual funds operate primarily in the mortgage market, one may expect some resistance from demanders of mortgage finance to any switch of funds towards production enterprises.

Finally, on the matter of indirect financial intermediation, there is the possibility of Central Bank rediscounting of DFC financial assets. At present, Central Bank rediscounting facilities to DFCs would necessitate similar regulatory treatment.

Credit risks, lending costs, and credit rationing

The Caribbean DFCs experience high lending costs where lending costs are defined as the sum of interest and non-interest costs of funds, loan administration costs, and risk costs. Because of the large grant element in external funds and the non-commercial nature of most loan capital provided by local governments, interest costs are not a large proportion of total lending costs in some DFCs, although since 1980, most of them have had to seek higher cost financial resources. Administration costs are a significant component, amounting to more than 30% of total lending costs in some DFCs. Risk costs are the loss of loan capital and income resulting from loan delinquency. These costs are a major danger to DFCs. Loan default costs crippled the Jamaica Development Bank in 1980, forcing a redesign of the institutional framework for providing development finance. Similarly acute problems were experienced by DFCs in St Vincent, Grenada, St Kitts-

Nevis, and Trinidad and Tobago during the 1970s and early 1980s. High lending costs combined with policy-determined concessionary loan rates of interest undermine the financial viability of DFCs and ultimately impair their ability to expand or maintain the supply of credit. At the same time, some credit practices intended to ensure viability by reducing administration and risk costs result in reduced access to credit. This dilemma and the solutions to it warrant closer analysis.

It may be useful to begin by indicating the interest cost of lending by relating it to the size of the loan portfolio. During the 1980s, interest costs rose as a percentage of loan balances. For the Barbados Development Bank, interest expenses increased from an average of 2% between 1975 and 1979 to 7.4% in 1988. Interest expenses per unit of loan balances averaged 5.8% during 1980–6 for the Trinidad and Tobago DFC, and 5% during 1983–8 for the St Lucia Development Bank. In all cases, unit interest costs were higher at the end of the decade than at the start.

Administration costs have been a similarly large proportion of total loan balances in recent years. In the case of the St Lucia Development Bank, unit administration costs varied between 5.4% and 6.2%. For the Trinidad and Tobago DFC, it rose from 4.8% in 1980 to as much as 9.9% in 1986. However, some DFCs have managed to keep unit administration costs at a low level. A case in point is the Barbados Development Bank where unit costs decreased from 2.4% in 1977 to 0.5% in 1980 and remained below 1% for most of the decade.

Loan administration costs arise in processing loan applications, disbursing loans, and recovering loans. There is an element of fixity and discontinuity in several of these costs (e.g. minimum levels of capital stock and staff). Furthermore, the unit costs of loan appraisal, disbursement and recovery decrease with the average loan size. DFCs can force a reduction in unit costs by increasing the sizes of individual loan accounts (i.e. by rationing out small borrowers). Risk costs can also be reduced by credit rationing, especially by minimising credit to new ventures and potential new clients. To the extent that enterprises rationed out of the loan market have higher rates of return than those accommodated by the DFCs, allocative efficiency and economic growth are adversely affected. From a national welfare perspective, one must seek other solutions to the problems of administration costs and risk costs.

With respect to administration costs, it is possible to achieve economies of scale by increasing portfolio size. An increase in the total volume of lending activity enables the spreading of overheads, including the more intensive utilisation of staff over a large number of loan accounts. Another possibility is economies of scale through spreading costs over a wider range of output. This requires DFCs to add other financial services such as commercial banking and financial advice to those they currently provide.

Loan delinquency has been extremely burdensome on Caribbean DFCs. Bad debt, comprising as much as 9% of the total loan balances of the Barbados Development Bank in 1986 and somewhat more in 1987, resulted in cumulative operating losses of Bds$25.7 million between 1985 and 1986 which exceeded the Bds$0.3 million accumulated profits for the preceding eleven years. Loss provisions comprised as much as 48% of the Trinidad and Tobago DFC's assets in 1987. In the cases of the St Lucia Development Bank and the Development Bank of St Kitts-Nevis, an indication of the incidence of bad debt is provided by statistics on the proportion of principal payments due that are in arrears. For St Lucia, this amounted to 20% approximately in each year of the 1985–87 period and 18% in 1988. In St Kitts-Nevis, this measure of the arrears rate rose from 9.2% in 1982 to 23% in 1984 and 24% in 1985, before decreasing to 17% in 1987.[7]

The problem of loan default costs may be less tractable than that of administration costs. Borrowers may involuntarily default because of structural weaknesses in the production environment, marketing failures, inflation, or foreign exchange problems.

Within the agricultural sector, adverse weather conditions, pests and diseases, and seed failures are fairly common problems in less developed countries. While the first two are susceptible to control through investments in irrigation and drainage, and applications of chemicals, their role is limited in the present context of Caribbean agriculture. The small sizes and fragmentation of farm holdings seem to render capital investment in drainage and irrigation uneconomic from the perspective of the farm operator. The availability of imported improved inputs is subject to the vagaries of the country's foreign exchange situation, and their costs are influenced by unanticipated exchange rate depreciations. The noteworthy feature of these potential sources of production failure is that they are structural (i.e. they arise from either the structure of the agricultural sector or from the structure of the economy). Being structural in nature, these sources of production failure are not unique to individual enterprises and will tend to affect many enterprises at any point in time. As a consequence, there is rather limited scope for reducing these kinds of credit risks by increasing the number of loan accounts within the sector. In other words, portfolio diversification by DFCs may not help much.

Other sectors and industries are also susceptible to structural sources of production failures. Manufacturing output has a high import content, as does tourism even in economies with sizeable domestic food production capacities. These sectors are therefore vulnerable to structurally-determined movements in the price and availability of inputs. Jamaican experience in the second half of the 1970s and Trinidad and Tobago experience in 1986 and 1987 reveal how sensitive manufacturing output is to national foreign exchange resources and exchange rate policy. In both countries, manufacturing output decreased sharply and production costs rose when foreign exchange restrictions tightened and the foreign exchange rate was devalued.

To the extent that the balance of payments has a pervasive effect on production in small economies, one should have modest expectations of the scope for credit risk minimisation through portfolio diversification across sectors. This is not to say that there are no gains to be had. Since not all production risks will be positively correlated inter-sectorally, pooling of loans across sectors will tend to reduce the overall variance in expected returns on the loan portfolio. The point being made, however, is that to a large extent, individual variances are likely to be correlated under certain structural conditions.

It should not be difficult in all countries to identify many DFC loan projects where market performance has turned out to be considerably poorer than projected. This negative divergence is termed marketing failure. The reasons include errors in estimation of potential commodity demand, unanticipated commodity price depression, insufficient knowledge of and accounting for competing supply, and fluctuations in domestic purchasing power. It is possible for DFCs to reduce credit risks associated with market failure by improving upon their methods of estimating demand and future price trends. It is also possible to improve information systems with respect to competitive supply. However, there are likely to be persistent information deficiencies in relation to the production and supply plans of non-client enterprises within the domestic economy and more so of those located in other countries including members of the Caribbean Community.

Moreover, shifts in foreign trade policies can impact adversely on market prospects. Import liberalisation in particular and commodity aid programmes (e.g. the sale of US surplus grain, milk, and dairy products) can present acute short-term problems in Caribbean commodity markets. Likewise, abrupt shifts in the trade policies of developed countries could restrict market entry for Caribbean products or make them more vulnerable to competition from other suppliers. Fluctuations in consumer incomes or reversal of growth trends also affect market performance. For domestically-marketed output, the pertinent variables are national income and its distribution. Although frequently ignored, the distribution of income is important because changes in the functional distribution of personal income and changes in the distribution of income between the government and the personal sector influence both the level and composition of consumption expenditures. For export commodities, including tourism services, it is the trend in foreign income which matters. Its significance can be appreciated, for instance, by the slump and recovery in the tourism industry during the 1970s synchronously with economic recession and recovery in the USA.

For the export industries, exchange rate policy may also be influential because the local currency price of output is the product of the exchange rate and the exogenous foreign currency commodity price. To the extent that home goods are substitutable for foreign goods in domestic production and consumption and to the extent that the prices of home goods are independent of the exchange rate, exchange rate policy may also affect market outcomes for domestically-marketed output. In practice, the structure of Caribbean economies is such that the elasticity of substitution between home and foreign goods is weak and there is a strong causal relationship between the exchange rate and prices of home goods. As a result, the scope for improving market viability of home goods by exchange rate devaluation seems quite limited.

The third type of credit risk to be considered is inflation. One linkage is through the divergence between capital approvals and actual investment costs in the context of unanticipated inflation or erroneous inflation forecasts. This can be a serious problem if disbursement is protracted and supplementary financing is not readily available. Another linkage is the effects of the inflation rate on relative commodity prices. The structure of relative prices tends to be preserved under mild inflationary conditions and to be seriously distorted under rapid inflation. This implies that relative profitability changes under the condition of rapid inflation. Evidence for non-Caribbean countries indicates that the dispersion of profits shifts in favour of real estate, construction, and services, and against manufacturing and agriculture. If those findings are applicable to the Commonwealth Caribbean, then it may not be unreasonable to surmise that annual inflation rates in the region of 15% to 20% may have hurt those industries particularly favoured by DFCs.

The final source of involuntary default to be discussed here is exchange rate costs. Some attention has already been paid to exchange rate effects on commodity prices and production costs. We now turn to exchange rate effects on debt service (including amortisation). In most cases where the DFC's line of credit is funded in foreign exchange, credit to a domestic client is a foreign currency obligation. The debtor is required to amortise the fixed foreign currency value of the loan. This means that the local currency obligation varies with the foreign exchange rate. Because the interest rate is a fixed percentage of loan balances, interest payments in local currency would also vary with the foreign exchange rate. Credit customers therefore face the risk of substantial unanticipated increases in debt service obligations, depending upon the magnitude and frequency of currency devaluations. With devaluations of the cumulative order of 30% and 50% combined with commodity price rigidity, foreign exchange risks are unlikely to be manageable by individual enterprises, especially small ones. Another kind of exchange risk arises in the context of generalised floating of the world's major currencies, especially the US dollar and the £ sterling. Since the Commonwealth Caribbean countries, except Guyana, peg their currencies to the US dollar, their multilateral exchange rates adapt passively to movements in the US multilateral exchange rate. To the extent that commodity prices are quoted in a depreciating currency and inputs are purchased in an appreciating currency, multilateral exchange rate movements introduce a further profit risk and therefore another source of credit risk. This point, it is claimed, has some force in the OECS economies where the main agricultural exports are sterling-denominated. Sterling depreciated relative to the US dollar between 1981 and 1985 but appreciated during 1986 and 1987. Generalised floating presents opportunities for both loss and gain.

Many of the credit risks discussed here in the economic structure of Caribbean countries are largely outside the direct control of the DFCs. The pursuit of financial viability therefore requires considerable attention to general economic policy. Some illustrations are appropriate. Firstly, production risks emanating from input supply irregularities have their fundamental solution in the foreign exchange capacity of the economy, in the development of production technology favouring local resources, and in the production of local inputs. Secondly, marketing risks may be alleviated by rationalisation of industrial activities both domestically and regionally; by the harmonisation of foreign trade policy, exchange rate policy, and industrial and agricultural production policy; and by economic stabilisation. As a third example, exchange rate policy and factor cost policy could be employed to influence the domestic price level. Since one cannot realistically expect exchange rate policy to be tailored to the debt service obligations of DFC customers or even the DFCs themselves, this aspect of viability is perhaps better pursued by developing mechanisms for transferring foreign exchange risk to the government or to the Central Bank.

The preceding discussion of the general economic policy requisite for DFC viability is not intended to absolve the DFCs of responsibility for improving their own systems of credit risk evaluation and management. But the point has to be stressed that the viability of the economies *per se* is critical, and that policies affecting the economy as a whole have strong, pervasive effects on DFC viability.

The prospects for loan repayment are not unrelated to the strength of incentives to repay. One important incentive is the sanctions which lenders can impose in order to enforce compliance with repayment obligations. Enforcement is partly a legal matter; it is also a matter of social mores and political attitudes. Recent work on credit markets identifies expectations of future credit flows as an important incentive to repayment.[8] If expected flows exceed repayment flows, loan delinquency and default is less likely. For rational debtors, these expectations would reflect not only their judgment about the willingness of lenders to terminate a line of credit and the existence or lack of debt morality among the collective of debtors, but would also reflect their assessment of future funding prospects of the lender. A vicious circle may well ensue: financial fragility causing loan default which then further intensifies fragility. Matters are further complicated for DFCs by their emergent tradition of fixed capital as opposed to working capital lending. If there is no working capital relationship, credit flows to any borrower cease with the final disbursement on the investment project. Expectations of future flows are then zero, unless new investment projects are contemplated in the immediate future, which is hardly likely. Rural financial market specialists also point to frustrations and costs experienced during loan negotiation and disbursement as additional reasons for loan delinquency. The poor quality of the credit service destroys the debtor's goodwill towards the lender and undermines the willingness to repay. Although 'poor quality of service' may be a somewhat self-servicing argument for loan default, interviews with loan customers do indicate considerable dissatisfaction among the DFCs' clientele.

The establishment and maintenance of a continuing, harmonious relationship between DFCs and their credit customers would involve a change in credit policy to permit greater working capital financing, expansion of the menu of services actually provided by DFCs, simplifications and speeding up of loan appraisal and disbursement procedures, and strengthening of their loan capacity.

Income and wealth distribution roles of DFCs

The last role to be discussed in this chapter is that of achieving a more egalitarian distribution of income and wealth. Credit programmes may influence income and wealth distribution through two distinct mechanisms. They may increase utilisation of productive inputs and the productivity of credit beneficiaries *vis-à-vis* non-beneficiaries. Furthermore, the substantial credit subsidies accrue only to credit recipients and raise their income and wealth by amounts directly proportional to the credit received. Whether this credit role reduces or increases inequality of income and wealth depends upon the differential access of credit applicants classified by income and wealth status. There is considerable scepticism on this count. Many persons believe that political influence and privilege, reinforced by social class and kinship ties, result in disproportionate access by the already wealthy to the financial resources of DFCs. This is a matter that requires careful study. The only empirical analysis of this issue has been with regard to the Jamaican rural financial markets; this established an unambiguous egalitarian influence (Bourne, 1983), but this result is not necessarily generalisable elsewhere, not even to the Jamaican financial sector as a whole.

DFCs as credit wholesalers

Jamaican DFCs have had a new *modus operandi* since the early 1980s. Wishing to sidestep the problems of loan delinquency and high administration costs in direct lending to development enterprises, the Jamaican economic authorities in 1981 refashioned the Jamaica Development Bank into two new institutions, the Agricultural Credit Bank and the National Development Bank. Unlike their predecessor, the two new institutions do not lend directly to development enterprises. Instead, they provide credit tranched to commercial banks, selected community-level agricultural banks (i.e. some People's Co-operative Banks), and other private financial institutions for on-lending. This new operational system has considerably lowered lending costs for the two Jamaican DFCs. It does mean, however, that DFCs operating as credit wholesalers are not in a position to apply social cost-benefit criteria at the level of the individual enterprise since the micro-level loan decision is taken by the on-lending institution.

Conclusions

DFCs have been ascribed an important role in the financial sector and economic development policies of many Commonwealth Caribbean countries. Their actual quantitative significance has tended to vary both across countries and over time. The status of DFCs is greater in those countries where the financial sector has not grown greatly and is not extensively layered. DFCs also seem to lose significance in the complex of government institutions and policies when there is less need of foreign grant funds.

The general funding capacity of DFCs is a dominant factor in determining whether they can play a major role in expanding the volume and improving the quality of credit, or occupy a position on the fringe of the financial sector. Their dependence on resource flows from local government and international agencies is a source of financial fragility which may be overcome by diversification of funding activities to include local deposit mobilisation, bond issue, and debt instruments to other local financial institutions.

DFCs also have to direct attention towards reducing the level of their lending costs and increasing their rates of return. Considerable progress can be achieved through improvement in the DFCs' operational policies and practices, and by institutional reorganisation. However, financial viability of DFCs is critically dependent on overall economic policy, on the policies laid down by their predominant contributors of loan capital, and by public perception of DFCs as welfare dispensing agencies. Removal of these constraints is necessary for realisation of the intended role of DFCs as promoters of economic development.

Notes

1 Callender (1965) reports that Jamaica established the Agricultural Development Corporation in 1951. However, development financing was being provided through the Agricultural Loan Societies Board from as early as 1912.
2 Among the new institutions are privately-owned finance companies specialising in medium and long-term lending, mortgage finance companies, and merchant banks. Secondary mortgage markets, unit trusts, and stock exchanges have been established in several countries.
3 The institutions called 'national development foundations' have been established as adjuncts of United States foreign assistance programmes and have been funded with the financial proceeds of PL 480 commodity sales. However, they are rapidly evolving into locally funded entities with particular credit market niches, including venture capital financing.
4 Jamaica moved from a policy of credit retailing through its major DFCs to one of credit wholesaling. Trinidad and Tobago is in the process of revamping the operations of its Development Finance Corporation and Agricultural Development Bank.
5 The solvency problems of finance companies in Trinidad and Tobago and Barbados are salutary. For detailed discussions of the Trinidad and Tobago case, see Bourne (1986) and Farrell (1988).
6 See for instance, Adams and Neyman (1979) and Saito and Villanueva (1981).
7 This depiction of the state of affairs for St Lucia and St Kitts-Nevis may come as a surprise to those who measure loan delinquency by the ratio of principal arrears to total financing outstanding. This latter measure may generate a false sense of security, as should now be appreciated.
8 See for instance, Stiglitz and Weiss (1983).

CHAPTER 11

Small business financing: The role and performance of the National Development Foundations in the Caribbean

Stanley Lalta

Most writers and practitioners in the area of small business have identified financing and financial management as the critical factors influencing the development of the sector. Commercial banks have, with the exception of a few limited innovative programmes, tended to ignore small businesses in their loan portfolios. State-sponsored development banks and institutions have generally adopted a paternalistic approach to small businesses with the result that their resources dry up very quickly and their portfolios show a high percentage of bad loans.

This chapter undertakes a preliminary assessment of the role and performance of National Development Foundations (NDFs) – private, non-profit organisations established in most Caribbean countries between 1981 and 1988 to provide credit and technical assistance to small businesses. It begins with a general overview of the financial environment in which small businesses operate, focusing on the ways in which access to finance and financial management determine the establishment and/or expansion of a small business. It then examines the objectives, functions and performance of the NDFs in the short period of their existence, and ends by identifying ways of enhancing the role of the NDFs in the future.

Overview of the financial environment facing small businesses

The majority of small businesses are started with the personal funds of the owners or funds borrowed from family members and friends. Failing these, the prospective business person may seek funds from the informal financial market (local money-lenders), approaching a commercial bank only as the last resort. (Sometimes the order is reversed with respect to the banks and money-lenders.) The general perception that banks are unsympathetic to small business applicants can be traced to the following factors:

- the administrative costs of small loans are disproportionately high;
- small businesses lack adequate collateral (land title deeds, property, fixed incomes, etc.);
- small business persons do not usually have verifiable credit histories;
- small businesses lack audited financial statements and proper business and financial projections;
- small business loans are generally high risk with relatively little salvage value if the project collapses; and
- credit restrictions on bank lending may cause attention to be focused on other more profitable sectors.

At the same time, it may be argued that the small business person is often reluctant to approach the bank either because of past experience or a perception that the banks are unhelpful. This attitude derives from:

- the size of the equity contribution required by the bank;
- the rate of interest charged which is generally higher for small than for large businesses (except where special funds are available);
- the reluctance of the bank to fund working capital even though this is a short-term requirement;
- the relative inflexibility of bank loan arrangements and funds which impedes quick changes in the operations of the business; and
- the lack of knowledge of the services and facilities available at the bank.

Unless the banker is well-known to the small business person, or *vice versa*, start-up or expansion funds will not be forthcoming and the project may be dropped or modified.

Public-sector financing institutions (whether specifically established to cater to the needs of the small business sector, to guarantee small business loans or to make funds available to the sector through intermediaries) are generally deficient in their portfolio management, exhausting what were intended to be revolving funds. The Caribbean is replete with examples of such institutions – the Small Business Loan Board (1956) and later the Small Enterprise Development Company and the Small Industry Finance Company in the 1960s in Jamaica are examples of the lack of recognition of the full costs (operational and developmental) of concessionary lending to small businesses.

It should be mentioned also that a number of private voluntary organisations and public welfare agencies are present in the financial market catering to the needs of the small business person. Their funds, though flexible in terms of usage by the small business person, are essentially for micro-enterprise operations and do not generally 'revolve'.

Apart from these institutional and subjective factors, one also has to consider the financial management competence of the small business borrower. His credit and collection systems may be very suspect and lax; record-keeping and budgeting may be absent or minimal ('Why keep records when the business is making money?' or 'I have no time for that' are common excuses) and his purchasing policies (e.g. securing new or additional machinery at full cost while hire purchasing may be more appropriate) could drain away the resources of the business.

One can identify a clear need for a financing institution which:

- provides funds at reasonable cost (that does not include a subsidy to the borrower);
- has a balanced portfolio of projects;
- provides guidance and technical assistance to the small business manager; and
- ensures that the loan funds are revolving.

Policies and performance of the NDFs

Objective and functions

At present, NDFs have been established in 11 Caribbean countries – Jamaica and Dominica (1981), Barbados (1982), St Lucia and Belize (1983), Grenada, Antigua and St Kitts (1985), St Vincent and Guyana (1986), and Montserrat (1988). The NDFs are private limited liability non-profit organisations whose mission is to strengthen and develop entrepreneurial skills and practices in the region through the provision of credit, business guidance and technical assistance to individuals and groups which are unable to access traditional commercial sources. Initial capital for their operations came from donor agencies such as the Pan American Development Fund (PADF), USAID, the Canadian International Development Agency (CIDA) and the German Technical Co-operation Agency (GTZ), and from domestic banks, business houses and national governments. The NDFs in the East Caribbean – including the Women in Development Project in Barbados – are recipients of a five-year US$10 million programme of technical assistance, credit funds and training from USAID called the Small Enterprise Assistance Project. This will expire in 1991.

NDFs are permitted to charge such fees and interest rates as necessary to ensure the revolving nature of the funds they manage. Sometimes, however, specific allocations are made by the donor agencies for particular sectors and activities.

NDFs are one-stop entrepreneurial centres offering loans, advice, training and technical assistance. Every prospective client must undergo a certain period of basic management training while his application is being processed. Lending limits vary from US$10,000 loan per individual in the East Caribbean to US$85,000 in Jamaica. Average loan sizes, however, have been much lower – about US$2,000 in the East Caribbean and US$3,000 in Jamaica.

NDFs accept intangible collateral in lieu of physical assets or where owner equity is minimal. For example, good character and community standing, sound business intentions and experience, commitment and initiative have, at various times, been accepted as sufficient guarantee by the NDFs.

For costing and strategic purposes, the functions of banking and technical services and training (TST) are separated since it is generally expected that banking operations (loans and repayments) will cover the current expenses of the NDFs while TST, being a developmental activity, will have to be met from external sources. However, NDFs regard TST as an integral part of their credit programmes, the success of the latter being dependent on the effectiveness of the former. Banking operations cover:

- project development and analysis;
- loan packaging and monitoring; and
- business advice.

TST activities cover:

- business counselling and 'trouble-shooting';
- agricultural extension services;
- seminars and workshops;
- information gathering and monitoring; and
- institutional support to other small business agencies.

The NDFs' portfolio

The analysis below covers data on the NDFs in the East Caribbean and Jamaica (which has four branches).[1] The NDF of Jamaica's (NDF/J) operations are summarised in Table 11.1 The NDF/J receives about 3-4,000 loan enquiries per year with approximately 70% of these becoming loan applications. Approvals, however, are 12 to 15% of total applicants. Between 1981 and 1989 there has been a rapid increase in both the value and number of loans approved annually. While the ideal loan period is about 36 months, most loans are repaid between 24–30 months with those in agricultural crops being retired in six months. Perhaps the most gratifying aspect

Table 11.1   National Development Fund of Jamaica.

Summary data, November 1981 – September 1989

(i)	Loans approved	2,524
(ii)	Percentage of applications	12%
(iii)	Value of disbursements	J$40.9 million
(iv)	Average loan size	J$16,197
(v)	Sectoral distribution	23% manufacturing (crafts, food processing, footwear, garments, furniture, building materials); 55% services (pantry/retail outlets, groceries, meatshops, transport, hairdressing, education); and 22% agriculture (agricultural business, livestock, aquaculture);
(vi)	Jobs created/saved	6,500
(vii)	Number of businesses expanded/established	1,700
(viii)	Number of persons trained	13,300
(ix)	Loan write-offs (i.e. delinquencies)	4.2% of disbursements at (iii)
(x)	Loan arrears (i.e. up to 90 days)	5.4%

Source: Annual Reports of NDF, Jamaica 1981–9.

of the credit operations is that write-offs averaged 4.2% and totalled less than J$2 million over the period 1981–9.

In terms of sectoral destination, the greatest demand and the most favourable repayment capacity is in the area of commerce and services, which accounts for 55% of funds disbursed while manufacturing received 23% and agriculture 22%. The NDF/J, however, maintains that it is not biased towards services as the interest rate here is approximately 20% while the rate for agriculture is 10–14%.

Data for the NDFs (and Women in Development, WID) in the East Caribbean are given in Tables 11.2 and 11.3. Over the period 1986 to June 1989 the eight NDFs and WID had disbursed 2,019 loans valued at US$4.02 million. Average loan size was US$2,000 and arrears about 5% of loans disbursed. There were 4,105 jobs created or saved, of which 2,481 were male and 1,624 female. Manufacturing received the largest share of loans with 30%, followed by services (22%) and retailing (20%). Of all disbursements 54% was spent on projects in the rural areas, compared with 45-48%

Table 11.2 NDFs in the East Caribbean: Summary data, 1986–June 1989.

Indicators	1986	1987	1988	1989 (Jan–June)	Total
Enquiries/applications	1,912	n.a.	2,563	1,391	
Approvals					
– number	428	n.a.	751	327	
– value (US$)	904,910	n.a.	1,600,000	671,300	
– % enquiries	22	n.a.	29	24	
Disbursements					
– number	409	613	701	296	2,019
– value	858,653	1,072,071	1,499,000	591,900	4,022,624
Average loan size (US$)	2,099	1,762	2,139	2,000	
Arrears (30 days+)	14.72%	3.73%	5.16%	5.18%	
Jobs created	1,088	1,205	1,283	529	4,105
– Male	769	675	741	296	2,481
– Female	319	530	542	233	1,624
Cost					
– per loan	2,040	n.a.	1,515	1,440	
– per job created	816	805	828	806	
Sectoral distribution					
– agriculture	71	88	155	68	382 (19%)
– fishing	18	22	33	13	86 (4%)

Table 11.2 (continued)   NDFs in the East Caribbean: Summary data, 1986–June 1989.

Indicators	1986	1987	1988	1989 (Jan–June)	Total	
– manufacturing	130	188	226	83	627	(30%)
– services	90	130	142	98	460	(22%)
– retailing	80	152	129	47	408	(20%)
Geographical distribution						
– urban	173	291	337	142	943	(46%)
– rural	236	331	368	173	1,108	(54%)
Distribution by sex						
– male	237	379	425	185	1,226	(60%)
– female	164	207	235	99	705	(34%)
– partnership	8	39	46	32	125	(6%)

Source: Caribbean Association of Industry and Commerce, Barbados, Small Enterprise Assistance Project, 1989.

Table 11.3 Caribbean Association of Industry and Commerce Small Enterprise Assistance Project, Micro-Enterprise Performance, January – December 1987 US$

| Summary | Loans disbursed | | | Portfolio | | | Jobs affected | | | Technical assistance | |
| | Number | Amount '000 | Average size | Amount receivable '000 | Recovery rate (%) | Arrears (over 90 days) % | Male | Female | Cost per job | Over 3 hrs. | Total reached |
Location											
NDF Antigua	64	172	2,688	200	80.70	1.68	108	86	575	6	49
NDF Barbados	75	119	1,590	312	66.20	3.75	90	77	969	69	174
WID Barbados	67	94	1,400	162	73.00	2.13	33	173	653	0	76
NDF Dominica	80	129	1,610	228	24.00	5.20	97	41	1,091	29	81
NDF Grenada	79	152	1,929	315	80.00	6.12	80	31	979	n.a.	n.a.
NDF St Kitts	150	214	1,423	206	77.00	3.03	90	50	636	16	83
NDF St Lucia	68	159	2,333	191	68.00	3.07	91	49	1,046	85	n.a.
NDF St Vincent	30	34	1,124	45	57.00	4.87	86	23	493	18	48
Total Jan – Dec. 1987	613	1,072	1,762	1,659	66.74	3.73	675	530	805	223	511
Regional total Jan – Dec. 1986	409	858	2,099	692	73.50	15.75	769	319	n.a.	n.a.	1,150

Source: Caribbean Association of Industry and Commerce, Barbados, Small Enterprise Assistance Project, 1989.

in Jamaica.   In Jamaica the distribution of loans between the sexes is even, but in the East Caribbean, males received approximately twice the number of loan disbursements as did females.

Main findings

(a) As agencies designed to finance small businesses exclusively, the NDFs start off at an immediate disadvantage since they cannot target low-risk, high-return ventures in their portfolio as favoured by commercial banks. That the NDFs have been able to show sustained annual growth in their assets, clientele, job impact and TST activities is indeed a laudable achievement especially in view of the fact that the delinquency rate (which plagues commercial banks and state-sponsored financing institutions) is quite low.

(b) Operating deficits are large but declining. While NDFs are almost self-sustaining in their banking operations (interest and principal repayments vs. disbursement costs), TST activities are quite costly and generally account for 40% of all operating costs. Since no fees are charged for these activities, the strain is placed on strict portfolio management to keep costs under control. TST activities are developmental and while their positive impact generally guarantees the repayment of loans it will become necessary to achieve a better balance between the costs and benefits of such activities.

(c) As private, non-profit-making organisations, NDFs are subject to a minimum of interference from governments but they are too dependent on external grants and loans for their existence. This dependence has led sometimes to the tying of grants and loans to specific sectors and activities which the NDFs may have been reluctant to get into. Such conflicts of purpose do not appear to have impeded the progress of NDFs.

(d) NDFs have concentrated on 'quality' loans, in keeping with their financial resources and expertise – and have proven to be quite effective and efficient. Repeat borrowers number no more than 10% of NDFs' clients, so that the role of NDFs in job creation and the establishment of new businesses, given their limited resources, and their geographical and gender distribution of loans, has been positive, increasing and well-managed.

Issues and considerations on NDFs' policies and programmes

Venture capital

In addition to the current operations, the NDFs are now considering a venture capital window. A venture capital company brings together potential investors and entrepreneurs who need financing. Since NDF clients can often bring very little capital of their own to a venture, it might be difficult to convince investors to place large sums of money at the disposal of a partner who has a much smaller financial commitment. The success of a venture capital window will depend upon the ability of the small business-man and the NDFs to convince potential investors that small businesses need not be high risk ventures.

A question also arises as to whether a venture capital facility is best operated by the NDFs or by some other small business organisation. The service would involve additional costs for staff and training, and perhaps more extensive physical facilities. In view of their financial limitations it may be unwise for the NDFs to attempt to provide this facility. Instead, the matter should be explored with other small business development agencies and development banks that may be better equipped to provide the service.

Small business lobby

Another problem facing the small business sector is the absence of an effective lobby to represent its interests. For example, the Small Businesses Association of Jamaica, established in 1974, is the primary organisation in this role, but it has not persuaded the government to articulate a national policy for small business development. The NDFs do not see lobbying as part of their function although they acknowledge the need to create a favourable environment for the development of small-scale operations.

After years of successful lending to clients who are ineligible for commercial bank loans, the NDFs are now in a position to assist commer-cial banks by providing them with information about non-lending services to reduce the riskiness of loans to small enterprises. NDFs have earned the respect of governments and institutions in the public and private sector. They should bring their reputation to bear and to influence small business policy nationally and regionally.

Graduation of customers

Once a business has developed the size and asset structure that makes it eligible for a commercial loan, it becomes ineligible for further assistance from the NDFs. The NDF's information on the client from its initial inves-tigation when the loan application was first made through the duration of the relationship, is not available to the commercial bank, which must carry out its own investigation.

The NDF's target of self-sufficiency forces it to give up its best clients. As the NDF increases its reliance upon loan interest and capital repayment to fund its operations and provide new loans, it needs to include in its portfolio loans that are made with profit as the primary goal. The establishment of 'second windows' in Jamaica, Dominica and St Lucia where funds are loaned at slightly higher terms to 'graduate' clients is to be supported.

Sectoral focus of the NDF of Jamaica

The Foundations deny any bias towards the service sector, and attribute its relatively large share of their portfolios to the high demand and favourable repayment capacity of the sector. Donors are often biased against the service sector whose activities are not considered to be developmental. However, services do contribute to employment, greater popular participation in management and a more equal distribution of income.

The NDFs provide special incentives for agriculture in the form of lower interest rates, and they secure low-cost funds specifically for this sector. For example, in December 1986 the Jamaica Agricultural Development Foundation approved loan and grant funds amounting to J$1.3 million for the purpose of providing financial and technical assistance to small farmers. The NDF of Jamaica has also collaborated with the IAF, the GTZ and the ACB to secure funds for the provision of credit and TST to persons engaged in agricultural activities. As part of its Hurricane Relief Assistance, the Foundation donated tools which were secured in collaboration with the PADF, to individual farmers and related organisations island-wide. The NDFs provided a wide range of services to farmers who have secured loans from the Foundations through the activities of their field extension officers.

The demand for the services of the NDFs is high in all sectors; effective portfolio management suggests that the Foundations should not arbitrarily or altruistically divide their portfolio equally among sectors but respond readily to good, bankable projects from all sectors.

The need for self-sufficiency

All indicators point to the need for self-sufficiency of the NDFs in the region. USAID, which has been a major contributor to the NDFs, has been forced by US budget stringency to cut back its contributions for future operations. For Jamaica, in 1986 USAID grants amounted to 51.9% of the funding for Operational and Technical Assistance and Training costs, and USAID loans accounted for 15.7% of sources of funding for lending. The executive director of the NDF/J, Dr. Blossom Stokes admits that although special grants were made available to the Foundation due to the abnormal situation created by Hurricane Gilbert in 1988, USAID funds had been declining and were generally more difficult to access. Other sources from which the Foundation received funding are: CIDA, the PADF, Inter-American Development Bank, and the National Development Bank (NDB) and the Jamaica Agricultural Development Foundation (JADF).

In an effort to become self-sufficient the NDF/J instituted a Strategic Development Plan in 1987, 'designed to put itself in a position of self-sufficiency within five years'. It calls for the separation of cost and profit centres (administration will be a cost centre and the branches will be profit centres) and the separation of banking and TST functions, each generating the resources necessary for its needs (NDF/J 1987 Annual Report). The NDF/J also underwent a USAID-sponsored operational review in 1988 which established a break-even portfolio size, target loan size and disbursement levels.

In 1987 it was decided to establish an Endowment Fund to attract substantial contributions from local and overseas sources. The income from the investment of these contributions is used exclusively for technical assistance and training (now called technical services and training) costs. By November 1989 the Endowment Fund had attracted J$4.4 million from CIDA, GTZ and local contributions including all fund-raising proceeds – at this rate it is unlikely that the target of J$13.763 million set for the end of 1989 will be met. While TST has been offered free of charge in the past, the NDF/J has decided to offer free training of up to 9 hours, and up to 20 hours free business counselling, after which clients will be charged. The NDF/J will also try to raise money by holding seminars and workshops.

The trend towards self-sufficiency at the NDF/J pre-dates this Strategic Development Plan. In its relatively short lifetime the NDF/J had made significant progress in this direction. In 1985, loan interest was the source of 20% of the Foundation's funding. In 1986 loan interest represented 39.6% of funding for operating and TST costs, and loan repayments represented 40.7% of funding for lending; in 1987 loan interest funded 39.55% of operating and TST costs, while loan repayment provided 37.5% of loan funds generated (See Table 11.4).

The Foundation has been operating at a deficit, which has increased annually, from $779,514 in 1984 to $2,503,521 in 1987. However, the percentage annual increase has been decreasing dramatically from 106% between 1984 and 1985, to only 8.61% between 1986 and 1987. TST costs amount to approximately half of the annual operating deficit (See Tables 11.5 and 11.6).

With the separation of the TST operations, the main sources of funding or saving will be:

- the Endowment Fund established in 1988;
- limiting the amount of TST available free of charge; and
- offering seminars and workshops as income-generating activities.

Table 11.4   NDF, Jamaica: Per cent of funding for operations (including technical services and training), 1986–7 (J$ M)

Year	USAID	CIDA	Loan interest	Other	JADF	IDB
1986	51.9	4.0	39.6	4.5	–	–
1987	39.0	7.1	39.55	7.62	5.65	1.10

Source: Annual Reports, NDF Jamaica.

Table 11.5   NDF, Jamaica: Performance, 1984–7 (J$ M)

Year	Assets	Deficit ($)	% Increase deficit
1984	4.2	0.8	n.a.
1985	5.1	1.7	106
1986	6.7	2.3	43.6
1987	9.3	2.5	8.6

Source: Annual Reports, NDF Jamaica.

Table 11.6   NDF, Jamaica: Expenses, 1984–7

Year	Expenses Deficit	Expenses TST	Expenses Operations	TST as % of Expenses	TST as % of Deficit
1984	0.8	0.5	0.8	38.9	61.9
1985	1.7	0.9	1.4	40.5	59.1
1986	2.3	1.1	2.1	34.9	47.8
1987	2.5	1.2	2.1	29.4	49.4

Source: Annual Reports, NDF Jamaica.

It is, however, unlikely that plans outlined for the funding of TST operations will generate sufficient income. The NDF/J must adopt a joint approach with other institutions that provide technical assistance and training: technical schools, youth camps, Boys' Town, Girls' Town, the Social Development Commission, the government-sponsored HEART training programme, the official promotional agency JAMPRO and the SBAJ. They must jointly:

* eliminate duplication of services;
* reach as many small businessmen as possible;
* secure maximum financial assistance from the government; and

- reduce the cost of providing the services by increasing co-operation between agencies.

In other NDFs, the situation is quite similar.

Currently self-sufficiency stands at 38% (the ratio of loan revenues to expenditure). It is targeted, in the strategic plan, for this figure to increase to 45% by 1990. NDFs should diversify their portfolios, subsidising less profitable loans with income earned on more profitable loans. The Foundations should also continue to respond favourably to demands in the service sector, which has the most favourable repayment capacity. The governments should provide special incentives to the agriculture and manufacturing sectors.

As NDFs expand their client base and activities, dependence on donors should be reduced. Each NDF needs a strategic mix of loan funds mobilisation, portfolio expansion management, services pricing, collections, cost savings, training fees, second window facilities and new services to reach sustainability by the targeted dates.

The NDFs, the governments and the need for small business policy

Governments have demonstrated keen interest in the role of the NDFs in promoting small businesses, and they may enhance this role by making grants to the NDFs, and offering guarantees to donor agencies. However, if the NDFs court governments' assistance, they may also have to endure a certain amount of government interference.

The articulation of a policy for small business development is necessary to confirm the governments' commitment to the sector and to ensure that macro-economic and adjustment measures (tariffs, incentives, foreign exchange, etc.) do not discriminate against the sector.

An official small business policy might incorporate the following:

- establishment of priority sub-sectors within the small business sector and providing incentives to firms in these sub-sectors;
- reduction of the bureaucracy involved in establishing and operating a small business;
- easier access to imported raw materials and foreign exchange;
- encouragement through fiscal incentives of production using local raw materials where possible;
- assistance with the sale of the finished product, for example, setting aside some portion of state procurement contracts for small businesses;
- encouragement of expansion and linkages with large firms; and
- provision of grants for training and R&D for the sector.

Note

1 Data for Belize and Guyana could not be accessed in time for preparing this chapter, though in informal discussions with the executive directors of the NDFs in Belize and Guyana, there seemed to be many similarities with the experiences of the other NDFs in the region.

Part IV

Equity and securities markets

CHAPTER 12

The development of equity markets in the Caribbean

Courtney Blackman

Equity markets in a theory of finance and development

If there is one thing known about economic development it is that invest-ment must increase relative to consumption as a proportion of the national income. Investment, in the words of John Maynard Keynes, is the engine of growth. Investment is made possible through savings. According to Sir Arthur Lewis, any industrial revolution cannot be explained 'until it can be explained why savings increased relative to the national income'.[1] Economic development, then, is about accelerating the rate of capital formation.

Capital formation implies investment expenditures over and above the level required to offset the depreciation of existing capital goods. A firm may confine the extent of its capital expansion programme to the limits of its retained earnings. More often than not a firm's expansion programme is accomplished through borrowing from other firms and households which have surplus funds at their disposal. The credit transaction is usually carried out through the intermediation of the financial institutions which comprise the financial market. The function of financial markets is to facilitate the transfer of savings from surplus units to deficit spending units, which are then able to invest more than they have saved. The more numerous the participants and the more frequent the transactions, the more extensive is the market and the larger the volume of investment and hence, of potential for economic growth.

The investment decision, then, as Professor Hyman Minsky aptly puts it, is 'a decision both to acquire tangible assets and to emit financial liabilities (including the implicit emission of liabilities by way of retained earnings)'.[2] Professors Albert Hart and Peter Kenen make essentially the same point when they observe that 'the growth of debt is a counterpart of economic growth'.[3]

As an economy develops, the gestation period of investment projects tends to lengthen and the pay-back period to become more extended.

Surplus lending units must therefore be persuaded to hold the liabilities of deficit spending units over longer and longer maturities – up to thirty years in the case of government and corporate bonds and indefinitely in the case of equities. The incentive for them to do so is greatly increased if, in the event of some contingency, the liabilities of the deficit spending units can be readily liquidated without significant loss of value (i.e. if the securities held by the surplus unit are liquid).

In this respect, J.G. Gurley and E.S. Shaw make an important point in their paper, 'Financial Aspects of Economic Development'. They argue that the Keynesian model:

> is not an efficient instrument for studying economic development in either its real or its financial aspects. On the side of goods, the model is inefficient because it does not allow for the effects of investment and of growth in the labor supply on output capacity. Once these effects are admitted . . . investment appears in a dual role. As an element in effective demand, it is an economic stimulant, but as an increment in capacity its effects may be depressing. On the side of finance, the Keynesian model is inefficient because it does not allow for the effects of spending and deficits on debt and on the financial capacity of spending units to sustain their spending. Deficits, like investment, leave an economic residue. In the case of deficits, the residue is debt and a change in financial capacity.[4]

Their charge that Keynes failed to take account of the residue of additional capacity and debt is unfair. Keynes' model assumed an economy in a temporarily depressed state, but with considerable idle capacity and with mature financial markets capable of absorbing any likely increase in debt. However, their insight that deficits, like investment, leave an economic residue is most important in the case of developing countries with limited production capacity and poorly developed financial markets. They highlight the fact that each wave of real investment makes an imposition upon the capacity of the economy to sustain the liquidity of the additional debt created by that investment. They describe this as the 'financial capacity of the economy'.

In this respect, financial markets need not only be extensive, but deep as well, if they are to sustain the liquidity of thirty-year bonds and perpetual equities. The institution of the stock market in the US is not primarily important as a source of new capital. The vast proportion of new capital investment derives from retained earnings, commercial banks and corporate bonds. Between 1958 and 1966, net new issues of corporate stocks in the US in no year exceeded $3 billion during a period in which net investment funds averaged $33 billion. Between 1982 and 1987 the net supply of credit issued through financial institutions other than new corporate stock was $8.6 trillion, while net issuance of corporate stock was a negative $260 billion.

The critical importance of the stock market is that it sustains the liquidity of trillions worth of common stock accumulated by the public for over one hundred years. The accumulated market value of shares on the US stock market exceeds $2.5 trillion, more than half the GDP of the United States. The ability of firms to finance new investment from retained earnings also derives from the existence of the stock market. Shareholders are prepared to forego current dividend payments in return for the prospect of capital gains, which are predicated upon a flourishing stock market.

The absence of adequate financial capacity also explains the strong bias towards consumption in developing countries. The illiquidity of medium- and long-term corporate, and even of government securities, is a disincentive for surplus economic units to hold the long-term debt needed to support capital investments. This situation favours deficit spending units that are willing to finance consumer goods through the emission of short-term liabilities. It is fair to say that sustainable growth in a mixed economy is unlikely in the absence of an effective stock market. This, in turn, explains much of the Caribbean's dependence on foreign sources for investment capital.

But the most important long-run benefit of a formalised market for equities is the increased sense of participation in wealth-creating activities brought about by the wider distribution of stockholders in the society. The fact that over 50 million Americans have investments in stocks or in stock mutual funds and that over 130 million participate in the stock market indirectly through pension funds, life insurance companies, or other financial institutions, goes far to explain why the US is one of the most politically stable societies in the world. Indeed, the most important political success of Margaret Thatcher's strategy of privatisation in the UK has been the transformation of millions of 'workers' into bourgeois property owners.

Measures to promote the market for equities in CARICOM

Except for the Bank of Guyana, all central banks in the region have been involved in the deliberate development of money and capital markets as charged by their statutes. In Jamaica, Trinidad and Tobago, and Barbados, these efforts eventually culminated in the formation of formal stock exchanges. In the Bahamas, Belize and the OECS the process has been less advanced. There are indications that the Bank of Guyana may, in the not too distant future, be motivated to follow the lead of its neighbours.

The standard approach to the development of financial markets is to start with the promotion of the money market. The central bank requires commercial banks to hold a stipulated proportion of their assets in government treasury bills and makes a market, as far as is possible, for commercial banks wishing to improve the liquidity of their portfolios. The key to the success of this exercise is for borrowing governments to accept interest rate levels which reflect demand and supply conditions in the money markets. The next step is to improve the marketing of medium- and long-term government paper. Here again the commercial banks are required to hold some proportion of their assets in longer-term paper, but the most important potential buyers are life insurance companies, for whom long-dated government paper is an important element of their portfolio as required by supervisory authorities to be invested in domestic assets.

As explained in the following section, the formal establishment of a stock exchange has usually required special legislation facilitating the timely transfer of securities from sellers to buyers, providing incentives for companies to list, and regulating the conduct of players on the stock exchange. In this exercise, central banks have usually played a catalytic role as promoter and provider of start-up funds, accommodation and sometimes a nucleus of staff.

To supplement the specific legislation establishing a stock exchange, several other legislative and administrative measures are necessary. These vary according to local circumstances and government objectives. These measures may be divided into those designed to stimulate the supply of equities and those which are designed to stimulate the demand for equities.

The supply of equities depends first of all on the existence of companies eligible for listing on the stock exchange. Once a minimum number of eligible companies exists, they can be motivated through appropriate incentives to list on the stock exchange. Publicly-held companies are naturally inclined to list; some privately-held companies, as seems to be the case in the Bahamas, may avoid the risk of the dilution of ownership.

One of the motivations of the indigenisation programme of Trinidad and Tobago in the 1960s, was to stimulate the increased ownership by nationals of the shares of foreign companies. In nationalising foreign companies, the government contemplated the later sale of some shares to nationals. The indigenised commercial banks, in particular, have become important sources of tradeable equities. Previously, the parent corporations traded on their national stock exchanges and were unavailable to Trinidad and Tobago resident nationals.

The original intent of the Trinidad and Tobago government to divest shares in favour of its nationals was not diligently pursued. However, with the rapid deterioration of the national finances, the Robinson Administration has embarked on a policy of privatisation which should considerably increase the number of enterprises eligible for listing on the stock exchange.

The Seaga Administration, for ideological as well as pragmatic reasons, also embarked on a program of privatisation which contributed to a revival of interest in the Jamaican stock market. In December 1986 a highly successful issue of National Commercial Bank stock encouraged many new investors to enter the market. In 1987 the government unloaded more of its holdings in the Caribbean Cement Company, although only 72% of the offering was taken up. In 1988 the government made a successful divestment of part of its holdings in the Jamaica Telephone Company.

The Central Bank of Barbados has sent forward to the government proposals for the establishment of a Venture Capital Corporation which would invest in the equity of new and promising companies. The proposed corporation would eventually become eligible for listing on the stock exchange.

One technique of stimulating the demand for equities is to reduce the risk to investors through participation in unit trusts. In Jamaica the initiative to establish unit trusts was taken by the private sector. In 1981 the Trinidad and Tobago Parliament passed legislation establishing the Unit Trust Corporation. This Corporation, which became operational in 1982, celebrated its fifth anniversary during 1987 with a symposium entitled 'Trinidad and Tobago Unit Trust Corporation – A Project in Economic Democracy'. During 1987 gross unit sales of the Corporation rose 83.1% to TT$22.7 million, from the level of TT$12.4 million in 1986. The Corporation increased investments in equity by TT$7.8 million and held shares in twenty-one companies at year end, one less than a year earlier. The maximum holding by an investor was also increased from 40,000 units to 200,000 units, thereby enabling large institutions to participate more effectively in the fund.

In recent years both Barbados and Jamaica have offered incentives to investors in equity. Tax-payers in Barbados benefit from a maximum BDS$10,000.00 tax write-off on investment in new equity issues. Unfortunately, the 50% dividend tax credit previously available to investors has been reduced to 15%. Effective since 1988, Jamaican companies expanding their equity base from their own profits through the issue of bonus shares instead of distributing dividends, are entitled to a tax credit equivalent of 25% of the value of the bonus shares issued out of profits subject to tax in that year, provided that the value of the bonus shares does not exceed 50% of that year's after-tax profits. All three existing CARICOM stock exchanges have conducted extensive public relations programmes to attract potential investors to the stock market.

The Bahamas, the OECS and Belize are still in the early stages of capital market development. Their markets for government paper are still primitive. In each country the Central Bank is currently embarked on capital market programmes to improve the functioning of their financial markets. The possible participation of the OECS in the Securities Exchange of Barbados has been mooted.

Existing stock exchanges

The Securities Exchange of Barbados

The Act establishing the Securities Exchange of Barbados (SEB) was passed on 11 October 1982. However, the Exchange did not commence trading until 12 June 1987. The SEB has received considerable financial and other support from the Central Bank of Barbados in whose building it occupies rent-free offices. The purposes of the Exchange as set out in the Act are:

(1) to provide a public securities market to promote commerce by creating a facility for dealing in securities in Barbados;
(2) to maintain a reliable and reputable securities market for the protection of the investing public of Barbados;
(3) to enable the facility created by this Act to form and operate, by itself or with others, a company to deal in securities until such time as the market in Barbados is mature enough to support itself; and
(4) to provide such other exchange services as the commercial and industrial needs of Barbados might require.

Purpose (3) represents an interesting innovation. To enhance the liquidity of stocks traded on the Exchange, legislators made provision for the Exchange to set up a marketing company which would deal in securities. In fact, it was the Central Bank of Barbados that set up the Barbados Securities Marketing Company (BSMC) which holds its own portfolio of securities and performs, to some degree, the role of what the Americans describe as a 'specialist' and the English used to call a 'jobber'. It is anticipated that the BSMC will be wound up when the Exchange is deemed mature enough. That day will be long in coming.

The Exchange is administered by a board of six governors elected by the members. Members may be either corporations or individuals and include all the commercial banks. As of 31 December 1987, there were 13 companies listed on the Exchange. For the period 12 June to 31 December 1987, 1,536,865 shares changed hands at a purchase price of BDS$3,563,546. Over the same period, the value of the original ten listings rose from BDS$243 million to BDS$387 million. Even more encouraging is the fact that the fees earned by SEB were meeting its operating costs by the end of

1987. Trading activity slowed during 1988 when 1,480,057 shares were traded with a value of BDS$4,168,646, and no additional companies were listed. The Exchange commenced trading in the government-guaranteed Sugar Industry bonds in 1988.

The Jamaica Stock Exchange

The Jamaica Stock Exchange was incorporated with limited liability in September 1967 under the Companies Act of Jamaica and commenced operation in February 1969. Its principal objectives are:

(1) to promote the orderly development of the stock market and a Stock Exchange in Jamaica;
(2) to ensure that the stock market and its broker-members operate at the highest standards practicable;
(3) to develop, apply and enforce rules designed to ensure public confidence in the stock market and its broker-members;
(4) to provide facilities for the transaction of stock market business; and
(5) to conduct research, disseminate relevant information and maintain local and international relationships calculated to enhance the development of the Jamaican stock market.

Stock holding is restricted to broker-members who trade both as agents and as principals. In the latter capacity, certain restrictions apply to transactions between a broker and his own client. Provisions exist for associate membership, without trading privileges, by financial institutions such as trust companies and merchant banks. The broker-members comprise the directors of the Exchange, with the right to exercise all the powers of directors under the Companies Act of Jamaica. The Exchange is governed by a council to which the directors delegate their powers subject to the regulations of the Articles of Memorandum of Association of the company. Although independent of the Central Bank, the Exchange's general manager and staff are all seconded from the Central Bank.

Three types of stock are dealt on the Jamaican Stock Exchange: (i) ordinary/common stock, (ii) preference stock, and (iii) debenture/loan stocks. Government bonds are not listed but are traded principally by broker-members in an over-the-counter market regulated by the Bank of Jamaica. Subject to certain exceptions for commercial banks, only broker-members of the Jamaica Stock Exchange are allowed to deal in government bonds with the Bank of Jamaica.

The listing of securities on the Exchange is in the absolute discretion of the council which may delegate such powers to a duly appointed committee. The minimum requirements for listing of a company's securities are:

- Total issued share and loan capital of J$200,000.00 or more; the share capital portion being not less than J$100,000.00.
- In the case of ordinary shares/stock, a minimum of 100 shareholders holding in their own right not less than 20% of the issued ordinary capital (such percentage being not less than J$50,000.00 nominal value) excluding the holding of one or more controlling share/stock holder(s).

The Trinidad and Tobago Stock Exchange

An informal securities market existed in Trinidad and Tobago for over twenty years prior to the opening of the Trinidad and Tobago Stock Exchange. This informal market took on much greater significance when the government, as a matter of policy, decided to localise the foreign-owned commercial banking and manufacturing enterprises. These were required to divest and sell a majority of their shares to nationals. To effect this policy two institutions were set up – the Capital Market Issues Committee, established by the Minister of Finance in July 1970 to oversee developments in the primary market, and the Call Exchange (an association of dealers in stocks), which was organised in August 1975 under the tutelage of the Central Bank to monitor activities in the secondary market. Parallel to this development in the public sector was the rapid development of private sector institutions, such as trust companies and stock-broking firms, to satisfy the demands of investors in both the primary and the secondary markets.

With a reasonably well-developed infrastructure in place and a corresponding increase in the securities business, the decision was taken to establish a centralised securities market so as to facilitate the orderly development of the domestic capital market. The Securities Industry Act of 1981 formalised the securities market in Trinidad and Tobago. This Act was proclaimed on 23 October 1981, and the Stock Exchange formally opened on 26 October 1981, under the auspices of the Minister of Finance.

The affairs of the Exchange are managed by a Board of Directors consisting of nine individuals, including two members appointed by the Minister of Finance, two members who are stockbrokers and two members elected by all listed companies. The Board of Exchange is responsible for policy direction and normally takes or confirms all strategic decisions related to the Exchange. These decisions reflect the provisions of the Securities Industry Act, the Listing Requirements, and the Rules and Regulations of the Exchange.

There are also the Quotations Committee, the Membership Committee, and the Commission and Dealings Committee. The latter, in turn, delegates the conduct of the day to day operations of the Exchange to the general manager. The Board of Directors decides, through the Quotations Committee, which securities may be listed and traded on the Exchange. On the recommendation of the Commissions and Dealings Committee, the Board may delist or suspend trading in a stock. Through the Membership Committee the Board has the right to examine the financial condition and *modus operandi* of member firms. It also has the right to discipline members for violation of the Exchange rules through temporary suspension, or outright expulsion from the Exchange.

The two principal classes of shares traded on the Exchange are common stock and preferred stock. Trading in government securities is conducted under the aegis of the Investment Division of the Central Bank. At its opening in October 1981, the number of listed companies was 35, with an issued share capital of TT$415.4 million. By November 1982 the number listed had risen to 40 with issued share capital of TT$527.9 million. Between October 1981 and December 1982, listed companies raised additional capital of TT$144 million and the total market value of the securities of listed companies increased from TT$2,291.5 million to TT$3,605 million, an increase of 57.3%. However, 1982 was to prove the peak year; trading declined sharply in 1984 and steadily thereafter.

Obstacles to the further development of equity markets in the Caribbean

The quickening trend away from state ownership removes an important ideological obstacle to the development of equity markets in the region. The more private enterprises there are, the larger the potential supply of listable equities. There are also signs that the traditional hesitation of the black majority to enter business and to hold equity is diminishing. This is especially noticeable in Barbados where the call is for black economic enfranchisement. However, substantial obstacles to the deepening of equity markets still remain in the CARICOM Caribbean.

Low incomes

A fundamental obstacle, of course, is low incomes. Where incomes are relatively low, the sums available for investment in equities are limited. The scope for investment in equity was highest in the MDCs of CARICOM. Unfortunately, incomes in the hitherto oil-rich Trinidad and Tobago have slipped rapidly in recent years; Jamaica's GNP has been drastically cut; that of Barbados has stagnated, while Guyana has become the second poorest nation in the Caribbean.

However, one is shaken by Professor Karl Bennett's estimates of capital flight from the CARICOM Caribbean over the period 1976–85.[5] He estimates that from 1977 to 1985, US$132 million fled from Barbados, US$228 million left Guyana and US$506 million flowed out of Jamaica. His estimate of capital flight from Trinidad and Tobago between 1976 and 1984 is US$1,059 million. The suggestion is that, given an appropriate institutional framework and government policies which inspire confidence in the domestic economy, substantial funds would be available for investments of all types.

Critical mass

To explain the slow development of the market for equities in CARICOM, we must invoke the concept of 'critical mass'. The larger the number of buyers and sellers in a market, the more actively they trade, the greater is the liquidity of the assets being traded and the more willing are investors to enter that market. Unfortunately, ideological pluralism and insularity have combined to create financial compartments within CARICOM, each too small to support a viable stock market. However, if Singapore, with a population of only three million, can develop a vibrant stock exchange capable of attracting foreign investors, then it is just possible that the integrated equity markets of Jamaica, Trinidad and Tobago, Barbados, the OECS, the Bahamas and a recapitalised Guyana, with a population of over five million and natural resources far outstripping those of Singapore, might jointly achieve the critical mass required for a viable stock exchange operation.

The concept of critical mass also applies to the potential size of enterprises. Currently less than 100 enterprises are listed on the three existing stock exchanges. Very few of these are large enough to compete effectively in the international market place. In a world of global production-sharing and global marketing, CARICOM enterprises have been fenced in by restrictions which severely impede region-wide operations.

There is a glimmer of hope on the horizon. Only within the last year the minimal requirement for a regional stock exchange – the CARICOM Enterprise Regime – was approved by all member states. The CARICOM Enterprise has 'full legal personality in every Member State in which it is registered as such, as if it were a company incorporated and registered under the general statutes relating to the incorporation, registration and management of companies.' Each member state undertakes to grant to a CARICOM Enterprise registered in its territory 'terms no less favourable than are accorded to any other similar enterprise of that member state . . . ' in areas required for its effective operation. The CARICOM Enterprise

Regime implicitly allows qualified companies to be listed on any CARICOM stock exchange, thereby opening the door for a regional market for equities.

Regional economic environment

Another obstacle is the unfavourable environment for business operations within the Caribbean. It is certainly easier to conduct business between Barbados and the US than between Jamaica and Trinidad and Tobago – not to speak of Guyana. Exchange control regulations of remarkable complexity inhibit capital flows between the member states of CARICOM; import licensing restrictions, theoretically for monitoring purposes only, have slowed regional trade to a trickle; the intra-regional payments system – CMCF – has collapsed; Barbadian fishermen are fined for catching flying fish in the waters off Trinidad and Tobago; double taxation agreements exist between Barbados and Canada and between Barbados and the US, but not between Barbados and any other CARICOM state; and member states alter their exchange rates and other economic variables without the slightest consultation with each other. In fact, the degree of harmonisation of trade and macro-economic policy is closer between the OECD countries and Japan than among CARICOM member states, theoretically bound by the Treaty of Chaguaramas.

Technical considerations

Of all the obstacles, the technical aspects of the integration of equity markets in CARICOM are by far the least formidable. In fact, the stock markets of the major financial centres of the world are already effectively integrated. The following are the essential features of a viable CARICOM stock exchange.

(1) Format.
   The existing stock exchanges would have to be federated. Provision would be made for the OECS, Guyana, Belize, and the Bahamas to join the system when they establish their own exchanges. CARICOM enterprises could be listed on any or all Exchanges. The partial model would be that of the UK where in 1965 the regional stock exchanges of England, Ireland and Scotland were united to form the Federated Stock Exchange of Great Britain and Ireland.

(2) Centralised clearing system.
   A centralised clearing house would be required for the prompt settlement of transactions involving mutually listed stocks and for the accurate maintenance of records.

(3) Communications.

A communications system linking the three Exchanges would have to be set up. It would involve overseas telephone lines connecting the trading floors of each Exchange, with computerised display units permitting real time display of market information. With the recent advances in computer and telecommunications, the linkage would be neither difficult nor prohibitively expensive.

(4) Shift from call to auction market.

All three existing Exchanges are essentially call systems – with the Trinidad and Tobago Exchange incorporating some elements of an auction. A pure call system would be difficult to operate with players so widely dispersed. The computerised telecommunications system required to link the exchanges also provides the basis for a continuous auction system, allowing for trading both on and off the floor.

(5) Exchange control.

The successful operation of a CARICOM stock exchange requires that the investors of any member state be free to purchase any shares listed on any participating Exchange. Investors would also expect automatic settlement of transactions between investors from different member states. Member states would need to grant blanket exemption from exchange control for all transactions resulting from the operations of a CARICOM stock exchange.

(6) Standardised listing and reporting requirements.

Minimal listing and reporting requirements would have to be established and standardised for all participating Exchanges.

(7) A common unit of account and settlement.

In the absence of an international currency market for the continuous determination of the relative value of CARICOM currencies, a common unit of account, probably the US dollar, would have to be established for the valuation of stocks listed on more than one participating Exchange. The US dollar might also serve as the unit for the settlement of intra-regional transactions.

(8) Surveillance.

A CARICOM stock exchange would have to be supervised by some external authority. Because of their experience in bank supervision, the regional central banks might be assigned the 'watch-dog' duties which the Securities Exchange Commission performs in the US.

Recommendations and concluding observations

The recommendations emerging from the above discussion of the development of equity markets in the CARICOM Caribbean may be summarised as follows:

- exchange control barriers between member states should be removed immediately with respect to transactions in equities, and completely by the early 1990s;
- alien land-holding restrictions and any other barriers to property owner-ship by CARICOM citizens in other member states should be abolished;
- the free movement of capital, enterprise, and technical and professional skills should be institutionalised within CARICOM;
- double taxation treaties should be negotiated among CARICOM mem-ber states and tax policies harmonised as far as possible;
- import licensing arrangements with respect to CARICOM trade should be abolished;
- collaboration between CARICOM member states on exchange rate and other macro-economic policies should be resumed and discussions com-menced towards eventual monetary union;
- the privileges of the CARICOM Enterprise Regime should be extended to all enterprises owned and controlled by CARICOM residents;
- CARICOM governments should divest themselves of commercial enter-prises as soon as the 'infant industry' principle has lost its validity;
- the OECS should seek listing for their eligible enterprises on the Secu-rities Exchange of Barbados; and
- CARICOM member states should commence discussions towards the integration of regional stock exchanges within five years.

If embarked upon, a region-wide stock exchange would take CARICOM states well past the point of no return towards full economic integration. Member states would soon learn that the concessions required to bring it about were not so costly after all, and indeed brought substantial benefits to them both individually and collectively.

On the other hand, failure to 'Caribbeanise' these equity markets would condemn the region to reliance on fragmented and primitive finan-cial institutions and seriously jeopardise future growth. Saddest of all, it would exclude the Caribbean from the growing cast of players in the unfolding drama of the internationalisation of capital markets and the emer-gence of a global economy.

Notes

1 Lewis, Sir Arthur W. (1963) 'Economic Development with Unlimited Supplies of Labour', Agarwala, A.N. and Singh, S.P., eds, *The Economics of Underde-velopment*, New York, OUP, p. 416.
2 Minsky, H. (1967) 'Money Market and Savings Intermediation', Pontecorvo, G., Shay, R. and Hart, A., eds, *Issues in Banking and Monetary Analysis*, New York, Pinehart and Winston, Inc., p. 43.

3 Hart, A. and Kenen, P.B. (1961) *Money, Debt and Economic Activity*, Englewood, N.J., Prentice Hall, p. 122.
4 Gurley, J.G. and Shaw, E.S. (1955) 'Financial Aspects of Economic Development', *American Economic Review*, September p. 523.
5 Bennett, K. (1988) 'External Debt, Capital Flight and Stabilisation Policy: The Experiences of Barbados, Guyana, Jamaica and Trinidad and Tobago', *Social and Economic Studies*, Vol. 37, No. 4, December pp. 57–77.

CHAPTER 13

Venture capital, new investment and the development of stock exchanges in the Caribbean

Marion Williams

This chapter analyses the role which venture capital can play in the economic development of the Caribbean, explains the costs which Caribbean countries pay for the absence of such regimes and examines the kind of fiscal and other support necessary for the establishment of venture capital regimes in Caribbean countries.

The decision to invest in a new project or to set up a new company is based on an analysis of perceived profitability. The level of profitability desired is generally a function of the perceived risk of the undertaking. Venture capital is the term used to describe equity (or finance which involves equity) seeking investment in new ideas, new companies, new products or new services that offer the potential of high return on an investment which bears a high risk. Risk capital (as distinct from venture capital) is generally defined as capital, either equity or loan, invested in a business enterprise where it is at relatively greater risk than collateralised loans to the same enterprise or where the risk for the investor is greater than for common alternative investment opportunities. All venture capital is therefore risk capital though some capital at high risk may not qualify as venture capital.

Risks involved in a venture are both non-diversifiable and diversifiable. It is not possible for an investor to do anything about his non-diversifiable risk though the actions of governments can affect such risk through changes in general economic conditions, inflation rates and generalised tax structure. Where the diversifiable risks are high and returns are low, such ventures are off the curve of feasible options. Governments may take action to alter this risk/return trade-off through fiscal measures designed to assist specific types of investors, altering diversifiable risks for a limited period of time and altering the returns of investment candidates through tax concessions.

Generally speaking, most new ventures in sectors such as retail trade, distribution and, to a lesser extent, services, are not considered high risk operations. Risky operations are those which require investment in substantial equipment, fixed assets, tools, know-how and engineering and must face the uncertainty of product acceptance, marketability, appropriate pricing and, where such goods are exported, foreign exchange variability. In the Caribbean context, venture capital operations tend to be in the manufacturing and export sectors.

In the Caribbean, many existing operations in manufacturing and export industry are not at the high profitability end of the market, yet the risks are high. This explains why export ventures have tended to be slow in coming on-stream. One may conclude that the conditions which give rise to venture capital do not exist in the Caribbean. In Caribbean countries constrained by the need to earn foreign exchange, there is a strong case for artificially improving the potential profitability of these ventures and in so doing, taking some of the risks out of the ventures and adjusting the risk/return trade-off to attract venture capitalists.

In the past, Caribbean governments have paid considerable attention to the need to attract new capital by altering returns of companies in specific activities, principally by way of incentives and tax concessions. Where those concessions differ from those of a venture capital regime is that the company must be in operation in order to benefit from these concessions. The potential investor must therefore look to the profitability of the operation in order to recover his investment.

Very little has been done to alter the diversifiable risk of the investor. The rationale behind the establishment of venture capital regimes is to permit the investor or the venture capital company to recover most or all of his investment independently of the profitability of the operation of the company in which he invests, while at the same time permitting him to share in its potential returns for the duration of his investment. Specific divestment rules invariably assume his exiting the operation by way of sale of his interests thereafter, thus transferring ownership to the venturer. An examination of other venture capital regimes suggest that in order for such regimes to be successful a whole package of tax and other fiscal support must be offered to the investor at the stage of investment as distinct from the stage of operations.

Gross capital formation in many Caribbean countries has been declining (see Table 13.1) and private capital inflows have dwindled (see Table 13.2). In Barbados, for example, the past five years show negative capital flows. This compares with positive flows for the most part in the years prior to 1983. Data for Trinidad and Tobago demonstrate the same trend, while Jamaica experienced both net inflows in some years and net outflows in others.

Venture capital regimes help to pool resources, assisting in the process of domestic resource mobilisation. In the Caribbean, a highly competitive market for export products suggests the need for increased scale of opera-

Table 13.1   *Private gross capital formation of selected CARICOM countries, 1982–8 (in current prices) US$'000.*

	Barbados	Jamaica	Trinidad and Tobago
1982	192	408	n.a.
1983	186	570	1,560
1984	179	425	2,619
1985	164	392	1,911
1986	164	326	3,584
1987	200	n.a.	2,811
1988	235	n.a.	n.a.

Source: Central Bank of Barbados *Annual Statistical Digest*, IMF Reports.

Table 13.2   *CARICOM countries: Private capital flows, 1983–8 (BDS $ million)*

	Barbados	Guyana	Jamaica	Trinidad and Tobago
1983	–13.1	–	–220.4	118.7
1984	–47.3	3.1	239.6	–116.7
1985	–34.3	–	110.0	–84.2
1986	–81.9	–	–46.8	–135.0
1987	–12.4	–	435.2	9.1
1988	–23.9	–	n.a.	41.9

Source: Central Bank of Barbados, *Balance of payments* and *Annual Statistical Digest.*

tions, more advanced levels of technology in equipment and engineering and therefore higher levels of equity participation. Generally, the limited savings of the owner of the company or the sponsor of the idea are insufficient to provide sufficient equity to finance large- or medium-sized projects. The establishment of venture capital regimes provide a basis for the establishment of larger and better technologically equipped companies and thus more competitive operations.

A random sample of the gearing ratios of applicants for credit at one financial institution in Barbados for example, disclosed that gearing ratios tend to average 2.75:1. The samples selected further suggested that medium-sized borrowers in the portfolio were particularly thinly capitalised. Large companies, here defined as those with market value of equity in excess of $3.0 million, had gearing ratios averaging 0.5:1 (see Table 13.3). In the cases of both Trinidad and Barbados, new investment by existing companies tended to be financed through internally generated funds. (The

Table 13.3 Barbados: Gearing of companies.

	Total debt to equity	
	Small and medium-sized companies[1]	Selected large companies[2]
Tourism	2.36	n.a.
Industry	3.07	.64
Manufacturing	1.89	.41
Small business	2.00	n.a.
Fishing	4.43	n.a.
	2.75	.55[3]

Source: 1 Sample of companies, clients with Barbados Development
Bank.
2 Calculated from data in *Performance '89* published by Arthur
Young.
3 Average for two categories only.

Trinidad survey was conducted in 1983 while the evidence for Barbados is
for 1989 and includes 18 of the largest firms in the island). For Trinidad
31% of the companies surveyed used overdraft facilities to finance some
proportion of capital investment. As in Barbados, firms in distribution in
Trinidad and Tobago tended to have higher debt/equity ratios. Perhaps the
nature of their business lent itself to collateralising of security. Sixteen per
cent of firms in the sample had total debt/equity ratios in excess of 5:1 and
45% of those firms were in the distributive sector.

Normally, high gearing reduces the profitability of companies since
additional interest expense on high levels of debt is a charge on profits.
(This is less so in regimes where interest rates are low and where dividend
tax credits are generous). Adequate equity through the systematic establishment of venture capital regimes in the Caribbean could help to provide the
depth of capital needed for growing companies as under-capitalisation of
even promising companies can hasten bankruptcy.

Most policymakers agree that fiscal incentives relating to the operation of manufacturing enterprises are not producing the required results;
that rapid technological advances have left the Caribbean behind; that stiff
competition from other destinations, and a slowdown in private foreign
capital inflows have combined with regional trade problems to place manufacturing and export sectors under some pressure. However, Caribbean
governments struggling to balance their budgets will most likely be highly
sceptical about ceding further potential revenues through a scheme of tax
concessions designed to increase equity in new venture capital companies.

The Caribbean must use the surpluses of the private sector to avert a loss of viability of its foreign exchange earning sectors and reverse the trend towards declining exports evident in many countries over the past five years. Improved access to risk capital and improved profitability are essential ingredients for a turn-around.

Potential new businessmen have tended to take their chances in the lower risk retailing, distribution and service sectors, where there are fewer new skills to be acquired and no new geographical markets to breach. The areas of highest growth tend to be in distribution or in production for the domestic market. In 1989, of the four companies which had the Return on Capital Employed in excess of 20%, three were manufacturing principally for the domestic market. Yet these traditional high-earning activities cannot survive indefinitely unless other sectors earn the foreign exchange to finance their activities.

Demand-dampening measures put in place to stem the outflow of foreign exchange in almost every Caribbean country tend to have the effect of reducing the profitability of companies at the margin, many of them in foreign exchange earning or saving sectors. New business start-ups tend to rise when the economy is buoyant but if a proportionately higher percentage of new businesses are involved in foreign exchange-using activities this growth can be short-lived as foreign exchange needs force countries to adopt demand-dampening measures. For example, the recession of 1981–3 was accompanied by increased bankruptcies in Barbados (see Table 13.4) while the 1984–8 years of positive growth were accompanied by an increase in start-ups. One of the most critical factors in an economic turn-around is to effect a change in the structure of the industrial sector – a shift to encourage entrepreneurs to reinvest surpluses in foreign exchange earn-

Table 13.4   Barbados: Annual liquidations by number of years in operation, 1982–5

	0–4 yrs (4 yrs)	5–8 yrs (4 yrs)	9–12 yrs (4 yrs)	13–16 yrs (4 yrs)	Over 16
1982	5	2	4	4	10
1983	6	6	4	6	8
1984	16	7	6	8	7
1985	10	2	1	1	5
Total 1982–5	37	17	15	19	30

Source: Registrar of Companies.

ing or saving activities. The risk/return trade-offs must be altered to attract surplus-earning companies to reinvest in these activities.

Many countries have established venture capital companies to meet the need for equity capital in desired activities. In developed countries many large profitable companies opt to search for viable projects or use their funds for research and development partly because fiscal systems permit either write-off of research and development costs or credits against tax payable.

In the US, venture capital companies have been set up in this way, many being subsidiaries of a high profit-making parent firm. In other countries they have been given official support either through a series of tax allowances or through the direct involvement of the government in the establishment of a firm to hold equity in companies. In the UK, in addition to the several private venture capital companies, a company was set up by the Bank of England and the clearing banks as a vehicle for providing venture capital to small- and medium-sized businesses. Canada, and Quebec in particular, has paid particular attention to the establishment of a vibrant venture capital regime to encourage new and expanding companies. In Korea, a Korean Technology Advancement Corporation was sponsored by the government and another venture capital company was set up jointly with foreign financial institutions. In Australia, a programme called Management and Investment Companies (MIC) Programme has become a model for other venture capital regimes. The government had no direct involvement but offered a regime of tax incentives for equity investors in licensed MICs. Other developing countries where such regimes have been established are Singapore, Korea, Brazil, India, Mexico and Kenya.

The venture capital industry provides early-stage finance, expansion finance and finance for acquisition or managerial buyouts. This latter is most applicable to Caribbean countries faced with the departure of foreign firms when fiscal incentives expire. Also, if further venture capital is not available for expansion many businesses cannot develop. While this is by no means an explanation of the demise of Barbados' manufacturing sector (the reasons are many and much more complex), some Caribbean manufacturers did suffer for lack of further capital at the critical point when expansion was indicated. The survey conducted by the Central Bank of Trinidad and Tobago in 1983 indicated that 21% of the companies sampled had either to scale down or abandon projects for lack of financing. (The survey was conducted during the boom years.)[1]

Presently, fiscal regimes in the Caribbean tend to give encouragement to investing in public rather than private companies. However, in Barbados, one of the few concessions which encourages investment of new capital is the ability to claim up to $10,000 invested in new shares of public companies and $7,000 invested in the shares of private companies, as of 1990. Caribbean countries could usefully extend tax concessions of this kind to include venture capital defined in a manner which suits the financial needs of each Caribbean economy.

Tax incentives to venture capital may take several forms. Among them are tax credits, tax rebates, deductions from tax payable or taxable income of amounts invested in eligible venture capital companies. In Korea and Brazil, income received from investments is tax free in the hands of the venture capital company and, in addition, some countries make payments to the venture capital company tax-deductible expenses (e.g. Brazil). Investors in the venture capital company may be subject to a lower tax rate or may be tax exempt – usually after a certain minimum period of investment. It has been suggested by some writers on venture capital regimes that the existence of capital gains taxes works to discourage reinvestment in high risk ventures by taking away some of the returns which companies earn through growth, so discouraging venture capital regimes. Some Caribbean countries do have in place capital gains taxes which may well have this effect.

Venture capital is also often required for private companies to go public. Private companies may need a bridge of equity or long-term finance to satisfy listing criteria before going public. Stock exchanges therefore have a role to play in the development of venture capital regimes. Stock exchanges traditionally have not filled the venture capital vacuum since their rules require that the company must first of all be public, its asset base must be fairly large and it must be paying annual dividends. The private company which is young and which is interested in retaining its earnings for future growth rather than paying out dividends is not accommodated.

An active market for company stocks is a crucial factor which makes venture capital feasible as it provides a vehicle for investors to off-load shares when the time for divestment comes. Not all venture capital companies can reach the stage of listing by the time divestment comes and they often need other vehicles to effect transfers of ownership.

Several countries have provided a vehicle to facilitate the needs of small- and medium-sized businesses in the exchange of shares. North American, European and some developing countries, among them Nigeria, have created special exchanges for shares of small companies. The listing requirements of such exchanges are lower (e.g. only a minimum percentage of shares need be held by the public, reporting of shareholders is less frequent and there need be no profitability record or a lower profitability record is acceptable). In some cases, mutual funds and special investment trusts have been authorised to invest in stocks if companies trade in these over-the-counter markets or special exchanges. The development of a special arm to the stock exchanges of the region or the development of an over-the-counter market seems indicated for Caribbean countries.

Venture capital companies do exist in the Caribbean. The Caribbean Financial Services Corporation (CFSC) is a small but critically important source of venture capital. With funding from USAID, the IDB, and the EIB, it provides up to 15% of net worth to any one company or up to US$500,000. The Agricultural Venture Trust, an organisation established by USAID to serve Barbados and the OECS region invests up to 49% of the equity in a corporation or up to 49% of the total capitalisation other than loans in a project involving a small farmer. The CFSC was set up in 1984 and the Caribbean Venture Trust in 1986. These institutions do not benefit from tax and other fiscal concessions and their capital comes almost entirely from overseas rather than from domestic surpluses.

It is probably unrealistic to envisage transnational or trans-Caribbean venture capital companies in different Caribbean countries, working jointly on projects which need substantial resources, each regime being supported by a range of tax and other fiscal concessions. However, large projects requiring capital, technological know-how and perhaps raw materials which reside in different locations may well be candidates for the transnational venture capital company.

The experience of venture capital regimes has been that operations need to be supported by providing technical assistance and advisory services and by facilitating contracts between businessmen and potential overseas marketing and technical partners. The provision of capital is therefore only one part of the entire thrust, but it is a vital part. As Peter Wall (1986) has noted, 'a risk capital industry is a national necessity for any country which puts value on a healthy dynamic private sector.'[2]

Notes

1 Farrell, T, Najjar A., Marcelle H. (1983) *Corporate Financing and Business Use of Bank Credit in Trinidad and Tobago*, Central Bank of Trinidad and Tobago.
2 Wall, P. (1986) *Venture Capital Activities in Selected Countries*, International Finance Corporation.

Part V

Regulatory framework

CHAPTER 14

Problems of regulation and intervention in a small financial system: Trinidad and Tobago in the 1980s

Terrence Farrell

Perhaps more than any other Caribbean country, Trinidad and Tobago has experienced severe difficulties in its financial system from which lessons may be drawn for other countries in respect of bank regulation and intervention by the Central Bank. This chapter discusses the evolution of the regulatory framework in Trinidad and Tobago, the cases of difficulty which prompted certain changes in the approach to and legal basis of regulation and intervention and then points to continuing problems which underscore the need for further legislative change, as well as changes in regulatory practice. It is argued as well that countries in the Caribbean should stoutly resist pressures for the 'de-regulation' of the financial system which is very much in vogue in the industrialised countries.

The evolution of regulation

The regulation of banks in Trinidad and Tobago is provided for in the legislation establishing the Central Bank and the legislation governing the activities of commercial banks, both of which were promulgated in 1964. The legislation provides for the appointment by the President, which means in effect the Cabinet, of an Inspector of Banks who might be (and in fact has always been) an officer of the Central Bank. The functions of the Inspector are:

- to recommend to the Central Bank and to the Minister the issuance of commercial bank licences;
- to determine the financial condition of a licensed institution; and
- to examine and report whether it is in compliance with the provisions of the Banking Act and the Central Bank Act.

If the Inspector finds that an institution is insolvent or is unlikely to be able to meet the demands of its depositors, he reports these findings to the

Minister and to the Central Bank. The Central Bank may then, with the approval of the Minister, suspend the business of the institution for a period of not more than 30 days, and can either re-open the institution with or without conditions, or apply to the court for its winding up. The Inspector has no power to act independently of the Central Bank, which must in turn obtain the approval of the Minister.

The Central Bank created an inspection department in 1968, headed by Mr A.K. Basu who was recruited under the auspices of the International Monetary Fund. The Bank did not intend to establish an inspection function so early in its life, but Governor McLeod was disturbed by the varying practices of the British, Canadian and American banks and took the view that it was important for the Central Bank to have a good understanding of how the system functioned. However, because the commercial banks were all subsidiaries of expatriate banks, most of considerable international re-pute – Citibank, Scotiabank, Chase Manhattan, CIBC, Barclays Bank DCO, and the Royal Bank of Canada – the approach to bank supervision was less to examine for insolvency or potential inability to pay depositors, than to ensure consistency of reporting and compliance with the legislation and the specific monetary policy and exchange control regulations issued from time to time by the Central Bank. The local subsidiaries all made use of well-documented and in some respects rigid procedures and practices laid down by their head offices, and large loans had to be reviewed by the head office before approval was granted. This system gave comfort to the regulatory authority in respect of the solvency of the banks operating locally. Neither was liquidity support a problem, since the head office could be counted on to provide liquidity, if required.

This relaxed approach to bank supervision, focusing on policy and legislative compliance, continued throughout the 1970s. However, there were two important developments in the financial system in the 1970s which were to have profound implications for supervision of banks in the 1980s. Firstly, there was the process of localisation of banks and the growth of 'indigenous' banking institutions. Secondly, there was the rapid growth of non-bank financial institutions. The government, partly in response to social pressures, created the National Commercial Bank in 1970 by buying out the operations of the Bank of London and Montreal. In 1971, the Workers' Bank was created by the trade union movement, with some government participation and a great deal of government encouragement. In 1976, the Trinidad Co-operative Bank was granted a commercial bank licence, transforming overnight a 60-year-old thrift institution into a fully-fledged commercial bank, in a highly competitive environment. In addition, the government persuaded the expatriate banks to incorporate locally and divest a majority of their shares to locals. All the expatriate banks localised their operations with the exception of Chase Manhattan, which elected to sell its total operations rather than localise. Its operations were bought by the National Commercial Bank.

The second factor was the proliferation of non-bank financial institutions. These were created by both banks and by non-financial companies and their numbers and assets grew rapidly during the 1970s, since their operations were unregulated. Indeed non-bank activity – finance companies, trust business, mortgage financing and subsequently merchant banking – became important areas of competition for commercial banks in what was a booming economy. The entry of non-financial enterprises was a source of concern to the banks and to the authorities, but the authorities were slow to put a regulatory framework in place to deal with the new sector. This eventually came with the passage of the Financial Institutions (Non-Banking) – NFI – Act in 1979. This Act, however, was not proclaimed until May 1981, when the relevant regulations were published.

The NFI Act contained many of the provisions of the Banking Act, the only difference being that it demarcated commercial banking from non-bank activity. Non-banks were restricted to the acceptance of deposits and to the granting of loans for a period of not less than one year, with exceptions for merchant banking and trade confirming. It also provided for the annual application and issuance of licences, whereas banks merely paid a fee annually once they had been initially licensed. The NFI Act made no advance in respect of the functions of the Inspector who was merely given the additional responsibility for supervising all non-bank financial institutions covered by the Act.

The system of regulation prevailing in 1980 may be described as follows. Firstly, regulation extended only to commercial banks while other deposit-taking institutions were not yet regulated, and institutions such as credit unions and development finance institutions were not subject to regulation. Bank supervision focused on compliance, and was therefore backward-looking. There was no power to prescribe or to enforce. Secondly, self-regulation was not in use. The commercial banks had created an informal pricing cartel in the 1960s and early 1970s, but this broke down, and the banks had established no formal mechanism that addressed prudential self-regulation. The informal meetings of bankers may have softened the sharper edges of competition in the market-place, but could not really be considered a viable or useful self-regulatory mechanism. Thirdly, unwittingly, the principle of *caveat emptor* was the effective organising principle of regulation in a financial system where the average investor or depositor was quite unsophisticated, new institutions were being created and the institutions themselves were introducing new products at a rapid pace, with the average client unable to evaluate properly the risk characteristics of the products. Yet the scramble to try to maintain relative real incomes prompted many of these individuals to accept risks, which became larger and crystallised as the economy slowed and began to decline. Fourthly, there was no deposit insurance, nor indeed was the introduction of deposit insurance on the policy or legislative agenda of the monetary authorities.

If the system of regulation in the early 1980s was little different from a decade earlier, the regulatory environment was markedly different. The Inspection Department now had to supervise new commercial banks which did not have the comfort of an overseas head office in respect of liquidity and solvency, with new boards of directors reflecting local shareholding in formerly wholly foreign-owned banks, and in some cases, new management comprising mainly local professional bankers, and over 20 new non-bank financial institutions. In addition, the economy began to decline at an accelerating rate, depressing the real estate market and the construction sector first and hardest, and then spreading to all areas of economic activity. Before very long the financial system was in trouble, and required not only a regulatory response but also direct intervention by the Central Bank as lender of last resort.

The shaking of the system

While the difficulties experienced in the financial system in Trinidad and Tobago can be dated back to August 1983 when the International Trust Limited (ITL) crisis broke, the genesis of the problems was much earlier. During the boom years, liquidity in the banking system reached historically high levels and there was intense competition to lend in a highly buoyant market-place. The new finance companies, especially those owned by non-financial enterprises (the so-called 'independent' finance companies) were particularly aggressive in their lending and often ignored prudential norms such as loan to capital ratio, loan to deposit ratio and the adequacy of collateral security. There was a concentration of lending to the construction sector and a significant proportion of loans were secured by real estate. Moreover, lending to affiliated or related companies far exceeded prudential norms.

When the NFI Act came into force in May 1981, many of these finance companies were seriously in breach of the legislation in respect of:

• the acquisition and holding of land; and
• the extent of unsecured lending to associate companies, employees or directors.

Under the legislation, the options available to the regulatory authorities were to refuse to licence those institutions which were in breach of the law and thereby cause them to be wound up by their depositors and creditors, or to licence them conditionally, allowing them a period of time to put their houses in order by ensuring full compliance with the Act. At that stage, the regulatory authorities could have dealt only with the issue of compliance, since without the benefit of an on-site inspection, the solvency or otherwise of these institutions could not be assessed.

The Bank Inspection Department of the Central Bank set about trying to organise itself to undertake the required examinations. However, it was hampered by both technical and resource constraints. The department now had three times as many institutions with which to deal and therefore required a substantial increase in manpower, since bank examination is a highly labour-intensive activity. In addition, the nature of the examination required was different from the compliance-type examinations it had been accustomed to undertake. It was required to make a judgement on the condition of the business as a going concern, its liquidity and its managerial capacity. These judgements necessitated a higher order and greater amount of skill and knowledge than was then resident in the Inspection Department. Importantly, a judgement on the solvency of the institutions required an assessment of the likely evolution of the economy and the financial system as a whole.

Circumstances did not permit the regulatory authorities to get their house in order to deal with a radically different regulatory environment. One finance company, Pinnacle Finance Co. Ltd., was refused even a conditional licence under the NFI Act, since its paid-up capital was the princely sum of TT$3. In March 1982, the officer of that company fled the country leaving behind depositors who were unable to recover their funds. In August 1983, a magistrate fined the managing director of International Trust Limited (ITL) the sum of TT$7.2 million in respect of an exchange control violation. The announcement of this fine precipitated a run on the institution, which continued notwithstanding reassurances from the Governor of the Central Bank. Eventually, the Bank, in order to stop the run, declared that the institution did not have to meet demands for fixed deposits until the maturity date of the deposit. This had the effect of slowing the run to a 'walk'. However, public confidence had been rudely shaken. ITL had a fairly large deposit base and about 4,000 depositors.

The Central Bank suspended the operations of ITL under the Act on 15 September, 1983. It seemed unlikely that the institution could be successfully reopened without new management and a substantial injection of capital. The Central Bank sought unsuccessfully to obtain the assistance of the other banks and financial institutions since it did not have the legal authority to inject new capital. However, there were other parties interested in purchasing the company. Because the 30-day period of suspension was coming to an end, and to give the interested parties the opportunity to bid for purchase, the Central Bank exercised the only other option available under the Act. It applied to the High Court for the institution to be put into receivership on 14 October 1983. The application was challenged by the directors of ITL and the court case on the receivership, which went to appeal and lasted a few years, revealed a sorry and sordid tale of unsecured lending, self-dealing and mismanagement which began to reflect badly on all of the independent finance companies.

Several of the other independent finance companies began to come under pressure as depositors withdrew their funds on maturity despite the efforts of their managements to have deposits rolled over at even higher interest rates. In March 1984 the Central Bank suspended the business of another non-bank finance company, Southern Finance, which was unable to meet the demands of its depositors. The company was allowed to reopen for business after the 30-day suspension period under certain conditions. Efforts to arrange the restructuring and recapitalisation of this institution by finding a buyer were frustrated by the company's management and eventually proved fruitless.

After the experiences of ITL and Southern Finance, and the continuing pressure on other finance companies, the Central Bank and the Inspector of Banks recognised that substantive changes to the legislation were required so as to give the Bank powers which would extend beyond suspension and liquidation and which would offer depositors a greater measure of protection than was available through court action on a liquidation. The Bank also recognised a need to provide liquidity support for the problem institutions pending the promulgation of the new legislation.

Accordingly, in July 1984, the Central Bank arranged a liquidity support facility through the commercial banks for the problem institutions. The support mechanism was arranged through the banks partly because the Bank felt that a demonstration of support by the banking system for the problem institutions would help to contain the erosion of confidence and prevent it from spreading to other institutions, including the banks themselves, and partly because of the legal restrictions in the Central Bank's own legislation on the terms of lending to financial institutions. Section 36(i) of the Central Bank Act permits the Bank to lend to commercial banks and NFIs for fixed periods not exceeding six months with approved security. The appropriate security was a vexing problem for the Bank since many of the problem institutions could offer only real estate which the Bank could not accept, and they usually did not have treasury bills, bills of exchange or other similar security appropriate to an advance from the Central Bank.

The amendments and additions to the legislation were long in coming and it was not until February 1986 that both the Central Bank and NFI Acts were amended. In the intervening period, the Bank provided TT$142 million in support to the problem non-bank institutions, which were unable to improve their situations notwithstanding.

The amendments introduced in 1986 gave the Bank the power, with the approval of the Minister of Finance, to take over the management of an institution, dismiss its board of directors, and restructure its business and recapitalise its operations. The powers of the Bank may be exercised where the interests of depositors or creditors are threatened, when the institution threatens to default on its obligations or when it does not maintain high standards of financial probity. The powers given to the Bank under these amendments are for emergencies and may be used only if the Bank is of the opinion that the financial system is in danger of disruption or damage. The amendments also provide for the creation of a Deposit Insurance Corporation (DIC) to provide protection up to TT$50,000 for eligible depositors in member institutions of the Deposit Insurance Fund. All licensed institutions are required to be members of the Fund.

The amendments make no mention of the role of the Inspector of Banks in the process of the exercise of the powers conferred on the Bank, save that the Central Bank may appoint the Inspector of Banks to perform some of its functions. The amendments therefore left the role of the Inspector essentially as a recommender and without power to enforce or direct in his own right.

Perhaps surprisingly, the first institution to be affected by the Bank's new emergency powers was not an NFI but a commercial bank. The Trinidad Co-operative Bank had been granted a commercial banking licence in 1976. Over the decade to 1986 it was quite unable to make an impression in a highly competitive, oligopolistic market-place. The other commercial banks had many more branches in far superior locations, and had invested heavily in new technologies and services such as ATMs, interest-bearing cheque accounts and easy consumer loans. The 'Penny Bank', as it is called, found it difficult to mobilise deposits given its four small, badly-located branches. It therefore gravitated into the wholesale deposit market in order to support a loan portfolio that was weak because of a high proportion of high-risk assets.

The issue which precipitated Central Bank intervention was that the bank, as a company listed on the stock exchange, had to publish its accounts which would have shown a massive loss for the financial year. Fearing the effect this publication might have on a public already fearful and of waning confidence, the Central Bank assumed control of the institution under the newly-granted emergency powers. This it did in perhaps the smoothest intervention to date. The Penny Bank was never suspended or closed. The Central Bank assumed control over a weekend and on the Monday morning it had its inspection staff temporarily in control until new management, drawn from the National Commercial Bank, was put in place. There was no run or loss of confidence, aided by the fact that the problems of the bank were not generally known to the public and the media, and it was a relatively small institution. The Central Bank also stressed that it would not allow an institution which was under its care to fail. The intervention subsequently involved the purchase by the Central Bank of the portfolio of doubtful loans of the Penny Bank, and the appointment of a new board of directors. This latter exercise proved to be quite difficult since the Bank discovered that although its emergency powers allowed it to dismiss a board and the management of a financial institution, it did not have the power to appoint a new board. The Penny Bank remains under the control of the Central Bank up to this time, and although it has managed to record small profits in the last two financial years, it still carries a substantial accumulated loss position.

In September 1986, the Central Bank moved to close the independent finance companies which it had been supporting pending the introduction of the legislation and the establishment of the Deposit Insurance Corporation (DIC). The Bank took the view that deposit insurance was a key element in the restoration of public confidence in the financial system, since it was clear that it would be impossible to restructure successfully the independent companies so as to protect depositors to any reasonable degree. Once the DIC had been established, therefore, and the problem companies – Trade Confirmers, SWAIT Finance, Summit Finance, Commercial Finance and MAT Securities – had been registered as members, the Bank moved to suspend their operations and subsequently appointed the DIC to liquidate their operations. MAT Securities was given a reprieve since several large depositors agreed to convert their deposits into equity and developed a business plan for that institution which the Bank accepted. That plan failed, and in September 1988, MAT Securities too was put into liquidation.

Towards the end of 1988, the Central Bank became increasingly concerned about the Workers' Bank and its subsidiary trust company. The Inspector of Banks' evaluation of the portfolio of both institutions suggested that they were technically insolvent. The trust company's portfolio was mainly in mortgages and many of these were based on a variable payment amortisation plan which had assumed that mortgagors' incomes would be rising into the medium- and long-term future. With the decline in the economy, this assumption was no longer valid. The loan portfolio of the bank was also in poor shape since the bank had been able to attract only marginal and therefore high-risk or speculative business. Moreover, the bank had only eight branches, which limited the raising of retail deposits and caused an inordinate reliance on wholesale corporate deposits and interbank borrowings for funding. These deposits were not only high cost but also volatile. Borrowings from the Central Bank, ostensibly for liquidity support, had developed into hard core borrowing which reached 19% of total liabilities.

Attempts at suasion by the Inspector's office over the years had failed to bring results and this helped to confirm the Bank's view that the management of the institution was not up to the task of restructuring without intervention. The state of the portfolio was so weak that the option of closure could not be ruled out. The regulatory authorities elected to attempt to restructure and recapitalise the institution because closure would have been costly to the Deposit Insurance Corporation and would have weakened the confidence of the community in the banking system as a whole. Political, social and psychological factors combined to push the Bank towards restructuring.

The intervention was not as smooth as in the Trinidad Co-operative Bank's case. The institution had to be suspended, which meant that depositors were denied access to their accounts for the 30-day period, and a new institution incorporated in which the assets of the Workers' Bank and its trust company were vested. The Central Bank assumed control of both the new and old institutions in order to effect the transfer and to provide some assurance to the depositors and creditors who now had to deal with the new institution, which is called Workers' Bank (1989) Limited.

Issues in regulation

The experience of Trinidad and Tobago in the 1980s highlights a number of issues in the regulation of financial institutions in small financial systems, and might be especially pertinent to other Caribbean territories whose financial histories are similar, and which may experience similar problems. The first issue surrounds the coverage of regulation. In Trinidad and Tobago, a large class of deposit-taking institutions remained outside the regulatory framework until as late as 1981. This class of institution – trust and mortgage finance institutions and finance companies – had been in existence when the Banking Act was promulgated although their numbers and significance were not great, and ought to have been included in coverage of regulated institutions at that time or soon after. As we have seen, a great deal of mismanagement, misfeasance and mischief had already occurred, and the economic environment was not conducive to a speedy rectification of the problems.

Regulatory authorities also need to be concerned about institutions which are not deposit-taking, but whose activities may impact directly on the banking system. In Trinidad and Tobago, there have also been failures among insurance companies and the casualty rate among credit unions is increasing. While the Central Bank and the office of the Inspector of Banks cannot be expected to supervise these institutions as well, there is need for co-ordination among the various regulatory authorities. In Trinidad and Tobago, the supervision of insurance companies has been attended by several problems including late submission of data and problems of enforcement, and it is only recently that the position of Supervisor of Insurance has been vested in a position separate from the Permanent Secretary in the Ministry of Finance. Credit unions are not regulated in the same sense as non-banks, or even insurance companies. Yet, some of these institutions have become major mobilisers of funds from the public and place large deposits with, and have substantial borrowings from, the commercial banks.

The second issue is the need to supplement regulation with deposit insurance, and if possible with some form of self-regulation. It should be noted that we do not view these as alternatives. Indeed some neo-classical analysts argue that regulation is inefficient and costly, and that therefore it should be replaced with deposit insurance and further, that the deposit insurance premium must in some way be related to the risks assumed by institutions. In small economies with small financial systems, portfolio diversification in order to minimise risk is constrained by the skewness of the economy and the limited number of firms and therefore of risks which may be assumed. In small financial systems, therefore, particularly where the economy is subject to external shocks, the overall riskiness of the portfolios of financial institutions is likely to be greater than that of institutions in larger and more diversified economies. In addition, in developing countries, the average investor is less sophisticated and less well informed than his counterpart in an industrialised country. He is therefore less able to evaluate the risk/return profile of the financial institutions in which he may place his funds, and is more vulnerable to losses.

These arguments are sufficiently persuasive of the need for regulation and some form of deposit insurance. Deposit insurance, without regulation, would be especially prone to the problems of moral hazard in an environment in which the diversification of risk is less possible on account of small size. Regulation alone would not be sufficient since failures are likely to occur notwithstanding, and without deposit insurance, public confidence would always be low and this would make the process of financial intermediation less efficient. Authorities in small financial systems would therefore do well to introduce a deposit insurance scheme at an early stage, especially in a situation in which the financial institutions do not have a lender of first resort in the form of a parent or head office.

The question of self-regulation can only now be raised in the financial system of Trinidad and Tobago. The commercial banks have recently formed an Institute of Banking, which can admit non-bank institutions as members. Although the principal purpose of the institute is professional education of bankers, it has embraced a 'code of ethics' and it is not inconceivable that the Institute may be persuaded to adopt prudential norms binding on its members. This type of initiative could certainly help in regulation and could make the moral suasion of the Inspector and the Bank more effective.

Thirdly, localisation and the licensing of a commercial bank or a thrift institution meant that the new entities did not enjoy the first line of defence which foreign-owned institutions had, and therefore in the event of difficulty, they came immediately and directly to the lender of last resort. Indigenous institutions also had to develop their own procedures and systems, and did not always have experienced bankers at the helm. Moreover, the new indigenous institutions had to carve out a niche in the market-place for themselves and often found themselves with marginal business, poor locations, high risk accounts and a volatile deposit base. This meant that their portfolios were even more risky than might be indicated by the size of the economy and the availability of business opportunities.

A fourth issue concerns what may be described as the regulatory capacity. As earlier noted, in 1981, the Inspector of Banks found his office having to deal with over 20 new institutions of varying sizes and types of business, and also with real concerns about the basic viability of certain finance companies. While it is true that the legislation was passed in 1979, and therefore the Central Bank, in which the Inspector's office is housed, had two years to prepare, the recruitment of staff with the level and mix of skills needed to be addressed (not only compliance, but also liquidity and solvency and to design strategies of intervention) proved to be difficult in a buoyant economy in which persons with those kinds of skills were being employed at high rates of pay elsewhere in the economy.

A fifth issue surrounds the question of intervention. Regulation is intended to avoid intervention, but experience world-wide has shown that at some time it becomes necessary to intervene in an institution either to cause it to take action to make certain changes in its operations or to close it down, or to restructure its management or capital base or its scope of operations. In a small financial system in a small country, an intervention may become highly politicised. The interests of depositors, creditors and shareholders compete and conflict and inevitably cause reactions in the political sphere. These reactions may put additional pressure on the regulatory authorities. In the case of the Workers' Bank, the fact that it was an institution owned by workers and their representatives, immediately brought a resolution of its deep-seated problems into the realm of politics. It also raised questions of ethnicity in what is a plural society in which the ownership and control of resources follows ethnic lines to a significant degree. The Trinidad and Tobago experience also suggests that legislation should provide for Central Bank's application for liquidation or receivership through the courts to be made *ex parte* and unchallenged on account of the length of the process, the publicity generated and the cost of litigation. This has been most evident in the ITL case which has only recently been resolved, and where because of the length of time and the numerous legal battles, depositors have experienced a severe erosion of the value of their deposits.

The Trinidad and Tobago experience also suggests that it is useful for the Inspector of Banks to have certain directive powers, and powers of sanction before the Central Bank and the Ministry of Finance become formally involved. The Inspector should be able, after consultation with the Bank, to issue 'cease and desist' orders to financial institutions, and require that certain managers be removed. The power to determine the board of directors of an institution is best left in the hands of the Bank since it is a serious step, indicating that the affairs of the institution are in disarray. The options available to the regulatory authorities should therefore span the spectrum from suasion to directives, to powers of appointment and dismissal of management and boards to restructuring or outright closure of an institution which cannot be salvaged, with the safety net of deposit insurance to protect the smallest and least sophisticated depositors.

A final observation is that the experience of Trinidad and Tobago has been that changes in the regulatory framework came only after a crisis had emerged and the inadequacies of the existing legislation were made crystal clear in actual practice. Even in a situation of crisis, the political directorate and the drafters of the legislation moved slowly to put new measures in place, and as experience subsequent to the new measures has shown, there are still gaps and loopholes in the legal framework of regulation. Admittedly, lawmakers have to be concerned about the protection of the fundamental rights and freedoms of individuals, and removal of certain powers from the judicial realm to the administrative realm can be fraught with danger if these powers are abused. However, where judicial restraint of administrative power and judicial resolution is given prominence, there may be the perverse result of mismanagement and even fraud being protected on grounds of constitutional rights of the individual, while the rights of depositors to the access to and enjoyment of the property takes second place. As far as the financial system is concerned, the preference is for the administrative exercise of power in the interest of depositors and creditors, with managers and directors having recourse to the courts *ex post facto* if they feel that they have been aggrieved by the intervention of the regulatory authorities.

Summary and conclusion

This chapter has sought to review the experience of regulation in Trinidad and Tobago. This experience is particularly instructive because the financial system has been shaken by several failures over the last seven years, which in turn have precipitated changes in the framework of regulation. Several issues in regulation in the context of small financial institutions were identified, based on the experience of the financial system in Trinidad and Tobago in the 1980s. These were:

- the institutions which should be covered by regulation;
- the need for deposit insurance and if possible, some form of self-regulation to supplement and complement regulation;
- the special problem for regulation and for the lender of last resort posed by the localisation of financial institutions and the growth of indigenous institutions;
- regulatory capacity;
- the 'political sociology' of intervention in a small, plural society; and
- the problems which attend judicial *vis-à-vis* administrative resolution of problems in the financial system.

In conclusion, policymakers and their advisers in small open economies should at all costs avoid the 'deregulation' of their financial systems in the interest of the efficiencies which are presumed to flow from such a move. These financial systems need more and closer regulation, not less. It is also important that adequate regulatory and insurance measures be put in place before a crisis occurs. The loss of confidence which results from inadequate intervention is far more costly to the economy than concerns that administrative power will be abused.

CHAPTER 15

The regulatory framework for financial institutions in the OECS

Eustace Liburd

The OECS (Organisation of East Caribbean States) financial sector consists broadly of three categories of institutions. The commercial banking sector, in which both foreign and indigenous banks operate, provides the basic infrastructure to the financial system and is well linked to the world financial markets. An emerging non-bank financial sector includes credit unions and finance companies. The third category includes the providers of long-term funds, namely the development banks and the national insurance schemes. Except for one mortgage and one general finance company, the non-bank financial intermediaries are locally incorporated and operate only within their home country. The commercial banks and the non-bank financial institutions tend to operate in different segments of the market with little competition between the two groups.

There are two factors which give rise to the need for banking regulations. The first involves the bank loans and investment which lead to the creation of deposits. Since these deposits make up the major portion of a country's money supply, the quality of bank credit underlies the value of money. The second factor is the nature of the financial intermediary role that banks fulfill in the economy. Banks receive deposits that are highly liquid. These deposits are invested by banks in other less-liquid assets. To prevent a liquidity crisis banks must hold some liquid assets, have adequate capital and maintain professional management. In the OECS, two agencies have responsibilities in a regulatory process that is just evolving: member countries' Ministries of Finance and the Eastern Caribbean Central Bank (ECCB).

Existing legal framework

In the OECS, Ministers of Finance are entrusted with the power to grant banking licences and to implement each territory's banking act. The legislation does not establish a comprehensive framework for the regulation of financial institutions; it governs the operations of banks (including development banks) but does not apply to non-bank financial institutions which are governed by separate pieces of legislation. Generally, the banking acts do not go beyond stipulating the capital requirement for establishing a bank and certain regulatory ratios to be observed.

The operating ratios applied to banks include the reserve fund ratio that requires the banks to channel at least 25% of their profits into a reserve fund up to the amount of the paid-up capital. This regulation can be varied by the Minister of Finance for banks that are considered to be in sound financial condition. As a result of this provision, foreign banks have generally been exempt from having to comply with this ratio. There is also a stipulation that deposit liabilities may not exceed twenty times the paid-up capital and reserves of the bank. In practice these minimum capital requirements have been applied only to locally-incorporated banks. In the case of the branches of overseas banks, the capital of the head office is considered to have satisfied the minimum capitalisation criteria.

In most OECS jurisdictions the acts also restrict the size of loans that a bank may grant to individual customers to a certain proportion of the bank's capital and reserves. The extent of banks' involvement in the equity holding of commercial, industrial, agricultural and other enterprises is limited. Generally, banks are permitted to hold real assets only for their own use.

The acts do not, in general, provide a basis for regulating lending policies or influencing the structure of interest rates. In Dominica, Antigua and Barbuda and St Lucia, they provide for regular inspection by a banking inspector appointed by the Minister of Finance. However, prior to the establishment of the ECCB in October 1983 and the subsequent introduction of a Bank Supervision Department in the Central Bank, this provision for inspection was rarely implemented.

The agreement establishing the ECCB provides the Bank with powers to regulate the activities of the financial institutions in the area. These powers are derived from Article 3(2) of the agreement which states that the Bank will have power to 'regulate banking business on behalf and in collaboration with participating governments'. Since licences for establishment of banks are given by the participating governments in the respective territories, any supervisory role exercised by the Central Bank in this regard has to be with the acquiescence and collaboration of the individual participating government.

Other powers to exercise regulation come from Article 35(1) of the agreement, which requires financial institutions to furnish information and data to ensure compliance with reserve requirements and other stipulations such as interest rates on deposits, loans, margins on loans, etc. The Central Bank has a limited supervisory role in respect of offshore financial institutions and it may administer or participate in schemes for insuring bank deposits.

Even though these and other powers conferred in the articles of agreement are broad, in most instances they do not specify the type of penal action the Bank can take in case any financial institution has failed to observe the regulations. Only participating governments can take appropriate measures to rectify deficiencies in the operation of banks in their respective jurisdictions, especially when it relates to the management of funds.

The draft uniform Banking Act

Partly in an effort to overhaul and update the existing legislation and partly to give greater effect to the regulatory powers conferred in the Central Bank Agreement referred to earlier, the participating governments have agreed to the implementation of a uniform Banking Act for the area. This upgrading is in response to developments in the financial sector, including the establishment of locally-incorporated commercial banks which lacked the support and close supervision to which the overseas offices of foreign banks have traditionally been subjected. Also, the non-bank financial institutions (including credit unions and finance houses) have emerged as significant providers of financial services, and the existing legislation governing their activities is inadequate.

Two categories of financial institution are subject to supervision under the proposed Banking Act: banks and credit institutions. A bank is distinguished by the acceptance of the chequeing deposits. While credit unions, building societies, finance companies and other similar institutions will come under the ambit of the Act, it will be left to a decision of the Monetary Council to determine when the relevant provisions relating to such institutions may be invoked.

Implementation of the uniform act will greatly enhance the role of the Central Bank in the supervision of the financial systems. The authority to grant licences continues to reside with the respective ministers of finance but an advisory role is envisaged for the Central Bank in that process. There is provision for the minister, before the granting of a licence, to request the Bank to conduct an investigation into the financial condition and history of the applicant, the characters of the persons to be involved in the management, the adequacy of the capital structure, the validity of documents submitted and the needs of the community to be served by the granting of the licence. Provision is made for the Bank to examine financial institutions from time to time or whenever it is necessary or expedient.

The proposed Act prescribes new minimum capital requirements for financial institutions, including an assigned capital in the case of financial institutions incorporated abroad. If operating as a bank, the minimum capital is not to be less than EC$5 million, but in the case of credit institutions, the Act empowers the Minister, after consultation with the Central Bank, to prescribe the minimum capital.

Other financial requirements to be observed under the proposed Act include the maintenance of a reserve fund; a ratio of 20:1 for total liabilities to paid-up capital and reserves; credit limitations to single and interconnected borrowers of 15% of capital and reserves; and provisions to limit insider loans. To facilitate monetary policy objectives, the Act also provides that financial institutions can be required to maintain specified assets expressed as a percentage of specified liabilities. This provision reinforces that of Article 33 of the Central Bank Agreement, which deals with minimum required reserves.

The supervisory process

The basic objective of regulating the operations of banks is to safeguard the interest of the depositors and to build up and maintain a sound banking system to meet the social requirements and economic objectives of the particular country. At the micro level, there are periodical inspections of individual financial institutions and guidelines are set for the amount, type and nature of individual assets banks can acquire using deposit resources. At the monetary policy level, there are currently not many regulations in force. The cash reserve requirement stipulates that banks keep a minimum of 6% of their deposit liabilities as balances with the Central Bank. Cash reserves are required both as a tool of monetary policy and for the protection of depositors, although these funds provide only minimum backing for deposits and are not generally considered adequate for an institution in crisis. The Central Bank has stipulated that banks pay a minimum of 4% rate of interest per annum on savings deposits. The policy stance in relation to interest rates has been that they ought to be established by the free interplay of market forces. However, given the small and imperfect market, it became necessary to establish a minimum rate for savings deposits.

At the ECCB, the supervisory process at present consists of on-site inspections and analysis of prudential and other returns submitted by banks periodically. At this early stage of development of the Bank Supervision Department, in-depth on-site inspections have been confined mainly, although not exclusively, to indigenous or locally incorporated banks. They encompass examination of the quality and soundness of assets – in particular the loan portfolio – a review of capital adequacy, liquidity and external and/or currency exposure. Annual meetings with bankers provide an avenue for discussing general problems and specific issues facing individual banks. Inspection reports on individual banks are sent to the respective banks for comments and to the government of the territory for information and such action as is deemed necessary.

Analysis of monthly balance sheets, quarterly returns on ownership and maturity of deposits, structure of loans and advances, interest rates on deposits and loans provide information on bank activity and progress. They may be used, for example, to analyse the riskiness of lending activity in the light of the maturity structure of deposits and the prevailing economic situation. The interest margin between deposits and advances, and past information on operating expenditures, give an indication of the direction in which profitability of the bank is moving. The final picture is, of course, assessed by the annual return on earnings and expenses submitted by the banks. The supervisors pay special attention to the adequacy of provisions made for bad and doubtful debts.

During 1988, banks in the ECCB area earned a return of 2.5% on assets, well above the rate earned by banks in many countries. For the large majority of locally incorporated banks net worth as a proportion of risk assets was well above 15% and capital and reserves well above 7% of deposits. A small minority of these banks, however, do need strengthening of capital to meet the standards stipulated by supervising authorities in many developed countries.

The regulatory framework for the supervision of financial institutions in the OECS is just evolving. To date, efforts at prudential supervision by the Central Bank have been concentrated mainly on the commercial banks. This is justifiable on the basis of the need for widespread confidence in banks as the main providers of the community's means of payment.

There is also the recognition that a safe and well-run banking system is central to the economic and financial health of the countries.

Due to the absence of uniform banking legislation, the ECCB is unable to articulate an independent and comprehensive supervisory role in respect of financial and management systems and performance of banks but it appears that banks in the territories are acquitting themselves well, and following sound practices. There is scope for improvement. This should come when ECCB takes on new powers envisaged in the uniform banking legislation.

Part VI

External financial flows, debt and capital flight

External financial flows to developing countries with particular reference to the Commonwealth Caribbean: Trends and issues

Dinesh Dodhia

Overview

Net flows

According to the OECD, total net financial flows[1] to developing countries, in current dollar terms, after declining sharply from the peak of $138 billion in 1981 to $84 billion in 1986, rose for the third successive year to $109 billion in 1989 (see Table 16.1). In real terms (i.e. when adjustments are made for inflation and the changes in the dollar exchange rate), however, flows in 1981 were only about 55% of the 1981 level.

Commercial bank lending and export credits were largely responsible for the dramatic decline in overall flows to developing countries during the 1980s, in particular after the outbreak of the debt crisis in 1982. Flows of official development assistance[2] (ODA) or aid, after a drop in 1981–3, rose steadily in nominal terms although in real terms in 1989 they were only marginally above the 1981 level. Flows of non-concessional ODF – official development finance[3] also rose strongly during the 1980s, while direct investment flows, after falling sharply between 1981 and 1985, recovered during the 1986-9 period. Overall, the share of financing provided by international capital markets, which comprised nearly 40% of the total flows in 1981, fell to 9% of the total in 1989. Similarly, the share of export credits[4] in the total flows fell from 13% in 1981 to 1% in 1989. By contrast, ODA flows comprised 47%, non-concessional ODF about 15% and direct investment about 20% of the total in 1989, compared to around 30%, 6% and 13% respectively in 1981.

For the twelve independent countries of the Commonwealth Caribbean (Antigua and Barbuda, the Bahamas, Barbados, Belize, Dominica, Grenada, Guyana, Jamaica, St Kitts-Nevis, St Lucia, St Vincent and the Grenadines, and Trinidad and Tobago), estimates based on OECD data indicate that during the 1980s net flows to the region were subject to wild

Table 16.1 Net financial flows to developing countries,[i] 1981 and 1985–9

	US$ billion						Per cent of total			
	1981	1985	1986	1987	1988	1989[ii]	1981	1985	1988	1989
I Official Development Finance (ODF)	45.5	48.9	56.2	61.6	66.1	67.1	33.1	58.0	63.4	61.6
1 Official development assistance (ODA)	36.8	37.3	44.4	48.3	51.7	51.3	26.8	44.2	49.6	47.1
of which: Bilateral	28.9	28.8	34.9	38.2	40.3	39.8	21.0	34.2	38.6	36.5
Multilateral	7.9	8.5	9.5	10.1	11.4	11.5	5.7	10.1	10.9	10.6
2 Other ODF	8.7	11.6	11.8	13.3	14.4	15.8	6.3	13.8	13.8	14.5
of which: Bilateral	3.0	3.7	4.0	6.6	7.9	9.0	2.2	4.4	7.6	8.3
Multilateral	5.7	7.9	7.8	6.7	6.5	6.8	4.1	9.4	6.2	6.2
II Total export credits	17.6	4.0	-0.7	-2.6	-0.5	1.2	12.8	4.7	-0.5	1.1
1 DAC countries	16.2	3.4	-0.9	-2.9	-0.9	1.0	11.8	4.0	-0.9	0.9
of which: Medium and Long-term	13.3	0.2	-2.1	-1.2	-1.1	–	9.7	0.2	1.1	–
Short-term	2.9	3.2	3.0	4.1	2.0	1.0	2.1	3.8	1.9	0.9
2 Other countries	1.4	0.6	0.2	0.3	0.4	0.2	1.0	0.7	0.4	0.2
III Private flows	74.3	31.4	28.2	34.4	38.7	40.7	54.1	37.2	37.1	37.3
1 Direct investment (OECD)	17.2	6.6	11.3	20.9	23.4	22.0	12.5	7.8	22.4	20.2
of which: Offshore centres	4.1	3.7	6.8	13.5	9.9	n.a.	3.0	4.4	9.5	n.a.
2 International bank lending	52.3	15.2	7.0	7.0	5.8	8.5	38.1	18.0	5.6	7.8
of which: Short-term	22.0	12.0	-4.0	5.0	2.0	4.0	16.0	14.2	1.9	3.7

Table 16.1 (continued)   Net financial flows to developing countries,(i) 1981 and 1985–9

	US$ billion						Per cent of total			
	1981	1985	1986	1987	1988	1989(ii)	1981	1985	1988	1989
3 Total bond lending	1.3	5.4	2.7	0.5	0.4	1.0	0.9	6.4	0.4	0.9
4 Other private	1.5	1.3	3.9	2.5	4.9	5.0	1.1	1.5	4.7	4.6
5 Grants by non-governmental organisations	2.0	2.9	3.3	3.5	4.2	4.2	1.5	3.4	4.0	3.9
TOTAL NET RESOURCE FLOWS (I, II and III)	137.4	84.3	83.7	93.4	104.3	109.0	100.0	100.0	100.0	100.0
Memorandum item:										
Total net credits from IMF	6.6	0.8	-1.4	-4.7	-4.0	-3.2				
At 1988 prices and exchange rates										
Total net resource flows	201.9	128.3	103.3	100.2	104.3	110.1				
Total Official Development Finance	66.8	74.5	69.3	66.1	66.1	67.8				
Total ODA receipts from all sources	54.1	56.8	54.8	51.8	51.7	51.8				
Total ODA from DAC countries	37.6	44.8	45.3	44.6	48.2	47.2				

(i)   Excluding Taiwan.
(ii) Provisional.

Source: OECD Press Release, SG/Press (90) 34, Paris, 14 June 1990.

gyrations: about $810 million in 1981; $1,360 million in 1983; $510 million in 1984; $1,560 million in 1987; and $1,250 million in 1988 (see Table 16.2). However, net flows to the region are to a significant extent inflated by the offshore direct investment and international bank lending activities in the Bahamas. If such flows are excluded, the region's net flows, which averaged around $630 million during 1981–2, were only about $430 million annually during 1987–8. Barbados, Guyana, Jamaica, St Lucia and Trinidad and Tobago suffered declines in net flows, while other countries registered increases.

The main reason for the dramatic decline in overall flows was the sharp about-turn in export credits from an average annual inflow of $125 million in 1981–2 (or 20% of the total) to an annual average outflow of $175 million in 1987–8 (or about 40% of the net inflows). ODA, non-concessional ODF and direct foreign investment showed only marginal or no improvement while the contribution of international financial markets changed from a small net outflow in 1981–2 to a small net inflow in 1987–8. However, because of the decline in the overall total, the shares of all other flows except export credits showed significant increases, with ODA flows equal to 80% of the total net inflows in 1988.

Debt and net transfers

World Bank estimates indicate that total external indebtedness of all developing countries rose rapidly in the early and mid-1980s, but over the 1987–9 period virtually stagnated, with external debt outstanding in 1989 at $1,290 billion ($1,165.5 billion for 111 countries which reported debt to World Bank; see Table 16.3). The near stagnation in the growth of debt reflects both a much slower growth in all debt-creating flows (compared to non-debt creating flows such as grant aid and private direct investment) as well as significant amounts of debt conversion transactions (such as debt-equity swaps, debt buy backs and debt to debt conversions with lower face values) which served to reduce the outstanding debt from what it otherwise would have been.

Growth in indebtedness and persistent high interest rates also meant that interest payments by developing countries increased sharply during the 1980s. Since 1983, interest payments abroad by developing countries have exceeded net debt-creating inflows into them and by a larger margin each year. This difference, the so-called debt-related net transfer, was negative to the tune of some $52 billion in 1989 for the 111 countries which report their debt to the World Bank. It is estimated that over the period 1983–9 these countries transferred about $243 billion to their creditors in this way. Such transfers have been mainly concentrated in the heavily-indebted middle-income countries.

Table 16.2   Net financial flows to the Commonwealth Caribbean^(i) 1981 and 1985–8

	US$ million					Per cent of total^(iii)			
	1981	1985	1986	1987	1988	1981	1985	1987	1988
I Official Development Finance (ODF)	467.7	468.0	487.5	475.3	518.7	82.5	270.2	113.4	118.1
1 Official development assistance (ODA)	303.6	304.7	331.5	333.1	354.9	53.5	175.7	79.5	80.8
of which: Bilateral	187.7	238.8	252.4	255.3	256.1	33.1	137.7	60.9	58.3
Multilateral	115.9	65.8	78.9	77.0	98.6	20.4	37.9	18.4	22.4
2 Non-concessional ODF	164.2	163.9	156.0	142.2	163.8	28.9	94.5	33.9	37.3
of which: Bilateral	73.7	55.1	1.8	13.1	91.6	13.0	31.8	3.1	20.9
Multilateral	90.5	108.4	154.2	129.1	72.2	15.9	62.5	30.8	16.4
II Total export credits	139.4	4.3	57.1	−168.0	−183.8	24.6	2.5	−40.1	−41.8
of which: Official	49.8	72.1	53.9	−33.7	−24.9	8.8	41.6	−8.0	−5.6
Private	89.6	−67.8	2.8	−134.3	−158.9	15.8	−39.1	−32.0	36.2
III Direct investment (OECD)	343.7	−318.4	436.8	719.0	738.4				
Excluding the Bahamas	33.2	−444.6	−77.1	34.9	42.7	5.9	−256.4	8.3	9.7
IV International bank and other private lending	−136.6	495.1	223.7	538.6	180.9				
Excluding the Bahamas	−73.5	145.3	27.2	77.4	61.6	−13.0	83.7	18.4	14.0
Total Net Financial Flows (I, II, III and IV)^(iii)	814.6	649.4	1204.5	1564.7	1253.7				

Table 16.2 (continued)   Net financial flows to the Commonwealth Caribbean[i] 1981 and 1985–8

	US$ million					Per cent of total[iii]			
	1981	1985	1986	1987	1988	1981	1985	1987	1988
Excluding direct investment and international bank and other private lending to the Bahamas[iii]	567.2	173.4	494.1	419.2	439.2	100.0	100.0	100.0	100.0

(i) Includes twelve independent countries of the Commonwealth Caribbean, i.e. Antigua and Barbuda, the Bahamas, Barbados, Belize, Dominica, Grenada, Guyana, Jamaica, St Kitts-Nevis, St Lucia, St Vincent and the Grenadines and Trinidad and Tobago.

(ii) Total net financial flows excluding direct investment and international bank and other private lending to the Bahamas.

(iii) Totals may not necessarily add due to rounding.

Source: Calculated from data in OECD, Geographical Distribution of Financial Flows to Developing Countries, various issues.

Table 16.3 Developing countries and Caribbean economies: Debt and net transfers of financial resources, 1981–9 (US$ billion).

	1981	1982	1983	1984	1985	1986	1987	1988(i)	1989(ii)
A Developing countries(iii)									
Total debt	672.0	752.9	818.9	854.6	952.3	1,046.8	1,176.3	1,155.9	1,165.5
Net transfers on debt creating flows(iv)	25.2	6.4	−2.4	−21.9	−36.2	−38.2	−40.3	−52.0	−51.6
Net transfer on all flows(v)	33.8	7.0	−1.2	−10.6	−19.4	−11.1	−16.6	−22.1	−7
of which: through official flows(vi)	33.7	32.5	28.2	24.5	15.1	11.5	7.5	10.2	13
private grants	1.2	1.2	1.9	2.1	2.5	3.4	3.5	4.2	4
direct investment(vii)	−0.9	−3.0	−3.3	−2.5	−1.2	−0.8	1.7	6.3	4
medium and long-term private credit(viii)	17.0	3.4	−8.7	−22.0	−27.3	−27.0	−32.5	−32.8	−36
short-term borrowing and domestic outflows net(ix)	−17.3	−27.2	−18.9	−12.7	−8.6	1.8	3.2	−10.1	7
B Caribbean Economies(x)									
Total debt	4.63	5.75	6.96	5.96	6.81	7.72	8.33	8.42	8.83
Net transfer on debt creating flows(iv)	0.45	0.53	0.17	−0.04	0.08	0.06	−0.54	−0.22	−0.25
Net transfer on all flows(v)	0.64	1.07	0.37	−0.20	−0.11	−0.29	0.11	−0.06	n.a.

Table 16.3 (continued) Developing countries and Caribbean economies: Debt and net transfers of financial resources, 1981–9 (US$ billion).

(i) Estimates.

(ii) Preliminary estimates.

(iii) Data for total debt and net transfers on debt creating flows refer to 111 World Bank DRS Countries, and that for net transfer on all flows relate to a sample of 96 countries for which data is available to the UN.

(iv) Net flows through all (official and private) borrowings by developing countries less interest payments on all debt, as estimated by the World Bank.

(v) Including transfers on non-debt creating flows.

(vi) Grants as well as net official credit (including IMF credit) less interest paid (including IMF charges).

(vii) Direct investment (net of reinvested earnings) less net dividends and other income.

(viii) Net medium and long-term private credit inflow less interest paid.

(ix) Calculated as a residual (including short-term trade financing, normal and unusual outflows ('capital flight'), arrears on interest due, and other flows captured in balance-of-payments data as 'errors and omissions' and presumed to be financial flows).

(x) Data for total and net transfers on debt creating flows refer to eight countries which report their debt to the World Bank (i.e. the Bahamas, Barbados, Belize, Grenada, Guyana, Jamaica, St Vincent and Trinidad and Tobago) and that for net transfer on all flows relate to all 12 independent Commonwealth Caribbean countries.

Sources: World Bank, World Debt Tables, 1989–90, UN, World Economic Survey 1990, and author's calculations from data supplied by United Nations Department of International Economic and Social Affairs.

The UN Secretariat works on a much broader definition of net transfers which includes, *inter alia*, inflows of official and private grant aid and private direct investment as well as outflows of profits and dividend and private capital (including capital flight) by residents. Of a sample of 96 countries for which data are available, the UN Secretariat estimates that the negative net transfers were some $7 billion in 1989, considerably lower than $22 billion in 1988 and an average of $17 billion over 1984–8. However, this was largely a result of significant positive flows on account of short-term capital (including capital flight repatriation) in 1989. Excluding such short-term flows, which by their very nature are very volatile, the transfers on account of long-term flows were negative at an annual average level of about $14 billion during the 1985–9 period.

Estimates for eight Caribbean countries, which report their debt to the World Bank, indicate that their external debt rose from about $4.6 billion in 1981 to around $8.8 billion in 1989 (see Table 16.3). Taking account of interest payments by them on their debt, debt-related transfer to them turned from a positive of around $450 million in 1981 to a negative of about $250 million in 1989. Over the 1987–9 period, these Caribbean economies transferred close to $1 billion in this way. Even by the UN definition, net transfers to the twelve Caribbean economies were negative during the 1984–8 period at an average annual level of about $100 million compared to a positive transfer of $650 million in 1981. Negative net transfer was a feature mostly of the larger countries; most OECS countries generally continued to enjoy positive net transfers.

With a large number of developing countries, including those in the Caribbean, transferring real resources abroad and some receiving very low levels of real resources from abroad, domestic investment and consequently growth in many developing countries has been particularly adversely affected. For financial transfers to be consistent with their investment and growth needs, measures would be required to improve their receipts of all types of financial flows as well as, where appropriate, to reduce their outstanding stock of debt or debt service. The purpose of this chapter is to review the trends and issues in relation to the main types of flows to developing countries generally and the Caribbean economies in particular.

Official Development Assistance (ODA)

Global trends

In current dollar terms, total ODA receipts of developing countries, after falling between 1981 and 1983, rose steadily to reach around $51 billion in 1989. However, in real terms these receipts fell between 1985 and 1987, and in 1989 were only marginally above the 1981 level (see Table 16.1).

The decline in aid is largely attributable to a contraction in ODA from Arab countries, which fell even in nominal terms from $9.5 billion in 1980 to $1.2 billion in 1989. Aid from the USSR and East European countries, which having risen somewhat between 1980 and 1987, showed a significant reduction for a second consecutive year in 1989. By contrast, bilateral aid from the Development Assistance Committee (DAC) (which comprises most industrial countries) rose steadily between 1983 and 1989 to reach $34.5 billion in 1989. Aid by multilateral agencies (which are largely funded by DAC countries) also rose from $7.9 billion in 1981 to $11.5 billion in 1989.

Despite a steady increase in both DAC bilateral ODA and multilateral aid to developing countries, total DAC ODA has been subject to significant year to year variations because of uneven yearly DAC contributions to multilateral agencies. If the effects of the latter are smoothed out, DAC ODA grew in real terms at an average rate of about 2.2% per annum between 1983–4 and 1988-9. This growth in aid, however, falls short of the growth in their combined GNP during the period. If present trends continue, the ODA/GNP ratio, which averaged 0.36% during 1980–5 (and which fell in 1989 to 0.33% largely because of the decline in contributions to multilateral institutions), could fall to 0.31% in 1995, representing retrogression rather than progress in reaching the ODA/GNP target of 0.7%.

The overall average growth in DAC aid also masks conflicting trends among individual donor countries (see Table 16.4). Countries registering the sharpest annual real increases between 1983–4 and 1988–9 were Finland (16.8%), Italy (13.8%), Denmark (5.4%), Sweden (4.9%), Norway (4.3%), Canada (4%), France (3.8%) and Japan (3.6%). By contrast, some countries recorded sharp annual declines, *inter alia*, Belgium (–3.0%), United States (–2.0%) and New Zealand (–1.4%). In terms of ODA/GNP ratios, Norway, Denmark, Sweden and the Netherlands stand out as countries with the highest ratios, significantly above the 0.7% target. The first three as well as Finland, Italy, France and Japan also registered significant improvements in their ODA/GNP ratios. In the case of Japan, which overtook the US as the largest donor in 1989, while the overall ratio improved from 0.30% in 1980–5 to 0.32% in 1988–9, this still remained below the DAC average. By 1992, however, Japan intends to raise the share of its ODA in total DAC aid to a level commensurate with the share of Japan in DAC GNP (i.e. to the DAC average). A particularly disappointing performance was that of the US whose ODA/GNP ratio fell from 0.24% in 1983–4 to 0.18% in 1988–9. Britain's ODA/GNP ratio at 0.32% in 1983–9 was substantially lower than the average of 0.37% and 0.43% registered respectively during 1981–5 and 1976–80. Austria, Ireland, Switzerland and New Zealand are other countries with below DAC average performance.

The share of multilateral aid in total ODA receipts of developing

Table 16.4 ODA performance of DAC countries in 1989 and recent years (Net disbursements).

	US$ million			Per cent of GNP						Per cent change 1989/88			Annual average % change in volume[iii] 1983-4, 1988-9
	1989 actual[i]	1988 actual[i]	1989 at 1988 prices and exchange rates	1976-80 average	1981-5 average	1988-9 average	1987	1988	1989	In national currency	In $	In volume terms[iii]	
Australia	1,017	1,101	933	0.48	0.48	0.41	0.34	0.46	0.37	-8.6	-7.6	-15.2	1.5
Austria	282	301	295	0.21	0.32	0.22	0.17	0.24	0.23	0.3	-6.4	-2.1	0.0
Belgium	716	618	740	0.52	0.58	0.44	0.48	0.41	0.47	24.2	15.9	19.6	-3.0
Canada	2,302	2,347	2,114	0.48	0.46	0.46	0.47	0.50	0.44	-5.6	-1.9	-9.9	4.0
Denmark	1,003	922	1,048	0.66	0.77	0.95	0.88	0.89	1.00	18.2	8.9	13.6	5.4
Finland	705	608	673	0.19	0.33	0.61	0.49	0.59	0.63	19.0	16.0	10.8	16.8
France incl. DOM/TOM	7,467	6,865	7,731	0.60	0.75	0.75	0.74	0.72	0.78	16.5	8.8	12.6	3.0
France excl. DOM/TOM	5,140	4,777	5,322	0.34	0.49	0.52	0.51	0.50	0.54	15.2	7.6	11.4	3.8
Germany	4,953	4,731	5,168	0.40	0.47	0.40	0.39	0.39	0.41	12.0	4.7	9.2	-0.3
Ireland	49	57	51	0.16	0.22	0.19	0.19	0.20	0.17	-6.4	-12.9	-10.2	-0.4
Italy	3,325	3,193	3,290	0.12	0.22	0.39	0.35	0.39	0.39	9.8	4.1	3.0	13.8
Japan	8,958	9,134	9,500	0.25	0.30	0.32	0.31	0.32	0.32	5.6	-1.9	4.0	3.6
Netherlands	2,094	2,231	2,228	0.87	1.00	0.96	0.98	0.98	0.94	0.7	-6.2	-0.1	2.4
New Zealand	87	104	90	0.35	0.27	0.24	0.26	0.27	0.22	-7.9	-16.0	-12.9	-1.4
Norway	919	985	956	0.87	1.00	1.06	1.09	1.10	1.02	-1.1	-6.7	-2.9	4.3
Sweden	1,809	1,534	1,767	0.85	0.87	0.92	0.88	0.86	0.98	24.1	18.0	15.2	4.9

Table 16.4 (continued) ODA performance of DAC countries in 1989 and recent years (Net disbursements).

	US$ million			Per cent of GNP						Per cent change 1989/88			Annual average % change in volume[ii]	
	1989 actual[i]	1988 actual[i]	1989 at 1988 prices and exchange rates	1976–80 average	1981–5 average	1988–9 average	1987	1988	1989	In national currency	In $	In volume terms[iii]	1983–4,	1988–9
Switzerland	559	617	604	0.21	0.28	0.31	0.31	0.32	0.30	1.2	−9.5	−2.1		3.2
United Kingdom	2,588	2,645	2,637	0.43	0.37	0.32	0.28	0.32	0.31	6.3	−2.1	−0.3		1.1
United States	7,664[iii]	10,141	7,362	0.24	0.24	0.18	0.20	0.21	0.15	−24.4	−24.4	−27.4		−2.0
TOTAL DAC	46,498	48,132	47,188	0.35	0.36	0.35	0.35	0.36	0.33	1.6	−3.4	−2.0		2.2
Memo: Unweighted average	–	–	–	0.44	0.50	0.51	0.49	0.51	0.51	–	–	–		–

(i) At current prices and dollar exchange rates.

(ii) At 1988 exchange rates and prices.

(iii) The decline in 1989 results mainly from two 1988/1989 instalments on IDA payments, both made in 1988.

Source: OECD Press Release, SG/PRESS (90) 34, Paris, 14 June 1990.

countries remained virtually unchanged over the 1980s at a little over one-fifth of the total. There were, however, significant shifts in the position of different multilateral agencies as providers of concessional assistance (see Table 16.5). On the one hand, the shares provided by UN agencies fell from 36% in 1981 to 33% in 1988, and by Arab agencies from 5% to less than 1% in 1988. On the other hand, the shares provided by major international financial institutions rose sharply from 35% in 1981 to 43% in 1988 and EC

Table 16.5   Concessional and non-concessional flows from multilateral agencies, 1981–8 (US$ million).

	1981	1982	1983	1984	1985	1986	1987	1988
Concessional flows								
Major Financial Institutions								
IDA	1918	2363	2336	2492	2599	3327	3530	3567
IBRD	88	58	47	41	34	4	–	–
IDB	438	366	365	438	351	283	121	134
African Development Fund	90	122	158	111	210	272	374	351
Asian Development Fund	146	177	223	304	393	416	540	660
IFAD	75	104	144	170	270	286	366	102
Sub-total	2756	3190	3272	3556	3857	4588	4931	4814
United Nations								
WFP	542	595	630	679	779	649	720	878
UNDP	790	714	617	596	635	769	786	914
UNHCR	437	366	356	397	418	386	398	(400)
UNWRA	170	235	211	191	187	187	207	(210)
UNICEF	214	204	246	244	279	326	365	400
UNTA	210	196	253	217	295	254	314	268
UNFPA	129	113	122	119	127	101	107	129
Other UN	356	332	304	319	327	380	426	479
Sub-total	2848	2755	2739	2763	3047	3052	3322	(3678)
Other institutions	475	39	35	17	29	29	38	(40)
Total above	6079	5984	6046	6336	6933	7669	8291	(8532)
EC	1440	1143	1215	1287	1407	1659	1747	2723
Arab Funds	407	398	314	147	133	144	73	60
Total concessional	7926	7525	7575	7770	8472	9472	10111	(11315)

Table 16.5 (continued) Concessional and non-concessional flows from
multilateral agencies, 1981–8 (US$ million).

	1981	1982	1983	1984	1985	1986	1987	1988
Non-concessional flows								
Major Financial Institutions								
IBRD	3603	4534	5117	5628	5041	5418	4395	3417
IFC	510	291	166	127	94	156	208	356
IDB	643	832	957	1550	1398	1224	928	1093
African Development Bank	70	115	145	110	235	282	416	625
Asian Development Bank	390	473	550	513	400	364	253	598
Others	16	13	9	14	306	290	431	(433)
Sub-total	5232	6258	6944	7942	7474	7734	6631	(6522)
EC	241	320	202	84	152	190	140	–3
Arab Funds	243	48	80	187	286	–137	–101	–84
Total non-concessional	5716	6626	7226	8213	7912	7787	6670	(6435)

Source: OECD, Development Co-operation, 1989 Report.

agencies from 18% to 24%. Among international financial institutions, the
share of the soft arm of the World Bank Group (International Development
Association (IDA)), rose sharply from 24% to 32%. The soft arm of the
African Development Bank also increased its share, but the shares provided
by the soft arms of the Asian Development Bank and the Inter-American
Development Bank (IADB) fell, the latter very sharply from over 5% in
1981 to just over 1% in 1988.

Trends in aid to the Caribbean economies

In current dollar terms, aid flows to the twelve Caribbean economies in
1985 were virtually unchanged from the 1981 level, and in 1988 only 12%
higher. In real terms, these flows showed a decline of more than 20%
between 1981 and 1988. As a consequence, the Commonwealth Caribbean's share in the total ODA receipts of developing countries fell from
0.82% to 0.69% between 1981 and 1988. Barbados and Guyana saw sharp
nominal declines in their aid receipts and these two, together with Jamaica
and Dominica, registered declines in real terms. The other eight Com-

monwealth Caribbean countries registered real increases, particularly sharply in the cases of Belize, Grenada and St Kitts-Nevis.

In nominal terms, bilateral aid to the Caribbean increased throughout the 1981–8 period, but multilateral aid fell very sharply between 1981 and 1985, and although it recovered somewhat, the 1988 level was still well below that of 1981. Among bilateral sources, aid from Canada rose sharply, comprising around 29% of total bilateral aid in 1988 compared to 14% in 1981. The shares provided by West Germany, Japan and other smaller donors also increased, although at 4% in 1988, Japan's share in the total remained particularly small. By contrast, the share provided by the United States fell sharply from 53% to 33% and Britain's share also declined marginally (to 11% in 1988). Canadian and British assistance was widely distributed throughout the Commonwealth Caribbean, whereas assistance by other countries was more concentrated (see Table 16.6).

As for multilateral concessional flows, for the seven Commonwealth Caribbean countries for which data is available (see Table 16.7), while gross disbursements from the World Bank Group (IDA) were around $3 million annually during 1981–8, net disbursements (after repayments of previous loans) averaged practically zero and net transfers (after also taking account of interest payments on previous loans) were negative to the tune of $2.5 million annually throughout the period. Net disbursements to these seven countries from the IADB fell very sharply from an average of $25 million during 1980–5 to about $8 million during 1986–8, primarily as a result of a sharp decline in gross disbursements. Net transfers were even lower at an average of $4 million during 1986–8 compared with an annual level of about $23 million during 1980–5. Net disbursements to the seven countries from the Caribbean Development Bank (CDB) averaged just over $3 million during the 1984–6 period compared to an average of $18 million over 1981–3, while net transfers averaged only $0.7 million compared to $17 million over the same period. While there was a marked revival of flows in 1987, preliminary indications suggest that both net disbursements and net transfers were nil or negative in 1988.

Issues for developing countries as a whole

The actual and prospective slow growth in DAC ODA as well as the contrasting performance of different donors raise important issues about ways of increasing aid. There is clearly a need for each donor to adopt the most effective means for expanding its own aid programme. All donor governments which have declared a timetable for reaching the 0.7% target could adopt the practice of setting intermediate targets to achieve their stated objectives, while for other donors various self-imposed targets may

Table 16.6 Sources of bilateral ODA to the Commonwealth Caribbean countries – 1981, 1988 (US$ million).

		USA	Canada	West Germany	UK	Netherlands	Japan	Other	Total
Antigua and Barbuda	1981	n.a.	n.a.	n.a.	n.a.	n.a.	n.a.	n.a.	n.a.
	1988	1.0	2.5	–	1.7	–	–	–	5.3
Bahamas	1981	–	–	–	0.1	–	–	–	0.1
	1988	–	–	–	–	0.1	–	–	0.1
Barbados	1981	–	2.6	–	1.0	–	–	–	4.0
	1988	–	2.0	0.3	-1.4	0.8	0.1	0.6[1]	2.3
Belize	1981	–	–	–	8.0	–	–	–	8.4
	1988	10.0	1.3	0.1	4.9	0.3	0.1	–	16.6
Dominica	1981	n.a.	n.a.	n.a.	n.a.	n.a.	n.a.	n.a.	n.a.
	1988	–	4.9	0.2	3.4	–	0.2	–	9.1
Grenada	1981	n.a.	n.a.	n.a.	n.a.	n.a.	n.a.	n.a.	n.a.
	1988	–	4.9	0.3	2.1	0.1	0.2	–	7.6
Guyana	1981	6.0	3.7	–	–	–	3.2	–	16.2
	1988	6.0	6.2	0.1	0.9	–	2.0	C.3[2]	15.6
Jamaica	1981	63.0	11.2	11.1	13.5	–	–	–	110.1
	1988	60.0	43.2	28.7	8.5	4.7	5.6	22.3[3]	173.1

Table 16.6 (continued) Sources of bilateral ODA to the Commonwealth Caribbean countries – 1981, 1988 (US$ million).

		USA	Canada	West Germany	UK	Netherlands	Japan	Other	Total
St Kitts-Nevis	1981	n.a.	n.a.	n.a.	n.a.	n.a.	n.a.	n.a.	n.a.
	1988	3.0	3.7	–	3.6	–	0.1	–	10.4
St Lucia	1981	n.a.	n.a.	n.a.	n.a.	n.a.	n.a.	n.a.	n.a.
	1988	–	4.4	0.2	1.5	–	1.1	–	7.2
St Vincent and Grenadines	1981	n.a.	n.a.	n.a.	n.a.	n.a.	n.a.	n.a.	n.a.
	1988	2.0	1.3	0.1	1.4	–	1.4	–	6.2
Trinidad and Tobago	1981	–	0.7	–	-7.2	–	–	0.2[4]	-5.9
	1988	2.0	–	-1.1	0.2	0.7	0.3	0.7[5]	2.6
TOTAL	1981	69.0	18.2	11.1	15.4	..	3.2	0.2	132.9
	1988	84.0	74.4	28.9	26.8	6.7	11.1	23.9	256.1

1 Finland ($0.5 million) and Belgium ($0.1 million).
2 Norway.
3 Italy ($17.6 million), Norway ($3.0 million), Sweden ($0.7 million), France ($0.3 million), Switzerland ($0.2 million), Belgium ($0.2 million), Australia ($0.2 million) and Finland ($0.1 million).
4 France.
5 France ($0.3 million), Finland ($0.1 million), Norway ($0.1 million) and Switzerland ($0.1 million).

Source: OECD, Geographical Distribution of Financial Flows to Developing Countries, various issues.

Table 16.7 Flows from selected multilateral agencies to Commonwealth Caribbean countries[1] 1981–8 (US$ million)

	CONCESSIONAL			NON-CONCESSIONAL		
	Gross disburse-ments	*Net disburse-ments*	*Net transfers*	*Gross disburse-ments*	*Net disburse-ments*	*Net transfers*
World Bank: IDA/IBRD						
1981	7.8	3.8	1.3	58.7	47.9	29.3
1982	0.3	−1.9	−4.0	148.8	134.3	110.2
1983	–	−2.4	−4.3	77.7	57.7	23.8
1984	0.3	−2.3	−3.9	63.2	38.2	−1.0
1985	2.3	−0.6	−2.1	88.3	62.3	20.3
1986	8.4	4.3	2.6	30.5	−9.1	−66.2
1987	1.8	−1.5	−3.2	72.5	19.4	−43.7
1988[2]	4.6	0.1	−1.6	37.8	−41.5	−123.2
Inter-American Development Bank						
1981	36.2	36.0	34.1	7.9	5.9	4.0
1982	32.6	31.9	29.5	12.0	9.9	7.3
1983	25.4	24.6	21.8	30.8	27.9	23.8
1984	18.2	16.8	13.9	21.0	18.0	11.6
1985	19.4	17.4	14.3	44.2	38.0	27.6
1986	12.3	9.8	6.3	52.1	46.0	30.0
1987	10.8	7.2	3.5	67.8	54.5	26.1
1988[2]	12.3	7.7	3.6	40.9	15.3	−15.3
Caribbean Development Bank						
1981	28.7	28.3	26.8	13.1	11.3	9.3
1982	13.5	13.0	11.2	8.2	6.0	3.6
1983	15.0	14.6	12.5	4.3	1.9	−0.2
1984	4.0	3.3	0.2	5.8	4.5	2.2
1985	3.9	2.6	−0.4	10.2	8.7	6.3
1986	5.7	4.1	0.9	13.5	11.6	9.0
1987	13.3	10.5	7.2	10.2	5.8	1.2
1988[2]	3.9	−1.7	−6.0	6.3	−1.4	−9.7

1 The Bahamas, Barbados, Grenada, Guyana, Jamaica, St Vincent, Trinidad and Tobago.
2 Provisional.

Source: Calculated from World Bank and other data.

be helpful. As a minimum, these latter donors need to avoid any decline in ODA/GNP ratios, as has been occurring in some countries. The scope for expanding ODA has increased because of reduced East-West tensions and the prospect of a 'peace dividend' accruing from reductions in military expenditures. For example, a cut of just 10% in defence spending of the North Atlantic Treaty Organisation (NATO) countries could make possible a doubling of aid.

But profound political and economic changes taking place in Eastern Europe have added new claimants for aid. Already Western governments have offered aid and other assistance in support of political and economic reforms in these countries, and there is a danger that this aid could be at the expense of aid flows to developing countries. Although there have been assurances to the contrary by some countries, these assurances could be consistent with the maintaining of real ODA flows to developing countries while diverting incremental ODA to East European countries. If that were to be the case, ODA flows to developing countries as a proportion of DAC GNP could fall sharply to 0.27% by 1995. In this respect, all donors need to consider closely an Italian government proposal to raising EC countries' ODA/GNP ratio to 1% from the present 0.4%, with 50% of the incremental ODA (0.3% of GNP) being devoted to East and South European countries and the other 50% (0.3% of GNP) to developing countries. Such assistance would go a significant way to reconciling increased aid to Eastern European countries on the one hand, with the increase in EC ODA to developing countries towards the 0.7% of its GNP, on the other.

There is also a question of geographical distribution of aid amongst developing countries themselves. Political, strategic and commercial considerations weigh heavily in bilateral aid allocations (although multilateral aid is allocated on developmental grounds mainly to low-income countries). There is a strong body of opinion which considers that aid should be reallocated to low-income countries (which currently receive only little more than one-half of the total aid) and within the low-income group towards sub-Saharan African countries, given the latter's dismal performance during the 1980s. But the possibilities of reallocating aid within the low-income group are limited because: firstly, over the past 10–15 years, sub-Saharan Africa's share in DAC ODA has risen sharply from 23% in 1975–6 to 31% in 1986–7 (while South Asia's share has fallen from 23.5% to 14.2% over the same period); secondly, a significant proportion of the population of large countries in Asia remain in absolute poverty and the domestic resources of these countries are too limited to make the major social investments required to provide even minimum acceptable standards; and thirdly, curtailment of concessional assistance could create debt servicing difficulties for countries such as India by preventing them from achieving a blend of concessional and non-concessional flows at an overall reasonable cost, which is consistent with effective debt management. It would thus seem highly desirable that a reallocation of ODA should take place from middle-income to low-income countries. But there are several limitations on the extent to which this can be undertaken, which are particularly relevant to the Caribbean economies.

Issues for the Caribbean

The World Bank uses the criteria of per capita income to determine eligibility for its concessional resources, although other criteria are also used to determine allocation of resources amongst eligible countries. There are strong arguments which suggest that the criteria of per capita income in determining eligibility may be misplaced, especially in relation to small economies like those in the Caribbean. The graduation of five OECS states from IDA has been temporarily postponed while these countries gain full creditworthiness of market-related funds of the World Bank (i.e. ordinary resources of the International Bank for Reconstruction and Development (IBRD). However, the size of these economies poses severe limitations on the economies of scale they can foster and the degree of structural transformation they can achieve without concessional assistance over a significant period of time to build up their physical and social infrastructure. Continued efforts, therefore, would be required to ensure that premature graduation of OECS countries from IDA does not take place.

A shift of ODA from other lower middle-income countries facing problems of indebtedness and structural adjustment such as Jamaica, can also be highly disruptive. Aid-dependence of Jamaica is particularly high, about 7.7% of GNP in 1987–8. Indeed, if countries like Jamaica which have built up a large amount of non-concessional debt, particularly with multilateral agencies, are to see their way through their current difficulties, additional concessional assistance for structural adjustment would seem to be highly desirable. In particular, efforts need to be made to ensure access for such countries to the concessional resources of the IMF's Enhanced Structural Adjustment Facility (ESAF) currently restricted to IDA-eligible countries only. This task could be made easier by securing additional contributions to this facility from donors.

For tactical reasons, Caribbean policymakers need also to consider whether they should not seek greatly enhanced regional soft-arm funds such as those of the IADB and CDB, which, unlike IDA and ESAF, do not include claimants from low-income Africa and Asia which are much poorer than the Caribbean economies. Given also the overall paucity of multilateral concessional assistance, the Caribbean economies need to look increasingly for bilateral concessional resources, especially from countries with fast-expanding aid budgets. With some of the West European countries in this category likely to be increasingly preoccupied with the needs of East European economies, it would seem that Japan, from which the Caribbean countries have so far tapped few resources, could be a major focus of attention. There is also a greater onus on countries like Canada and Britain, with traditional ties with the Caribbean, to ensure that aid flows to these economies are not squeezed disproportionately.

Non-concessional ODF (official development finance)

Global trends

Non-concessional ODF, though relatively small compared with ODA, has been one of the few sources of finance which has shown a significant increase during the 1980s (Table 16.1). Such flows rose from about $8.7 billion in 1981 to $15.8 billion in 1989, to comprise 14.5% of the total flows in 1989 compared with only 6.3% in 1981.

A strong rise in bilateral disbursements (from $3 billion in 1981 to $9 billion in 1989) represented both the capitalisation of substantial amounts of interest arrears in debt consolidations as a result of action in the Paris Club, as well as disbursements of untied non-concessional loans by the Japanese Export-Import Bank (Jexim) Bank under Japan's recycling programme. Japan had earmarked $9 billion to be channelled through the Jexim Bank (out of a $30 billion recycling programme) over a three-year period ending in March 1990. Multilateral disbursements also rose strongly between 1981 ($5.7 billion) and 1984 ($8.2 billion), but stagnated at a lower level ($6.5 to $6.8 billion) over the three years 1987–9. More than half of the non-concessional multilateral lending is accounted for by the IBRD, flows from which declined significantly between 1986 and 1988. Among the regional banks, flows from the African Development Bank increased steadily throughout the 1980s, while those from Asian and the Inter-American Development Banks after falling between 1986 and 1987, showed some recovery in 1988.

Trends for the Caribbean

Flows of non-concessional ODF to the twelve Caribbean economies were virtually unchanged at $164 million in 1981, 1985 and 1988, although for most other years the amounts were below this figure. Between 1981 and 1985 bilateral flows fell, but these were offset by increases in multilateral flows. Between 1985 and 1988 the trends were reversed. Bilateral flows increased while multilateral flows fell back.

IBRD gross disbursements to these seven Commonwealth Caribbean countries for which data is available, fell from an average of about $87 million during 1981–5 to about $47 million during 1986–8 (see Table 16.7). Because of rising principal and interest repayments, net disbursements turned from a positive $68 million to a negative $10 million and net transfers from a positive $61 million to a negative $78 million over the same period. Gross disbursements, net disbursements and net transfers from the Inter-American Development Bank to the seven Commonwealth Caribbean countries rose very strongly between 1981 and 1987, but in 1988 both gross and net disbursements were down very significantly ($40 million and $15 million respectively) and net transfers turned from a positive of $26 million in 1987 to a negative $15 million in 1988. Gross disbursements, net disbursements and net transfers from the Caribbean Development Bank, after showing significant improvement up to 1986, also fell back, with preliminary estimates for 1988 indicating negative figures for both net disbursements and net transfers.

Issues

The stagnation of non-concessional ODF to Caribbean countries, and in particular the recent poor performance of multilateral flows generally, raise important questions about improving these flows. With regard to bilateral flows, at the 1989 Western Economic Summit, Japan enlarged its recycling programme from $30 billion to $65 billion and extended it over a longer period. A significant portion of the amount is being channelled through the Jexim Bank to support direct operations as well as to co-finance with the World Bank and the IMF. In particular, $10 billion has been earmarked to support voluntary commercial bank debt reduction operations in conjunction with the IMF and the World Bank. Japan's programme is likely to give a significant boost to flows of non-concessional ODF, and the Caribbean economies would need to make special efforts to ensure that they too benefit from this programme. It is important that other industrial countries also make special efforts to supplement lending from the multilateral agencies. At the same time, capitalisation of interest arrears in debt reschedulings can continue to ease the financial strain facing many severely-indebted developing countries.

The size of non-concessional lending by multilateral development institutions depends largely on their capital bases. Agreement on an 80% increase in the IBRD capital to $171.4 billion which was reached in 1988, allowed the Bank to expand its commitments in 1988 and 1989 although at a lower end of the planning range set by the Bank. But if the IBRD is once more to become a significant source of resource transfers for developing countries, it is imperative that commitments should rise sharply and amounts be disbursed more rapidly.

A major issue for the Caribbean countries in relation to the IBRD concerns the graduation of countries with high per capita incomes from access to its resources. The Bahamas and Barbados have faced this question recently, while Trinidad and Tobago, after a considerable period of uncertainty, has gained access to IBRD resources. While compared to IDA graduation, procedures are more flexible and there is a phase-out period once a country reaches a GNP per capita benchmark, there is still no assurance that these countries will continue to have adequate access to capital markets upon graduation, nor can self-sustaining development be assured, particularly when these small economies continue to require long-term finance for infrastructure development.

Among the regional development banks, an increase of 200% in the case of the African Development Bank in 1987 has already permitted it to embark upon a lending programme over a five-year period, twice the size of the previous such programme while a general capital increase for the Asian Development Bank is also due. From the perspective of the Commonwealth Caribbean, however, the capital bases of the IADB and CDB are more relevant. Agreement in 1989 on a $26.4 billion capital increase for the IADB will enable it to make commitments of $22.5 billion over 1990–3, roughly double the current programme. As for the CDB, while the admission of Italy and West Germany as members will relieve the shortage of loanable funds up to 1991, a substantial increase on the current capital of $50 million is required if the Bank is not to start the 1990s with a serious liquidity crisis.

In addition to direct lending, multilateral institutions play an important role in catalysing other sources of external finance. The IMF's adjustment lending and its policy advice and conditionality have often become a necessary condition for concerted lending by commercial banks and other sources of finance to the severely-indebted countries. The World Bank and regional development banks can also play an important role in mobilising other sources of finance through their co-financing operations with export credit agencies and international financial markets (this is discussed below). With the decline in general purpose external lending to developing countries as well as constrained domestic public finances, international institutions and developing country policymakers need also to address the role that private finance can play in public projects such as power generation, water supply, etc. The World Bank has already set up a pilot project in Pakistan for the purpose of attracting such project finance, a process that needs further encouragement.

Export credits

Trends

Net export credit finance to developing countries fell very sharply from an average of $16 billion in 1980–2 to about $5 billion during 1983–5 and turned negative during 1986–8. While there was a small positive flow in 1989 ($1.2 billion), it mainly reflected short-term business (see Table 16.1). The main reason for the decline was a sharp downturn in medium- to long-term credits from DAC countries (which fell from $13 billion in 1981 to a negative $6.7 billion in 1987), principally as export credit agencies removed cover from a number of severely-indebted countries in arrears and seeking reschedulings, and also as most developing countries curtailed or restructured their investment programmes. DAC short-term export credits suffered a decline during 1983–4, but then revived at an average of about $3–$4 billion during 1985–7 as both debtors and creditors gave greater priority to the servicing of short-term credits. While DAC short-term credits were only $1–$2 billion during 1988-9, figures for medium and long-term credit (a negative $1.2 billion in 1988 and almost zero in 1989) appear to indicate an end to the continuing decline in such credits. As in recent years, gross disbursements of medium- to long-term credits amounted to $20 billion in 1989, although this was almost offset by repayments.

Export credit flows to the Caribbean economies were even more strongly affected during the 1980s, falling from a positive $140 million in 1981 to a negative $184 million in 1988; but, in contrast to the experience of developing countries as a whole, an end to the decline in such flows to these countries was not apparent in 1988-9.

Issues

Both supply and demand factors have been in play to keep such credits at negative or nil levels. While export credit agencies (ECAs) have generally maintained an open stance for countries without debt servicing difficulties and those with Paris Club reschedulings and good records of adjustment policy implementation, for other countries they have maintained a very cautious stance (except for short-term cover). Also, where they have terminated lending, ECAs have been slow to resume operations. Moreover, most liberalisations have taken place on a case by case basis and, occasionally, agencies or their governments have taken decisions that affect a broad group of countries. Furthermore, ECAs have not yet gained confidence enough to lend to the private sector in developing countries, despite the greater emphasis placed by governments on the role of that sector.

The demand for export credit finance has also been affected by the disproportionate cutbacks in investment in adjusting countries which is recovering only slowly; and also by the terms of export credit finance. Repayment periods often do nòt match the requirements of projects, posing difficult issues for countries that have little access to general purpose borrowing from international capital markets. At the same time, progressive reduction in the subsidy on interest rates has led some creditworthy borrowers to seek alternative sources of finance in the capital markets. There has also been a significant growth in mixed credits which combine aid with export credits.

The pace at which the Paris Club and adjusting countries reach agreement on official debt rescheduling and developing countries reorient their expenditures towards investment, will to a large degree determine the growth in new commitments, particularly to indebted countries. But export credit agencies, multilateral agencies and developing country governments can all play an important role in significantly enhancing these flows. Export credit agencies could be more innovative in raising long-term finance at a reasonable cost that is compatible with the needs of the project, for example, through floating of specific instruments in the international capital markets to generate specifically-tailored financing measures conducive to developing country needs, while enabling the different risks involved to be priced and assessed separately. In this respect, agencies which are separately incorporated and borrow directly from the markets such as the Swedish and Canadian agencies are better placed through the utilisation of newer market techniques, to have the full efficiency of the markets being translated directly from investors to borrowers. Even other agencies, such as the UK's ECGD have been in the forefront in seeking ways to reduce the impact on their balance sheets of bank-financed export credits by creating new capital market products (consisting either of a portfolio of a single country export credits or a more diversified portfolio) attracting a full range of international retail and institutional investors.

Multilateral institutions through their co-financing operations can also play a much stronger catalytic role in reviving export credits. Over 1985/6–1988/9, 18% of the planned external financing of World Bank projects was accounted for by export credits. In 1990 the World Bank and major international ECAs put in place a scheme called the Export Credit Enhanced Leverage (EXCEL) Programme which will serve to·provide export credits, repayable at prevailing OECD rates, to private sector borrowers in developing countries through local development banks and other financial institutions. Under the scheme, amortisation of the loans supported by ECA cover would be completed ahead of amortisation of the Bank's loan, and while ECAs would not benefit directly from the World Bank's preferred creditor status, the Bank would pledge 'best efforts' to seek full repayment.

Developing countries in severe debt servicing difficulties themselves could also encourage the flow of export credits to viable private sector projects, through limited recourse financing where this is seen as appropriate (e.g. some utilities and infrastructure projects). Such financing makes an explicit link between project viability and repayments, and is not directly dependent on the overall financial strength of the borrowing country. Export credit finance for the export-oriented projects could also be encouraged through escrow accounts, under which all or part of the foreign exchange earned by the project is deposited in an account held abroad.

From the perspective of the Caribbean economies, the above considerations highlight the critical importance for them to step up investment and to carry out thorough assessments of the financing needs of projects. They also need to build up a good track record in their dealings with ECAs and to shop around, as agencies differ in their openness to different developing countries, in the financing terms they provide, including their innovativeness in raising finance at appropriate terms, and in the support they provide to the private sector.

International financial markets

Trends

The amounts raised by developing countries in the international capital markets fell very sharply, particularly in the aftermath of the outbreak of the debt crisis. Borrowings fell from $49.5 billion in 1981 to $17.1 billion in 1989 (see Table 16.8). While the figure for 1987 indicates a modest revival, both the 1987 and 1988 figures were affected by concerted or managed loans extended by commercial banks in the context of debt restructuring agreements and IMF-supported programmes for some heavily indebted middle-income countries. Excluding such loans, borrowing from international capital markets by developing countries was fairly stable at around $16–17 billion annually during 1987–9.

The decline in syndicated credits (loans from banks) accounted for practically all of the fall-off in lending to developing countries (from $46.1 billion in 1981 to $12.5 billion in 1989), although voluntary lending (excluding managed loans) by banks showed some improvement between 1986–9. Utilisation of bond markets, which have generally been accessible to the more creditworthy developing countries, also on the whole, showed remarkable stability during the 1980s averaging about $4 billion during 1981–8, although the amount raised fell to $2.5 billion in 1989, particularly as Chinese borrowing encountered resistance following the June 1989

Table 16.8   Funds raised by developing countries[i] in the international capital markets, 1984–9 (US$ billion)

	1984	1985	1986	1987	1988	1989
Total	32.6	25.8	19.5	26.3	22.5	17.1
excluding managed loans[ii]	23.1	18.7	19.5	16.7	17.3	17.1
Loans	21.2	16.4	11.9	20.1	15.5	12.5
excluding managed loans[ii]	11.7	9.3	11.9	10.5	10.3	12.5
Bonds	3.6	7.2	4.3	3.1	4.2	2.5
Borrowing facilities[iii]	7.8	2.2	3.3	3.1	2.8	2.1

(i)   Excludes Greece, Turkey, Portugal, Malta, East European countries, and South Africa.

(ii) New money in the form of syndicated credits provided under the umbrella of rescheduling packages and IMF-supported programmes.

(iii) Includes both committed medium-term facilities – multi-component facilities, note issuance facilities and other international facilities underwritten by banks – as well as euro-commercial paper and other non-underwritten facilities.

Sources: OECD, Financial Market Trends (various issues) and Financial Statistics (various issues).

Tiananmen Square events. Since 1982, the most creditworthy developing countries also made some use of the international borrowing facilities. Initially they were all underwritten, but with the advent, in the mid-1980s, of euro-commercial paper and other non-underwritten facilities they started to use these facilities too. Of all the financing (excluding managed loans) raised by developing countries in recent years, about two-thirds was accounted for by six Asian countries – China, India, Indonesia, Malaysia, South Korea and Thailand.

In the Caribbean, four countries – the Bahamas, Barbados, Jamaica and Trinidad and Tobago – raised funds in the international capital markets (see Table 16.9), but the total amounts raised fell very sharply from $469 million in 1981, to an average of $229 million during 1982–5 and, after an abnormal spurt in 1986, declined for the third successive year to $53 million in 1989. The amount raised varied with the requirements of individual countries as well as the market assessments of their creditworthiness. For example, borrowings by Trinidad and Tobago, the largest borrower, varied in the early 1980s largely with its borrowing needs but since 1986 appears to have been increasingly affected by creditworthiness considerations; in 1989 it did not raise any amount. Jamaica, whose position may also have been affected by creditworthiness considerations, only managed to raise

Table 16.9 Funds raised by Caribbean economies in the international financial markets, 1981–9 (US$ million)

	1981	1982	1983	1984	1985	1986	1987	1988	1989
Total	469.3	119.0	317.5	262.9	215.9	461.5	180.8	119.0	53.0
of which:									
Bahamas	177.3	16.5	–	–	–	125.0	–	–	28.0
Barbados	50.0	–	–	–	44.2	99.8	45.5	40.1	25.0
Jamaica	196.2	–	12.6	–	–	–	30.0	–	–
Trinidad and Tobago	45.8	102.5	304.9	262.9	171.7	236.7	105.3	78.9	–
International Loans									
Total	469.3	119.0	267.5	95.5	75.0	401.7	75.5	–	53.0
of which:									
Bahamas	177.3	16.5	–	–	–	125.0	–	–	28.0
Barbados	50.0	–	–	–	25.0	40.0	45.5	–	25.0
Jamaica	196.2	–	12.6	–	–	–	30.0	–	–
Trinidad and Tobago	45.8	102.5	254.9	95.5	50.0	236.7	–	–	–
Foreign Loans									
Total	–	–	–	60.0	21.1	–	–	–	–
of which:									
Trinidad and Tobago	–	–	–	60.0	21.1	–	–	–	–
International Bonds									
Total	–	–	50.0	–	–	–	–	–	–
of which:									
Trinidad and Tobago	–	–	50.0	–	–	–	–	–	–
Foreign Bonds									
Total	–	–	–	107.4	119.8	59.8	105.3	119.0	–
of which:									
Barbados	–	–	–	–	19.2	59.8	–	40.1	–
Trinidad and Tobago	–	–	–	107.4	100.6	–	105.3	78.9	–

Sources: OECD, Financial Market Trends (various issues) and Financial Statistics (various issues).

one loan after 1983. Barbados borrowed in every year between 1985 and 1989, while the Bahamas borrowed only occasionally according to need.

Prior to 1983 all borrowings were through bank loans. But since then the issuance of bonds became much more significant. In particular, foreign bonds (which, unlike Eurobonds, need to conform to the securities registration requirements of the host countries) were widely used. For instance, the entire $119 million raised in capital markets by Barbados and Trinidad and Tobago in 1988 was through issuance of foreign bonds. By contrast, only one Eurobond has so far been issued. Also, no Caribbean country has so far used the borrowing facilities, even those which are underwritten.

On a net disbursement basis (after taking account of repayments), OECD estimates indicate that international bank lending (including managed lending) to developing countries averaged only $7 billion over 1987–9 (compared to $49 billion in 1981), with only about one-half of this in the form of medium- to long-term lending (see Table 16.1). Net bond lending was only $1 billion in 1989, a figure not too dissimilar to 1980–1; but only a quarter of the 1985–6 levels, indicating that some of the recent issues may have in fact been used to refinance redemptions of earlier bonds. For the 12 Caribbean economies, net disbursements on account of bank and bond lending, after being negative in some of the earlier years, turned positive after 1985 (see Table 16.2), although the effects of the slowdown in gross borrowings in 1989 could mark a reversal of this turnaround.

Issues

In discussing the problems affecting developing countries' access to capital markets, it is necessary to distinguish between three groups of countries on the basis of their varying access to the markets: the more creditworthy countries, the marginally creditworthy countries and the problem-debtor countries. Generally, the more creditworthy countries (among them the Bahamas and Barbados) have good access to capital markets. They need to continue to explore newer techniques of borrowing and hedging to improve terms and reduce risk. Some of them may see an advantage in co-financing with the World Bank to obtain substantially enhanced credits and longer maturities particularly through its B loan programme under which the World Bank either takes a share of the parallel loan concentrated on the longer maturities or guarantees repayment of these longer maturities to commercial banks.

For marginally creditworthy countries which have not recently rescheduled or which are without debt servicing difficulties but have difficulties of access, in the past World Bank B loans have helped avoid reschedulings and maintain some standing in the international capital markets. Under the new Expanded Co-financing Operations (ECO) agreed in 1990 (which has now broadened this co-financing beyond the syndicated lending market to bond issues), the Bank can guarantee early maturities or interest payments which could be particularly helpful to countries facing immediate liquidity problems. However, no country which has rescheduled its debt in the past five years can have access to the ECO. This leaves at present a fairly narrow group of countries for whom this facility would be useful, and could exclude countries such as Trinidad and Tobago, for whom the B loan and ECO programmes could be particularly useful to retain access to the markets. Co-financing and guarantees also provide a suitable method of raising capital for commercially viable projects in the less developed countries of the Caribbean which have difficulties in access.

The difficulties of the problem-debtor countries could only be resolved through a wider menu of options including concerted new lending and substantial debt reduction/conversion, as appropriate. It is important that countries such as Jamaica benefit under the Brady Plan which provides official support for voluntary commercial bank debt reduction operations. Such debt reduction/restructuring may in fact provide increased opportunities for both public and private sector enterprises in restructuring countries to undertake bond issuance in the markets, as was demonstrated in 1990 by Mexico.

Direct foreign investment

Trends

Direct investment from OECD countries to developing countries, after falling very sharply from $17.2 billion in 1981 to $6.7 billion in 1985, recovered to an average flow of about $22 billion during 1987–9. Direct investment by Japan increased from an average of $2.1 billion in 1982–3 to $7.4 billion in 1987, while investment by the United States, which had fallen during the 1982–6 period, rebounded sharply to reach a record $8 billion in 1987 (see Table 16.10). However, the destination of these flows remains very uncertain because about one-half of them are channelled through offshore financial centres. Excluding such offshore investment, direct investment to developing countries showed a steady increase between 1986 and 1989. But the improvement partly also reflected the growing importance of debt-equity conversions, particularly in the Latin American countries, which tend to inflate the figures for equity flows (while reducing the overall stock of debt). East and South-east Asian countries were the main beneficiaries of the rise in genuinely new foreign investment, increasing from an average of $3 billion in 1985–6 to $7.4 billion in 1987, and Japanese companies were the main source as these companies sought to take advantage of cheaper locations and retain access to Western markets. Mexico also seemed to have benefited following the announcement of its debt reduction agreement with commercial banks under the Brady Plan in

Table 16.10   Major sources of direct investment to developing countries, 1978-87 (US$ billion).

	Average 1978–9	1981	Average 1982–3	1984	1985	1986	1987
Canada	0.4	0.3	0.3	0.5	0.1	0.1	–0.1
France	0.5	1.1	0.7	0.3	0.6	0.6	0.7
Germany	0.9	1.4	0.9	0.7	–0.1	0.4	0.7
Italy	0.3	0.1	0.6	0.4	0.4	0.3	0.4
Japan	1.7	3.9	2.1	1.7	1.0	3.1	7.4
Netherlands	0.3	0.4	0.1	0.4	0.5	0.2	0.3
Norway	–	–	0.1	–	–	–	–
United Kingdom	0.8	2.3	1.4	2.1	2.1	1.9	1.9
United States	6.8	6.5	3.9	4.4	0.9	3.1	8.0
Other countries	1.0	1.2	1.0	0.8	1.0	1.6	0.9
Total OECD	12.7	17.2	11.1	11.3	6.6	11.3	20.2

Source: OECD, Financing and External Debt of Developing Countries, 1988 survey.

1989. For the majority of developing countries however, genuine new direct investment remains elusive.

Direct investment by OECD countries to the Commonwealth Caribbean, after a sharp decline between 1980 and 1985, picked up very strongly, to reach $740 million in 1988. But much of it reflected offshore investment activities in the Bahamas. Excluding such offshore investment, direct investment was negative throughout the 1983–6 period, and while there was a mild recovery after that to positive flows, the figure for 1988, at $43 million, remained moderate. Moreover, some of it, especially in relation to Jamaica, reflected debt-equity swaps. While national balance of payments statistics sometimes continued to show significant inflows of direct investment, much of it reflected retained earnings. The larger countries accounted for much of the poor performance while the OECS countries continued to attract positive flows, albeit at a lower level than the early 1980s. Therefore, for the Caribbean region, as for the majority of the developing world, therefore, attracting genuinely new direct investment remains a priority.

Issues

The attraction of foreign investment in part depends on the policy of host countries. Most Caribbean economies have always had fairly liberal regimes welcoming foreign investment, while many other developing countries, with previously unfavourable environments for foreign investment have made numerous policy changes, including provision of special incentives, to attract such investment. But for some countries, despite these changes, foreign investment flows have not revived. Direct investment, private lending and export credits all have tended to move together, reflecting market perceptions of a country's creditworthiness, growth and export potential. Economic fundamentals have been much more important than specific inducements: growth, financial stability, absence of exchange controls governing essential imports and remittances, a realistic exchange rate, strong domestic savings and investment.

Nevertheless, countries can, to some extent, take advantage of the fact that direct foreign investment is not homogeneous and different companies have different motivations. Some are looking for large and rapidly growing internal markets; the small size of the Caribbean markets clearly pose severe limitations. Mining and oil companies are influenced by world market conditions and local raw material availability as well as specific contractual and tax regimes applicable in the sector, while export-oriented manufacturers would be largely concerned with labour costs and productivity. The Caribbean economies may have a considerable potential, especially in relation to the skill-intensive exports, given the preferential access arrangements they enjoy in relation to the North American and European markets.

There are also many variants of foreign investment that are not directly reflected in the statistics of foreign investment flows. These do not involve foreign equity in the conventional sense but may ensure in different ways, that returns from financial flows and contractual obligations to foreign collaborators are directly related to project performance. In the oil sector for example, there are arrangements which involve production or revenue sharing as well as service contracts and concessions. In other sectors – manufacturing, agriculture and tourism – there are licensing arrangements for technologies, management contracts for marketing or engineering and franchise arrangements relating payments to results. Joint ventures also offer a wide variety of possibilities for combining foreign, local, private and government equity, and they may provide assurance to foreign investors against political and economic risks. In this respect, foreign private investment in large public infrastructure projects, often referred to as build-operate-transfer (BOT) projects, may also offer some possibilities.

The international and national official agencies can also play a catalytic role in enhancing private investment flows. The IFC has continued to expand its direct lending under a recently completed five-year programme to encourage equity flows from other sources. To play a substantially enhanced role in the 1990s, it would require a major increase in its current capital of $1.3 billion. For the Caribbean economies the IFC's role in the past has been very limited because of the minimum size of investment it supports. It usually requires a minimum IFC investment of $1 million in a project of $4 million to justify IFC's administrative costs. In 1988, recognising the difficulties this had caused in funding small- and medium-sized projects for the African region, it set up an Africa Enterprise Fund (AEF) concentrating on projects whose total cost would not exceed $5 million, with AEF meeting up to 40% of the costs. There is no equivalent fund in the Caribbean. A Caribbean Enterprise Fund (CEF) to support small- and medium- sized projects could go some way to meeting an important gap and in promoting foreign direct investment. It would also be a useful adjunct to the Caribbean Project Development Facility which has been in existence for many years now and which helps in project identification and development.

Regional development banks also need to play a more active part in promoting private sector development and foreign investment financing. The IADB already has a private sector arm, established in 1986, the Inter-American Investment Corporation (IAIC), for supporting small- and medium-scale firms, but so far the institution has not been very active. National agencies such as the UK's Commonwealth Development Corporation and their counterparts in other industrial countries can also do much to catalyse private sector foreign investment in developing countries. The Overseas Private Investment Corporation (OPIC) in the US for example, has been instrumental in setting up an African Growth Fund. Similar initiatives should be taken to support investment in the Caribbean.

Increased provision of insurance against non-commercial risks for foreign investors in developing countries would also be helpful in encouraging foreign investment. The Multilateral Investment Guarantee Agency (MIGA), which became operational in December 1988 provides insurance for non-commercial risks, facilitating provision of cover to investors from countries without national schemes or to multinational companies which have difficulties in securing guarantees under national schemes. But MIGA's activities would invariably be limited by its capital which is very small ($1.08 billion) in relation to the global nature of its operations.

National schemes also have an important role to play. Japan has increased, on a case-by-case basis, its underwriting of investment (including debt-equity swaps and portfolio investment) by private Japanese companies in about 50 countries regarded as high investment risks. Given the difficulties of attracting investment in such countries, special measures by all major industrial countries may serve to provide additional motivation to companies to undertake new investments in the indebted countries. The support being provided to East European countries through credit and investment guarantees clearly demonstrates the importance Western governments attach to guarantees in generating investor confidence.

Portfolio investment

A noteworthy feature of financial flows in recent years has been the growing amount of portfolio investment in 'emerging stock markets' in a number of (mainly Asian) developing countries. Portfolio investment flows are estimated at about $4 billion in 1988 and close to $5 billion in 1989 compared to fairly small annual amounts during the early 1980s. The main reason for this increase has been the growth in the number and size of special, country-specific or multi-country funds which are listed on the major stock exchanges of developed countries, a number of which have been pioneered by the IFC. Country-specific funds exist for Brazil, Chile, India, Korea, Malaysia, Mexico, Portugal, Taiwan and Thailand, among others. At the turn of 1989 total market capitalisation of 41 such country funds was $7.8 billion. Since 1986 there has also been a growth of a number of diversified funds – the IFC's Emerging Markets Growth Fund, the private-sector Templeton Fund, and ADB's Asian Development Equity Fund. 1990 also saw the launch of a $56 million Commonwealth Equity Fund which would invest in the stock markets of Commonwealth developing countries. This successful initiative can be a spur to the development of regional funds, including one for the Commonwealth Caribbean.

Portfolio investment through country funds could bring substantial benefits to the host country in terms of the development of domestic financial markets as well as the wooing of a whole class of new institutional investors in developed countries, such as pension funds and life assurance companies. Moreover, as the aim of such funds is not to seek control of domestic enterprises but rather to maximise the returns on their investments, country funds, to some extent, serve to allay the fear many developing countries have regarding foreign control of enterprises. Furthermore, the closed-end nature of the funds guarantees a stabilising influence in the market as they do not represent 'hot' money. Regional or multi-country funds (where domestic markets are small) can protect investors from the vagaries of investing in one country alone as well as making their shareholding liquid. For the Caribbean countries, equity funds could be particularly important for attracting portfolio investment from the Caribbean community abroad.

To provide further encouragement to portfolio investment, developing countries would need to ensure that their taxation regimes, standards of disclosure, market information and investor protection as well as their regulatory, supervisory and enforcement bodies are such as to inspire confidence. For the Caribbean countries, an urgent need would be to strengthen their existing stock markets and to establish, as appropriate, a regional trading system for securities. Developed countries could also help by removing the remaining impediments placed on portfolio investment overseas such as any ceilings that may exist, and legal or administrative difficulties that may be faced by public sector bodies making investments. They might also provide enhanced financial and technical assistance to strengthen local capital markets in developing countries.

Main issues for consideration by Caribbean policymakers

There has been no real turnaround in financial flows to developing countries, which, after falling sharply in the early 1980s, in recent years were still only a little above one half the 1981 level in real terms. The Caribbean economies shared in this general decline in net flows. As a consequence, in many developing countries domestic investment was particularly adversely affected, constraining future prospects of growth. Measures are required to improve all types of financial flows to developing countries as well as, where appropriate, to reduce outstanding stock of debt or debt service. The latter would be particularly important for Jamaica and Guyana.

Some specific issues requiring attention by Caribbean policymakers in relation to improving financial flows are:

- tapping both official concessional and non-concessional resources from countries with fast expanding budgets of aid and other development finance, particularly Japan;
- avoiding premature graduation of five OECS countries from IDA and of the Bahamas, Barbados and Trinidad and Tobago from IBRD; supporting expanded regional soft-loan funds of IADB and CDB; urging extension of ESAF to lower middle-income countries like Jamaica with large official indebtedness;
- increasing the capital base of the Caribbean Development Bank;
- maintaining regular access to the capital markets by the Bahamas, Barbados and Trinidad and Tobago; utilising newer techniques of borrowing to reduce costs; encouraging the World Bank to utilise B-loan, ECO and other guarantee programmes for countries with difficulties of access to capital markets;
- promoting a stable economic environment for private foreign investment; calling upon the IFC to establish a Caribbean Enterprise Fund for small and medium-sized projects;
- developing Caribbean stock markets, including a regional market, and equity funds to attract portfolio investment;
- tapping export credit agency finance wisely and selectively to match project needs; and
- considering possibilities of financing public projects with private finance.

Notes

1 Total net financial flows comprise net flows on account of official development assistance, non-concessional official development finance, export credits, grants by private voluntary agencies and other long- and short-term private transactions (including bank and bond lending, private direct investment and portfolio investment).

2 Official development assistance or aid refers to grants and loans at concessional financial terms (with at least 25% grant element) undertaken by the official sector with the promotion of economic development or welfare as the main objectives. Grant element reflects the financial terms of a commitment (interest rate, maturity and grace period) and measures the concessionality (softness) of a loan in the form of the present value of interest rate below the market rate (usually taken at 10%) over the lifetime of a loan. ODA includes technical assistance which comprises grants (and a very small volume of loans) to nationals of developing countries receiving training at home or abroad and to defray the costs of teachers, administrators, advisers and similar personnel serving in developing countries.

3 Non-concessional ODF (official development finance) is defined as loans with less than 25% grant element so that they do not qualify as ODA. For the purposes of this chapter, non-concessional ODF does not include official export credits (i.e. credits which are provided directly by official institutions).

4 Total export credits include both official credits as well as private-sector credits, most of which are officially guaranteed.

CHAPTER 17

External borrowing: Source of development financing for CARICOM countries in the 1990s?

Byron Blake

CARICOM countries have historically had a situation of significant out-flows of resources (in the form of profits or adverse terms of trade) simultaneously with inflows of new direct investments, loans and grants. The net position had invariably been favourable, however, so that most of the countries in the group maintained positive external reserves and a manageable external debt. This situation changed dramatically in the 1980s. The total external debt of CARICOM countries increased significantly during the first five years of the current international debt crisis which began in 1982. In aggregate, the debt of eight of the 13 countries, which account for approximately 98% of the total debt of the region, increased from US$6.74 billion to US$8.63 billion, equivalent to a rise of 28%. The increase in the debt of the individual countries varied. In five of the eight countries this ranged between 25% and 40%. The extreme cases were the Bahamas, whose external debt declined by 12%, and St Vincent and the Grenadines where it increased by 62%.

In spite of this increase in indebtedness, total GDP declined and unemployment worsened significantly. The rate of inflow of external resources must be much faster to produce a positive impact on the rate of growth in GDP. CARICOM countries are small economies with high import propensities. This naturally high import tendency has been reinforced by policies designed to liberalise imports. Any increase in GDP requires foreign exchange to provide imported inputs into production. Also, the rapid decline in the commodity terms of trade for most of the major export products of the region in the 1980s reduced the amount of earned foreign exchange available.

Exports of goods and services have grown at a much slower rate than external indebtedness and external debt servicing. An increasing proportion of the earnings from the export of goods and services is being pre-empted to service the current external debt. The existing stock of debt constrains the ability of the region to augment development resources by contracting new debt, diverts foreign exchange earned from the export of goods and services from re-investment in imports for production, and may discourage new inflows of direct investment.

An analysis of the debt situation has been undertaken for the Bahamas, Barbados, Belize, Grenada, Guyana, Jamaica, St Vincent and the Grenadines and Trinidad and Tobago, using data for the period 1983 to 1987 from the *World Debt Tables* produced by the World Bank, supplemented for Belize, Guyana and Jamaica by data from country sources using the Commonwealth Secretariat Debt Reporting and Management System and from other sources. (Table 17.2).

The analysis covers the long-term debt, IMF credits and short-term debt as defined by the World Bank. Given the reporting capacity and practices of CARICOM countries, the data on private non-guaranteed long-term debt are estimates. This amount, fortunately, is sufficiently low as not to pose a problem for the overall analysis.

Extent of current external indebtedness

The total external debt of the eight countries under analysis was approximately US$8.6 billion in 1987, an increase of some 28% above the level in 1983. The total external debt fell by 4.6% in 1984 compared with 1983 (due to a reduction in the short-term debt of Barbados and Trinidad and Tobago and the long-term debt of the Bahamas), and increased in 1985 (13.4%), in 1986 (12.1%) and again in 1987 (5.7%).

There was a net inflow of additional resources, although at a declining rate, up to 1985 but the region experienced a total negative net transfer of US$104 million in 1986 and US$459 million in 1987. The build up in the debt in the later period reflects the rescheduling (voluntary and involuntary) and the use of new loans to meet debt servicing obligations.

The contribution of the various countries to the total debt differed significantly. Jamaica's contribution which was at 49% in 1983, varied between 46.2% and 51.5% over the period. The Jamaica debt grew significantly, if erratically, registering increases of 4% in 1984, 12.2% in 1985, 3.4% in 1986 and 11.2% in 1987. The relatively large increases in 1985 and 1987 reflected the large reschedulings by the commercial banks and some bilateral creditors in those years. Whilst the proportion of Jamaica's debt bears a close relationship to that country's proportion of the total population, it bore no relationship to the country's contribution to the region's production (GDP or GNP). Jamaica's contribution to the total GDP varied between 15% and 24%. The increase in Jamaica's external debt was not strictly related to increase in output. The largest annual increase in Jamaica's debt occurred in 1985 which coincided with a negative growth in output.

Trinidad and Tobago was the second largest contributor to the region's debt with a share of between 19% and 23%. Guyana, the third largest debtor, accounted for between 14% and 15%. The aggregate contribution of these three countries, which exhibited the slowest rate of growth of GDP over the period, to the total debt of the region ranged between 81% and 87%.

Long-term debt increased by 44% between 1983 and 1987 and the proportion of long-term debt in the total rose from 71.6% to 80.7%. Short-term debt decreased over the period but its contribution to the total debt decreased from 17.2% to 10%. The use of IMF credits remained relatively stable, varying between a high of 11.7% and a low of 9.4% of the total during the period.

Interest payments grew by US$67 million or 19% over the five-year period. There was an increase in interest payments in every year except in 1984 when interest payments fell by 6.2%. The relatively low growth in interest payments over the period was due to a fall in the overall rate of interest on loans, a fall in the debt and debt servicing of the Bahamas (which paid among the highest rates of interest) and the involuntary rescheduling of interest due by Guyana. Total interest payment by Guyana fell by US$12 million, from US$28 million to US$16 million between 1983 and 1987 despite the 32% increase in Guyana's total external debt.

The change in interest payments varied significantly among the countries. Although relatively small, outlay on interest by Grenada and St Vincent and the Grenadines more than doubled (125% and 117% respectively) over the period. Interest payments by Barbados, Belize and Jamaica also increased significantly by 88%, 74% and 50% respectively. The Bahamas, Guyana and Trinidad and Tobago were making lower outlays on interest at the end of the period by 50%, 43% and 0.8%, respectively.

Nature, structure and source of debt

The long-term debt of the CARICOM countries consists of public and publicly guaranteed loans, except for a minimal and declining amount of private non-guaranteed loans for Jamaica. Approximately two-thirds of the public and publicly-guaranteed loans have come from official creditors and the remainder from private sources. These proportions remained fairly constant for each of the five years to 1987. Three countries – the Bahamas, Barbados, and Trinidad and Tobago – accessed the private market for more than the regional average amount of loans. In the case of the Bahamas and Trinidad and Tobago, two-thirds of long-term loans come from private sources. The Bahamas, whose total long-term debt decreased over the period, reduced its private borrowings significantly. Private borrowings remained roughly 84% of a declining total debt over the first three years as official borrowings remained constant in both absolute and percentage terms. Borrowings from public sources, while small, more than doubled between 1985 and 1987 in absolute and relative terms reaching US$76.9 million or 35% of the total long-term debt. Trinidad and Tobago displayed the opposite tendency as private borrowings increased steadily each year in both absolute and relative terms rising from US$861 million, 63.6% of the total, in 1983 to US$1,364 million or 73.3% in 1987. In the case of Barbados, the proportion of private borrowings fluctuated but with a tendency to increase, reaching 50% of the total in 1987.

For the other five countries private long-term borrowing remained at less than 25% of total long-term debt with a tendency to decline. Private long-term borrowings declined steadily from 2.8% in 1983 to 0.5% in 1987 in the case of St Vincent and the Grenadines, 9.2% to 3.0% in Grenada and 18.0% to 10% in Belize. In the case of Guyana and Jamaica the proportion of private long-term borrowings was approximately 20% and 15% respectively, but with a tendency to decline.

There was a shift in the sources of long-term public and publicly-guaranteed debt from bilateral to multilateral sources. (See Table 17.1). Loans by bilateral creditors peaked at 42.3% of total long-term loans in 1984. This percentage has declined steadily since, falling to 37.0% in 1987. The exposure by the multilateral institutions increased steadily, from 26.5% in 1983 and 1984 to 30.8% in 1987. There was a 61.4% increase in multilateral credits over the period, compared with the 25.5% increase in bilateral credits. Suppliers credit, which grew relatively slowly over the period in absolute terms (13%), declined in relative terms from 5.5% to 4.5% of the total. The contribution of the financial markets remained constant, at 27%. Loans from the financial markets grew at roughly the same rate as the overall long-term debt.

Bilateral credits declined in all countries, with the exception of Grenada and Jamaica, in at least one of the five years. St Vincent and the Grenadines, which received the smallest amount of bilateral loans in 1983 (only US$2 million), had an increase in 1984 of almost 400% and this level was maintained over the period. Bilateral credits to Belize and Grenada more than doubled over the period (102% and 107% respectively). Jamaica, whose bilateral credits increased by 36%, was the only other country to exceed the regional average.

The multilateral institutions reduced their exposure to three countries – the Bahamas, Belize and Trinidad and Tobago in 1984 and again to the Bahamas in 1985. Their overall exposure, however, increased to all countries over the period. The 61% cumulative increase was exceeded by the increase to five countries – the Bahamas, Barbados, Grenada, Jamaica and St Vincent and the Grenadines. The lowest increase was to Belize.

Table 17.1 Summary of public and publicly-guaranteed long-term debt by source for selected CARICOM countries, 1983–7

Year	Total	Multilateral	% of total	Bilateral	% of total	Suppliers credit	% of total	Financial markets	% of total
1983	5,816.3	1,541.5	26.5	2,379.2	40.9	320.6	5.5	1,575.0	27.1
1984	6,309.9	1,670.3	26.5	2,667.0	42.3	309.0	4.9	1,663.6	26.4
1985	6,952.5	1,850.8	26.6	2,831.2	40.7	341.8	4.9	1,928.7	27.7
1986	7,340.8	2,079.3	28.3	2,832.4	38.6	326.8	4.5	2,102.3	28.6
1987	8,068.8	2,488.5	30.8	2,986.1	37.0	362.3	4.5	2,231.9	27.7
% Change 1983–7	38.7	61.4		25.5		13.0		41.7	

Sources: World Bank, World Debt Tables, country sources using Commonwealth Secretariat, Debt Reporting and Management System.

Five countries – the Bahamas, Grenada, Guyana, Jamaica, and St Vincent and the Grenadines – borrowed less from the financial markets in 1987 than they did in 1983. Only Trinidad and Tobago increased its borrowings from this source in each of the five years. While St Vincent and the Grenadines did not borrow on these markets after 1984, Barbados, Belize and Trinidad and Tobago, which were the only net borrowers on the private financial markets over the five-year period, all exceeded the average percentage increase in the exposure of the private markets to the region.

In Belize, there were only a few active lenders to the public sector in any one year. There was only one multilateral creditor in each year between 1984 and 1987 and there were no bilateral creditors either in 1986 or 1987. This compares with 1983 when four multilateral creditors contributed 51% of loans outstanding and two bilateral creditors contributed 48%, and in 1985 when five bilateral creditors extended 99% of the country's credits. Non-traditional creditors – the Eastern Caribbean Central Bank (ECCB), Barbados, Mexico and Venezuela – were active in 1985. Belize obtained almost twice as much credit in 1985 as in any other year.

Relatively few creditors made new commitments to Guyana during the 1983 to 1987 period. The IADB and OPEC were the only two creditors to make new loans in three of the five years. New commitments were very low in 1983 and 1986. Nationalisation and debt rescheduling amounted to approximately 80% of the total of new commitments in 1984, 230% in 1985 and 340% in 1987. Guyana had, at different points, mobilised loans from non-traditional sources such as the People's Republic of China (PRC), North Korea (DPRK), Barbados and IFAD.

Jamaica mobilised an increasing volume of external resources between 1983 and 1985 and again in 1987. A major portion – 61% in 1985 and 37% in 1987 – of these resources represented rescheduled commercial bank loans. When account is taken of the loans rescheduled by other creditors such as Mexico and Venezuela, rescheduling again amounted to more than 60% of the resources mobilised in 1987. Bilateral credits increased more than threefold in 1984 over 1983 mainly as a result of a near fivefold increase in loans by the United States of America. Bilateral credits, however, declined by almost 50% in 1985 and again in 1986. Credit from the United States fell by 40% between 1984 and 1985 and by a further 72% between 1985 and 1986 so that by 1986 loans from the United States were a mere 17% of the level in 1984.

A range of multilateral and bilateral institutions and agencies extended credit to Jamaica. Non-traditional bilateral lenders such as Italy, Japan, Libya (1986), Mexico, Trinidad and Tobago and Venezuela were active, particularly between 1983 and 1986. Among the traditional sources of finance the World Bank, IDA and the IMF, and the Federal Republic of Germany, Canada, the UK and the United States of America provided significant loans during the period. The United States extended more than 15% of total credits in all years except in 1987 when there were significant reschedulings by the commercial banks and certain bilateral creditors such as Venezuela and Mexico.

The terms (interest rates, maturity period, grace period and the grant element) on which the current stock of debt of the CARICOM countries had been accumulated have varied tremendously and erratically among the countries, over time for each country and between creditors (public and private). (Table 17.2).

It is difficult to identify any strong explanatory factors for the disparity in terms of borrowing. For example, the Bahamas with 84% private borrowings in 1983 and Jamaica with 83% of borrowings from official sources attracted the same average interest rate of 7.7% with the Bahamas attracting only a marginally shorter repayment period – 17 years compared to 18.9 years for Jamaica. In 1987, with the Bahamas still borrowing 65% from private sources and Jamaica 86% from public sources, the Bahamas paid interest at 4.1% compared with 6.8% for the same maturity of 15 years as Jamaica. Belize, Grenada and St Vincent and the Grenadines all received in excess of 80% of their loans from official sources but Belize invariably had terms which were much less advantageous than Grenada and St Vincent and the Grenadines. Interest rates on loans to Belize were always higher, often by as much as two or three times and the maturities invariably shorter. The 'grant element' for Belize was invariably lower than for the other two countries, never exceeding 50%.

Throughout the region, the average interest on new commitments was lower in 1987 than in 1983. In the case of the Bahamas, Grenada, Guyana and Trinidad and Tobago, the difference in interest rates over the period exceeded 3 percentage points. Only in the case of Jamaica – where interest rates averaged 7.7% in 1983 and 6.85% in 1987 – was the difference less than 1 percentage point. This improvement in the interest terms was not repeated in any of the other three areas.

The data for Belize do not reveal any particular pattern. In the case of Guyana a greater proportion of the bilateral and multilateral loans tended to be on fixed terms at less than 5% interest. This reflects the increasing perception of uncreditworthiness for commercial loans and the resultant reduced range of creditors. The weak bargaining power of the country is also reflected in the relatively high and constant spread of 2½% above LIBOR charged on rescheduled commercial loans in 1984, 1985 and 1987. (See Table 17.3)

The data for Jamaica show a strong tendency towards variable interest rates and fixed rates above 5%. The proportion of loans mobilised by Jamaica at lower than 5% fell from 31% in 1983 to 6% in 1987 compared with loans on variable interest rates which increased from 21% to 67%. The

Table 17.2 Inter-temporal and inter-country comparison of average terms
on new commitments of selected CARICOM countries, 1983–7

All creditors	1983	1984	1985	1986	1987
Interest %					
The Bahamas	7.7	10.7	n.a.	8.4	4.1
Barbados	9.0	8.5	8.8	7.5	8.3
Belize	7.6	3.8	3.6	9.1	6.7
Grenada	5.3	2.4	1.1	4.0	1.4
Guyana	6.2	8.3	5.9	6.5	2.0
Jamaica	7.7	7.3	8.0	6.7	6.8
St Vincent and Grenadines	4.2	2.6	4.8	4.2	2.8
Trinidad and Tobago	11.1	11.0	8.5	6.9	6.8
Maturity (years)					
The Bahamas	17.0	8.5	n.a.	11.5	14.5
Barbados	16.1	20.7	7.7	7.9	12.1
Belize	18.4	23.3	19.5	16.5	13.8
Grenada	13.2	20.6	34.4	20.2	25.5
Guyana	33.7	19.2	27.7	7.1	27.1
Jamaica	18.9	17.6	11.2	15.8	15.0
St Vincent and Grenadines	26.9	32.9	15.5	19.3	31.9
Trinidad and Tobago	8.4	8.3	7.4	9.9	7.1
Grace Period (years)					
The Bahamas	4.0	2.0	n.a.	2.3	2.8
Barbados	4.0	4.3	4.7	4.0	2.8
Belize	6.5	7.2	6.7	4.4	3.6
Grenada	4.1	5.6	7.4	4.9	8.7
Guyana	7.5	3.8	6.0	1.0	7.8
Jamaica	5.8	5.1	3.6	4.2	3.0
St Vincent and Grenadines	5.2	8.0	3.1	4.6	7.6
Trinidad and Tobago	3.2	4.1	3.9	2.2	4.0
Grant Element					
The Bahamas	12.8	−3.7	n.a.	7.2	31.2
Barbados	6.6	11.8	5.0	9.2	6.3
Belize	17.7	49.6	46.6	4.9	17.9
Grenada	26.1	48.1	71.7	39.2	65.3
Guyana	45.9	6.3	30.3	10.7	60.0
Jamaica	18.0	19.7	13.8	21.1	16.5
St Vincent and Grenadines	42.5	57.9	28.5	36.9	56.8
Trinidad and Tobago	−5.3	−4.1	6.0	11.5	13.1

Sources: World Bank, *World Debt Tables*; country sources using
Commonwealth Secretariat *Debt Reporting and Management
System.*

Table 17.3 Analysis of interest rates of government loan commitments as percentage of total government borrowing (Belize, Guyana and Jamaica) 1983–7

	1983	1984	1985	1986	1987
Belize					
Fixed interest rates					
Multilateral and					
bilateral creditors					
rate: under 5%	34.3	–	44.8	–	81.0
rate: 5% or over	36.4	–	14.7	100	–
Variable interest rates					
Multilateral and					
bilateral creditors	27.7	52.5	–	–	–
Guyana					
Fixed interest rates					
Multilateral and					
bilateral creditors					
rate: under 5%	n.a.	5.0	46.9	100	92.7
rate: 5% or over	n.a.	95.0	53.1	–	7.3
Memo item:					
Interest on rescheduled		LIBOR	LIBOR		LIBOR
commercial loans		+ 2¼%	+ 2½%	–	+ 2½%
Jamaica					
Fixed interest rates					
Multilateral and					
bilateral creditors					
rate: under 5%	30.6	30.6	5.9	9.4	6.2
rate: 5% or over	40.6	20.8	60.8	69.6	23.3
Commercial banks	0.3	0.2	–	–	–
Variable interest rates					
Multilateral and					
bilateral creditors	20.4	39.8	16.8	17.9	30.9
Commercial banks*	0.4	3.4	16.1	–	36.5
Memo item: margins	2¼% +	2¼ – 2⅜%	2½ % +		1¼%+
	LIBOR	+ LIBOR	LIBOR		LIBOR

* Includes rescheduled debt

Sources: Country sources using Commonwealth Secretariat *Debt Reporting and Management System.*

interest on commercial loans, the bulk of which represented reschedulings, ranged from the high of LIBOR plus 2¼% to LIBOR plus 2½% between 1983 and 1985. The rate of commercial loans fell to LIBOR plus 1¼% in 1987.

The maturity period for new borrowings shortened in six of the eight cases, by over three years in four cases (see Table 17.2). The maturity period lengthened significantly for Grenada and St Vincent and the Grenadines. The grace period also shortened for four countries but lengthened for four. The 'grant element' improved for five countries, deteriorated for two and remained the same for one. This element exceeded 50% for Grenada, Guyana and St Vincent and the Grenadines in 1987 whereas the highest grant element in 1983 was 46% in the case of Guyana.

Debt repayment capacity

The debt servicing capacity of a country or region is usually assessed by the relationship of the debt to total production (GDP or GNP) and perhaps more specifically by the ratio of debt service to export earnings. In countries such as those in CARICOM where export production has a high foreign import content, the export earnings to debt service ratio can only provide a rough guide. (See Tables 17.4 to 17.7).

In the CARICOM countries under study, total Gross Domestic Product fell from approximately US$14.07 billion in 1983 to an estimated US$12.17 billion in 1987. (The 1987 figure itself was a recovery from the $11.83 billion in 1986.) GNP displayed the same pattern falling from approximately US$14.4 billion in 1983 to an estimated US$11.3 billion in 1987. The fall in total production was accompanied by stagnation in total export earnings indicating that a higher proportion of total production was being

Table 17.4   Service payment on public external debt for selected CARICOM countries, 1983–7 (US$ millions).

	1983	1984	1985	1986	1987
Bahamas	44.3	55.1	51.0	42.9	49.6
Barbados	28.3	28.0	43.9	56.8	70.6
Guyana	51.3	36.0	24.6	32.2	25.4
Jamaica	263.8	260.6	395.1	434.8	437.2
Trinidad and Tobago	304.0	409.8	404.0	336.5	404.0
TOTAL	691.7	789.5	918.6	903.2	986.8

Source: IADB *Economic and Social Progress in Latin America,* 1989 Report.

Table 17.5 Comparative ratios of debt service to exports of goods and services (CARICOM, heavily-indebted and low-income African countries), 1983–7

Year	Jamaica	Guyana	Trinidad and Tobago	All CARICOM	15 heavily-indebted countries	Low-income African countries
1983	19.2	22.6	10.6	10.7	41.8	20.8
1984	19.2	14.6	7.2	8.7	41.7	26.9
1985	29.1	9.2	9.7	11.5	40.7	31.1
1986	29.7	12.5	17.8	14.6	45.3	27.5
1987	25.8	10.1	27.3	28.2	35.0	26.8

Source: CARICOM countries calculated from data in *World Debt Tables*. Heavily-indebted countries and low-income African countries, from IMF *World Economic Outlook*, 1989.

Table 17.6   Debt indicators for selected CARICOM countries, 1983–7 (external debt/GNP %)

Country	1983	1984	1985	1986	1987
Bahamas	16.4	12.0	10.0	10.9	9.1
Barbados	55.9	34.4	38.4	47.0	46.1
Belize	60.2	54.2	65.5	61.5	n.a.
Grenada	56.7	49.8	46.2	45.6	53.3
Guyana	228.5	277.6	205.2	313.9	520.3
Jamaica	105.6	160.7	222.0	186.3	175.9
St Vincent	27.1	24.1	24.0	27.9	32.7
Trinidad and Tobago	18.3	16.0	19.6	38.7	43.3

Sources: World Bank, *World Debt Tables*; country sources using
    Commonwealth Secretariat, *Debt Reporting and Management
    System.*

Table 17.7   Total debt service to GNP (%) for selected groups of debtor countries, 1983–7.

	1983	1984	1985	1986	1987
All developing countries[a]	3.6	3.8	4.4	4.5	n.a.
Sub-Saharan Africa[a]	3.3	4.2	5.0	4.3	n.a.
Highly-indebted countries[a]	4.7	4.8	5.2	4.9	n.a.
Low-income Africa[a]	2.5	3.2	3.5	3.9	n.a.
CARICOM countries[b]	4.7	4.2	5.9	7.9	8.9

Source: a   Commonwealth Secretariat, *Debt Distress: A Problem for
      Low-income Countries.*
     b   Calculated from *World Debt Tables.*

exported. Total earnings from the export of goods and services which amounted to US$6.24 billion in 1983 peaked at US$6.82 billion in 1985, but fell to about US$6.1 billion in 1986. This outturn reflects a fall in the performance of Guyana, Jamaica and Trinidad and Tobago, a combination of some fall in physical production and steep devaluations of the domestic currencies.

The percentage of total export earnings of the region devoted to debt servicing more than tripled, from 8.7% to 28.2%, between 1984 and 1987.

(Table 17.5) By 1987, the average debt service ratio for the CARICOM countries had exceeded the debt service ratio for the low-income African countries and was only 7 percentage points below the ratio for the 15 heavily-indebted countries. The situation for the CARICOM region deteriorated very rapidly. In 1984 the debt service ratio was almost five times higher in the heavily-indebted countries and three times higher in the low-income African countries than in the CARICOM group of countries.

In Guyana and Jamaica total external debt exceeded total production in all five years (Table 17.6). In the case of Guyana the ratio of total external debt was more than five times the country's GNP by 1987. The ratio of debt service to export earnings improved from 22.6% in 1983 to 10.1% in 1987, having fallen to as low as 9.2% in 1985, but this merely reflects Guyana's inability to meet debt service obligations. (Table 17.5).

In Jamaica, total external debt, which was at 106% of GNP in 1983, rose to 176% in 1987 having peaked at 222% in 1985. The total debt service to export earnings ratio increased from 19% in 1983 to 26% in 1987, having reached a high of 30% in 1986. Debt servicing exceeded 20% of GNP in both 1985 and 1986.

Total debt exceeded or approximated 50% of GNP in Belize and Grenada. The debt servicing burden of these two countries as measured by the ratio of total debt service to export earnings was, however, relatively low, being less than 10% except in Belize in 1985 when it was 11.7%. The total external debt to GNP for St Vincent and the Grenadines, the other LDC in the Group, was below 30% between 1983 and 1986 and only reached 33% in 1987. The debt service to export earnings was also low, amounting to no more than 3%.

In the case of Barbados, total external debt was less than 50% of GNP in every year except in 1983 when it amounted to 56%. In 1984 and 1985 the ratio was below 40%. Total debt service represented less than 7.5% of earnings from export of goods and services in each year between 1983 and 1986. The call on export earnings, however, more than doubled between 1984 and 1986.

In the case of Trinidad and Tobago, external debt more than doubled as a percentage of GNP between 1983 and 1987, increasing from 18% to 43%. Debt servicing as a percentage of export earnings virtually quadrupled – from 7% to 27% – in the four-year period, 1984–7.

In the case of the Bahamas, total external debt as a percentage of GNP decreased steadily, from 16% in 1983 to 9% in 1987. The percentage of total export earnings devoted to the servicing of the external debt also decreased from 3.5% to 2.7% between 1983 and 1986. The Bahamas and Grenada were the only countries in the region which were expending a smaller percentage of their foreign exchange earnings on debt servicing at the end of the period than at the beginning. Grenada was, however, using twice as large a percentage of its foreign earnings to service its debt as the Bahamas.

In 1983 Guyana and Jamaica were using almost the same percentage of their foreign exchange earnings to service their external debt as the low-income African countries and about one-half of the amount that was being used by the heavily-indebted countries. Guyana was in fact using a slightly higher percentage, 22.6% compared to 20.8% for the low-income African countries. The debt service ratio for Jamaica and the low-income African countries remained very close in each of the five years except in 1984 when the ratio for the low-income African countries increased to 26.9% and the ratio for Jamaica remained stable at 19.2%.

New external resources for CARICOM countries

In spite of the increasing burden of debt servicing, the CARICOM debtor countries, with the exception of Guyana, met their debt servicing obligations. The international creditor community has, against the background of its agreed strategy of the 'case by case' and 'menu' approach, intervened in different ways for the different countries, to ensure continued servicing of the debt. Among the issues of concern are a) whether such interventions are sufficient quantitatively and qualitatively to deal with the deteriorating debt situation? b) whether the CARICOM debtor countries are being treated on a par with, or less advantageously, than other similarly placed debtor countries? c) the extent to which current and proposed international strategies are likely to impact positively on the external debt stock and debt servicing burden of the CARICOM debtor countries; and d) the extent to which current strategies for treating the CARICOM countries' debt releases or provides new resources for development financing.

The most heavily exposed countries – Guyana, Jamaica and Trinidad and Tobago – have had to approach their external creditors for assistance with their current external debt. CARICOM countries as a group have also approached the international community to seek a focus on and treatment of the debt of small middle-income countries in a manner which would ensure that the productive capacity of these countries was not weakened and that they did not drift further into 'debt distress'.

The international creditor community has not yet responded with any common strategy to focus specifically on the debt situation of the middle-income CARICOM debtor countries. The current approaches towards debt reduction, as distinct from debt service amelioration through reschedulings, have all by-passed the CARICOM countries. No CARICOM debtor country was listed among the 15 potential beneficiaries under the Baker Plan. While Jamaica is included among the 39 debtor countries listed by the US Treasury as possible candidates for relief under the Brady Plan, the major prerequisite, substantial activity in the private secondary market, is unlikely to be met to any significant extent. The Toronto approach, on the other hand, focused on low-income countries in sub-Saharan Africa. In light of this geographic focus, a CARICOM debtor country such as Guyana, which on all objective bases must be considered a low-income heavily-indebted country, was at first refused Toronto terms in the Paris Club reschedulings which were concluded in 1989, although in 1990 it benefited under the terms.

Jamaica, with a total external debt of just over US$4 billion in 1987, owed 50% to bilateral creditors, 36% to the multilateral financial institutions and 14% to commercial banks and providers of suppliers credit. Jamaica has had to approach both the Paris Club of official creditors and the London Club of commercial bank creditors for restructuring. The commercial banks agreed in March 1987 to reschedule 100% of the principal falling due between April 1985 and the end of 1986 and 100% of the maturities falling due between January 1987 and 31 March 1990. The amounts involved were US$185 million and US$180 million. This followed reschedulings in 1983, 1984 and 1985. The terms on which the 1987 loans were rescheduled were perhaps average for reschedulings of commercial loans in that year. The interest rate of $1\frac{1}{4}$% above LIBOR, for example, was a significant improvement on the interest rates in earlier Jamaica reschedulings – $2\frac{1}{4}$%, $2\frac{1}{4}$–$2\frac{3}{8}$% and $2\frac{1}{2}$% above LIBOR in 1983, 1984 and 1985 respectively. Debtor countries such as Argentina, Brazil, Chile, Mexico, Honduras, Mozambique, the Philippines and Venezuela, had reschedulings on better terms than Jamaica in 1987 while debtor countries such as the Congo, Côte d'Ivoire, Morocco, Romania, Poland, Uruguay and Zaïre, were on less favourable terms. The terms obtained by the Dominican Republic and Nigeria were very similar to those received by Jamaica.

The international creditor community is fundamentally interested in ensuring debt servicing and maintaining the liquidity of the debt. There has been no effort to reduce the stock of debt either through forgiveness, write off or write-down. The techniques applied – interest capitalisation and the rescheduling of principal at variable (generally increasing) interest rates – have the effect of enlarging the stock of debt. The Jamaica and Guyana experiences also demonstrate that the approaches are also not designed to make any significant volume of new resources available. In the case of Guyana, rescheduled loans were several times more than new resources mobilised in 1985 and 1987. For Jamaica, rescheduled loans represented slightly more than one dollar for each dollar of new resources borrowed.

Given the weight of Guyana, Jamaica and Trinidad and Tobago in the external resource requirement of the region and the current strategy of treating the debt of these countries, the clear direction is towards the preempting of external resources rather than the release of new resources for development. This trend will worsen on present policies.

Conclusions and recommendations

CARICOM as a region, and several of the individual states, are now highly exposed, either from the standpoint of total external debt to total production exports or the debt servicing ratios. These measures of exposure worsened in the post-1987 period as a result of the combined effect of increased borrowing (mainly to maintain the solvency of the existing debt stock) and reschedulings, the fall in the value of the Guyana, Trinidad and Tobago and Jamaica domestic currencies, and increasing interest rates.

The current external debt and its servicing requirements have exceeded the critical levels (from the perspective of creditors) for the region as a whole and for some of the individual countries. The ability of some of the countries to raise new loans, especially loans to be guaranteed by the public sector, has been constrained both by creditors' assessment of their continued creditworthiness and by limits set in international agreements with the World Bank and the International Monetary Fund.

The government of Jamaica was unable to give a letter of comfort to OPIC in October 1989 for a private sector loan while the government of Guyana was unable to commit itself to a soft loan from the EC in 1989 because of their external ceilings. The loans were for projects in priority areas of agriculture and telecommunications. Excluding the Bahamas and Barbados, the CARICOM countries where the existing debt would permit further borrowing, the smaller countries have been consistently rated as either not having or just barely having the capacity to take commercial resources.

Improvement in the credit standing of the countries and the region as a whole will require major improvements in production and exports. This, however, is not likely to be sufficient. Even if production and exports doubled by the mid-1990s, there were no additional borrowings and no further depreciation of the exchange rates, the debt to GDP ratio would still be in excess of 30%. Increased production and export must be accompanied by significant debt reduction. The current stock of debt is a major constraint to further external borrowing and its servicing a most inefficient use of new resources.

The general approach of the international creditor community to the region has not been towards debt reduction or even towards debt restructuring and rescheduling on the most favourable terms. There is the underlying assumption that, as middle-income countries, these debtors can or can be made to service their outstanding debt. Yet, any detailed analysis of the size and composition of the current stock of debt, the terms on which it has accumulated and the export capacity of the debtor countries would show that the debt servicing cannot be sustained. The resources available to support the required new export production are not available, and there are no strong indications that the prices of the region's major primary exports are likely to increase significantly. A strategy to release a part of the current outflow for productive investment is necessary to ensure the long-term viability of the debtor countries and the sustainability of debt repayment. The strategy must be comprehensive and involve a contribution by all parties. It must involve a significant element of debt reduction and improvements in payments terms. There is a pivotal role for the multilateral financial institutions, holders of a major share of the outstanding debt of the region; these institutions have previously played no direct role in debt reduction in the region or elsewhere.

Multilateral financial institutions (MFIs) – in particular, the World Bank and the International Monetary Fund – should reduce their own stock of outstanding loans and increase support for the reduction of the debt outstanding to private commercial creditors.

A comprehensive approach to the debt reduction issue, could involve the following elements:

- the MFIs would make a grant equivalent to about one-third of their outstanding loans and interest (calculated for about seven years into the future) to an agreed financial institution for investment to meet payments on the total debt (rescheduled and unrescheduled) from year 8. The institution charged with investing the grant – the Guardian Institution – would be free to decide on the nature, placement, spread, etc. but with due regard to the objective of the debt servicing at the agreed time;
- private commercial creditors would reschedule principal and interest with a grace period of seven years. The interest foregone in the grace period would be the commercial creditors' contribution to the debt reduction scheme; and
- bilateral creditors would reschedule the outstanding loans – principal and interest – with a grace period of seven years. They could also assist the debt reduction process further by measures such as the conversion of a portion of their outstanding loans into grants and the provision of a larger portion of any new resources on a grant basis.

The debtor countries would be required to:

- service the current debt to the multilateral financial institutions during the grace period. Resources for servicing these loans would be from export earnings and new soft loans by the MFIs on a 50:50 basis. The soft loans would be added to the total MFIs' loans at the end of the grace period; and

• place 25% of the yearly debt servicing payments on the rescheduled loans – that is the outstanding loans to the private and bilateral creditors – in a fund with the Guardian Institution.

The interest charged on the rescheduled loans and by the multilateral financial institutions would be at a fixed and concessional rate. New borrowings by the debtor countries would be severely restricted in the grace period, with a view to bringing the debt service ratios within some agreed limits.

The Guardian Institution could be the main development bank servicing the debtor countries concerned. In the case of the CARICOM countries, this would be the Caribbean Development Bank. (The African Development Bank could play the role for African debtor countries, Central American Bank for Economic Integration (CABEI) for Central America and the Inter-American Development Bank for Latin America and Caribbean countries not covered by CABEI and the CDB).

This debt reduction strategy recognises the constraints of, and provides a role within those constraints for, each of the parties involved. There are no 'Free Riders'.

The analysis of the debt accumulation in relation to production and export growth in the 1980s suggests strongly that borrowed resources were, in significant measure, inefficiently used to finance consumption and, in some cases, to facilitate capital flight. An increasing proportion of any new external loan resources mobilised must be directed to projects and to provide foreign exchange for production and exports. External grant resources should also be significantly project-related to build-up the domestic infrastructure – physical and human – required to facilitate efficient production in the short and long term. Resources released to the governments by way of reduced payment obligations should be identified and used to strengthen the general infrastructure of the countries. The reduced external obligation should not provide opportunity for reduced fiscal or budgetary discipline on the part of central governments.

The constraint implicit in the current debt burden and the undesirability of increasing the present stock of debt of the region and of several of the individual countries, suggest the need for greater emphasis to be placed on new sources of non-debt creating inflows. One potential source is the large Caribbean community overseas. Caribbean nationals could be encouraged to save or invest in the region. Apart from appropriate institutional facilities to mobilise such savings, certain policy changes and incentives would be necessary. These would include stability of exchange rates or at least the rates applicable to such investments, the ability to repatriate principal and interest freely and the ability to earn interest in foreign exchange. The rate of interest would need to be competitive with international rates, provide for a risk element, but not be based on domestic interest rates.

Notes

1 The Grant Element of the loan which is used to measure the overall cost of the borrowing is the committed present value less the discounted present value of the contractual debt service. This definition does not take account of the tied nature of much of the official resources, especially from the bilateral sources. This often results in procurement at prices much higher than could be obtained with untied resources permitting international tenders. In such cases interest is being paid on a higher principal. The definition also ignores the impact of variable exchange rates.

2 The Inter-American Development Bank has argued that for Latin America as a whole, improved disbursement of loans reflected the different use of some of the external capital, for balance of payments rather than investment purposes. (See *Economic and Social Progress in Latin America: 1989 Report*, p. 25). The data for Guyana and Jamaica – two of the major CARICOM debtors – confirm this for the Caribbean. At the end of 1987 only 23% of the outstanding debt of Jamaica and 52% of that for Guyana were identified as attributed to projects.

CHAPTER 18

Capital flight, and its implications for Caribbean development

Karl Bennett

A major problem facing CARICOM countries is that of mobilising adequate finance to help restore their economies to a positive growth path for the remaining years of this century. In this study, special attention will be directed towards an identification of the kinds of policy initiatives necessary to ensure that the financing problems with which these countries will have to cope will not be compounded by capital flight.

The first section of the study will be devoted to an assessment of the magnitude of capital flight from Barbados, Guyana, Jamaica and Trinidad and Tobago, from 1976 to 1986. During this period each of these countries has experienced economic difficulties. The Barbadian economy, after experiencing an annual average growth rate of GDP in excess of 4% between 1976 and 1980, went into decline in 1981 and 1982 and the slow subsequent recovery has resulted in real GDP at the end of 1986 being approximately the same as at the end of 1980. The Guyanese economy declined throughout the period. The Jamaican economy experienced negative growth rates up to 1980 and since that time a modest recovery was followed by a decline associated with the slump in the bauxite/alumina industry. Consequently, real GDP in 1986 was at approximately the same level as in 1981. The economy of Trinidad and Tobago, after undergoing a petroleum driven boom up to 1981, has experienced negative growth with the severe weakening of the international petroleum market after 1982.

In assessing the magnitude of capital flight from these countries, an attempt will be made to estimate not only the value of outflows of financial assets but, in addition, the value of human capital outflows. With respect to the latter, a specific effort will be made to arrive at an estimate of the cost to the countries arising from the emigration of highly trained personnel. Emigration of this type of personnel has important implications for countries in the region, in that it is widely acknowledged that one of the major impediments to growth is the scarcity of highly skilled individuals. This will be followed by an effort to identify the major causes of capital flight. This will provide important insights into what might be appropriate measures for limiting such outflows in the future, as well as potentially reversing past outflows. In the final section attention will be directed towards identifying the various ways in which the savings of Caribbean expatriates could be tapped to support economic growth in the region.

Estimating financial outflows

Economic principles do not provide a guide to a unique or natural definition of capital flight (Cumby and Levich, 1987, p. 4). As a consequence, there is an unavoidable element of arbitrariness involved in the estimating procedures which have been adopted in the past. One of the broadest concepts of capital flight has been that used by the World Bank in its studies. Their estimation procedure is based on the residual method and does not distinguish between so-called normal and abnormal capital outflows. The World Bank estimates capital flight from a country by subtracting from capital inflows in the form of increases in external debt and net foreign direct investment, the deficit on current account and increases in official reserves. Another version of the residual approach has been used by Morgan Guaranty. In addition to the current account deficit and increases in official reserves, the increase in short-term assets of the banking system is also subtracted from total capital inflows (Cumby and Levich, 1987, p. 10). The Morgan approach is frequently criticised on the basis that there is no obvious justification for treating the acquisition of short-term assets by non-bank agents as capital flight while not including similar acquisitions by the banking system.

In this study two estimates of capital flight will be reported for each of the countries. The first estimate will be based on the World Bank procedure subject to the following amendments when estimates are reported for Guyana and Jamaica. In both countries during the period covered there were years in which there were substantial payments arrears, as well as special financing received in support of the balance of payments. Consequently, these types of transactions, which are recorded in the *Balance of Payments Yearbook* as exceptional financing, will be treated as an additional financing source to external borrowing and net direct investment. Hence capital flight was estimated for Barbados and Trinidad and Tobago as:

$$K_F = X_D + C_B + DFI + R \tag{1}$$

and for Guyana and Jamaica:

$$K_F = X_D + EF + CB + DFI + R \tag{2}$$

where,

X_D = the change in external debt.
CB = the balance on current account.
DFI = net direct foreign investment.
R = the change in official reserves.
EF = exceptional balance of payments financing.

The second method used attempted to arrive at an estimate of unrecorded or illegal capital outflows. In so doing, the broader concept of net private capital transactions was substituted for net direct foreign investment. Hence all recorded capital movements supplying or using foreign exchange would be exempted from capital flight. Accordingly, for Barbados and Trinidad and Tobago, estimates of unrecorded or illegal capital outflows would be:

$$K_1F = X_D \pm C_B \pm NP_C \pm R \qquad (3)$$

and for Guyana and Jamaica:

$$K_1F = X_D + EF + CB + NP_C + R \qquad (4)$$

where,

K^1F = illegal or unrecorded outflows.

NP_C = net private capital movements.

The use of this technique is likely to provide a significant upward bias to the estimates of capital flight for Guyana. As indicated earlier, there was a major decline in the economy of the country in the period covered by the study. This period of decline was associated with a major expansion of the informal sector. Many of the participants in the informal sector were involved in the retailing of consumer goods, including imported consumer goods.

One would normally expect that a period of economic decline would be associated with a reduction in imports of all goods, including consumer goods. However, the reported decline in imports for Guyana in this period would lead one to believe that the activities of the informal sector were not fully reflected in the official statistics. The total volume of imports in 1984 was only 43% of that in 1976.[1] Furthermore the amount reported as being spent on imported consumer goods in 1984 was one-third of that for 1976.[2]

Since it is widely acknowledged that the informal sector in Guyana is of major significance, it would seem reasonable to conclude that the current account deficits reported in official publications which were used in our estimates were too low. Consequently, a part of what was estimated as capital flight was likely used to finance imports distributed through the informal sector. Given the size of informal sector activity, it is likely that actual spending on imported consumer products during the 1980s might have been as much as 50% more than the amounts reported in official statistics. To place such an adjustment in context, this would still leave such spending below that of 1976. In light of these considerations concerning spending on imported consumer goods, the actual amounts spent on all imports might have been 5% more than that reported. Consequently, the capital flight estimates reported in Table 18.1 might be subject to a margin of error of approximately 15%.

Estimates of capital outflows for the four countries using the estimating techniques described above are presented in Table 18.1. In the case of

Barbados, capital outflows using the World Bank method would appear to be insignificant for the entire 1976-86 period. In fact, the alternative method revealed a small net inflow. However, when one considers the sub-period 1981–6, a period (as reported earlier) of relative economic stagnation in the country, the outflow as estimated by the World Bank method amounted to US$151.6 million. The alternative measure geared towards estimating illegal movements was much less, amounting to US$68.7 million. Over this same period, the external debt of the country rose by US$394 million. During the 1976–80 period, when the country experienced high annual growth rates, there were annual net inflows of capital and very little growth in external debt. This is in keeping with what one would expect with a growing economy. The outflows of the later period are also consistent with what one would expect in a depressed economic environment with associated limited attractive investment opportunities.

In the case of Guyana, capital outflows over the period were clearly significant. However, as was the case with Barbados, most of the outflows occurred during the 1980s. By 1981 the country found itself in a position where it was no longer able to negotiate any further external loans of significance. Between 1982 and 1985 net additional external borrowing amounted to only US$31 million. However, because of the country's inability to meet interest and amortisation payments, there was a rapid build-up of arrears. As a result, the public debt, inclusive of arrears, increased by approximately US$915.2 million between 1981 and 1986. As the economic situation worsened during the 1980s there was an increase in capital outflows.

There were very large capital outflows from Jamaica during the period. Estimated outflows using the World Bank technique amounted to US$1,611.9 million. The alternative technique geared towards estimating illegal outflows yielded an estimate of US$1,323.8 million. At the same time, there was an increase of US$2,788.6 million in public and publicly-guaranteed external debt. This suggests that around one-half of the funds borrowed was lost through capital outflows. The periods of massive outflows occurred during the second term of the Manley government, between 1977 and 1980, and during the first term of the Seaga government, between 1981 and 1983. The outflows were generally higher in the latter period. The differences were most noticeable in the estimating procedure geared towards determining illegal outflows. Outflows which were estimated at US$893 million between 1981 and 1983 were more than twice that, estimated at US$429 million, between 1977 and 1980. The period from 1981 to 1983 also witnessed a dramatic increase in external public indebtedness of US$1,400 million.

The post-1983 period was associated with radical changes in the administration of exchange rate and monetary policies. An auction system

Table 18.1 Estimates of capital outflows (Barbados, Guyana, Jamaica, Trinidad and Tobago), 1976–86 (US$ million).

Country	1976–86	1976–80	1981–6	1977–80	1981–3
Barbados					
K_F	18.2	−133.4	151.6		
K^1_F	−26.4	−95.1	68.7		
Guyana					
K_F	622.8	104.3	518.5		
K^1_F	769.9	124.2	645.7		
Jamaica					
K_F	1611.9	924.3	687.6	833.1	952.2
K^1_F	1323.8	486.7	837.1	429.2	892.9
Trinidad/Tobago					
K_F	947.3	83.8	863.5		
K^1_F	1255.5	359.4	896.1		

(−) Capital inflows.
K_F World Bank method.
K^1_F Alternative method.

Sources: Calculated from data in Central Bank of Barbados, *Annual Statistical Digest*; IMF, *Balance of Payments Yearbook*; IDB, *Economic & Social Progress in Latin America.*

was adopted for exchange rate determination, which signalled a desire on the part of the government to place more reliance on market forces in setting rates. This led to a substantial depreciation in the exchange rate. At the same time, the introduction of highly restrictive monetary measures led to dramatic increases in interest rates. There was no net public external borrowing in 1984 and the amounts borrowed in 1985 and 1986 were far below the US$400–$500 million of the earlier period. The capital outflows of the earlier period were reversed dramatically in 1984. Estimated inflows based on the World Bank method amounted to US$453 million and by the alternative method US$346 million. The capital inflows, against a background of a major depreciation in the exchange rate combined with a steep rise in interest rates, would appear to be consistent with one of the standard explanations of capital flows. It is often argued that a major cause of capital flight is that the rate of return on domestic financial assets is kept artificially low because of policies which keep interest rates depressed and an exchange rate resulting in a major overvaluation of the currency. Although, on the basis of the World Bank estimating method, there were also inflows in 1985, the return to major outflows in 1986, against a background of a deceleration in the rate of inflation, suggests that it might be premature to draw any conclusions concerning the linkage between rate of return on assets and capital movements, in this context.

Trinidad and Tobago also experienced substantial capital outflows between 1976 and 1986. Most of the outflows occurred in the post-1982 period, in particular 1984 and 1985. This period, as indicated earlier, was coincidental with the decline in the country's economy arising from the depression in the international petroleum market. There was also a substantial increase in the level of external public indebtedness, between 1981 and 1986, of US$1,091.5 million. Estimates of capital outflows for the same period suggest they amounted to approximately 79% of the increase in debt.

The alternative estimating technique which is geared towards illegal outflows results in the estimated outflows for the period rising by more than US$300 million to US$1,255.5 million. Although, as mentioned above, the heaviest outflows were in the 1980s, there were, as shown in the table, substantial outflows between 1976 and 1980. These large outflows occurred at a time of rapid expansion in the economy. Consequently, unlike the situation in Guyana and Jamaica where capital outflows were linked to the poor performance of the economy, in this instance capital outflows might be attributed to limited domestic absorptive capacity.

In summary, it would appear that, with the exception of Barbados, there were significant outflows of capital from the countries under consideration. There were also a number of factors which seemed common to all countries. The heaviest outflows occurred in the post-1980 period. The periods associated with the heaviest outflows were also the ones in which there occurred the largest increases in external debt. In all instances, the growth in external debt was associated with a downturn in the economies of the respective countries.

Human capital outflows

There is widespread agreement that a scarcity of human resources is a major impediment to economic growth in the region. This scarcity is particularly acute in the professional and managerial categories, as well as among skilled workers. In this section, attention is directed to the level of emigration of individuals from the four countries falling within those occupational categories, and the potential cost to the economies of those countries arising from this emigration. The cost estimates will be based on the implicit assumption that these people would have been fully employed had they not emigrated.

In Table 18.2, information is provided on the number of emigrants from these two groups for the 1976–86 period and for two sub-periods. Jamaica had by far the largest number of emigrants. Guyana ranked a distant second, but when it is considered that the population of Guyana is approximately one-third that of Jamaica, the relative levels of emigration were quite similar. A proper assessment of the significance of the numbers presented in the table, would require some knowledge as to the total number of individuals turned out by both domestic and foreign educational institutions, who would fall within those occupational groups. Such comprehensive information is, unfortunately, not available. There is, however, some less complete information which can provide some useful insights. A study conducted on Jamaican emigration to North America during the 1970s concluded that between 1977 and 1980 the number of emigrants falling in the occupational category of managerial, professional and technical, amounted to 38% of the output of institutions in the country producing such individuals.[3] The annual average rate of emigration of technical, professional and managerial personnel between 1976 and 1986 was slightly in excess of 2,000. Such persons would all be graduates of tertiary institutions. The UNESCO *Statistical Yearbook* provides periodic data on the number of graduates from tertiary institutions. In 1980, the total number of graduates was 4,266 and in 1986, 3,537. If one were to assume the number of graduates averaged 4,000 per year over the 1976–86 period, then the findings for the 1977-80 sub-period might be deemed to be representative of the entire period, with at least one-half of the individuals produced locally with these skills lost to emigration.

In the case of Guyana, emigration of managerial, professional and technical personnel was at an annual average rate of approximately 700 between 1976 and 1980 and 800 between 1981 and 1986. In four of the five years from 1981 to 1985, the total number of graduates from tertiary institutions ranged from a low of 511 to a high of 791, averaging 667. In 1978, 965 individuals graduated from tertiary institutions.[4] It would then appear that output from these institutions during the period was completely offset by emigration.

Over an eight-year period, 1975–6 to 1982–3, 2,804 Trinidadians, an average of 350 per year, graduated from the St Augustine campus of the University of the West Indies.[5] It is recognised that not all emigrants in the technical, professional and management category, would be university graduates. Furthermore, the St Augustine campus is clearly not the sole source of graduates for the country. However, it is noteworthy that between 1976 and 1986 emigration of managerial, professional and technical personnel averaged 471 per year.

There were, on an annual average basis, approximately 200 Barbadian emigrants who fell in the managerial professional, technical category, during the period. Unlike the other countries, emigration relative to the total

Table 18.2 Emigration to North America in the occupational categories managerial, professional and technical and skilled workers (Barbados, Guyana, Jamaica, Trinidad and Tobago), 1976–86.

Country/occupational group	Total 1976–86	Average annual	Total 1976–80	Average annual	Total 1981–6	Average annual
Barbados						
Managerial, professional technical	2,321	211	1,287	257	1,034	172
Skilled workers	1,957	178	1,075	215	882	147
Guyana						
Managerial, professional technical	8,471	770	3,554	711	4,917	820
Skilled workers	5,950	541	2,195	439	3,755	626
Jamaica						
Managerial, professional technical	22,512	2,047	10,592	2,118	11,920	1,987
Skilled workers	16,070	1,461	5,478	1,096	10,592	1,765
Trinidad and Tobago						
Managerial, professional technical	5,181	471	2,906	581	2,275	379
Skilled workers	3,614	329	2,178	436	1,436	239

Sources: Employment and Immigration Canada, *Immigration Statistics*, Annual.
Jamaica National Planning Agency, *Emigration to North America from Jamaica 1910–1980*.
US Department of Justice, Immigration and Naturalisation Service, *Statistical Yearbook*, Annual.

number of graduates from tertiary institutions, does not appear to be particularly large. For example, in 1983 and 1984 there were 1,486 and 1,764 graduates respectively from tertiary institutions.[6] Emigration would appear to have had a relatively small impact on the supply of individuals with such skills.

Turning to the second category, skilled workers, Jamaica, once again, had the largest number of emigrants, averaging just under 1,500 per year. It was estimated that emigration offset 54% of the output of training institutions producing both skilled and semi-skilled workers between 1977 and 1980.[7] Emigration levels averaging in excess of 500 per year for Guyana and 300 per year for Trinidad would seem quite significant given the generally acknowledged scarcity of skilled workers.

The emigration data suggests that in quantitative terms the losses to three of the four countries in these two broad occupational categories was significant. We will now turn to a consideration of the economic costs associated with the reported levels of emigration.

The overall costs to the economies of the respective countries would comprise a direct replacement cost associated with training individuals to replace those lost to emigration. In addition, there would be an opportunity cost representing the contribution to national income which would have been made by the emigrants. In estimating the direct replacement costs for individuals in the managerial, professional and technical category, it was assumed that all these emigrants were graduates of tertiary institutions. Consequently, replacing the emigrants would involve absorbing additional graduates from the secondary level into tertiary institutions. It was also assumed that skilled workers are graduates of secondary level institutions and hence their replacement would involve absorbing a larger number of primary level graduates into these institutions.

The costs to the respective countries for replacing the emigrants are set out in Table 18.3. The cost estimates were derived in the following way. In the first column, the direct costs for Barbados, Guyana and Trinidad and Tobago were derived from estimates reported in the UNESCO *Statistical Yearbook* on current expenditures at the secondary and tertiary educational levels during 1982. It was assumed that, on average, students would take five years to complete the secondary level and three years for the tertiary level. Per capita spending estimates during 1982 were then multiplied by the respective number of years to estimate the incremental direct costs associated with training a student to the two levels indicated. These per capita costs were then multiplied by the number of emigrants to determine total direct costs. The Jamaican cost estimates were derived from a National Planning Agency study, which provided estimates on costs associated with different levels of training during the 1981–2 period.[8] In the Jamaican case the costs include capital expenditures.

Table 18.3   Estimated costs of replacing emigrants in the occupational categories, managerial, professional and technical and skilled workers (Barbados, Guyana, Jamaica, Trinidad and Tobago), 1976–86 (US$000's)

Country/ Occupational group	Direct replacement costs	Opportunity costs	Total costs
Barbados			
Managerial, professional			
technical	14,266	5,777	20,043
Skilled workers	6,240	6,866	13,106
Total	20,506	12,643	33,149
Guyana			
Managerial, professional			
technical	61,838	25,040	86,878
Skilled workers	3,738	4,113	7,851
Total	65,576	29,153	94,729
Jamaica			
Managerial, professional			
technical	327,528	132,625	460,153
Skilled workers	81,248	89,401	170,649
Total	408,776	222,026	630,802
Trinidad and Tobago			
Managerial, professional			
technical	88,326	35,766	124,092
Skilled workers	25,479	28,036	53,515
Total	113,805	63,802	177,607

Sources: Calculated from data in UNESCO *Statistical Yearbook*; Jamaica, *National Planning Agency Study*, 1982.

The opportunity cost estimates were derived in the following way. These costs, as indicated earlier, are a reflection of income foregone during the period when individuals are being trained to replace the emigrants. The social rate of return was deemed to be the appropriate measure of the contribution to national output by individuals. The marginal social rates of return to education at the tertiary and secondary level were used for the two occupational groups. The actual rates used were 12% for the tertiary level and 16% for secondary level education. These were reflective of average estimates reported in a study on social rates of return to education across developing countries in Africa, Asia and Latin America (Psacharopoulos, 1985). The estimates for the managerial, professional and technical group were then derived by applying the 12% social rate of return to the direct cost outlay for three years. The estimates for skilled workers were arrived at by applying the 16% social rate of return to the direct cost outlay for five years. This approach to estimating the costs to the economy from emigration is based on the assumption that there would be full employment within these occupational groups in each country.

The full employment assumption might be challenged on the grounds that the period of economic decline which started for Guyana and Jamaica during the late 1970s, and which was experienced by all countries during the 1980s, would likely have resulted in some measure of open unemployment or under-employment of individuals in these occupations. Nevertheless, throughout this period officials in both the public as well as private sectors complained of a shortage of individuals with managerial and technical skills. One must then conclude that unemployment rates among emigrants if they had remained at home would have been considerably below national averages. National average rates of unemployment during this period ranged between 12 – 30%. Barbados and Trinidad and Tobago for most of the period experienced rates at the lower end. In the circumstances, the opportunity cost estimates might be subject to a margin of error of 10% in the case of Guyana and Jamaica and 5% for Barbados and Trinidad and Tobago.

The total cost to the Jamaican economy for replacing these designated emigrants would be US$630.8 million in terms of 1981–2 costs. Given the earlier estimates of financial outflows, the inclusion of human capital would raise the value of outflows by at least 40%. Alternatively, the estimated cost to the economy would amount to 26% of GDP for 1986. In the case of Guyana, the country which ranked second in terms of total number of emigrants in these categories, the total replacement cost was estimated at US$95 million. This represents approximately 15% of our estimates of capital outflows over the 1976–86 period and 43% of the value of GDP in 1986. The cost to the economy of Trinidad and Tobago was estimated at US$178 million over the period. This would increase the estimates of capital outflows from that country by a minimum of 15%. In the case of Barbados where, as reported earlier, the outflows were concentrated in the 1981–6 period, the US$33 million replacement cost would represent 22% or 48% respectively, of the estimated outflows in that period depending on whether the World Bank or alternative estimation procedure was used.

These estimates, in so far as they consider as part of the cost to the economy only the output foregone while replacements are being trained, are clearly biased in a downward direction. Given the scarcities of individuals with these high-level skills, it might be argued that this cost element should be based on the remaining productive working life of the emigrant. Furthermore, it is also the case that because of the additional scarcities created in the short run through emigration, additional costs in some instances might have been incurred in the recruitment of foreigners to offset temporary shortages. Such bottlenecks might have been particularly acute in the managerial professional category, given the high rate of emigration relative to output of graduates from tertiary institutions. Nevertheless, our cost estimates were significant for all countries, with the possible exception of Barbados.

Causes of capital flight

It is usually the case that when consideration is given to the causes of capital flight, whether in the form of financial assets or human capital, attention is directed to differentials in rates of return to capital in the home country, as opposed to foreign centres. In the case of financial assets, the following factors are usually put forward to explain differentials in rates of return. The existence of financial repression, as reflected in interest rate ceilings on both loans and deposits, could give rise to a situation where the real rate of return on financial assets could be zero or negative, particularly in countries experiencing high rates of inflation. Another causal factor could be exchange rate overvaluation. This usually occurs when a country operates a fixed or managed exchange rate regime and fails to make adjustments in the rate to reflect changes in the international competitive position of the country. This could arise, for example, from differences in inflation rates between the country and its major trading partners. Further evidence of an inappropriate level for the exchange rate is claimed to be found, where in the face of a severe shortage of foreign exchange, rigid controls are employed to guide allocation of foreign exchange.

Another factor which has a significant bearing on capital flight is the risk of loss of asset value. This risk is related to such things as unanticipated inflation and currency devaluation, the imposition of limits on the convertibility of domestic assets, confiscatory taxation, as well as the possibility of outright confiscation of assets (Williamson and Lessard, 1987). Capital flight will then occur when the risk-adjusted rate of return on assets is not sufficient to encourage residents of the country to hold domestic financial assets.

A number of empirical studies have been conducted to determine whether the factors cited above were indeed major contributors to capital flight. Cuddington, for example, investigated the cause of capital flight for a number of countries, four of which, Argentina, Mexico, Uruguay and

Venezuela, had experienced large outflows (Cuddington, 1986). The model he used was a portfolio adjustment model in which an investor's decisions are based on relative rates of return and perceived risk. He then proceeded to try to establish the extent to which capital flight could be explained by domestic interest rates, the domestic inflation rate and the foreign interest rate augmented by the expected rate of depreciation of the domestic currency (Cuddington, 1986, Chapter 4).

He found that for each of the four countries the extent of currency overvaluation was a highly significant determinant of capital flight. However, he also argued that in the cases of Argentina and Uruguay, although in the late 1970s and early 1980s domestic interest rates exceeded foreign interest rates by margins much higher than the expected depreciation of domestic currencies, uncertainty with respect to the government's ability to manage the domestic financial system triggered massive capital flight. Cuddington's findings were in keeping with those of other studies which concluded that by and large, capital flight was a consequence of macroeconomic mismanagement by the governments of the various countries (Williamson and Lessard, 1987, p. 25).

As for the factors which might have contributed to capital flight from four Caribbean countries, a recent empirical study (Bennett, 1988) attempted to determine whether differentials in rates of return on domestic and foreign assets were a major determinant of capital flight. The approach adopted in the study was somewhat indirect for the following reasons. In the Caribbean, the principal financial assets are bank balances. The capital flight issue was then approached by considering what were the major determinants of the demand for money balances. Quarterly money demand functions, using both M_1 and M_2 as dependent variables were estimated for each of the four countries. The independent variables used were real exports as a proxy for national income, the 90-day US treasury bill rate and the 90-day treasury bill rate for each of the countries, and as a proxy for expected depreciation of the exchange rate, changes in the domestic rate of inflation. Inflation lowers the value of domestic financial assets and consequently should encourage capital flight. Furthermore, in view of the fact that most domestic products of those countries are substitutes for foreign products, an increase in the rate of inflation would encourage residents to make a greater effort to secure foreign exchange to support their general spending.

The equations were estimated for Barbados and Jamaica covering a period from the second quarter of 1977 through the fourth quarter of 1985, and for Guyana and Trinidad and Tobago from the second quarter of 1977 through the third and fourth quarters, respectively, of 1984.

Changes in the domestic rate of inflation were found in all instances to be a highly significant determinant of the demand for real money balances. Neither the income proxy nor the rate of return variables were found to have a significant impact on the demand for money in that period. The principal conclusion drawn was that capital flight from the region was primarily motivated by a desire to secure or to defend asset values rather than by a desire to earn a higher rate of return. This is in keeping with some of the earlier findings referred to above where it was government mismanagement of the economy, or a public perception of government inability to manage the economy, which contributed to capital flight.

This matter of lack of confidence in the ability of government to manage the economy also appeared to have played a role in the flight of human capital from the region. This certainly appears to have been the case for the two countries with the highest emigration levels, Guyana and Jamaica. In the case of Guyana, economic conditions became increasingly worse during the period. The average annual rates of emigration for the two categories of emigrants reported in Table 18.2, were higher during the 1981–6 period than between 1976 and 1980. In the case of Jamaica, the highest emigration levels among the managerial, professional and technical group took place between 1976 and 1980. This was a period characterised by a severe decline in the performance of the economy which was attributed directly to government mismanagement. There was also an escalation in crime and political violence which the government seemed unable to control. The outflow of skilled workers was at its highest level after 1982. The inability of the government to cope with the problems created for the economy arising from the collapse of the bauxite/alumina industry between 1982 and 1985 did nothing to enhance public confidence in the government.

Policy implications

It was suggested that changes in the domestic rate of inflation appeared to have been an important contributor to capital flight from the Caribbean. Increases in the domestic rate of inflation, in the context of a fixed exchange rate regime, contribute to currency overvaluation. The more the currency becomes overvalued the greater would be the expectation of a devaluation. Governments, in order to avoid currency overvaluation, should then not hesitate to adjust exchange rates.

The three countries most seriously affected by capital flight all devalued their currencies during the period covered by the study. The Guyana exchange rate, which stood at G$2.55 = US$1 at the end of 1980, had fallen to G$10 = US$1 by 1987. These devaluations had no discernible impact on the outflow of capital from the country. The Guyanese situation suggests that an attempt to correct a deficiency in the application of a policy instrument will be unsuccessful where there is a basic lack of confidence on the part of the public in the government's ability to manage the economy.

Trinidad and Tobago first devalued its currency late in 1985, after experiencing massive reserve losses in 1983 and 1984. The 50% devaluation, raising the rate from TT$2.40 = US$1 to TT$3.60 = US$1, was the first adjustment in the exchange rate in a decade. In view of the fact that over the same period consumer prices, as reflected in changes in the consumer price index, had more than tripled, the public might still have considered the currency to be overvalued after the devaluation. There was no significant improvement in the external payments position of the country, and there was a further devaluation in 1988 leaving the rate at TT$4.24 = US$1.

The Jamaican dollar was devalued on four occasions between April 1977 and May 1978. Then, as part of an IMF stabilisation package, there was a series of monthly devaluations from June 1978 to May 1979 of 1.5% for the first four months and 1% subsequently. These devaluations did little to halt the large outflows of capital from the country during the 1977–80 period. The situation in Jamaica at that time, like that of Guyana for the entire period, could be attributed to a lack of confidence in government ability to manage the economy. In November 1983, there was a further 77% devaluation of the currency. At the same time, it was decided to introduce an auction system for setting the level of the exchange rate in the future. The currency depreciated rapidly in the two-year period following the introduction of the auction, falling from J$3.15 = US$1 in November 1983 to J$6.40 = US$1 in October 1985. The substantial devaluation combined with the application of highly restrictive monetary measures was associated with very large inflows of capital during 1984. This lends some support to the notion that eliminating currency overvaluation can work to curtail capital flight.

Since November 1985, the government has succeeded, primarily through the pursuit of strict demand management, in stabilising the exchange rate. Consequently, although the outward trappings of an auction system was retained, the government had in a real sense returned to a managed exchange rate standard. A true auction is unlikely in the Caribbean context to be an appropriate mechanism for avoiding currency overvaluation. The existing imbalances between the demand and supply of foreign exchange would in an unrestrained auction system inevitably lead to an open-ended downward movement in the exchange rate. Given the extreme openness of these economies, such a development would inevitably lead to an increase in the rate of inflation. The avoidance of currency overvaluation would have to be achieved through discrete adjustment in the exchange rate where the impact would be on the price level rather than on the rate of inflation. As argued elsewhere (Bennett, 1985), this could be achieved by means of a crawling peg exchange rate regime.

Policy initiatives

Before turning to some of the policy initiatives which might be undertaken
to reverse capital flight, it seems clear that the following conditions would
have to be satisfied in order to make it attractive for residents to repatriate
external asset holdings. They would have to be convinced that no major
obstacles would be imposed on future conversion of repatriated assets.
Furthermore, the rate of return which could be realised from repatriated
assets would have to be comparable to that which could have been earned
abroad. In other words, residents would have to be satisfied that they could
realise their objectives with respect to yield, risk and liquidity.

One initiative which has been tried by the Jamaican government, is to
allow residents of the country to maintain foreign currency accounts in the
domestic banking system. This scheme was introduced in 1984. Such accounts could be opened with funds transferred from abroad through the
banking system. All earnings on these deposits would be credited in foreign
currency. There were no restrictions on the disposition of funds held in
these accounts. Although these accounts seemed to embody the requisite
element of liquidity and would seem to expose the holder to minimum risk,
the available evidence suggests that this measure did not contribute to
significant inflows of funds from abroad. For example, in 1987, deposits to
all types of foreign currency accounts amounted to only US$35.2 million,
with a balance of US$13.2 million remaining as of 31 December.[9] One must
conclude that the small amounts in these accounts relative to our estimates
of capital outflows, indicates a lingering concern on the part of residents
with respect to the security of holding assets at home.

Raising interest rates to premium levels would create other problems.
With high interest rates paid in foreign exchange, loans would have to be
channelled to borrowers who were foreign exchange earners. This might
mean directing loans to firms engaged in export activity, which, on the
surface, would appear to be an ideal way to employ such funds. However,
such firms faced with paying what would amount to premium borrowing
rates, would find themselves at a distinct disadvantage in competing for
export markets.

In all countries, periods when capital flight was at a peak also witnessed substantial growth in external indebtedness. A similar association
has also been noted in many of the heavily-indebted Latin American countries. A number of those countries have employed debt/equity swap arrangements as part of a strategy designed to bring about a reversal of capital
outflows. The Chilean scheme embodied special provisions for residents of
the country. It is claimed to have been successful in bringing about a return
flow of US$1.6 billion over a 19-month period from June 1985 through to

the end of January 1987 (Davies, 1988, p. 155). The Chilean scheme was alleged to suffer from a serious flaw in that it encouraged so-called 'round tripping'. This occurs when residents who purchased debt at a discount use the local currency proceeds to purchase foreign exchange on the black market. These black market purchases are then transferred out of the country. Nevertheless, it was estimated that the amount of capital repatriated amounted to, approximately, 5% of the country's external debt (Williamson and Lessard, 1987, p. 51).

Jamaica introduced a debt/equity swap arrangement in 1987. The Jamaica scheme was aimed at reducing the amount owed to commercial banks, which at the time was US$400 million, to US$200 million over a five-year period. Residents of the country were explicitly prevented from participating in the programme, and hence it was clearly not directed at repatriating capital, along with reducing external indebtedness. The programme was aimed at attracting additional investment proceeds into certain designated economic sectors, such as tourism and manufacturing. The programme was monitored in an effort to ensure that funds which would normally be invested in the country would not be subsidised.

There was a very positive response on the part of external investors to the programme. In the first year of its operation, applications in excess of US$100 million were received and six applications amounting to US$60.1 million were approved. Actual conversions of US$2.1 million had been completed.[10] The strong response on the part of foreign investors and the high rate of approvals is worthy of note, given the emphasis on directing investments into specific areas and excluding those investors who would normally have invested in the country. The basic thinking which guided the formulation of the operational principles appeared sound. However, in spite of the monitoring one must retain some serious doubts as to whether such principles could in fact be enforced. Residents of the country were excluded from participation because of fear of 'round tripping'. However, the Chilean experience would suggest that the potential benefits to be derived from the repatriation of funds by opening the scheme to residents outweigh the potential costs which might arise from 'round tripping'.

The question as to whether other Caribbean countries ought to pursue a debt conversion strategy as a means of repatriating capital and mobilising funds for investment will depend on the amount of external debt owed to foreign private sector lenders. In the case of Trinidad and Tobago, a country which has experienced substantial capital outflows and where a major portion of the external debt is owed to the private sector, such a strategy ought to be pursued. The major part of the Guyanese external debt is owed to foreign governments and international institutions. Consequently, debt conversion schemes would likely make a minimal contribution to debt reduction and capital repatriation.

In the final analysis, the level of interest on the part of foreigners and residents in purchasing government debt as a means of reducing the cost of investment in a country will depend on the range of attractive investment opportunities which exist there. Although schemes such as debt/equity swaps could conceivably work to repatriate capital, they do provide a reward to those who might have illegally exported capital in the past. Having been rewarded in this fashion, residents might be encouraged to again resort to illegal capital outflows at the onset of a subsequent crisis. Consequently, it would be a mistake to place too much emphasis on capital repatriation schemes. In the final analysis capital flight will most likely be curtailed and potentially reversed, if governments in the region could succeed in restoring their respective economies to a stable growth path. Success in the realisation of this objective will depend on how far they can succeed in mobilising sufficient external financing.

Mobilising external capital

A successful mobilisation effort requires an ability to identify the appropriate group towards which the effort should be directed. In addition, a range of financial instruments must be provided which are sufficiently broad to satisfy differential needs in terms of earnings, liquidity and risk avoidance.

The Caribbean community resident in North America would seem to be an ideal group on which to base the mobilisation effort. Between 1976 and 1986 Caribbean emigration to the area from Barbados, Guyana, Jamaica and Trinidad and Tobago amounted to 436,000 persons. Of that number, 189,000, approximately 43%, entered directly into the labour force. Large-scale emigration from the Caribbean to North America started in the late 1960s. In addition, the size of the community has been supplemented by a movement to North America by some emigrants and their dependants who had settled in the United Kingdom at an earlier date. Taking all of these factors into consideration, it would be reasonable to estimate the size of the Caribbean community in North America to be at least 1 million, of whom a minimum of 40% would be in the labour force. This group would be dominated by first generation emigrants with strong ties to the Caribbean and hence could be persuaded to devote a part of their savings to support development in the region.

As for the potential size of the pool of savings which could be tapped from the Caribbean community in North America, a rough approximation might be derived from an examination of the occupational breakdown and earnings potential of emigrants over the 1976–86 period. In Table 18.4 are set out the cumulative totals of emigrants to North America falling within occupational categories which account for 95% of emigrants entering di-

Table 18.4 Total number of Caribbean emigrants to North America 1976–86 and their estimated earnings in 1986 by occupational groups.

Occupational group	Total number emigrants	Estimated[1] US earnings 1986 ($M)
Managerial	13,460	353.6
Professional technical	25,025	540.8
Clerical	32,114	499.2
Sales	6,707	124.8
Skilled workers	27,591	587.6
Labourers	34,301	535.5
Service	40,151	468.0
TOTAL	179,349	3,109.5

[1] Based on median weekly earnings in the United States.

Sources: Employment and Immigration Canada, *Immigration Statistics*, Annual; Jamaica National Planning Agency, *Emigration to North America from Jamaica 1970–1980*; United States Department of Commerce, *Statistical Abstract of the United States*, 1988; United States Department of Justice, Immigration and Naturalisation Service, *Statistical Yearbook*, Annual.

rectly into the labour force. The actual number of labour force participants in the categories listed arising from the flow of emigrants over the period would have been greater than the total indicated in the table. In each year more than 50% of emigrants, many of whom were dependant children, did not enter the labour force directly. Several of those would, by 1986, be labour force participants.

In the second column on Table 18.4 estimates of earnings in 1986 are reported for the flow of emigrants over the 1976–86 period in the designated occupational categories. These estimates were based on the median weekly earnings of workers falling within these occupational categories in the United States during 1986. The North American Caribbean community is resident both in the United States and Canada. The largest portion of the community is resident in the United States. Earnings across occupational groups are similar in the two countries. Consequently, use of United States earnings data is reasonable in this context. The estimates reported in the table are based on an implicit assumption of full employment. However, as indicated above, these estimates of the number of participants in the various occupational categories is likely to be on the low side, since they did not allow for those who were originally dependants entering the labour force.

Total earnings associated with emigrants arriving in North America between 1976 and 1986 were estimated at US$3,109.5 million. However, as indicated earlier, the actual size of the Caribbean community in North America and labour force is likely to be at least twice the size of that reflected in the flow of emigrants between 1976 and 1986. It is also the case that the percentage share of emigrants in the various occupational categories remained fairly constant in each year during that period. Consequently, we would estimate gross earnings of the community in 1986 to be around US$6,000 million. If one were to assume that members of this community on average saved between 5% and 10% of their income, this would imply a potential pool of savings in 1986 of between US$300 million to US$600 million.

With regard to the strategies which might be adopted to tap this pool of savings, it would appear that emphasis should be placed on encouraging Caribbean expatriates to use a part of their long-term savings to support economic growth in the region. This would involve each country directing its efforts towards its nationals. The strategy, especially in the case of the larger economies, should involve both public and private sector participation in the mobilisation of funds.

The public-sector effort should be geared towards attracting long-term support for development institutions such as agricultural and industrial development banks. Moreover, in the promotional effort emphasis should be placed on encouraging overseas nationals to act more as investors rather than as creditors to the country. The financial instrument which should be marketed by these institutions is par value preferred shares, as opposed to traditional bond financing. Such instruments would have no specific date of maturity, relieving governments of amortisation obligations. Such securities would be attractive to the expatriate community only if they embodied the necessary elements of yield, liquidity and risk.

These shares would have to pay a return reflecting yields on comparable instruments on North American financial markets (e.g. long-term government bonds) at time of issue. The dividend should be set for an initial period of seven years. Subsequently, the dividend could be adjusted to reflect more closely earnings on the investments of the development institutions. Moreover, in order to provide liquidity to the shares in the absence of a secondary market, the government could guarantee that after the seven-year period of the dividend guarantee had expired, it would be prepared to repurchase at par value, up to a minimum value of, for example, $10,000 worth of shares offered by any individual. This guarantee could be supported by an insurance provision which might be financed through a premium charged to dividends payable to shareholders. This provision should prove to be particularly attractive to those with modest incomes who might desire to retain a part of their retirement savings in this form, but at the same time would need the assurance that their savings were not at risk.

An added incentive for holding such instruments as part of retirement savings would be provided if Caribbean governments could work out an agreement with governments of the United States and Canada, which would allow holders of these shares to accumulate up to $1,000 in any given year in a retirement account and gain a tax exemption on the outlay.

Turning to private-sector initiatives, the emphasis here should be on developing ways in which expatriates could invest in firms in the region. India has established a mutual fund which has allowed their expatriates to invest in Indian industry. In the Caribbean, the industrial base is very small and in most countries there is a great deal of concentration of economic power in the private sector. The dominant firms have no difficulty in financing their operations; the critical shortage is in the availability of venture capital to assist in the establishment of new firms and the expansion of smaller businesses. The merchant banks and possibly the insurance companies should establish a mutual fund which would be geared towards the acquisition of minority ownership positions in what might be called non-traditional companies. The portfolio of such a fund would also incorporate some of the equity of the dominant companies in order to maintain some reasonable balance between yield, liquidity and risk. Units of such a fund would be marketed to expatriates who would be willing to expose themselves to the risk inherent in such investments in the hope of realising potentially high returns. The success of such a venture would be clearly dependent on the ability of the fund managers to identify the winners among the new firms wishing to commence or expand operations.

Another area in which the private sector could attempt to mobilise savings would be to make it possible for expatriates who intend to reside, either on a full or part-time basis, in the region after retirement to save towards the purchase of a retirement property. Such a programme has already been initiated by the Jamaican building societies. Apart from the matter of retirement property, it is also the case that restrictions on the extension of mortgages to non-residents could be eased as a means of encouraging a greater flow of non-resident savings into residential and non-residential developments.

In conclusion, the savings of the large Caribbean expatriate community represents a potential major source of finance which could be tapped to support economic growth in the region. Given adequate promotion, measures of the type suggested above should be successful in encouraging the non-resident community to invest a part of their savings in the region. There is, however, a clear need to foster development of capital markets in the region offering a broad range of financial instruments. Specifically, there is a need to develop a broader market for equities. More developed capital markets would not only help attract funds from expatriates but could also, potentially, harness funds from external investors in general.

Notes

1 IMF, *IFS Supplement on Trade Statistics*, no. 15.
2 ECLA, *Economic Survey of Latin America and the Caribbean*, Vol. 11, 1984.
3 National Planning Agency, 1982, Table 1.2, p. 3.
4 UNESCO, *Statistical Yearbook*, Annual.
5 Central Statistical Office, Trinidad and Tobago, *Statistical Digest*, 1985.
6 UNESCO, *Statistical Yearbook*.
7 National Planning Agency, 1982, Table 1.2, p. 3.
8 *ibid.*
9 Bank of Jamaica, *Report and Statement of Accounts*, 1987, p. 30.
10 *ibid.*

Select bibliography

Adams, Dale W., and Neyman, G.I. (1979) 'Borrowing Costs and the Demand for Rural Credit', *Journal of Development Studies*, 15.

Anderson, D., and Khambata, F. (1985) 'Financing Small-Scale Industry and Agriculture in Developing countries: The Merits and Limitations of Commercial Policies', *Economic Development and Cultural Change*, 33, 2.

Barrow, C., and Green, J.E. (1989) 'Small Business in Barbados: A Base of Survival', Kingston, Jamaica, Institute of Social and Economic Research, University of the West Indies.

Bennett, K. (1985) 'A Note on Exchange Rate Policy and Caribbean Integration', *Social and Economic Studies*, 34, 5, Special Number.

Bennett, K. (1985) 'An Analysis of the Jamaican Foreign Exchange Auction', *Social and Economic Studies*, 35, 4, Special Number 1986; an earlier version of the paper presented at the *Annual Conference of the Regional Programme of Monetary Studies*, Nassau.

Bennett, K. (1988) 'An Analysis of the Jamaican Foreign Exchange Auction', *Social and Economic Studies*, 37, No. 4.

Bennett, K. (1988) 'External Debt, Capital Flight and Stabilization Policy: The Experiences of Barbados, Guyana, Jamaica and Trinidad and Tobago', *Social and Economic Studies*, 37, 4. An earlier version of the paper presented to the *Annual Conference of the Regional Programme of Monetary Studies*, Belize, 1987.

Bernstein, D., Yen (1988) *Japan's New Financial Empire and its threat to America*, New York, Simon and Schuster.

Bobb, E. (1986) 'Financial Stability, the problems of the Independent Finance Companies and the Role of the Central Bank', *Central Bank Quarterly Economic Bulletin*, 11, 2.

Bourne, C. (1983) 'Effects of Subsidized Credit on the Size Distribution of Farm Household Incomes', *Social and Economic Studies*, 31, 2.

Bourne, C. (1986) 'Potentials and Pitfalls of Rapid Financial Innovation in Less Developed Countries: The Case of Trinidad and Tobago Finance Companies', *Savings and Development*, 10, 3.

Bourne, C. (1988) 'Financial Deepening, Domestic Resource Mobilisation and Economic Growth in Trinidad and Tobago' in Ramsaran, R. and Bourne, C. *Money and Finance in Trinidad and Tobago*, Kingston, Jamaica, Institute of Scientific and Economic Research.

Bourne, C. (1988) *Caribbean Development to the Year 2000, Challenge, Prospects, and Policies*, London, Commonwealth Secretariat/Caribbean Community Secretariat.

Bourne, C. and Graham, D.H. (1980) 'Funding and Viability of Rural Development Banks', *Savings and Development*, 4, 4.

Bourne, C. and Graham, D.H. (1983) 'Economic Disequilibria and Rural Financial Market Performance in Developing Economies', *Canadian Journal of Agricultural Economics*, 31, 1.

Broad, R. and Cavanaugh, J. (1988) 'No More NIC's', *Foreign Policy*, Fall.

Brown, D. (1990) *History of Money and Banking in Trinidad and Tobago 1984-1989*, Port of Spain: Central Bank of Trinidad and Tobago.

Building Societies Association of Jamaica (BSAJ). Fact Book, Several issues. Building Societies Association of Jamaica, Kingston, Jamaica.

Callender, C.V. (1965) 'The Development of the Capital Market Institutions of Jamaica', Supplement to *Social and Economic Studies*, 14, 3.

Codrington, H. and Coppin, A. (1988) 'The Financial Structure and the Allocation of Credit in Barbados, 1977-1987', paper presented to the *Annual Conference of the Regional Programme of Monetary Studies*, Trinidad and Tobago.

COLAC (Latin American Confederation of Credit Unions and Savings), (1978) *Panorama of the Latin American System of Savings and Loan Co-operation*, Panama.

Crichton, N. and de Silva, C. (1988) 'Financial Development and Economic Growth in Trinidad and Tobago', paper presented to the *Annual Conference of the Regional Programme of Monetary Studies*, Trinidad and Tobago.

Croteau, J. (1963) *The Economics of the Credit Union*, Detroit, Wayne State University.

Cuddington, J.T. (1986) 'Capital Flight Estimates, Issues and Explanations', *Princeton Studies in International Finance*, No. 58, Princeton, N.J.; International Finance Section, Department of Economics, Princeton University.

Cumby, R.E, and Levich, R. (1987) 'On the Definition and Magnitude of Recent Capital Flight', *NBER Working Paper*, Series No. 2275, Cambridge, Mass.

Danns, D.E. (1988) 'Guyana's Debt Problem', *Social and Economic Studies*, 37, 4.

Davies, O., Fisseha, Y., and Kirton, C. (1980) 'Small-Scale Non-Farm Enterprise in Jamaica', *Social and Economics Studies*, 29, 1.

Davis, Novelette, (1988) 'Debt Conversion, The Jamaican Experience', *Social and Economic Studies*, 37, 4.

Drake, P. (1980) *Money, Finance and Development*, New York, Wiley.

Dublin, J. and S. (1983) *Credit Unions in a Changing World*, Wayne State University Press.

Farrell, T., Najjar, A. and Marcelle, H. (1983) *Corporate Financing and Business Use of Bank Credit in Trinidad and Tobago*, Central Bank of Trinidad and Tobago.

Farrell, T.W. (1988) 'The Development of Non-Bank Financial Institutions in Trinidad and Tobago 1973-1987', pp. 81-96, in Ryan S. (ed.) *Trinidad and Tobago: The Independence Experience 1962-1987*, St Augustine, Trinidad and Tobago, Institute of Social and Economic Research, University of the West Indies.

Foundation for International Training, (1988) 'Report on Regional Consultation on Small Business', St Kitts, April.

Francis, C.Y. (1983) 'An Econometric Study of Commercial Bank Deposit Liabilities in the Bahamas, 1973-1979', *Domestic Monetary Institutions and the Way They Affect Adjustment Policies, Fifteenth Annual Conference of the Regional Program of Monetary Studies*, ISER and IDS.

Fry, M.J. (1988) *Money, Interest, and Banking in Economic Development*, Baltimore, Johns Hopkins University Press.

Gardener, E.P, (ed.) (1986) *UK Banking Supervision*, London, Allen and Unwin.

Goldsmith, R. (1969) *Financial Structure and Development*, New Haven, Yale University Press.

Gonsalez-Vega, C. *et al.*, (1988) 'The Demand for Deposit Services in the Rural Areas of the Dominican Republic', *Studies in Rural Finance Economics and Sociology*, Occasional Paper No. 14654, Department of Agricultural Economics and Rural Sociology, Ohio State University.

Gonzales Arrieta, G.M. (1988) 'Interest Rates, Savings, and Growth in LDCs: An Assessment of Recent Empirical Research', *World Development*, 16, 5.

Gurley, J.G. and Shaw, E.S. (1955) 'Financial Aspects of Economic Development', *American Economic Review*, 45, 41.

Harker, T. (1989) 'Caribbean Economic Performance: An Overview', *Second Conference of Caribbean Economists*, Barbados, May.

Hart, A. and Kenen, P.B. (1961) *Money, Debt and Economic Activity*, Englewood, N.J., Prentice Hall.

Jamaica Credit Union League (1987) *National Member Survey*, Jamaica.

Jamaica National Planning Agency (1988) *Emigration to North America from Jamaica, 1970-1980*, Kingston.

Jones-Hendrickson, S.B. (1988) 'Financial Structure and Economic Development in the OECS', paper presented to the *Annual Conference of the Regional Programme of Monetary Studies*, Trinidad and Tobago.

Kang, A. (ed.) (1981-6) 'A Glimpse into the Asian Credit Union Movement, Bangkok, *Asian Confederation of Credit Unions*, Vol. 1 (1981) and Vol. 2 (1986).

Khatkhate, D.R. (1988) 'Assessing the Impact of Interest Rates on Less Developed Countries', *World Development*, 16, 5.

Kirton, C. (1987) 'Capital Flight and Foreign Debt: Notes on the Jamaican Experience', paper presented at the *Annual Conference of the Regional Programme of Monetary Studies*, Belize.

Leff, N. and Sato K. (1975) 'A Simultaneous Equations Model of Savings in Developing Countries', *Journal of Political Economy*, 83.

Lewis, Sir Arthur W. (1963) 'Economic Development with Unlimited Supplies of Labour', in Agarwala, A.N. and Singh, S.P. (eds), *The Economics of Underdevelopment*, New York, OUP.

Liburd, E., and Bain, L. (1988) 'Financial Intermediation and Economic Growth in the OECS', paper presented to the *Annual Conference of the Regional Programme of Monetary Studies*, Trinidad and Tobago.

Llewellyn, D.T. (1986) 'The Regulation and Supervision of Financial Institutions', Institute of Bankers, Gilbart Lecture.

Luben, M. (1983) 'The Financial System in Belize, 1965 to 1982', *Domestic Monetary Institutions and the Way they Affect Adjustment Policies*, Fifteenth Annual Conference of the Regional Programme of Monetary Studies.

Magill, J.H. (1985) 'Credit Union Financial Positioning in Jamaica. A Summary of Materials Developed For and During a Workshop Sponsored by the Jamaica Credit Union League', World Council of Credit Unions and the Caribbean Confederation of Credit Unions, July 1985.

Mannhertz, D. (1971) 'The Savings Process and Capital Formation with Particular reference to the Jamaica Experience', paper presented to the Caribbean Capital Market Conference, Jamaica.

McKinnon, R.I. (1973) *Money and Capital in Economic Development*, Washington D.C., The Brookings Institution.

Minsky, H. (1967) 'Money Market and Savings Intermediation', in Pontecorvo, G., Shay, R., and Hart, A. (eds) in *Issues in Banking and Monetary Analysis*, New York, Pinehart and Winston, Inc p. 43

Najjar, A. and Marcelle, H. (1984) 'Estimating a National Savings Series 1970-1983 and Preliminary Estimates of the Savings Function', paper presented to the *Annual Conference of the Regional Programme of Monetary Studies*, Jamaica.

Nanjundan, S. (1986) 'Small and Medium Enterprises - Some Basic Development Issues', UNIDO.

National Savings Committee (1972) *A Study of Credit Unions Operating in Jamaica*, Kingston, Jamaica.

National Savings Committee (1974) *A Guide to Savings and Investment*, Kingston, Jamaica.

National Savings Committee (1976) *Building Societies in Jamaica: Some Aspects of their Development*, Kingston, Jamaica.

National Savings Committee (1977) *Symposium on Methods and Techniques to Mobilise Savings*, Kingston, Jamaica.

Odle, M. (1972) *The Significance of Non-Bank Financial Intermediaries in the Caribbean*, Kingston, Jamaica, Institute of Social and Economic Research.

Ortmeyer, D. (1985) 'Portfolio Model of Korean Household Savings Behaviour, 1962-1976', *Economic Development and Cultural Change*, 33, 3.

Poyo, J. (1988) 'Deposit Mobilisation and the Political Economy of Specialized Financial Institutions: The Case of the Dominican Republic', *Studies in Rural Finance Economics and Sociology*, Occasional Paper No. 1467, Department of Agricultural Economics and Rural Sociology, The Ohio State University.

Psacharopoulos, G. (1985) 'Returns to Education: A Further International Update and Implications', *Journal of Human Resources*, 20, 4.

Ramsaran, R. (1988) 'Savings, Investment and Growth: Trends and Determinants in Selected Caribbean Countries in Recent Years', paper presented to the *Annual Conference of the Regional Programme of Monetary Studies*, Trinidad and Tobago.

Saito, K.A., and Villanueva, D.P. 'Transactions Cost of Credit to the Small-Sector in the Philippines', *Economic Development and Cultural Change*, 29, 1981.

Shaw, E.A. (1974) 'What is Savings?' in *Proceedings of the Seminar on Savings in Jamaica*, Kingston, Jamaica, National Savings Committee.

Shaw, E.S. (1973) *Financial Deepening in Economic Development*, New York, Oxford University Press.

Small Business Task Force, Jamaica (1983) 'Proposal for National Development Plan for Small Business Sector'.

Small Enterprise Assistance Project, 'Annual Summary of Operation, 1986-1988', *SEAP Magazine*, May 1989.

Snowden, P.N. (1987) 'Financial Market Liberalisation in LDCs: The Incidence of Risk Allocation Effects on Interest Rate Increases', *The Journal of Development Studies*, 24, 1.

Stein, H. (1983) 'Controlling the Budget Deficit. If Now, When? If not Us, Who?', *The Economist*, American Enterprise Institute for Public Policy Research, December.

Stemper, G. De (1987) 'The Role of Credit in Development Projects. The Credit Union Movement in Togo', *Savings and Investment*, 1.

Stiglitz, J.E., and Weiss, A. (1983) 'Incentive Effects of Terminations: Applications to the Credit and Labour Markets', *American Economic Review*, 73, 5.

Taylor, L. (1989) *Macro-models for Developing Countries*, New York, McGraw-Hill.

Theophilus, G. (1986) 'Viability of Development Banks in the Caribbean, Obstacles, Approaches and Prospects' *Seminar for Development Finance Corporations*, Caribbean Development Bank, Barbados.

Thirlwall, A.P. (1976) *Financing Economic Development*, London, Macmillan.

Thomas, C.Y. (1986) 'Caribbean Financial Structure: Retrospect and Prospect', paper presented to the *Annual Conference of the Regional Programme of Monetary Studies*, St Kitts.

United Nations, (1987) 'Economic Commission for Latin America and the Caribbean, *The Caribbean in the context of Global Economic Crisis'*, LC/CAR/G.225.

United Nations, *World Economic Survey*, New York, 1988, 1989 and 1990.

Victor, R. (1987) 'The Regulation of Non-Bank Financial Institutions in Trinidad and Tobago: The Financial Institutions Non-Banking Act, 1979', mimeo, Research Department, Central Bank of Trinidad and Tobago, 13 July.

Wadinambiaratchi, G. (1981) *Caribbean Cases in Small Business*, Kingston, Jamaica, Institute of Social and Economic Research.

Wai, U Tun, and Wong, Chorng-Huey (1982) 'Determinants of Private Investment in Developing Countries', *The Journal of Development Studies*, 19, 1.

Wall, P. (1986) *Venture Capital Activities in Selected Countries*, Washington, D.C., International Finance Corporation.

White, M. (1984) *Small Business: A Viable Development Option for the Caribbean*, Washington, D.C., Inter-American Foundation.

Williams, M. (1988) 'Regulation of Financial Institutions in the Caribbean and the Implications for Growth and Development', paper presented to the *Annual Conference of the Regional Programme of Monetary Studies*, Trinidad and Tobago.

Williamson, J. and Lessard, D. (1987) *Capital Flight: The Problem and Policy Responses, Policy Analyses in International Economics*, 23, Washington D.C., Institute for International Economics.

Woolcock, J. (1987) 'The Contribution of Building Societies to the Development of Jamaica', *Institute of Social and Economic Research*, University of the West Indies, Kingston, Jamaica.

World Bank (1988) *Caribbean Countries, Economic Situation, Regional Issues and Capital Flows*, Country Study.

World Bank (1989) *World Development Report*.

Worrell, D. (1986) 'Financial Aspects of Development Strategies in the Caribbean'. Collection of unpublished research papers, Central Bank of Barbados.

Index